Mary,
Thanks for being the best!
Happy Birthday, 1998!

Always,
Marjie

P.S. Grow well!!!.

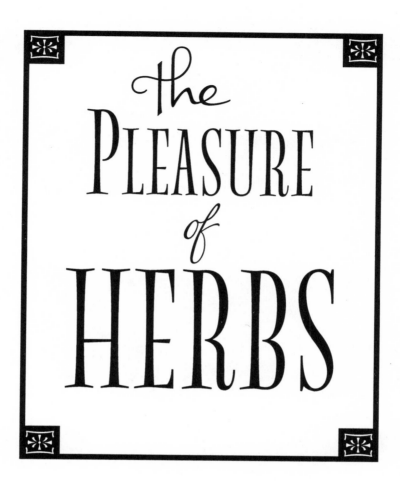

the
PLEASURE
of
HERBS

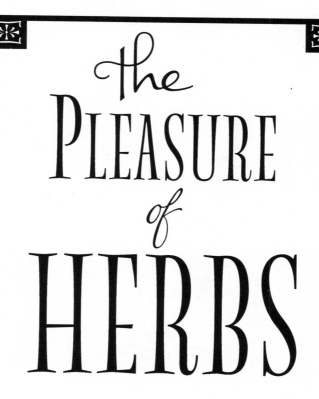

the PLEASURE of HERBS

A Month-by-Month
Guide to Growing, Using,
and Enjoying Herbs.

BY PHYLLIS SHAUDYS

BARNES
&NOBLE
BOOKS
NEW YORK

Illustrations by Charles Joslin, with the following exceptions: pages 8, 59, 60, 94, 95 by David Slyvester from TIPS FOR THE LAZY GARDENER by Linda Tilgner (Garden Way Publishing, 1985); small simple herb drawings by Cindy McFarland.
Diagrams by Cindy McFarland and Wanda Harper
Designed by Cindy McFarland
Edited by Deborah Burns
Typeset by QuadLeft Garphics, Burlington, Vermont in Garamond type

This edition published by Barnes & Noble, Inc.,
by arrangement with Storey Communications, Inc.

1997 Barnes & Noble Books

ISBN 0-76070-443-0

Printed and bound in the United States of America

97 98 99 00 01 M 9 8 7 6 5 4 3 2 1

MV

*This book is lovingly and gratefully dedicated to
the* Potpourri *family
(the readers of and contributors to my newsletter,
Potpourri From Herbal Acres),
because without their support, help, and encouragement,
there would be no book.*

About the Author 🖋

Phyllis Vandenbergh Shaudys is a homemaker, publisher, business-owner, author, and lecturer who specializes in herbs, the result of a hobby she started in 1960, when her three children were preschoolers. She has lived in Pennsylvania since her graduation from Bucknell University and marriage to Hugh Kirkbride Shaudys. She established her herbal business in 1976, and her publishing business in 1978, and has since produced five books — *Growing Fragrant Herbs for Profit, Gourmet Gardening, Sunbursts for the Spirit* (by Rev. C. W. Vandenbergh), *The Vegetable Spaghetti Cookbook* (with Derek Fell), and *Hobbying with Herbs* (now revised and reprinted as *The Pleasure of Herbs: A Month-by-Month Guide to Growing, Using, and Enjoying Herbs*). She also publishes a quarterly herbal newsletter, *Potpourri From Herbal Acres*. She is a member of the Herb Society of America, the American Horticultural Society, and the American Association of University Women.

Mrs. Shaudys' work has been published in *Woman's Day, Whitchappel's Herbal, Flower and Garden, The Mother Earth News, The Brooklyn Botanic Garden Record, Creative Ideas for Living,* and *Baer's Agricultural Almanac.*

CONTENTS

viii   **About the Author**

1   **Introduction**

5   **JANUARY**   Mints/Herb Teas/Spices/Herbs for Better Health/An Herbal Notebook/Bathing with Herbs/Potpourri

27   **FEBRUARY**   Scented Geraniums/Soups and Stews/Garden Designs/Growth and Use Chart/Herb Lore for Lovers

53   **MARCH**   Parsley and Chives/Herb Breads and Butters/Starting Herbs from Seed/Spring Sachets

69   **APRIL**   Thyme/Spring Care of Established Herbs/Beef with Herbs/Potpourri/Fixatives and Blenders

87   **MAY**   Marjoram/Omelets/Companion Planting/Starting Herbs from Seed Outside/Cat-a-Pillers/Catnip/Sweet Pillows/Bouquets

101   **JUNE**   Tarragon/Drying Herbs/Summer Salads/Herb Vinegars/Harvesting-Preserving/Tussie-Mussies/Showers & Weddings

121   **JULY**   Savory/Picnics/Pet Aids/Organic Sprays/Household Aromatics

133   **AUGUST**   Basil/Pesto and Pasta/Harvest Recipes/Nasturtiums/Harvesting/Indoor Herb Gardening

147   **SEPTEMBER**   Dill/Fish/Planning for Holidays/Wreaths/Potpourris

161   **OCTOBER**   Oregano/Herb Jellies/Apple Pulp Pomanders/Saffron and Garlic/Tricks and Treats

177   **NOVEMBER**   Sage/Poultry and Stuffings/November Baskets/Pressed Flowers/Potpourris/Garden Wrap-up

191   **DECEMBER**   Rosemary/Desserts/Beverages/Appetizers/Holiday Projects/Decorations

211   **APPENDIXES**   A. A Brief Encyclopedia of Herbs
B. Growing Fragrant Herbs for Profit
C. Directory of Herb Businesses and Gardens
D. Bibliography

267   **INDEX**

INTRODUCTION

*If the day and the night are such that you greet them with joy,
and life emits a fragrance like flowers and sweet-scented herbs...
that is your success.*

— Henry David Thoreau

THE PLEASURE OF HERBS is a month-by-month guide to the care, uses, and joys of herbs, based on my experience of 24 years. The satisfactions and pleasures of using herbs are countless. I know of no other year-round avocation that is as creative, sensual, healthful, economical, and useful, whether one is 16 or 76!

There is nothing difficult or mysterious about growing herbs. If you can grow marigolds, you can grow herbs. If you can scramble eggs, you can create a gourmet meal with herbs fresh from your garden. If you can follow a recipe, you can make a fragrant potpourri. And if you can use a pair of scissors, you can create lovely gifts for friends and family.

The pleasures I derive from my herb hobby are purely epicurean. I am entranced by the sensual, *alive* aspects of herbs — the flavors, fragrances, and beauty of these utilitarian plants. My hobby has brought me many thousands of hours of enjoyment in my gardens, my kitchen, and my herb room, where I create wreaths, arrangements, and fragrant gifts. An herb hobby is very compatible with a homemaker's life, as it adds spice, perfume, and a gourmet quality to everyday living.

My fascination with herbs began when I discovered the joy of drying them and using them all winter long, when the gardens were covered with snow. The initial hobby became a year-round delight because I could spend the dreary winter months enjoying my garden harvest inside.

Herbs are too special not to be shared. For the first sixteen years of my hobby, I knew no one else who grew her own herbs for home use. So I decided to share my love by writing about herbs. I wrote my first booklet because friends were interested in how I so quickly launched my business of selling fragrant gifts wholesale to local shops. *Growing Fragrant Herbs for Profit,* which is included at the end of this book, tells this story.

A year later I wrote a small book, *Gourmet Gardening,* because I wanted to share the culinary and gardening joys of herbs. This material appears in this book in the first two or three pages of each chapter. Related articles, recipes, crafts, and tips appropriate to each month follow, many excerpted from my quarterly newsletter, *Potpourri from Herbal Acres.* This is a seven-year-old periodical in which herb hobbyists and business owners "network" their experiences, crafts, and offerings. The unique format of *The Pleasure of Herbs* is thus a compilation of all my earlier writings, contributions from my newsletter readers, and many new articles from me.

You will find names of contributors to this book in boldface along with states and zip codes. This means that their full names and catalog information are listed in the Directory in the Appendix. The list shows which of these businesses have shops, gardens open to the public, mail-order catalogs, and so on. It is arranged by state so that you can easily find sources in your area.

For those of you new to the world of herbs, studying the "Brief Encyclopedia of Herbs" should give you a quick introduction to the varieties available. Not meant to be all-inclusive, this list covers the most popular herbs found in American gardens today, along with their botanical names, historical culture, and present-day uses. When planning your herb gardens, you may wish to refer to this list, especially for the plants that come in several varieties, such as thyme, basil, oregano, etc. I am most grateful to Ruth Chambers for sharing the list, on which she spent many long hours of research, and for allowing me to expand on it and add my own comments.

Many herbal books and periodicals are recommended throughout the chapters of this book. These are all listed alphabetically in the bibliography for your convenience.

I owe so much to so many wonderful souls who have supplied information to this book, but especially to Bertha Reppert. She offered me much encouragement when I started the newsletter and gave me free rein to publish a wealth of material from her own delightful writings.

My personal thanks to each one who has shared an idea or a recipe — I am indebted to you all. The book is far meatier for the splendid writings of Kathleen Gips on tussie-mussies, herb vinegars, and herb jellies. I have adapted many recipes from Rosemarie Vassalluzzo's column "Bucks County Kitchen," published in a local newspaper, *The Advance of Bucks County.* And a special thanks is due my dear friend, Jane Eimer, who came to my aid in several helpful ways, especially with many hours of painstaking proofreading.

Working with herbs is all play — the tasks are not chores when they give so much satisfaction. Join me in my year-round venture and share the joys from January through December. And I hope that every month for years to come you will turn to these pages for ideas and inspiration.

Phyllis Vandenbergh Shaudys
March 1986

Here's flowers for you,
Hot Lavender, sweet Mints,
Savory, Marjoram...
                    — William Shakespeare
                    The Winter's Tale, IV, 4

JANUARY

Peppermint *(Mentha piperita)*

JANUARY

Awake, O north wind, and come thou south!
Blow upon my garden,
that the spices thereof may flow out....

— Song of Solomon 4:16

JANUARY IS plan and dream, plot and scheme month. This is the time to order seed catalogs, if you're not already receiving them every year. Visualize the lush greenery that will give you fresh seasonings and vitamins all summer, and dried fragrance and flavor all winter. Dream about the spearmint that will flavor your summer iced drinks, garden peas, and cooked salads. Taste the fresh, pungent basil with your garden tomatoes, and smell the black peppermint, which will provide a healthful winter tea *next* January.

There is no comparison in flavor between store-bought herbs, which are dried quickly in large commercial ovens and then finely cut into tiny pieces, and your whole-leaf herbs, which you will harvest, dry slowly and naturally, and store yourself for year-round use. If you've never cooked with fresh or home-dried herbs before, each herb will be a whole new taste discovery for you and your family.

Plan now to make your own herbal mixes by the pint or the quart to store for use all next winter to flavor salads, soups, stews, breads, omelets, roasts, or poultry stuffings. Start saving all empty seasoning jars from your kitchen cupboards, as well as empty vitamin bottles with stoppers. You can spray-paint the lids in your favorite color and enclose your own herbal mixes in the jars next fall. You can share these culinary blends with friends and neighbors for Christmas giving, or donate them to your club or church bazaars and fairs.

January "plotting" involves decisions regarding location, space, size, and shape of your herb garden. You will need sun for most herbs. You can place individual perennial herbs among your existing flower beds or along the walls of your house. Southern exposures are best, but east- and west-facing areas that get a half day of sun will do for most herbs.

Gourmet Gardening — The Mints

The MINTS will be happy almost anywhere — applemint, for example, grows profusely on *all four* sides of our house — so if you have limited options you should save your sunniest spots for other herbs. There are many luscious mint flavors for kitchen delight (see Chart, p. 9). When you're doing your garden planning on paper this month, consider how you can grow a variety of mints *and keep them separated* — intermingling will tend to weaken their unique flavors.

The novice herbalist will have best luck buying starter plants of all the mints except catnip and lemon balm.

Mints can be easily contained, either by planting them in separate gardens or, if planting among other herbs or flowers, by using underground metal or brick barriers. They will spread vigorously by the second year through their underground root systems, but you can keep them under control by giving your unwanted rootings to friends or sharing them with other gardeners through fund-raising fairs or bazaars.

Contain mint in a chimney flue tile.

All mints can be kept compact and attractive by a monthly trimming of the tops of the plants. They will then branch out sideways, giving you more harvests for winter tea — and a neat, compact garden.

Recommended Mints

Treat your indoor herbs to a bath, rinse, and trim for the New Year!

If you are a beginner in herbcraft, or if you are a "pro" but have been discouraged about mints, start fresh with *well-labeled* plants or seeds from a reliable local nursery or an established herb mail-order firm. The label should give the full Latin botanical name for the herb (as should the mail-order catalog) so you will know exactly what seeds or plants you are getting.

The following list will help you decide which mints to start or start over with. These are all from the *Labiatae* family and although they require minimal care, they give optimal pleasure.

VARIETIES OF MINT

COMMON NAME *BOTANICAL GENUS & SPECIES* *"VARIETY"* AVG. HGT.	DESCRIPTION
APPLE MINT *Mentha suaveolens* (formerly *M. Rotundifolia*) 2½'	Often called "woolly mint". Delicate spearmint-apple flavor. Grayish-green hue, light purple flowers. Use for tea & to garnish applesauce.
BLACK PEPPERMINT *Mentha piperita* *'Vulgaris'* 15"	Superior fragrance and flavor! Forest-green leaves with deep purple veins and stems, purple flowers. Breathtaking freshness for tea, potpourri, tussie-mussies, bouquets. Used in Creme-de-Menthe.
ORANGE MINT *Mentha aquatica* (formerly *M. piperita, 'Vulgaris'*) *'crispa'* 18"	Also called "citrus mint" or "bergamot mint". Luscious lemon-orange scent. Grass-green leaves with reddish-purple stems and runners, lavender flowers. A bath mint, room deodorizer, tea or punch, and mice-repellent. "Eau-de-Cologne" mint is a superb fruity-sweet variation.
PENNYROYAL *Mentha Pulegium* (English) 12"	Creeping, matted growth style. Pungent medicinal aroma. Can be toxic, so not recommended for culinary use, especially by childbearing-age women. Small green leaves, violet-blue flowers. Superb flea and insect repellent. Aromatic ground cover. Easy to grow from seeds. Winter mulch necessary in cold climates.
PEPPERMINT *Mentha x piperita* *'officinalis'* 2'	Sometimes called "white peppermint". Will ward off harmful insects from members of the cabbage family in the vegetable garden. Grass-green leaves with reddish-purple undertones, violet flowers. Fresh bouquet, a bathroom or kitchen freshener and insect repellent; makes tea, potpourri, and tussie-mussies.
PINEAPPLE MINT *Mentha suaveolens* (formerly *M. Rotundifolia*) *'Variegata'* 12"	Stunning pineapple scent. Taste does not equal fragrance. Garden accent plant. Creamy patches of color on apple-green leaves, off-white flowers. Garnish for fruit salads; lovely in tussie-mussies or bouquets of yellow roses. A conversation piece in garden!
SPEARMINT *Mentha spicata* *'Viridis'* 2'	Also known as "lamb mint," "pea mint," "garden mint." Sensational fragrance and flavor! Nice for picnic table centerpiece; will deter flies. Light green leaves, violet-gray flowers. For mint sauce or juleps, jelly, tea, fruit salads or punch, with carrots or peas.

Keep the different kinds separated from each other and contained by barriers in the soil. And keep a record of where each mint is planted, because labels have a way of disappearing.

Each herb belongs to a "family" of its own, has a genus of its own and a species, of which there can be several variations or varieties. Much of the confusion about mints stems from the profusion of species and varieties resulting from cross-pollination. This is less likely to happen in *your* garden because you will know to keep the mints separated, and because you will be harvesting your mints often, which will prevent them from going to seed.

Although cross-pollination, deliberate or unintentional, has resulted in many of the marvelous varieties we enjoy, it can also result in weakened flavor and fragrance. Whenever someone tells me they had "some kind of mint and it wasn't very fragrant," I suggest that either it has been cross-pollinated or it has been left in the same spot for too long. This will also weaken the plant. Mints are among the perennial herbs that should be moved to fresh soil every four or five years.

Only the top three to five leaves of each branch of mint should be used for cooking. The lower leaves are too pungent, and the oils too strong, for culinary use.

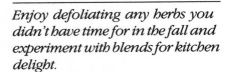

Enjoy defoliating any herbs you didn't have time for in the fall and experiment with blends for kitchen delight.

Herb Teas

There is no month of the year that our family doesn't use mints for tea, but I think the best cups of tea are those we enjoy when we're snowbound by a warm, cheerful fire. Plan now to luxuriate *next* January by your wood stove or fireplace with a pot of your very own homegrown herb tea and a couple of your best friends — or a good herb book!

Make herb tea by steeping one or two leaves per cup of boiling water in a covered, non-metallic cup or pot for ten minutes. I heat my china teapot, which makes four cups of tea, by rinsing it with boiling water, place six to eight herb leaves (or more, if the leaves are small or broken) in a tea strainer, and pour boiling water into the pot. We prefer a teaspoon of honey in each cup of herb tea, so I add this straight to the teapot before pouring the tea. If you're making just one cup, cover it with the saucer while it steeps. You can also enhance any cup or pot of storebought tea by adding mint leaves to the brew.

The first summer my children and I started our herb business, we tried a new herb tea each evening as we worked on the sachets and potpourri. We made a tea-taster's chart and each of us rated that evening's tea and commented on it.

Our Number One favorite tea is hot black peppermint tea. We drink it because it's delicious, but we have also used it very successfully to soothe upset stomachs and headaches. Black peppermint is distinguishable by its deep purple (not black) veins and stems. Regular white peppermint is also excellent in flavor, and we grow a lot of that separately.

I have served iced applemint tea to my family for twenty years, as this was the first live herb I ever met in person. Our first home was a rented one, and I was vigorously ripping out a stubborn "weed" from the side of the house where I wanted to plant zinnias and marigolds. I noticed that it smelled good, but it never occurred to me to taste it until a neighbor identified it as some kind of mint, and suggested I try it with some hot tea. We loved it so much that soon we were cooling it for iced tea. It became a staple in our household once I discovered that mint leaves could be dried for winter use.

That "weed" was the first plant I brought to our new house when we built it, and I planted it on all four sides to be sure it would grow in at least one area.

A very close third in our family list of favorites is lemon herb tea, from either lemon balm or lemon verbena. Lemon balm is easily grown outside from seed, and it's hardy, with thick roots.

Lemon verbena, on the other hand, is very tender and must be brought inside each winter in cold climates to "die down." I take cuttings of lemon verbena each year and grow them under lights. If you want a sensual experience, grow this herb. Its fragrance (the base of most of my herbal pillows) is breathtaking, like sweet lemon, and it makes a lovely tea.

Pineapple mint is another winner. In addition to being particularly attractive in the garden because of the creamy white patches on its leaves, it is very nice as a tea or to garnish salads using fresh or canned pineapple. (Incidentally, all of the mints make lovely garnishes for any fresh or canned fruit salad or cocktail.)

Spearmint is particularly good in any lime gelatin salad (see JUNE) and as a seasoning for cooked peas instead of salt and pepper. And of course spearmint is essential to mint juleps, if this is your "cup of tea"! It is a marvelous herb tea by itself, or as an addition to commercial tea.

Orange mint is favored by many herbalists to adorn tea or as its own tea with orange peel and a cinnamon stick added. It is also used to garnish fruit punches. Although orange mint is not at the top of my list as a culinary herb, I use it profusely in my "Citruscent" potpourri. I also love it in orange mint jelly (see OCTOBER) which we use all winter long to top-dress many of our Chinese wok dishes.

Add a pinch of cardamom to the liquid in baked apples and stewed fruits.

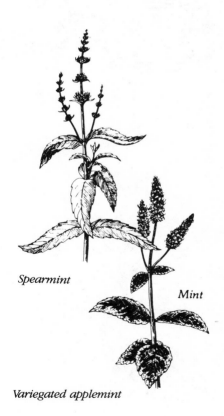

Spearmint

Mint

Variegated applemint

Orange or bergamot mint

Catnip is also from the mint family and makes a lovely tea, especially at bedtime, as it reputedly has sedative powers. (Interestingly, catnip gives the feline species a real "high," but affects the human family in the opposite way.) Catnip is easy to grow from seed and will "self-sow" or propagate itself, if some branches are left uncut to flower and go to seed.

There are many other herbs that make delicious teas, and there are an infinite number of combinations you should try. Scented geranium leaves make wonderful teas by themselves or added to commercial tea. The best flavors are rose, lemon-rose, apple, lemon, and orange-scented geraniums. (If you haven't known the sheer delight of growing these fragrant lovelies, see FEBRUARY.)

Three of my favorite herb tea blends ("tisanes") follow:

- Equal parts of *sage, thyme, marjoram* or *oregano,* and *camomile flowers.*
- Six parts of *peppermint* with one part each of *sage* and *rosemary* leaves.
- Equal parts *lemon verbena* or *lemon balm* and *peppermint* with a pinch of dried grated *lemon* or *orange peel.*

Dried calendula petals make a colorful addition to any of these blends. You can experiment with your favorite flavors and create attractive "gourmet" blends of your own from any of the edible, culinary herbs.

The colonists made their own teas for their healthful and medicinal effects. Folklore and most herbal manuals make many claims as to the health benefits of herb teas. I do not personally advocate self-diagnosis and self-medication with herbs, simply because I am not knowledgeable enough to do so, and because of my own experiences. For example, I often suggested comfrey tea to my arthritic mother, and supplied her with the herb, but I was so pleased that she had *not* followed my advice over the years when I later learned that there is now some doubt about the safety of continued, long-term ingestion of comfrey (see "Comfrey" in the Appendix).

To those who would still like to use herbs to heal themselves, I suggest very thorough research of the medicinal herbs (sources listed at the end of this section), adequate knowledge of the symptoms and causes of the illness, purchase of herbal medicinal blends *only* from reputable herbal authorities, and professional consultation for persistent illnesses.

Frankly, I feel the psychological effect of sitting down to savor a hot beverage from your very own garden is enough in itself to cheer the spirits! It seems logical to assume that herb teas are healthier than many other beverages, simply because they do not contain large amounts of caffeine or narcotics.

Comfrey

The following blends are traditionally reputed to have health benefits:

Equal amounts of *lavender, rosemary, and thyme* — for headaches and colds.

Sage, thyme, marjoram, and camomile — to calm the nerves.

Sage tea — to slow the aging process and halt wrinkles.

Yarrow — for relief from colds and flus.

Of course, there are hundreds of other historical herbal "remedies," as documented in the herbal encyclopedia in the Appendix.

Recommended Reading on the Medicinal Use of Herbs

WEINER'S HERBAL: The Guide to Herbal Medicine, Dr. Michael Weiner (Stein & Day, New York, 1980).

THE HONEST HERBAL: A Sensible Guide to Herbs and Related Remedies, Varro Tyler (George T. Stickley Co., Philadelphia, 1982).

THE AMERICAN HERB ASSOCIATION NEWSLETTER (P.O. Box 353, Rescue, CA 95672)

THE HERB REPORT (P.O. Box 1568, Hobe Sound, FL 33455).

BACK TO EDEN, Jethro Kloss (Bantam Books, New York, 1981).

THE HERB BOOK, John Lust (Bantam Books, New York, 1974).

SHAKER HERBS AND THEIR MEDICINAL USES, Dee Herbrandson (28 pp.; Shaker Heritage Society, Albany-Shaker Road, Watervliet, NY 12189, 1985).

Also, archival materials, including records and journals of Shaker herbalists, are available by appointment at Shaker museums and libraries.

Brighten your food on dreary days with dried calendula or nasturtium petals in soups, gravy, herb tea.

Calendula or Pot Marigold

SPICE UP YOUR LIFE

Some newspaper writers discuss herbs and spices as if they were one and the same. Not so! *Herbs* are garden plants grown in the northern temperate zones that are useful to humans aside from as decoration or shade for flavor, fragrance, cosmetics, medicine, or dyeing. Generally it is the leaf part of the plant that is useful. (You may pronounce herb with or without the "h" — just don't drop the "h" if you visit England!) *Spices,* in contrast, with their many uses for flavoring and fragrance, are primarily from the bark, root, seed, berry, or pod of vines, shrubs, or trees grown mostly in the tropical lands of the Eastern Hemisphere.

Many of the fixatives we use for potpourri are from the spice world and are discussed in the APRIL chapter. The aromatic culinary spices we are most familiar with are: ALLSPICE (the only true native aromatic spice grown in the Western Hemisphere, the West Indies), CARDAMOM (which may be spelled cardomon), CINNAMON (which is also cassia), CLOVES, GINGER, NUTMEG, MACE, PEPPER, SAFFRON, TURMERIC, and VANILLA. Many additional seasonings we use are *blends* of spices such as curry powder, chili powder, pickling spice, etc.

Crusades have been launched, wars fought, and continents discovered (ours, for instance)…for spices! Why are they so expensive? Many require special climatic conditions, and many must be hand-harvested. We pay not only for the container, but also for several middle-men before the spice reaches the grocer. Also, Americans are paying more and more for commodities such as spices — and oil — from Southeast Asia, Arabia, Africa, and the Middle East.

Saffron is the most expensive spice because 75,000 autumn crocuses have to be grown to harvest one pound. Then someone has to hand-pick 3 stigmas from each crocus — 225,000 to make a pound. You can grow your own saffron, however, if you can grow a crocus. (See OCTOBER.)

Cardamom is the second costliest spice because every seed pod has to be snipped by hand with shears. Cinnamon requires a complicated system of rotation and pruning, and then the bark needs to be hand-peeled, rolled into quills, and dried. Nutmeg is a tropical island plant from which the fruit is hand-picked with long poles containing special baskets. (Mace is the outer coating of the nutmeg, and so has similar flavor.)

It is best to buy *whole* spices because they retain their flavor longer, and then grind your own as you need them with a mortar and pestle or a nutmeg or pepper mill. Keep spices stored in tightly closed containers, away from light and heat, and in a dry place to preserve their volatile oils longer. Many of the mail-order catalogs listed in the Appendix offer quality spices, whole or ground, which are likely to be fresher and cheaper than what's on the grocer's shelf.

When your supplies are in, enjoy SPICE TEA to warm your soul. Combine 4 cups of cold water, 1 cinnamon stick, and 2 whole cloves. Bring to a boil, then simmer for 5 minutes. Remove from heat and add 2 tea bags or 1 T. tea leaves. Steep for 3 minutes. Strain the tea leaves or remove the tea bags. Sweeten with honey, if desired, to taste.

HERBS FOR BETTER HEALTH

January is the time for new beginnings, especially after all the excesses of the holidays. But *any* time is the right time to start heeding the medical advice we've been reading and hearing for many years. The reasons to reduce our intake of fats, cholesterol, salt, sugar, chemical additives, and excess calories are well documented. Herbs and spices are the key to making some basic changes in our eating habits — the key to creating exciting and delicious substitutions for the super-rich, salty, fatty, and sugary foods we've been growing up (and out) on!

It is infinitely easier for herb-lovers to de-program appetites and attitudes because we already know how herbs can transform basic foods into gourmet delights. The low-sodium diet given my mother-in-

"Awake, O north wind: and come thou south: blow upon my garden, that the spices thereof may flow out!"
Song of Solomon 4:16

Americans annually consume nearly 480 million pounds of herbs, spices, and seasonings.

Cold feet and hands? Sprinkle cayenne pepper in socks and gloves. This really works!
— *Barbara Bobo*
WOODSPIRITS SHOP OH 43972

law when she left the hospital this summer is chock-full of herbs and spices to use INSTEAD of salt. And the American Heart Association's pamphlet "Save Food Dollars and Help Your Heart" suggests growing one's own herbs for flavoring food.

Here are some basic guidelines for using herbs and spices for better health, followed by suggestions and recipes.

1. Use margarines, oils, salad dressings, and mayonnaise containing these polyunsaturated oils: corn, cottonseed, safflower, soybean, sesame seed, or sunflower. Select margarines that contain more polyunsaturated than completely hydrogenated fats. Season and cook meats and vegetables with these recommended fats, enhanced by herbs and spices rather than salt.

2. Use fortified, skimmed, non-fat milk and milk products and low-sodium cheeses made with skimmed milk and polyunsaturated fat. Flavor skim-milk drinks with almond, maple, vanilla, or walnut extracts or oils. Spice up low-fat cottage or creamed cheese with chives or garlic.

3. Make your own sauces, condiments, soups, broths, and dressings from herbs and spices and the recommended oils or fats to replace commercial varieties, which are *high* in sodium content. Low-sodium bouillon cubes and garlic powder are acceptable and helpful aids.

4. Make your own herb salt and keep it by the stove and on the table to season margarine, meats, vegetables, and soups.

5. Serve herb teas or punches instead of caffeine-laden beverages or heavily sugared bottled drinks. Serve unsweetened fruit juices flavored with mints and lemon-flavored herbs, and unsalted vegetable juices spiced with garlic, onion, basil, thyme, oregano, or bay.

6. Eat *fresh* fruits and vegetables as much as possible instead of highly sugared or salted canned commercial varieties. Serve fruits or fruit salads as desserts. Flavor with allspice, cinnamon, cloves, ginger, lemon balm or verbena, mace, marjoram, nutmeg or spearmint.

7. Serve *lean* meats, baked, broiled, roasted, or stewed. Remove all fatty portions and skim off fats from drippings. Flavor with herbs and spices. Serve poultry, veal, and fish often. Use beef, lamb, liver, and eggs less frequently, and pork products infrequently. (I've listed only the recommended protein sources here, from the American Heart Association's "Guide to a Man's Heart.")

Canned *mushrooms and* commercial *mustard are loaded with salt. Curry is strong; go light. Use fresh garlic or garlic powder. For best flavor, grind black peppercorns as needed. Limit egg yolks to 3 a week. Fresh white fish is best. Limit shellfish to oysters and 4 oz. of shrimp weekly. Use low-sodium-packed tuna and salmon. Use low-sodium tomato juice, vinegar, or red wine as base of slow-cooking stews and soups; add herbs and spices the last hour of cooking. Low-sodium cheese, mushrooms, onions or scallions enhance eggs.*

SEASONING VEGETABLES WITH HERBS & SPICES

I have listed only some of the complementary herbs and spices after each vegetable. Paprika, parsley, and freshly-ground black pepper can be added to any combinations except the spearminted peas and carrots, and the maple-flavored carrots. Nutmeg goes well with most vegetables, except those in the cabbage family.

A *GENERAL RULE* for making herb butters: for 1 lb. of vegetable use 2 T. of polyunsaturated oil or margarine (melted), ½ to 1 t. of herb(s), and ¼ t., or less, of spice(s). Gently toss the seasonings with the hot, drained vegetable.

To turn the "butter" into a sauce, add 2 T. lemon or tomato juice, sherry, vinegar, or the cooking liquid (or a combination of 2 of these).

Vegetables are best eaten *raw*. Next best is to steam them for the shortest time necessary.

VEGETABLE	SEASONINGS
ASPARAGUS	Lemon juice and dry mustard or thyme or marjoram
BROCCOLI	Lemon juice, dry mustard, and dill or nutmeg
BRUSSEL SPROUTS	Lemon juice or vinegar with dry mustard and dill
CABBAGE	Vinegar or lemon juice with marjoram, or with mustard and oregano or caraway seeds
CARROTS	Spearmint and marjoram; bay leaf and thyme or dill; honey and maple extract or maple syrup
CAULIFLOWER	Parsley with nutmeg or dill or tarragon or rosemary
CORN	Garlic powder or onion and paprika
EGGPLANT	Thyme, garlic, and oregano
GREEN BEANS	Savory and dry mustard; vinegar, garlic or onion, & dill
GREENS	Collard, endive, escarole, lettuce — oil, garlic, most herbs
LIMA BEANS	Lemon juice with parsley, onions, sage or savory
MUSHROOMS	(*fresh* only) — Lemon juice or sherry with onions, paprika and basil or thyme or tarragon; or ginger & rosemary
PEAS	Spearmint and/or marjoram; rosemary and thyme
POTATOES (white)	Onion or garlic, rosemary or mint
RUTABAGAS	Nutmeg or cinnamon
SUMMER SQUASH	Marjoram or parsley and paprika
SWEET POTATOES	Nutmeg or cinnamon and sherry
TOMATOES	Basil, bay leaf, chives, garlic, thyme
WATERCRESS	Lemon juice, paprika, parsley, and rosemary or sage
WINTER SQUASH	Nutmeg, ginger

(Some vegetables have been left off this list because they contain high amounts of sodium, such as kale, spinach, turnips, celery, chard, beet, dandelion, and mustard greens. Even carrots should be used with caution for this reason, if salt is a problem for you. Instant potato mixes and dried fruits processed with sodium are also forbidden on strict low-sodium diets, so use them with caution.)

My sources: American Heart Association's DAILY GUIDE TO GOOD NUTRITION and CRAIG CLAIBORNE'S GOURMET DIET.

SEASONING POULTRY, FISH, MEAT, & OTHER PROTEINS WITH HERBS/SPICES

Chives, paprika, parsley, and freshly-grated black pepper can be added to any or all of the blends, as can onions and fresh mushrooms. Novices should try one herb or spice at a time in order to develop a sense of the very individual flavors and a "feeling" for go-togethers. Eventually you will not miss the salt and butter tastes your body has acquired a craving for over the years. Be patient and creative!

PROTEIN	HERBS	SPICES
POULTRY	Basil, garlic, marjoram, rosemary, sage, tarragon, or thyme	Allspice, cayenne, cloves, curry, ginger, dry mustard, or nutmeg
FISH	Basil, bay leaf, chervil, chives, dill, marjoram, parsley, rosemary, scallions, thyme, or tarragon	Allspice, cayenne, curry, dry mustard, paprika
VEAL	Marjoram, oregano, parsley, or thyme	Curry or mace, paprika and freshly-ground pepper
BEEF	Basil, bay leaf, garlic, marjoram, oregano, onions or scallions, parsley, rosemary, thyme	Allspice, cayenne, chili powder, cloves, dry mustard, paprika, black pepper
LAMB	Garlic, marjoram, mint, onions or scallions, oregano, parsley, rosemary, sage, or thyme	Curry, black pepper
LIVER	Dill, onions or scallions, parsley, tarragon	Black pepper
EGGS	Basil, chives, marjoram, rosemary, tarragon, thyme	Paprika, pepper
DRIED BEANS OR PEAS	Use kidney, lima, or baked beans, lentils, or split peas as high-protein meat substitutes. Flavor with bay, mustard, marjoram, onions, parsley, black pepper, savory, thyme — your choice of blends.	

Even Popcorn Likes Herbs!

Herbs disguise the fact that you're not using butter — just substitute low-sodium herb margarine in any recipe calling for butter...even popcorn! When the family is sitting together around the fireplace you can treat them to something "special" without guilt. There are 40 calories in 1 cup of buttered popcorn, 32 in 1 cup of herb-margarined popcorn, and 25 in unbuttered (and 134 calories in a cup of caramel popcorn!). Here are examples of how herbs and spices can dress up "treat" food.

Herbed Popcorn For 8–10 cups of hot popcorn, melt ½ cup diet margarine seasoned with 1 tsp. oregano and parsley, and ½ tsp. each of basil, garlic powder, and onion powder. Let blend before stirring into hot popcorn. And pass the Parmesan!

Make a fresh or dried blend for veal or poultry using 2 parts lemon verbena and lemon thyme, and 1 part each of parsley, marjoram, thyme, and savory.

Spiced Popcorn For 2½ qts. hot popcorn, add ½ cup diet margarine in which you have blended:

Indian-Flavored: 1 tsp. each ground cardamom, cumin, and curry powder, and ½ tsp. each ground cinnamon, coriander, and nutmeg...plus a dash of ground cloves.

Mexican-Flavored: 1 tsp. each chili powder and ground cumin, and ½ tsp. each of paprika, crushed ground chilies, and garlic powder.

Oil-Free Popcorn Place a fry-pan over medium heat for 3 min., lower the heat, and add ½-cup unpopped corn or enough to cover the bottom of the pan. Cover and shake gently. Uncover when all sounds of popping have stopped. (If you must use oil in your corn-popper, make it *polyunsaturated,* as in safflower (best), sunflower, corn, soy, or cotton-seed.)

Herbs with Salad

Rose Canny shares the following salt-free recipes.

Salad Seasoning Blend Combine ⅓ cup toasted sesame seeds with 4½ T. onion powder, 2 T. poppy seeds, 1½ T. garlic powder, 1½ T. paprika, ¾ t. celery seed, and ¼ t. black pepper. Makes about 1 cup. (To make liquid dressing, mix 1 T. of this blend in a blender with ¾ cup oil and ¼ cup vinegar.)

No-Salt Herb Blend Combine 4 T. each of oregano leaves and onion powder with 4 t. each marjoram, basil, savory, garlic powder, thyme and rosemary, and 1 t. each sage and ground black pepper. Crush a small amount at a time in a mortar and pestle or in the blender. Spoon into a salt shaker. Makes about 1 cup.

Green Salad Rub a wooden salad bowl with a garlic bud, add crisp greens, and sprinkle with oregano or tarragon. Mix with vegetable oil and vinegar. Add a pinch of sugar if desired.

Check the Appendix for more books on healthy eating with herbs.

Resolution Recipes

These winter months after the holidays are perfect times to make fresh starts and new beginnings, especially for gardeners who now have more time to spend in the kitchen enjoying the harvests from our summer gardens...our dried herbs! The majority of nutritional diets stress eating more fish and poultry and less red meat. Here are several ways to serve these foods with your herbs and spices for variety of flavor and better health.

Phyl's Fish

1 6-oz. can *low-sodium* V-8 juice
2 T. polyunsaturated oil or unsalted margarine, melted
1 t. dill
1 t. paprika
1 lb. fresh white fish
1 thinly sliced onion

Gently heat the first 4 ingredients. Pour half of this herb sauce in the bottom of a baking pan. Place the fish in the pan and turn each piece over so that both sides are coated with the sauce.

Place onion rings on fish and pour or brush remaining sauce over all. Bake at 350 degrees for 30 minutes. *Serves 4.*

Double-Duty Salt-Free Dressing

Wonderful on tossed green salads or to baste chicken or fish before baking or broiling.

1 cup lemon juice
1 cup polyunsaturated oil
1 T. grated onion and juice
2 T. sugar
1 T. parsley
1 t. paprika
1 t. thyme or basil

½ t. dry mustard
¼ t. freshly-ground pepper

Combine all and beat in blender or mixer. Store in refrigerator. *Makes 2 cups.*

Herbed Fish Baste

For 4 servings of any baked or broiled fish

2 T. unsalted margarine or polyunsaturated oil
2 t. grated onion
1 t. lemon juice

1 t. rosemary or tarragon
1 t. parsley
Dash or two of pepper and paprika

Chive Butter for Chicken or Fish

For 4 servings

4 T. melted unsalted margarine
2 T. chopped chives

1 t. lemon juice
½ t. dry mustard

Rosemary Chicken Baste

2 T. unsalted margarine
2 T. sherry
1 t. paprika

1 t. rosemary
1 t. onion powder

Rosemary

And some other herbal treats for your winter pleasure.....

Tomato Sip for Six— Heat to boiling, then simmer for 10 minutes: 4 low-sodium beef bouillon packets, 3 cups water, 3 cups low-sodium tomato juice, 3 T. dry sherry, 2 T. lemon juice, 8 whole cloves, and 1 t. basil. Strain and serve in mugs. (6 lemon slices may be substituted for the lemon juice and floated in the mugs.) Serve with low-sodium crackers or pumpernickel sticks.

Salt-Less Salt — 3 T. each parsley, marjoram, basil, and thyme; 4½ t. chives; 2½ t. each rosemary, paprika, and onion powder. Grind all to a fine consistency in a mortar and pestle and place in your salt shaker or a used spice jar with shaker lid.
— **THE ROSEMARY HOUSE PA 17055**

THE HERBS OF SHAKESPEARE TEA

2 cups mints (peppermint or spearmint or 1 cup each)
½ cup marjoram
⅓ cup whole savory leaves
¼ cup lavender flowers

Mix thoroughly and store in tightly covered container. To use, steep 1 t. per cup of briskly boiling water for 10 min. or so to taste. Sweeten if desired. (Courtesy of Bertha Reppert and the Penn-Cumberland Garden Club)
— **THE ROSEMARY HOUSE PA 17055**

AN HERBAL NOTEBOOK

To begin the New Year right, start your own herbal looseleaf notebook, to compile information as you learn it from herb seed catalogs (see Appendix) or from any herbal books Santa brought you. To save yourself a lot of time hunting and rereading later, highlight all items, recipes, and so on that interest you with a felt-tip marker.

At the beginning of my well-worn notebook I still have my first "Herb Wish List" and three pages of "Things to Try", written after I had read my first literature on herbs (Adelma Simmons' early booklets and a few catalogs). I remember feeling overwhelmed at the time, and I devised the notebook to keep my accumulated knowledge in one easy-to-find place. I guarantee that you'll often refer to these pages!

Alphabetically list the herbs you'll grow, allowing at least three to four pages each. Record horticultural needs, growing habits, uses, and so on, for each herb as you learn about it.

Later you can use your notebook to note your gardening experiences — when and where you bought the seeds or plants, their botanical names, where, when, & how you planted them, and when and how they turned out. (If the results are disappointing, try new times, places, methods, and/or sources the next year!)

As you study, make lists of the culinary mixes and potpourri recipes you'd most like to try, along with the herbs, oils, flowers and fixatives needed for these creations. Then, if funds are limited you can start out with those items called for most often on your "Things to Try" list.

A fun project for the notebook is a comparison-shopping chart. My second year "into herbs" I had six catalogs to play with. (We're talking late '50s and early '60s — now it wouldn't be hard to have *60* herb catalogs.) My Wish List that year included more rose bushes and lavender plants, southernwood, tansy, several culinary herbs, orris root and more oils. I listed these in one column of my shopping chart, and the catalogs across the top of the page. The grid was filled in with prices and sizes or weights from each catalog. Very soon a pattern of consistency of pricing involved, and I ordered from the two that offered the most of what I wanted for the best price.

> *"Seed catalogs are a triumph of hope over experience. It's like having a second kid."*
>
> — *Anonymous*

BATHING WITH HERBS

January is the month I can take luxurious, leisurely baths. It's the one month I have very few pressures — no newsletter deadlines, no lectures (because of weather hazards), no outside gardening, and no rushed orders for my herbal products to deliver to stores. It is the month to pamper myself, to experiment with new scents and new pleasures, and to soak in the warm suds and dream of the spring to come. Time to read all the herbal catalogs and periodicals and plan new ventures for the summer gardens. Read on and join me!

Herbal Soaps

Glycerin soaps are the purest and mildest for the skin, containing the least amount of alkaline. The roots of Soapwort and Lamb's Quarters create suds when agitated in water and are excellent for skin and hair care. Camomile contains a soothing ingredient for the skin, called azulene, so is excellent for body care in the bath. This information is all from reader Dian Dincin Buchman's book, THE COMPLETE HERBAL GUIDE TO NATURAL HEALTH & BEAUTY, and she suggests an herb bath blend of ½ cup camomile flowers plus a dash of rosemary, horsetail, & pine needles (or extract).

English camomile

Camomile Jell Soap

Heat 6 cups water and 1½ cups of ground camomile flowers until boiling. Simmer for ½ hour and steep until cool. Meanwhile shred with a fine grater 2 cups of castile or other pure, mild soap. Re-heat 3 cups of the cooled camomile "tea" to a boil; add the soap and ½ cup of borax. Stir and boil for 3 min., then cool. Pour into pretty containers and keep covered. (Adapted from Jeanne Rose's HER-BAL BODY BOOK)

You can substitute the following herbs, but use *whole* leaves and strain after first cooling: Lemon Grass for oily skin, Peppermint for astringent soap, and Lavender for washing lingerie. You can also add ¼ oz. essential oil for scent, but not Bergamot or Pennyroyal — which could irritate sensitive skin.

Herb Soap Balls

Pour ¼ cup boiling water over 1 T. dried, pulverized herbs (Camomile or lavender flowers, leaves of peppermint, rosemary, sage, or thyme, or a combination of the last five!). Add 5 or 6 drops of a related essential oil, if desired, for a stronger scent. Steep 15 min. Reheat till bubbly, and pour over 2 cups shredded Ivory soap (1 "Personal size" bar). Mix well with hands and let stand 15 min. Mix again and divide into 3 or 6 parts, rolling each into a ball. Place on plastic wrap and dry for 3 days.

(Ruth Steber of Evansville, IN sent me the basis of this recipe from HERBCRAFT by Violet Schafer, and both Ruth and I experimented with it and made some adaptations. Ruth planned to wrap hers in nylon netting and ribbons for gifts.)

If you want to know all there is to know about scented home-made soap, your bookstore dealer can order Ann Bramson's SOAP, MAKING IT AND ENJOYING IT. For fancy soap molds, request the catalog of Pourette MFG. Co., PO Box 1520, Seattle, WA 98115.

Pamper Yourself

Bath Bags Make muslin or cheesecloth bags to hold ½ to 1 cup of herbs. Secure tightly with a ribbon or string long enough to hang from the faucet so the hot tap water will "steep" the oils and fragrances of the herbs, adding their benefits to your bath. An equal amount of fine oatmeal added to the herbs will act as a water softener and skin soother. Powdered milk may be included to simulate the skin-softening effects of a milk bath.

For softer skin, use camomile, calendula, and elder flowers in a blend with oatmeal and powdered milk. Rubbing the wet bag over your skin will bring extra benefits! *For a stimulating bath,* use rosemary, lemon verbena, marjoram, fennel, and lemon peel. (Or substitute thyme or sage.) *For a relaxing bath,* use camomile, calendula and lime flowers, rose geranium leaves, and a pinch of powdered valerian root or catnip leaves.

Rose geranium leaves

You can make an INFUSION by pouring 4 cups of boiling water over 4 T. of herb leaves and flowers; steep ½ hour, strain, and add to the bath water.

Make a DECOCTION by boiling 1 cup of herb seeds, barks or roots in 4 cups of water for 20 minutes. Strain and add to bath water. *For weary bones and aching muscles,* make a decoction of comfrey, sage, nettle, horsetail, and pine needles.

Dispersible Bath Oil (this will permeate the water) 4 parts Turkey Red Oil (from the pharmacist) and 1 part fragrant essential oil of your choice, such as lavender, jasmine, sandalwood. (Add sprig of fresh herb if desired.)

Floating Bath Oil 1 t. of almond oil will float on the water and coat your body as you leave the tub. (Or you can rub it on your body before the bath.) Scent the oil with an essential fragrance of choice.

The above information has been culled from an article by Emelie Tolley in a now defunct herbal newsletter, LIVING WITH HERBS.

Nancy McFayden, who sells essential oils and fragrant products wholesale, shares these two recipes.

Scented Bath Bubbles

2 cups Ivory Liquid
⅛ oz. essential oil

Let stand 1 week; use ¼ cup per bath.
— **GINGHAM 'N SPICE, PA 18926**

Bath Sachet

1 oz. **Lavender or Rosebuds & petals**
1 oz. **Peppermint or Rosemary leaves**
2 cups **Borax**

Combine and use 2 T. per bath. Fill muslin drawstring bag or cheesecloth, tie and float in water as tub fills. Hint: Add 2 T. oatmeal or cornmeal per bag if you have oily skin.
— **GINGHAM 'N SPICE, PA 18926**

Herbal Skin Oil

1 T. dried rosemary or sage
4 oz. safflower or wheat germ oil

Let stand in refrigerator for several days. Use for cleansing and lubricating. Soothes facial nerves.
— Martha Legg, Arkansas

Herbal Footbath

Add a handful of any or all of the following, tied in a cloth bag, to your footbath to soothe tired feet: fresh or dried comfrey, lavender, pennyroyal, rosemary, sage.

Lavender Bath

Equal amounts of lavender blossoms, comfrey leaves, and epsom salts, plus several drops of lavender oil. Blend well and store in a pretty container. Use a handful per bath to restore aching limbs.

Lavender Beauty Bath

Mix thoroughly 1 cup baking soda, 1 qt. Epsom salts, and 1 dram lavender oil. Place in a large bowl with a scoop. Add a scoopful to your hot bath and enjoy a fragrant, soothing soak. The mixture can be tied in muslin or cotton squares, too.

Bath bag

Camomile Skin Toner

Boil together ¼ cup camomile tea and 2 cups water. Divide in half. Keep half warm and half refrigerated. Alternate hot and cold compresses for a radiant look.

Oatmeal Beauty Scrub

4 oz. almonds
4 small hotel-sized soaps
1 dram rosemary oil
1 box oatmeal

Combine almonds and soaps in blender. Pulverize. Add to oatmeal. Mix in oil. Package in 4x4" cheesecloth squares to use for scrubs. Will stimulate circulation and act as a toner and cleanser.
— A BOUNTIFUL COLLECTION.

POTPOURRIS FOR JANUARY

New Year's Potpourri
"Reminiscent"

Recycle the greens from your holiday decorations and dry them to enjoy for the rest of the winter as fragrance "reminiscent" of Christmas.

1 qt. dried needles
2 cups dried red flowers
1 cup chopped patchouli leaves
½ cup broken cinnamon sticks
½ cup dried orange peel
½ cup frankincense tears, blend with:
1½ t. (45 drops) Christmas Fir* Essential Oil
1 T. each allspice, cinnamon, cloves, coriander seed, mace, and orris root, mixed

Dried cranberries and small cones (optional)

Place all ingredients in a brandy snifter or potpourri jar to use as a centerpiece.

*Available wholesale from GINGHAM AND SPICE PA 18926, the source of these recipes.

Check the store sales for wintery calicos and Christmas fabrics, nets, laces, and ribbons to make sachets and pillows for gifts from your fragrant herbs come fall.

Card Sachets

Save all your parchment-thin greeting cards to make *exquisite* re-cycled birthday, Christmas, get-well, or any-occasion cards. Fill the front and back with potpourri and machine-stitch together with colorful lace to match as a border. The potpourri can be loose or in maline or nylon net. (Or, hot-glue the edges together, in which case the potpourri should be enclosed in netting.) These are best sellers at craft fairs, according to Rose Rounds from Michigan.

Here are two mint recipes of mine that sell well at fall bazaars and make lovely Christmas gifts. The "Mintcense" makes a unique gift for a teacher, and children enjoy defoliating and sniffing the herbs used.

Herbal Acres Household Spice

A tablespoon of ground cinnamon, ground cloves, or vanilla extract may be substituted for the whole spices. For additional humidifying benefits, strain the steeped spice and use in a vaporizer to decrease static electricity and add fragrant moisture to a dry house.

1 cup dried peppermint
½ cup orange peel
1 cinnamon stick
1 T. whole cloves

½ vanilla bean or a tonka bean, sliced

Simmer gently in 6 cups water.

Mintcense

The colonists claimed that mint potpourri "cleared the head," and they placed it in covered china or apothecary jars for desk accessories. In the same tradition, this blend is an excellent room freshener when shaken and opened. Red bergamot flowers are a colorful, Christmas-ey addition.

2 cups each dried peppermint, orange mint, spearmint, and lavender

1 cup each thyme and rosemary
½ cup orris root blended with:
1 T. oil of lavender or pennyroyal

Winter Spice Incense

1 oz. frankincense tears
1 oz. myrrh pebbles
1 oz. vetiver
1 T. each allspice, cinnamon, cloves, coriander seed, mace, and orris root.
Lavender, rose petals, whole cloves,

or sandalwood or cinnamon chips (optional)

Place a few spoonfuls of this mixture in a metal dish on the back of your woodstove or in a slow oven and let smolder gently.

Peppermint

FEBRUARY

Rose geranium *(Pelargonium graveolens)*

FEBRUARY

*Herbs do comfort the wearied braine with fragrant smells
which yield a certain kinde of nourishment.*

— William Coles, 1656

IN LIEU OF the traditional candy or flowers, ask your Valentine to give you an herb book or two, from which you will learn many ways to say "I love you" in return all year round.

This is a good month to study those seed catalogs you ordered in January and to send your order for seeds and other planting equipment you might need. If you are fortunate enough to have a greenhouse or, like me, to have indoor lights, it is now time to visit local nurseries to purchase pots, sterile potting soil, seedling flats, and seeds of perennial herbs that can be started inside in February or March.

My gardening schedule here in the Northeast may not coincide with that of your gardening zone. Adjust your schedule according to your zone and the instructions in seed catalogs or on seed packages. Our climate allows for potted hardy perennial herbs to be put in the ground in April, and our frost-free date is mid-May, when we can safely plant *tender* perennials and annuals outside. By mid-October we must move all tender plants inside for winter protection. (The Harvesting Chart in JUNE elaborates on zonal differences.)

Purchase perennial herb seeds to be planted soon inside for a head start. Order perennial herb plants for spring delivery.

Get Ready for Spring ✄

February is a good month to perform the one gardening chore I dislike. But I am up to it this month because I am "itching" to get my hands into soil and am full of anticipation of the spring months to come. If you have a reserve cache of used potting soil and used pots and containers, now is the time to spend a few hours cleaning and sterilizing the pots and the soil to rid both of fungus, insect eggs, and bacteria. I soak the pots in a laundry sink-tub full of hot water to which I've added 3 or 4 cups of liquid bleach. When the water is cool, I use a scrub brush, and then rinse well with hot water again.

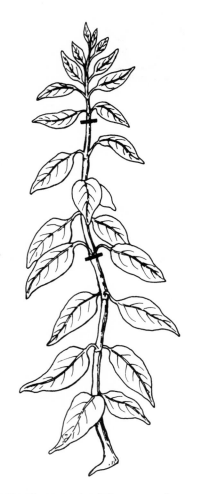

Cut plant stem just below a growing node.

The used soil (from plants that didn't make it through the winter!) can be sterilized in your oven some day when no one will be around to smell it. (About 200 degrees for 2 or 3 hours.) This should rid the soil of vermin or possible threats to your new creations this spring.

Start saving your eggshells for the sweet "lime-y" soil your herbs will want. Rinse them, and let them dry anywhere; then crumble them up and add to your potting soil. Or I put them in my blender with all vegetable peelings and discarded lettuce leaves and "liquefy." The strained solution is fed to the plants in my indoor garden all winter long, giving instant, fresh, natural nourishment to the herbs. What is left in the strainer goes right out to the compost pile for future mulch.

Save Citrus Peels

It is also time to get in the habit of saving all citrus peels for summer potpourris. Break the orange, lemon, or grapefruit rinds into pieces and dry anywhere on absorbent paper. (Paper towels or napkins are fine.) I place these in boxes on top of my metal reflectors holding my indoor garden lights. The heat hastens drying, but citrus peel will dry naturally if as much pith is removed as possible and if the pieces are not touching each other.

Oven drying, on lowest temperature with door ajar, is the quickest and best method, but requires careful attention to avoid overheating or burning as this destroys much of the flavor, fragrance, and color of citrus peel. Discard any peel that becomes discolored while drying, as this indicates the presence of unwanted fungus.

The winter months are good times to grind these dried peels, a handful at a time, in your blender, and store them separately in quart jars to display their bright golden hues. You can use these all year round to flavor herb teas and herb jellies, for any recipe that calls for orange or lemon flavoring and for use in scenting potpourri!

Take Cuttings

Next February you will delight in the winter joys of your indoor herbs and scented geraniums. This is a perfect month to prune them all and take cuttings to increase your summer harvest. The heavenly fragrances of the plants will help see you through the last weeks of winter.

Propagate indoor herbs and scented geraniums when growth has been vigorous by cutting at a slant just below a growing node, taking 4 or 5 inches from each branch. Strip all leaves except the top two or three and place the cuttings in wet vermiculite, perlite, sand, or peat. I use peat-packs that hold ten to twelve cuttings. Keep the soil wet, out of bright light, and in a warm place, such as on top of your indoor light reflectors, your clothes drier, a radiator, or the TV (which is warm every evening in many homes!).

In a week or so there should be signs of new growth, meaning the root system has started to develop. Now move the cuttings to a sunny window or under artificial lights and give weekly, but weak, feedings of a commercial indoor fertilizer when watering.

In a few weeks the cuttings will have strong enough root systems

Remove lowest set of leaves.

Insert cuttings about half their length into wet vermiculite, sand, perlite, or peat.

Transplant the cuttings into soil in a few weeks, when the roots are about an inch long.

to be transplanted into potting soil in individual peat pots. In mid-May I tear out the bottom of the pot and plant the new creation right in the garden, where it will provide new cuttings in August to bring inside in October.

Gourmet Gardening — Scented Geraniums

Scented-leaf geraniums have fascinated me ever since my mother-in-law, Anna Kirkbride Shaudys, gave me a rose-scented geranium many years ago that was a direct descendant from her mother's garden of the 1920s. The rose fragrance of the leaves was something of a miracle to me, as is the fact that three generations of the family, so far, have enjoyed the same plant and *its* descendants. I soon wanted other varieties and called a dozen nurseries within a 50-mile radius before I located one that sold these treasures — apple, lemon crispum, lemon rose, orange, lime, nutmeg, pine, musk, and peppermint scented geraniums. A collection of these will astound every visitor to your indoor and outdoor garden, and I always take a few bowls of freshly picked leaves to pass around the audience as I give a lecture, inviting them to take home the rose and fruit-scented treats to flavor their tea.

The culture and care of scented geraniums are very similar to those of the regular or zonal geraniums with which most gardeners are familiar. The flowers and leaves of the scented varieties are smaller and more delicate, and these plants are more noted for their fragrant, useful, and variously shaped leaves than for their visible beauty in the garden. They are excellent house plants, and share the other easy-to-tend attributes of the common geranium: they thrive in the garden or in pots or window-boxes outdoors, but will be killed by frost; they have succulent stems and can go a week or more without watering; they need a short "rest" when brought inside, but will eventually flower in a sunny window or under lights; they want a porous, loamy soil (I use the same sterile soil I recommend for herbs), and will perform beautifully with regular feedings and mistings; cuttings are easily

Make cuttings of scented geraniums and tender herbs you have wintered over.

Lavender

Start lavender from seed now with this method: sprinkle seeds on a wet paper towel and fold it four times. Place in a plastic bag and put on top of the refrigerator or in a top cupboard, preferably in a warm place where temperature stays around 70 degrees. In 4 or 5 days place germinated seeds 2 inches apart in flats filled with seed-sowing mix. Place in sunny window, water, and mist.
— from HARTMAN'S HERB FARM'S Annual Herbal Calendar MA 01005

rooted in sandy loam from the top 4–6 inches of the stems; they love SUN and like to live in cramped quarters with their relatives in pots. (I plant three mature plants in an 8–10" pot, and three new cuttings in a 4–6" pot).

I now have nearly 100 geraniums every year, both scented and zonal, in many colors and fragrances, all from a dozen "mother" plants purchased or inherited before 1977. Three times a year, during the indoor growing period, I spend a day giving them special TLC. Then it takes me two days to plant them in the ground or in planters in May and another two days in September to re-pot them so they will have time to adjust before I bring them in prior to our October frost. So, for one full week's work a year, I have lovely magenta, red, orange, and pink color in my gardens all summer and in my picture window all winter, as well as the dried blossoms of these regular geraniums for my Mintcense Potpourri. Even more importantly, I reap many *pounds* of sweet-scented leaves for my Sweet Bags, Citruscent, Sunshine and Rose-Geranium potpourris (see later in FEBRUARY). Of course, you can experience as much joy from a half dozen or a dozen each of both kinds of geraniums as I do from many dozens, for much less time.

My TLC Formula for Bountiful Geraniums

1. Bathe the plants by dipping them in a pail of tepid, sudsy water. Use mild dish soap or Fels Naptha bar soap, sliced with potato-peeler. I use the laundry tub in the winter, and pails and warm hose-water in summer. Set plants sideways on ground for a few minutes to absorb sudsy film. As with the bathing procedure, hold the dirt in the pot with your hand while rinsing off the suds. Let drip-dry. Your plants will be three shades greener and literally glowing with gratitude for being rid of insects and eggs.

2. Pull off dead or discolored leaves. Dry and store the scented ones.

3. Trim back plants by a third to a half of original height, making cuttings from the stems. (Cut diagonally below bottom node and cut straight across top, removing all leaves but the top two or three.) Root in a warm, shady place; outside or inside in sterile, sandy soil. Keep moist. Label all cuttings according to colors or scents. Feed at the first signs of new growth and move into the sunlight.

My geraniums get this TLC treatment in NOVEMBER, FEBRUARY, AND APRIL....and each time I feel *I've* had the therapy. Shortly after the April treatment, the plants are ready to go outside in the coldframe to "harden off" before their May entrance into the gardens. (They can be kept in pots all summer outside, but the scented geraniums will have much lusher foliage for harvesting if in the ground.)

The entire formula above is used in September when I uproot the plants to put them in new soil and clean pots, but then I also bathe

the *roots* in clear tepid water, after pruning the roots by a third. (This helps to eliminate insect larvae.)

I use a balanced fertilizer (20-20-20) for the scented varieties, as I am mainly interested in foliage development for my potpourri, but a regular houseplant or garden fertilizer is better for the zonal geraniums, to promote flowering.

All the geraniums come under the botanical name of *Pelargoniums.* Do yourself a favor and order some scented-leaf geraniums now from any of the catalogs in the Appendix listing herb plants for sale by mail. Start with the catalogs from **LOGEE'S NURSERY, CT 06239, SANDY MUSH HERBS, NC 28748,** or other herb firms selling plants locally.

Chervil

HERB SEASONINGS

Because this is a short month with fewer paychecks, the food budget must be stretched, at least at our house. In February you can make "gourmet" soup from any canned soup in your cupboard, by simply adding the crumbled leaves of the stored herbs from your summer harvest. Add a pinch of sage to chicken soup, thyme to fish chowder (especially cream of shrimp), basil to cream of tomato soup, and savory to vegetable or beef soups.

Even better, make your own herb mix by the pint or quart to add to all meat or vegetable soups or stews. Mix well the following dried herbs from your summer garden: One cup each of parsley, thyme, and marjoram (or oregano) leaves; ½ cup of summer savory; ¼ cup of either rosemary, basil, or sage; and 2 or 3 crushed bay leaves. Use a tablespoon at a time per 2 quarts of soup or stew stock, placed in a tea strainer or a cheesecloth bag during the last hour of cooking. (Best with beef, potatoes, onions, celery, carrots, and a little garlic powder.)

Turn canned soups into gourmet fare...add a pinch of rosemary and a teaspoon or two of both minced onion and lemon juice to asparagus soup; dried spearmint to pea soup; chervil, garlic, fennel, and/or bay leaf to fish soups.

Serve the soup or stew with a tossed salad and herb bread or rolls (see MARCH) and you will have a February meal fit for a king.

After your herb garden has become full-grown in two or three years, you will want to make enough of this mix (and others to follow in later chapters) to package up in plastic bags, with directions, to give to others to initiate them into the world of cooking with freshly-dried, home-grown herbs.

Note: all these soups can be dinner fare with the addition of hot herb bread and fresh fruit or a salad.

Herbed Corn Chowder

I use the following corn chowder recipe to stretch the budget and warm our hearts. I love it not only because it's delicious and easy to make, but also because it can be kept warm in my slow-cooker (on low) on nights when I'm not sure what time everyone will be home.

Thyme

6 slices bacon, diced and cooked,
   in large pan
1 medium chopped onion
1 medium diced green pepper (or
   ½ cup frozen green pepper)
2 1-lb. cans creamed corn
2 cans potato soup
2 cans milk

Sauté the onion and pepper in bacon fat in a large pan. Add the corn, potato soup, and milk to the pan and stir until smooth and hot.

While the chowder is warming up, add 1 T. chopped parsley and 1 T. chives and either 1 t. dill, 1 t. thyme OR 1 t. summer savory.

You may find you will want to stretch the recipe with more milk. I often add a third soup-can-full of milk if everyone seems unusually hungry and I want some leftovers to freeze for a quick weekend lunch. The recipe normally serves six generously.

We enjoy this chowder so much that I keep the ingredients on hand most of the time. I chop up my green peppers from the garden and freeze them in portions ready for this soup for winter use. Also, the chowder can be quickly prepared for unexpected company if the ingredients are in the larder. Hot herb bread and a salad make this a meal to remember.

Diet Soup

This will keep in refrigerator up to 2 weeks. Try this instead of a fattening snack. Or take to work for lunch in a thermos.

1 head shredded cabbage
1 large onion
2 cubes low-sodium beef bouillon
1 large can tomato juice
1 package frozen French-cut green
   beans
1 medium-size can tomatoes
1 t. each celery seed, garlic powder,
   parsley, thyme, and black pepper
Optional, but nice: celery, carrot,
   and green pepper slices

Add cabbage, onion, and bouillon cubes to tomato juice. When cabbage is half-cooked, add green beans, tomatoes, and seasonings.

(If using canned tomatoes and beans, you can remove most of the sodium content by rinsing the vegetables off in a strainer under cold water for 1 minute. Use low-sodium tomato juice.)

Fish Chowder

6 slices bacon
2 large onions, thinly sliced
4 medium potatoes, diced
2 cups water
1 bay leaf
1 lb. frozen flounder, haddock, or cod fillets, thawed & sliced into 1" chunks (check for bones)
1 t. each garlic powder, thyme, pepper
1 qt. milk
3 T. flour blended with 3 T. water
2 T. butter
1 T. parsley
Paprika

Cook bacon until crisp in a 3-qt. saucepan; remove, crumble, and set aside. Cook onion until golden in the bacon fat in saucepan. Add potatoes, water and bay leaf. Boil gently, covered, until potatoes are almost tender, about 15 min. Add fish, garlic, thyme and pepper; simmer gently until fish is cooked through, about 5 minutes. Meanwhile, gently scald milk and stir in flour mixture, cooking and stirring until thickened. Add to fish mixture. Just before serving, remove bay leaf and add bacon, butter, parsley and paprika. May be kept warm in slow-cooker on low. *Makes 2 quarts.*

Chicken Soup...Plus

4 lbs. chicken parts
3 cups tomatoes
2 cups sliced onion
6 cups sliced celery
3 cups sliced carrots
1 t. each: salt, garlic powder, pepper, celery salt, oregano
6 bay leaves
1 24-oz. pkg. frozen cut corn
1 24-oz. pkg. frozen baby lima beans
1 10-oz. pkg. frozen okra

Place chicken in 5-qt. pot. Fill to nearly the top with water. Add a dash of salt and pepper. Bring to boil then reduce heat, cover, and simmer for ½ hour.

Remove chicken from broth to cool and skim fat from broth. Measure broth and place in 10-qt. pot, adding enough water to make a total of 18 cups. Add seasonings and *fresh* vegetables and bring to a boil. Meanwhile remove skin and bones from chicken and cut meat into bite-size chunks. Add frozen vegetables and chicken. Bring to boil again. Reduce heat, cover, and simmer 1½ hours. Remove bay leaves before serving. *Serves 8–10 generously.*

Beef Chowder

1 lb. ground beef
1 cup each (chopped or sliced) onions, celery, carrots, and potatoes
4 cups water
1 t. brown bouquet sauce
1 t. garlic powder
½ t. basil
¼ t. ground pepper
1 bay leaf
1 28-oz. can tomatoes, with liquid

Brown meat in large saucepan, stirring occasionally. Remove most of fat from pan. Add onions and cook another 5 minutes. Stir in remaining ingredients and heat to boiling. Reduce heat, cover, and simmer gently about 30 minutes. Add salt to taste, if needed or desired. Remove bay leaf before serving. *Serves 4.*

Sweet bay

PLOTTING THE HERB BED

If you've postponed growing herbs until you can create an elaborate formal herb garden, you're wasting precious time that could be spent enjoying herbs planted among your perennial flowers, as a border to the house, or in the vegetable garden. (Place *perennial* herbs in the corners of the vegetable patch, so they won't be rototilled up each spring; see COMPANION PLANTING CHART in MAY.) By the time you have the funds, time, space, or energy to create a masterpiece of colonial perfection, you'll have well-established "mother" plants to propagate for your formal bed, and you'll be familiar with their growing habits and visual effects to help you plan the design.

For the first several years of my "herbing," my original sixteen herbs were placed among my hyacinths, daffodils, and shrubs bordering the house, and also in the perennial flower bed. I planted annual herbs in the vegetable garden in a patch of their own.

When I decided to start a small herb business in 1976, we felt the herbs should have a place of their own. The family helped me create three herb gardens that first summer, and the sixteen well-established "mother" plants were root-propagated into enough plants to fill the new beds. (For example, my three English lavenders mothered 25 healthy children, their well-spread root systems providing enough "heels" to multiply fruitfully.) Each year thereafter, we added a new bed or two until we reached the magic number of nine gardens in all, about seven more than I can take care of now that the children have left home and garden and I've become busy with indoor pursuits!

I didn't plan my gardens to be for "show." Rather they are "working" beds for continual harvesting, since my herb business requires large amounts of fragrant plants to produce the gift products I sell wholesale locally. But I did have fun designing them to please myself with contrasting forms, textures, heights, and shades of gray and green, interspersed with colorful flowers for accent.

I have culinary and fragrance beds, a rose garden of 34 bushes, a perennial bed with wedge-shaped patches which somewhat resembles a formal garden, and separate beds for the herbs I use most for my business — lavender, catnip, lemon southernwood and Silver King artemisia.

Five of my beds are 15' by 30'. There's nothing magical about this size, except that this was the size of our original vegetable garden, which became my "colonial" bed in 1976. (I wanted the fertile soil for my herbs because our land is so acidic.) So Hugh dug up a new vegetable garden next to it, the same size as the first so it would look planned. I soon needed this second garden for my lavender bed. And number 3 for the southernwood. And number 4 for the catnip. Number 5 remains vegetable, and probably will forever (unless I get a new husband).

The last four vegetable gardens required chicken wire fences, since we have deer, rabbits, and other fauna who like our flora. I've

Chart out your garden plans on paper, according to the herbs you want, their sizes at maturity, their sun and soil needs, and their textures, shapes, and colors.

Wash and sterilize clay pots in the dishwasher.

grown all kinds of fun things to disguise the fences and enhance the herbs. Wormwood borders the lavender and southernwood beds, tall marigolds add color to the catnip patch along with spectacular golden blooms of luffa plants draped gracefully over its fence, and the vegetable garden is adorned with a border of spaghetti squash plants.

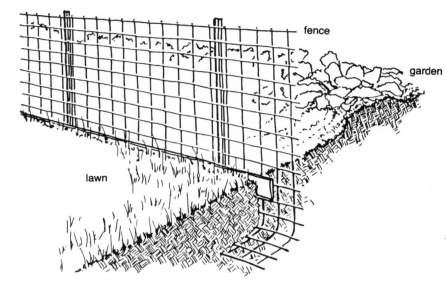

This pest-proof fence is three feet above ground (stretched on metal fence posts) and one foot below ground, and runs one foot out horizontally underground to discourage burrowers. To build it, dig a trench a foot deep and a foot wide around the entire garden, install the fencing, fill in the trench — and, if necessary, reseed the lawn! Around the bottom of the fence sink four-inch-high plastic edging to keep weeds from growing into the garden.

We used treated (pressure-treated, not creosote) 2" x 4" wood barriers to contain our perennial fragrance garden several years ago. They have not rotted but they need reinforcement and stamping down every few years because of their light weight. (The nails holding them together come loose.) After adding vegetable/leaf/lime compost as an organic mulch every other year or so, the garden sections are now raised beds about 4" higher than the paths, a condition beloved by herbs. So now we need to make *higher* and *deeper barriers*. If you happen to be related to a mason, you can solve the barrier problem forever — with deep concrete trenches around the borders, disguised on top with a brick edging!

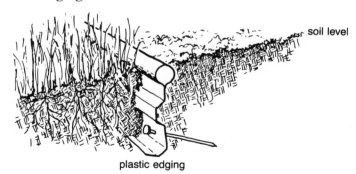

Commercial polyethylene edging with a rounded top can be shaped into curves for a curved bed, and then sunk into the earth so that only the top lip shows. A flange on the bottom keeps it from popping up, and a steel spike driven in every four or five inches prevents frost heaving. This keeps mulch in *and grass* out *of the bed.*

While many people have periodic yens to redecorate inside, I long to start all over again *outside,* rearranging everything and adding new accents, colors, and textures. The patterns that follow are based on what I have tried or on what I hope to try. Once you have determined *where* to plant your herbs, sun-wise, the locale may determine the size and shape of the beds.

This 3' x 14' culinary herb bed should be located along a south- or southeast-facing wall of your house, close to the kitchen door. Back row is mostly perennials; front row, mostly annuals.

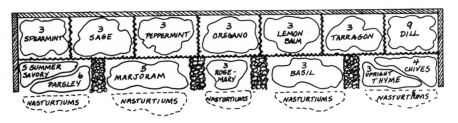

Basic culinary bed (3' x 14')

<u>KEY</u>

TP = Tender perennial

Lay down pebble or brick mini-paths to allow access to back plants.

〰〰〰 Use metallic, brick, or concrete dividers, placed at least 8" deep and 3" above soil level, to prevent spreading roots from intermingling and getting out of hand.

Border the sunniest side of the house with a fragrance bed.

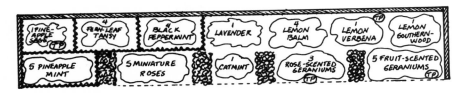

Basic fragrance bed (3' x 14')

Try the "add-a-bed-a-year" plan if you have limited time, space, or funds. A 3'x3' bed holds five different culinary herbs and yields enough harvest for a small family. Add an adjoining plot of the same size the next year, and another the year after that, etc. Each year you'll become familiar with five new gourmet treasures, and you'll eventually own a twenty-herb culinary bed, framed by paths among the four gardens. You could add a fence or border and a central object of interest, my favorite being a small bench. Carve out the bottoms of four large (12") green plastic pots. Bury these in the center of each square to contain the tall spreading herbs, leaving 3 or 4" above the soil level. These will be the focal unit of each bed. Caution: always allow enough space between beds for the lawn mower (until you create paths with pebbles or bark) and to allow enough space for sitting comfort while weeding and harvesting.

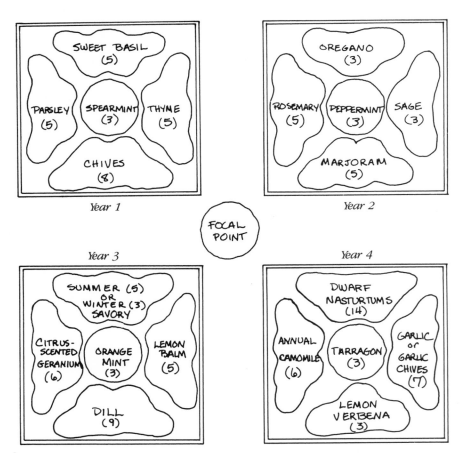

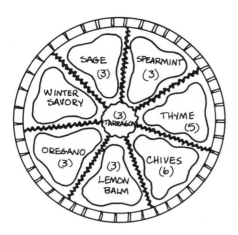

Perennial culinary wheel (3'–4' wide)
(must have permanent dividers).

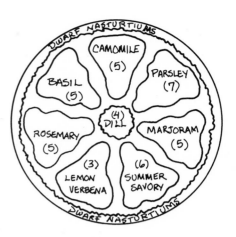

Annual culinary wheel (3'–4')

Annual all-basil culinary wheel (or all-lemon, all-thyme, etc.)

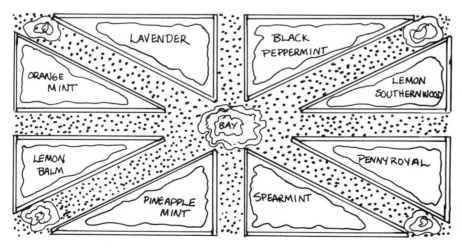

Perennial fragrance bed (15' x 30') — enhanced by fragrant annuals in summer.

<u>KEY</u>

 = paths of fragrant perennial camomile, cocoa bean hulls, or pine bark.

 = in summer, place potted bay tree in center of garden and lemon verbena, scented geraniums, and pineapple sage in the corners, leaving 4 exits open.

Designing Your First Herb Garden

by Bertha Reppert

Any small garden area can be your herbal playground. Size has nothing to do with productivity and usefulness. It is most important, however, to think of your herb plot, be it great or small, in terms of an overall design. Circles within squares; triangles, overlapping or extending into another plot; short rows of the same herb, straight or curved — these will give your herbal plot an interest, an inner beauty, that will set it apart from all other gardens.

The way to start herb gardening is with those herbs you already know. If you enjoy mint, chives, and parsley, then add to these three more herbs with which you are not familiar — let's say basil, thyme, and tarragon. Now, you see, you have six flavorful kinds of plants to grow, learn about, use, and enjoy. Assuming that your plot is a small rectangle, approximately 2 by 5 feet, let's plant it as in figure 1. This design is suitable for a kitchen garden and would lend itself admirably to the addition of a small garden feature such as a sundial, figurine, or birdbath. Plant the mint around the garden feature and keep it neatly clipped.

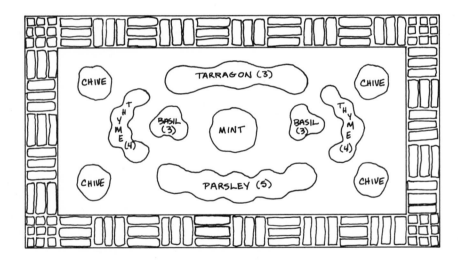

Figure 1. A small 2' x 5' kitchen garden.

Another plan, this for an 8-foot square area, might include a small walk within the design. Using an entirely different assortment of herbs, this could be planted as in Figure 2, featuring predominantly soft and lovely grays. The edging can be the creeping thyme plants, a mat that will crawl into the paths and release its fragrance as it is trodden upon. Or, if more color is desired, use cheerful pansies (heartsease) in spring and dwarf nasturtiums for summer and fall. Plant the pansies in bloom and tuck the plump nasturtium seeds in between. They will sprout, grow, and take over when summer heat curtails the pansies' blooming.

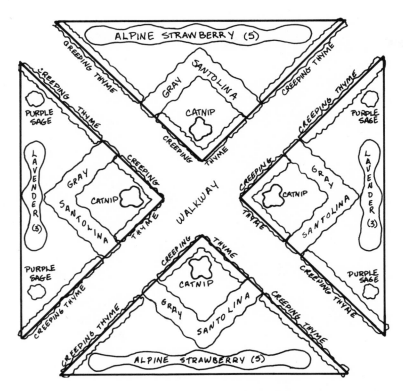

Figure 2. An 8-foot-square garden.

Each of these compact herb gardens would be an asset to a property, a joy to tend, and a pride to own. They would, despite their small dimensions, yield a generous harvest. In both instances the design of the garden depends upon careful clipping and continual harvesting of the plants. Overgrown herbs, weakened and spindly, would quickly obscure the original design of the garden.

It is entirely possible to do a small herb garden for $25.00. There can be no greater pleasure possible for so small an investment.
THE ROSEMARY HOUSE, PA 17055

HERB GROWTH & USE CHART

HERB	BOTANICAL NAME	LIFE CYCLE	AV. HGT.	GROWING	SPECIFIC NEEDS	BASIC USES
AMBROSIA	*Chenopodium Botrys*	HA	18"	Sow inside or outside; SS		Fragrant fresh or dried arrangements and wreaths
ANGELICA	*Angelica archangelica*	BI	4'	Sow outside in fall; SS	Moist, rich soil; part shade	Culinary, medicinal, potpourri fixative
ANISE	*Pimpinella anisum*	A	24"	Sow outside		Culinary, medicinal, cosmetic
ARTEMISIA (Silver)	(Ornamental Silver Mound, King, Queen)	P	6-24"	Root divisions		Fresh or dried wreaths and arrangements
BASIL	*Oscimum basilicum* and family	A	18"	Sow indoors in late spring	Rich soil; Bush B. best for pot culture	Culinary, potpourri, fly deterrent, cosmetics
BAY, SWEET	*Laurus nobilis*	TP (in pots)	2-6'	Stem cuttings	Pot culture in cold climates	Culinary, potpourri, cosmetics
BERGAMOT	*Monarda didyma* ("Beebalm")	P	36"	Root divisions	Part shade	Tea, potpourri, cosmetics
BORAGE	*Borago officinalis*	A	30"	Sow inside for early start	Rich soil	Cucumber flavor for salads; candied petals; medicinal
CALENDULA	*Calendula officinalis* ("Pot Marigold")	A	24"	Sow inside in early spring	Sow in peat pots	Culinary, food coloring, medicinal, cosmetic
CAMOMILE (Annual)	*Matricaria recutita* ("German" C.)	A	18"	Sow inside; SS		Tea, medicinal, dye, potpourri
CAMOMILE (Perennial)	*Chamaemelum nobile* ("Roman" C.)	P	6"	Sow inside; SS		Hair rinse; ground cover
CARAWAY	*Carum Carvi*	BI	24"	Sow outside in fall or inside in spring		Culinary, cosmetics
CATMINT	*Nepeta mussinii*	P	18"	Root divisions		Lovely purple flowers; ant & insect repellent
CATNIP	*Nepeta cataria*	P	18"	Root divisions or sow inside; SS		Tea, cat tonic insect repellent, cosmetics
CHERVIL	*Anthriscus cerefolium*	HA	24"	Sow outside in fall	Shade	Culinary
CHIVES	*Allium schoenoprasum*	P	12"	Sow inside or outside early spring	Rich soil	Culinary, fresh or dried floral arrangements
CLARY SAGE	*Salvia viridis*	BI	12"	Sow outside in late summer or inside in early spring	Sandy, dry soil	Arrangements, potpourri fixative, cosmetics
COMFREY	*Symphytum officinalis*	P	36"	Root division in early spring	Rich, moist soil	External healing, cosmetics, composting*

HERB	BOTANICAL NAME	LIFE CYCLE	AV. HGT.	GROWING	SPECIFIC NEEDS	BASIC USES
CORIANDER	*Coriandrum sativum* ("Chinese parsley")	HA	24"	Sow inside; SS		Culinary, potpourri
COSTMARY	*Chrysanthemum Balsamita* ("Bible Leaf")	P	36"	Root division	Will grow in shade but not blossom	Culinary, potpourri, cosmetics
DILL	*Anethum graveolens*	A	30"	Sow outside	Rich soil	Culinary
FENNEL	*Foeniculum vulgare*	A	30"	Sow outside by itself	Well-limed soil	Culinary, cosmetic
FENUGREEK	*Trigonella Foenumgraecum*	A	18"	Sow outside	Rich soil	Maple flavoring, sugar substitute, medicinal
FEVERFEW	*Chrysanthemum Parthenium*	P	36"	Early spring sowing or root division	*May not remain perennial if winter soil too wet or if allowed to go to seed*	Arrangements, insect repellent, cosmetics, potpourri
GARLIC	*Allium Sativum*	P	24"	Plant bulbs in fall, bulb division	Moist, rich soil	Culinary, medicinal, cosmetic
GERANIUMS (Scented)	*Pelargonium*	TP	18"	Stem cuttings		Culinary, potpourri, cosmetics
HOREHOUND	*Marrubium vulgare* (White)	P	18"	Sow indoors; SS; root division	Loves hot, dry soil	Garden edgings, bouquets, candy, coughdrops
HYSSOP	*Hyssopus officinalis* and family	P	24"	Sow indoors	Well-limed soil; partial shade OK	Potpourri fixative, white fly deterrent, cosmetics
LADY'S MANTLE	*Alchemilla vulgaris*	P	12"	Root division; SS		Sleep pillows, arrangements, medicinal, cosmetic
LAVENDER (English)	*Lavendula angustifolia*	P	24"	Sow indoors, stem cuttings, root division, layering		Potpourri, cosmetics, arrangements, medicinal
LEMON BALM	*Melissa officinalis*	P	24"	Sow inside; SS; root division	Part shade OK	Culinary, potpourri, cosmetic
LEMON VERBENA	*Aloysia triphylla*	TP	36"	Stem cuttings	Rich soil	Culinary, potpourri, medicinal, cosmetic
LOVAGE	*Levisticum officinale*	P	6'	Sow inside or outside	Moist, rich soil; part shade OK	Celery flavor for cooking, salt substitute; cosmetics
MARJORAM (Sweet)	*Origanum Majorana*	TP	12"	Sow inside or outside	Rich soil	Culinary, potpourri, medicinal
MINTS	*Mentha* family	P	18-30"	Root divisions, generally	Most like moist soil & part shade	Culinary, potpourri, bouquets, medicinal, cosmetic
OREGANO	*Oreganum vulgare*	P	24"	Root division		Culinary
PARSLEY (Curly)	*Petroselinum crispum*	BI	12"	Sow outside	Rich soil; part shade OK. *2nd yr. harvest negligible*	Very nutritious when fresh; cosmetics

HERB	BOTANICAL NAME	LIFE CYCLE	AV. HGT.	GROWING	SPECIFIC NEEDS	BASIC USES
PENNYROYAL (English)	*Mentha pulegium*	P	12" +	Sow inside	Moist soil; part shade OK	Insect repellent, cosmetics, potpourri**
PINEAPPLE SAGE	*Salvia elegans*	TP	36"	Stem cuttings		Culinary, potpourri, bouquets
ROSEMARY	*Rosmarinus officinalis*	TP	1-4'	Stem cuttings	Loves misting of foliage	Culinary, potpourri, cosmetics, incense
RUE	*Ruta graveolens*	P	24"	Sow inside; root division	Part shade OK	Insect deterrent, hedges, bouquets
SAFFLOWER	*Carthamus tinctorius*	A	30"	Sow inside midspring		Coloring & flavoring food, dye, cosmetics
SAFFRON	*Crocus sativus*	P	8"	Plant bulbs in fall	Rich soil, part shade	Coloring & flavoring food
SAGE	*Salvia officinalis*	P	24"	Sow inside; stem cuttings, root divisions	Well-limed soil	Culinary, cosmetic, medicinal
SALAD BURNET	*Poterium sanguisorba*	P	18"	Sow inside; root division		Cucumber flavor for salads
SANTOLINA (Gray)	*Santolina chamaecyparissus*	P	24"	Stem cuttings		Hedges & knot gardens, potpourri
SHALLOT	*Allium ascalonicum*	P	15"	Plant bulbs in early spring; bulb division	Rich soil	Onion flavor & substitute
SORREL (French)	*Rumex scutatus*	P	18"	Sow outside; SS	Re-sow every 3 yrs.	Culinary
SOUTHERN-WOOD	*Artemisia abrotanum*	P	3'	Root divisions; layerings, cuttings		Insect deterrent, potpourri, cosmetics, arrangements, wreaths
SUMMER SAVORY	*Satureja hortensus*	A	18"	Sow inside in peat pots, or outside		Culinary — the "Green Bean" herb
SWEET CICELY	*Myrrhis odorata*	P	3'	Root division or seeds outside in fall	Rich soil; part shade OK	Anise-flavor sugar substitute, cosmetics, arrangements
SWEET WOODRUFF	*Gallium odoratum*	P	10"	Root divisions; stem cuttings	All-shade, leafy moist soil	Culinary, potpourri, ground cover
SWEET WORMWOOD	*Artemisia annua*	HA	5'	Sow inside or out; SS	Needs plenty of room (3' wide)	Fragrant wreaths, arrangements, potpourri
TANSY	*Tanecetum vulgare*	P	3'	Root division	Toxic to cattle; do not plant where livestock graze	Ant & insect deterrent, fresh & dried arrangements, dye, cosmetics
TARRAGON (French)	*A. dracunculus* variety *sativa*	P	30"	Root divisions or layering		Culinary, cosmetic, medicinal
THYME (Upright)	*T. vulgaris*	P	12"	Root division or layering		Culinary, cosmetic, medicinal

HERB	BOTANICAL NAME	LIFE CYCLE	AV. HGT.	GROWING	SPECIFIC NEEDS	BASIC USES
WINTER SAVORY	*Satureja montana*	P	12"	Sow inside; layering		Culinary
WORMWOOD	*Artemisia Absinthium*	P	36"	Sow inside; root division	Part shade OK	Insect repellent, wreaths, arrangements, medicinal
YARROW	*Achillea species*	P	24"	Root division		Wreaths, arrangements, cosmetics

Explanation of Terms

This chart lists some of the herbs most commonly grown by hobbyists. Other herbs, and a break-down of the many "families" of herbs, will be discussed in future issues of *'Potpourri'*. If some of the botanical names look strange to you, it is because I have tried to use the latest terminology, whenever possible, provided by the definitive source, *HORTUS THIRD,* compiled by the L. H. Bailey Hortorium, Cornell University (Macmillan, 1976).

Life Cycle: A stands for Annual, a plant having life for one growing season only; started by seed.

HA means Hardy Annual, having a one-year life cycle, but self-sowing freely.

P is for Perennial, which should come back each spring, the roots surviving the winter.

TP stands for Tender Perennial, which will be killed by frost or severe cold weather. In cold climates these plants should be wintered over in the house, greenhouse, or coldframe. In warm climates these herbs should be given protection if a freeze is expected.

BI means Biennial, a plant which takes two years to mature, but quickly goes to seed the second year, necessitating annual plantings for consistent harvests.

Average Height: an approximate measure of the height of the mature plant, if not cut back during the growing season. Especially useful when designing the garden.

Starting and Propagating: Sow Inside = start seeds in house, greenhouse, or coldframe several weeks before frost-free date in cold climates to give a head start before transplanting in garden. This allows time for the plant to mature during shorter growing seasons. Those with long growing seasons can start the seeds directly outside when the soil is warm. **Sow Outside** = when soil and climate are warm, after frost-free date for your area, unless otherwise noted. **SS** = Self-Sows, so allow some of the plants to go to seed and dry in the garden. If soil and climatic conditions are cooperative, you'll find seedlings in the spring. **Root Division** — means you should purchase a plant rather than to try to grow it from seed, and propagate by root division, usually in the spring, when the "mother" plant is well-established. **Stem Cuttings** = purchase plant; propagate by cuttings.

Specific Needs: Exceptions to the general requirements for most herbs (SUN, SWEET AND WELL-DRAINED SOIL). If you've had poor success with some herbs, the clue may be here! **Rich Soil** = full of organic nutrients, such as vegetable and leaf compost. Well-decomposed manure can be used for some herbs, but NOT for any of the large mint family, on which it can cause rust.

*COMFREY: There is currently some question about the safety of *consistent, long-term* use of comfrey internally. Until research proves otherwise, internal use of *mature* comfrey *leaves* (only) is recommended. Comfrey has been a well-documented healing herb for centuries, without any blemishes on its reputation. Hopefully, it will be vindicated soon.

**PENNYROYAL: although occasional consumption of pennyroyal tea is not harmful, consistent use of large amounts is not recommended. *Under no circumstances* should the oil of pennyroyal, which can be very toxic to humans, be consumed by anyone, but especially by pregnant women or those hoping to become pregnant, as it can cause abortion.

This chart, combined with my Harvesting and Preserving Chart (see JUNE), has been published in the newsletter, POTPOURRI FROM HERBAL ACRES, and is available free to subscribers of that publication for distribution at herb shops, nurseries, and lectures. Write to Dept. POH for details.

When you're ready to get fancy with your gardens, you'll want all kinds of "specialty" beds. Here are some of the designs currently on my own dreaming and scheming list....

Had you thought of a breath-taking Silver Garden? (And beautiful Christmas Wreaths.) Try gray santolina, dittany of Crete (see "Oregano" in Appendix), eucalyptus, horehound, lamb's ear, lavender, mugwort (Artemisia vulgaris), and other artemisias: Silver King, Silver Queen, Silver Mound, Versicolor, and wormwood.

- An all-purple-flowering bed, topped by lavender-flowered bergamot, edged with purple basil, with lavender, oregano, peppermint, and purple sage in between.
- A special biennial bed — to help keep track of what needs to be preserved for seed and/or re-seeded for constant supply. (Caraway, coriander, anise, chervil, angelica, honesty, clary sage, and parsley.)
- A 5' x 45' "everlastings" bed, with a flagstone path down the middle and long rows of globe amaranth, statice, celosia, and strawflowers.
- A "tea" garden of herbs for tea blends, such as the mints, bergamot, camomile, scented geraniums, and most of the culinary herbs. How about having tea parties where guests can pick their own "tea" and take some home?
- An insect-chaser garden with wormwood, rue, tansy, camphor and other southernwoods, pennyroyal, and cat*mint,* all to be harvested for moth and insect-deterrent sachets.
- A rock garden featuring the thymes, both upright and creeping. (See "Thyme" in Appendix for partial listing of varieties available.)
- And my *pièce de résistance:* a perennial Christmas Wreath Garden, shaped like a wreath, with herbs to be harvested for wreath-making — featuring the southernwoods on the outside (tall and green), Silver King Artemisia in the middle, lavender, and an inner edging of Silver Mound Artemisia. It would be centered and pathed with white gravel (to symbolize white ribbons and the hole in the wreath), with lamb's ears at the core, surrounded by gray santolina.

Your own desires might include a Biblical garden, a medicinal bed, one featuring the dye herbs, a Salad Bowl herb garden, or perhaps colonial designs like those featured at Williamsburg. Designs for these gardens and many others (51 in all!) are outlined in a brand new book on this subject alone, HERB GARDEN DESIGN. It's for novices as well as professionals, including beginner's gardens, hillside and terrace plans, formal, historic, specialty, and educational designs, and *much more.*

And *an absolute must* for novices is THE BEGINNER'S HERB GARDEN from The Herb Society of America.

A word about this prestigious organization. Membership is limited to those who are experienced in the use of herbs and who have made contributions in the form of the studious pursuit of herbs or in creating educational programs or gardens for the benefit of the public. The focus of the Society is to share knowledge about herbs and this is accomplished through regional symposiums and programs and many public herb gardens throughout the country, primarily the National Herb Garden, a gift from the HSA to the nation. (Send for pamphlets about this to: Information Center, National Herb Garden, U.S. National Arboretum, Washington, DC 20016.)

Bergamot

Regional and Climatic Differences in Herb Growth Patterns

If you live in extremely hot or cold regions, some herbs will be more difficult to grow than others. If your climate is very dry or very wet, you will have another set of problems. Basically, the warmer climates have longer growing seasons (sometimes all year!), in which case those herbs needing a dormant cold spell (such as English lavender, French tarragon, and sweet woodruff) will not grow well as perennials or easily survive the long hot summer heat. On the other hand, perennials that are *tender* in the north (such as rosemary, marjoram, sweet bay, lemon verbena) will grow all year long in many southern regions, needing only mulch protection or temporary cover if a frost is predicted.

Many southern gardeners find it easiest to protect herbs from the intense heat and light of the direct summer sun by growing them in pots, thus also providing richer organic soil and more adequate moisture control...and keeping them in locations with diffused light, such as under shade trees. (No more than 4 or 5 hours of sun a day for herbs in pots in the south.) Raised beds are also recommended for herbs in those parts of the south (or *any* region) with heavy rainfall, especially for lavender and sage. Wherever there are long, hot, and *humid* summers, it is wise to plant French tarragon, the gray-leafed oreganoes, and most of the gray or woolly herbs in wire containers with peat or sphagnum moss for the excellent drainage these provide. These containers can be moved about to avoid the rains. The gray artemisias do not generally do well in extreme southern humidity.

If you live in the far *northern* regions, your main problems will be the severe winter cold and the short growing season in the summer for the annuals and tender perennials. Heavy winter mulches should cut down on the winter-kill devastation of perennials. Also, be sure you don't prune these in the fall, lessening their protective cover. The growing season can be extended with the use of heated coldframes, protected raised beds, greenhouses, or indoor gardening *under lights* (not enough winter sun in the far north for window gardening). Container gardening is also advantageous in the colder regions, as the potted herbs can be easily moved under cover for protection against sudden impending late or early frosts.

In extreme *dry* climates and soils, herbs will need the same help necessary for any greenery—plenty of rich organic humus added to the soil, heavy mulching to preserve the moisture in the soil, and some irrigation system or plan to insure that the roots do not dry out. And protection from the continual rays of the hot sun is a must. Container gardening in lath sheds would be advantageous.

In each area, and in all regions, planting times will depend upon your hardiness zone frost-free dates, depicted on many seed packages, for your specific locale. Call or write your State and County Agricultural Extension Departments for information about herb growing in your area.

See Bibliography for recommended books for southern gardeners. PARK'S SUCCESS WITH SEEDS is recommended reading for all.

While planning your exterior decorating, consider a colorful perennial pink-to-purple herbal rainbow, combining several varieties of lavender, sage, and oregano with a background of rose, crimson, and purple bergamot.

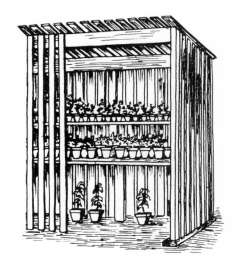

A lath house protects tender seedlings from summer sun.

February Fantasies: Herb Lore for Lovers

By Betty Wold

Valentine's Day, love, magic and herbs...they all come to mind in February. Gardeners and lovers who were foresighted enough to plant an herb garden will now have the ingredients for many romantic amulets and love potions.

Perhaps you are still searching for the true love of your life. According to ancient lore, you will dream of your true love if you sleep with yarrow under your pillow. To make marriage certain and soon, slip some orange leaves in with the yarrow.

The course of true love is not always smooth, though, and it is possible that the vision of your dreams does not realize he or she is the mate for you. Do not despair. There are any number of herbal charms you can use to your advantage. The first step, if you are a woman, is to offer your intended a sprig of basil. If he accepts it, you have won him. Should that fail, bathe in warm water to which a cupful of rose petals and teaspoon of dill seeds have been added. You will surely attract any suitor you desire.

The gentleman who wishes to make himself equally irresistible should approach his love with a bit of dried sage hidden under his tongue. Chicory root is also reputed to be a potent elixir, but only if it is given secretly. Perhaps this explains the Louisiana custom of mixing it with coffee.

For additional power, make tiny sachets of lovage and orris root and tuck them on your person. Passion will surely be aroused by the addition of lavender and southernwood, so use good judgment when incorporating these materials.

Now that you have attracted a lover who is all you desire, you still feel a little insecure. One effective measure is to tie three laurel leaves to the foot of the bed, and your lover will be blind to everyone but you. A more complicated, and temporary, spell can be performed secretly and may be more suited to your needs. Mix a handful of heartsease (johnny jump-up) with a lock of hair and some ashes from a burned piece of your lover's clothing. Wrap all in a fine white handkerchief and bury it under your porch at the new moon. The object of your affection is sure to be true to you for one month. You may decide at the end of that time, though, that that's not the one after all, and it's back to step one.

If you are pleased with this romance, however, and wish to ensure fidelity, dig up some soil on which your lover has walked and pot some marigolds in it. Your chosen one will be faithful forever.

For those lovers who are not gardeners, some of the kitchen condiments will be effective. Dill seed added to a drink has been reputed to be a powerful aphrodisiac. Cumin seed steeped in wine will insure faithfulness.

And if companionship, rather than *amour,* is your objective, make two small bags of red silk, fill them with cloves and tie with ribbon. Give one to your friend, wear one yourself and your friendship will never fade.

SEQUOYAH GARDENS, OK 74435

"I took my love to the garden so the roses could see her."
— Author unknown

Narrow-leaf sage

VALENTINE POTIONS

Massage Oil

4 ounces Sweet Almond Oil
½ t. your favorite essential oil

Blend and store. Shake before using.
— **GINGHAM 'N SPICE PA 18926**

Herbal Love Bath

7 cups lavender
6 cups rosemary
5 cups rose petals
4 cups lovage
3 cups lemon verbena
1 cup each: thyme, mint, sage, marjoram, orris root

Mix all dried herbs together and keep in covered container.

Place ¼-cup in muslin square and tie securely. Boil the bath ball in 1 qt. water for 10 min. Add to the hot bath water and scrub with the bath ball. Think serene thoughts and luxuriate! — from Bertha Reppert's *A HERITAGE OF HERBS,* **The Rosemary House PA 17055**

Rose geranium

Rose Geranium Potpourri

Combine equal parts of red or pink rose petals and crushed rose-scented geranium leaves. To each quart add 1 t. rose or rose geranium oil blended with 3 T. orris root. (Allow this to "set" for a few days, covered, before adding to the dried herbs. The orris root will absorb the oil, keeping the petals and leaves crisper.)

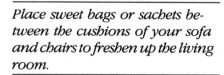

Place sweet bags or sachets between the cushions of your sofa and chairs to freshen up the living room.

Carnation Spice

6 cups petals of carnations and "pinks"
2 cups petals of any pink or red flowers, such as geraniums, roses, peonies, strawflowers
3 T. bay leaves, crushed
2 T. each nutmeg and cinnamon

3 T. ground frankincense
4 T. carnation oil in 6 tbls. orris root, mixed and "set"
2 t. rose geranium oil in 3 tbls. orris root, mixed & "set"
1 t. ambergris oil with either mixture

Citruscent

Sometimes I call this "SUNSHINE" potpourri and offer it as stored summer sunshine to combat winter blues and remind the recipients of next spring's promise...adding extra flowers for more vivid color.

4 cups lemon verbena leaves
2 cups lemon balm leaves
2 cups orange mint
2 cups lemon, lime, and/or orange scented geranium leaves
1 cup pineapple or apple mint
4 cups ground citrus peel

4 cups marigold or calendula petals (or any other yellow and orange flowers, such as lilies, daffodils, forsythia, etc.)
2 cups orris root, mixed with:
1 T. sweet orange oil and
1 T. sweet lemon oil

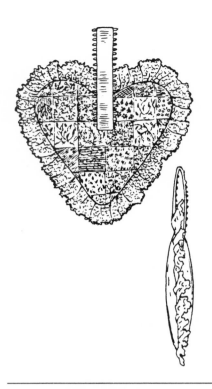

Odds and Ends on the February Agenda

If you shopped for fabric during the after-Christmas sales, this is a great time to cut out and sew for next summer's harvest. Experiment with quilted hot dish pads, pin cushions, & rag dolls or stuffed animals to hold your potpourri for fall gifts or bazaars.

Even making the simplest sachets is a time-consuming project later on when garden harvesting and potpourri-making can fill one's days! Sachets can be made by simply pinking the edges of 6" x 6" squares of fabrics sheer enough to permit the fragrance to emanate through, such as organdy, muslin, or cotton polyester.

Later, when your potpourri is ready, place 2 or 3 tablespoons in the center of each square, pull the corners up and tie them securely in the center with heavy thread. A pretty velvet or satin matching ribbon is the finishing touch. Or, you can machine-stitch heart, oblong, or circular shapes to create your own special bags.

Have a Heart...
For Remembrance

"Place this heart sachet on a closet hanger or in your clothing or linen chest for a pleasant scent to remind you throughout the year that you are loved and remembered."

(From the label on my heart sachets. — PVS)

Overnight Hearty Bean Soup

1½ cups dried navy beans
¼ lb. bacon, cut in 1" cubes
2 cups elbow macaroni
2 T. olive oil
½ lb. mushrooms, sliced
1 large onion, chopped
2 cups celery, sliced
2 cups carrots, sliced
1 clove garlic, finely chopped
3 cups tomatoes
1 t. each sage, thyme, oregano
1 bay leaf
Parsley, pepper, grated Parmesan cheese

Combine beans with 6 cups cold water in large bowl. Refrigerate overnight. Next day simmer beans, bacon and 1 t. salt for 2 hours, covered. Meanwhile, gently sauté mushrooms, onions, celery, carrots, and garlic in hot oil. Do not brown. Add tomatoes, sage, thyme, oregano, and bay. Stir to blend, then add to bean mixture. Cook macaroni, drain, and add to soup. Simmer gently. Add parsley, pepper, and cheese to taste before serving. (Adapted from "Bucks County Kitchen" column, Rosemarie Vassalluzzo.)

Easy-on-the-Heart Veal Stew

In Dutch oven heat 3 T. oil over medium heat. Add 2 lbs. veal, cut in 1" cubes. Brown well. Pour off excess fat. Stir in 1½ cups chopped onion, ¼ tsp. pepper, 1½ cups chicken or veg. broth, and ½ cup white wine. Cover. Bake at 350° for 45 min. Add 1 tsp. dill, 2 cups each celery and mushrooms, & 1 pkg. thawed frozen peas. Bake 30 minutes longer. ("Bucks County Kitchen")

Berry-Nice

Make heart-shaped sachets, edged with lace, with a ribbon for hanging, for each of your valentines this year! This potpourri goes well in delicate red fabrics, making it particularly appropriate for Valentine Sachets (as are all the potpourri recipes in this chapter).

2 oz. sweet woodruff
1 oz. each red rose petals and red clover tops
3 oz. rose hips
3 tonka beans, sliced

1 oz. orris root, cut
30 drops "Strawberry Fields" oil
— from GINGHAM 'N SPICE PA 18926

Basic Sweet Bag Potpourri

This is my favorite and most original potpourri, and I rarely make it the same way twice!

2 qts. rose-scented geranium leaves
1 qt. lemon verbena or balm
1 pt. lavender flowers
1 pt. pineapple sage or mint
2 cups ground citrus peel
1 cup ground tonka beans

Optional
1 or 2 cups basil, camomile, marjoram, or tarragon

Variation
1 t. rose geranium
oil added to ½ cup orris root
AND/OR
1 t. lemon or orange oil added to

½ cup orris root (These will add longer life and more vivid fragrance, if desired.)

My Sweet Bags are packaged in rectangular fabric bags, cut 4x8", with stitched sides, and the top folded down under about 2 inches, tied with a looped ribbon for hanging. My label defines them as "herbal perfume for refreshing your clothing or linen closet, bureau drawer, car, suitcase, or purse."

Sweet Bags

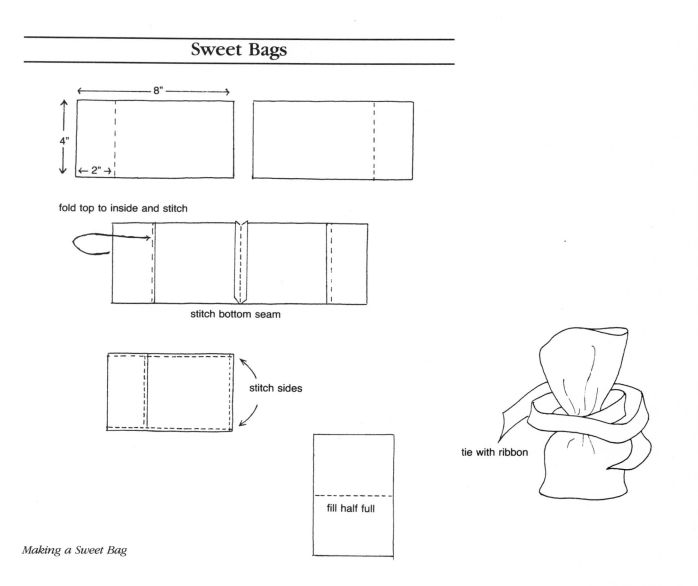

← 8" →

4"

← 2" →

fold top to inside and stitch

stitch bottom seam

stitch sides

fill half full

tie with ribbon

Making a Sweet Bag

MARCH

*I knew a wench
married in an afternoon
as she went to the garden
for parsley to stuff a rabbit.*

— William Shakespeare,
The Taming of the Shrew, IV, 4

Curly parsley *(Petroselinum crispum)*

MARCH

When daffodils begin to peer,
With hey! the doxy over the dale,
Why then comes in the sweet o' the year;
For the red blood reigns in the winter's pale.

— William Shakespeare, *The Winter's Tale,* IV, 3

BY MARCH in the Northeast, we "perennial" gardeners are using any excuse at all to be outside to reunite with the fresh air, the soil, and, on non-gusty days, the warmth of the sun! As soon as the soil is workable (unfrozen and not muddy), you can start to cultivate the ground where you will later plant herbs, whether you will be using existing beds or establishing new ones.

New beds will require the use of a rototiller or a handcultivator (or a spade and a lot of elbow grease!), to turn over the soil several times. Add lime (sparingly; according to manufacturer's directions), dried manure (except where you will plant mints) — I prefer the weedless commercial variety, but farm manure will last longer and go further, peat and sand if you have clayey soil, and a good commercial garden fertilizer (unless you have your own rich compost). For small spots in your existing gardens, this cultivation and enrichment can be done by hand with a spade and a digger.

As a rule herbs don't really need a super-rich soil, but new plants should have all the benefits of good soil while they are becoming established. Give them a good basic "foundation" and, once they are sturdy and well-rooted, they will require very little care in the following years (like children!). Mix in enough peat, sand, and humus to make the soil friable, lightweight, and airy.

Freeze chopped parsley and chives for winter freshness in soups and stews.

Herbs want well-drained soil (they don't like "wet feet"), and once established, they can go at least a week without water. *Newly planted* herbs, however, should not be allowed to get too dry until the roots are firmly established.

During this month you can re-till your new areas several times, so that the food additives are well mixed and absorbed in the soil by the time your herbs can be planted.

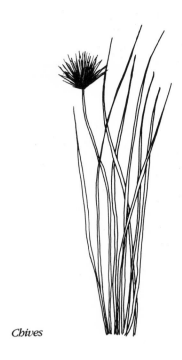

Chives

PARSLEY and CHIVE seeds can be planted outside as soon in spring as the ground can be worked. Chives yield more the second and subsequent years, but biennial parsley is lushest the first year (it goes to seed early the second summer). I plant it each spring in order to have a fresh supply each year. Both parsley and chives require cool weather and spring rains to grow.

I place the seeds in the sunny areas of my culinary bed where they will stay, near and around my existing clumps. I barely cover the seeds with sphagnum moss or a very fine soil, and then lightly sprinkle hay, chopped-up leaves or compost on top.

Timing will vary according to the variety of seeds and the zone you live in. I generally have plenty of parsley and chive seedlings by mid-to-late April. Neither will transplant well, so it's best to thin them out, leaving the strongest plants intact. The chives should be grouped in clusters.

These plants will thrive if you give them a "haircut" about twice a month from May until frost. Both can be easily dried and frozen for winter enjoyment. Chives are useful for a mild onion flavor in recipes, and are delicious in cottage cheese with some garlic powder. Parsley complements almost any meat or vegetable dish and, fresh or frozen, is full of Vitamin C.

HERB BREADS AND BUTTERS

In March you can delight your family on cold blustery days with hot herb bread that you either made yourself, or concocted from a loaf of store bread or rolls with your own homemade herb butter! Next fall or winter, after you have stored your herb harvests for kitchen use, mix up any or all of the following blends and store in mason jars or plastic bags to use to your heart's content. Be sure to label the blends.

You can add one tablespoon of any herb combination to each loaf of homemade bread dough. Or add one tablespoon of any blend to ¼ lb. melted butter or oleo, spread with a pastry brush on a sliced loaf of bread or on two dozen rolls, and heat in the oven in aluminum foil till warm. Or you can add 2 teaspoons herb blend per biscuit mix for 12.

- 2 cups SUMMER SAVORY
  1 cup PARSLEY
  ½ cup THYME
  ½ cup MARJORAM
  ½ cup minced onions or
  chives (optional)

  Herb breads of this blend are divine with any meat, but are especially good with beef or stews.

- Equal parts SAGE and PARMESAN CHEESE.
  Delicious with poultry, ham, or pork meals.

- Equal parts OREGANO and dried GARLIC CHIPS and PARMESAN CHEESE (optional)
  Good with spaghetti or lasagna.

- Equal parts BASIL and CHIVES
Complements (with compliments!) tomato dishes, soups, and stews.

Once you have tried these, and found out how easy it is to make any meal a gourmet treat with herb bread, you will want to make up enough mixes next year to share with friends. Many times at our house a simple leftover meal or a soup and salad meal was mouth-watering because of the addition of herb bread or rolls.

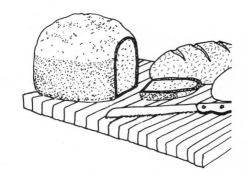

Annie's Dilly Bread in a Casserole

1 pkg. active dry yeast
¼ cup warm water
1 cup creamed cottage cheese
  (small curd)
2 T. sugar
1 T. instant minced onion
1 T. softened butter
2 t. dried dill, minced
1 t. salt
¼ t. baking soda
1 egg, beaten
2¼ to 2½ cups all-purpose flour

Soften yeast in warm water. Heat cottage cheese to lukewarm and combine with yeast mixture. Add rest of ingredients, except flour, and blend together.

Add enough flour, in several additions, beating well after each, to form a stiff dough. Cover with buttered wax paper and a linen towel. Let rise in warm place (80–90°) until light and double in size, about 50–60 minutes.

Stir down dough and turn into a well-buttered 8"-round ceramic or glass casserole (1½–2 qt. size). Cover and let rise again in a warm place until light, about 30–40 minutes.

Bake in preheated 350° oven for 40–50 minutes until golden brown. Brush with melted butter and sprinkle lightly with salt. Remove from casserole and cool on rack. Serve warm.

Makes one round loaf.

Quick Caraway Cheese Bread

4 cups flour
½ cup sugar
2 T. baking powder
2 t. salt
2 eggs, slightly beaten
2 cups milk
½ cup vegetable oil
2 cups grated Cheddar cheese
⅔ cup crumbled bacon
2 t. caraway seeds

Grease bottom and sides of two 9x5x3" loaf pans. Place all ingredients except bacon, cheese, and caraway into large mixing bowl; beat on medium speed ½ minute, scraping sides and bottom constantly. Stir in remaining ingredients; divide batter into prepared pans. Bake at 350° for 45 to 50 minutes. Cool in pans for 10 minutes; remove from pans and cool thoroughly. *Makes two loaves; freezes well.*

Caraway

Whipped Garlic Butter

1 cup softened butter or margarine
4 small garlic cloves, crushed

Beat ingredients together in small bowl of mixer at high speed until fluffy and light. Refrigerate in a tightly-covered container for up to one week. Use on hot rice, warm bread or rolls, hamburger buns, hot vegetables or broiled steaks.

Herb Biscuits

2 cups flour
4 t. baking powder
1 T. sugar
½ t. cream of tartar
½ t. salt
½ cup shortening
⅔ cup milk
½ t. each of parsley, dill, and
  caraway seed

Stir together thoroughly all of the dry ingredients. Cut in shortening until the mixture resembles coarse crumbs. Make a well in center; add milk all at once. Stir just until dough clings together. Knead gently on lightly floured surface. Roll or pat to ½-inch thickness. Dip 2½" biscuit cutter in flour; cut dough straight down. Bake on ungreased baking sheet at 450° for 10–12 minutes. Rosemarie Vassalluzzo, "Bucks County Kitchen," *The Advance of Bucks County.*

Oregano Cheddar Bread

Oregano

1 pkg. active dry yeast
5¼ cups all-purpose flour
2½ cups shredded sharp Cheddar
  cheese
1¾ cup milk
3 T. salad oil
2 T. sugar
2 T. minced oregano (4 if fresh)
1 t. salt

Stir together the yeast and *two cups* of the flour in large mixing bowl. Heat together the remaining ingredients (except rest of flour) until lukewarm. Add to flour-yeast mixture. Beat on low speed for 30 seconds, scraping bowl constantly. Beat at high speed for 3 minutes. Stir in as much of the remaining flour as you can mix in with a spoon.

On a lightly floured surface knead in enough of the remaining flour to make a stiff dough. Knead another 8 to 9 minutes until dough is elastic and smooth. Shape into a ball and place in a lightly greased bowl, turning once to grease all sides of surface. Cover and let rise in warm place until double in size (about 1 hour and 15 minutes).

Punch down dough and divide in half. Cover and let sit for 10 minutes. Shape into 2 loaves and place in 2 buttered 8 x 4" loaf pans. Cover and let rise until nearly double, about 45 minutes.

Bake in 350° oven for 40–45 minutes. Cover with foil for last few minutes of baking to prevent over-browning. Cool on wire rack. *Makes 2 loaves.*

Herb Cheese Wedges

2 cups Bisquick
1 T. sugar
2 t. dried minced onion
½ t. each dried dill, basil, oregano
1 egg
½ cup milk
¼ cup melted butter
¼ cup sauterne wine
⅓ cup shredded Cheddar cheese

Combine Bisquick, onion, sugar, and herbs. Mix the egg and milk together; beat slightly. Add this, the butter and wine to the dry ingredients. Beat until blended.

Turn out into a well-greased round 8" cake pan. Sprinkle the cheese on top. Bake at 400° until brown and crusty, about 25 minutes. Allow to sit for 10 minutes; cut in wedges and serve with butter. *Serves 6–8.*

(This bread is perfect with a luncheon salad. It doesn't taste as though it starts with biscuit mix!) — from BACKDOOR HERB GARDEN RECIPES.

Herb Butter

1 cup softened butter
1 t. each of minced dried marjoram, thyme, and rosemary leaves
¼ t. each of garlic powder and dried basil and sage

Beat all together at high speed in small mixer bowl until fluffy. Keep in tightly covered container in refrigerator. Melt some to brush on hot corn-on-the-cob; excellent with hot vegetables or broiled fish, steak or poultry.

The Slim Gourmet's Lemon-Garlic Butter

2 T. lemon juice
2 T. diet margarine
1 t. finely minced garlic

Mash ingredients together with the back of a spoon. Spread on 1 pound fish fillets or on chicken cutlets or beef flank steak. Enough for 4 servings, 30 calories each.

Seasoned Bread Crumbs

Buy bargain bread or use some that is several days old. Toast it in the oven. Place in a plastic bag and roll into crumbs with rolling pin. Then add garlic powder, dried oregano and parsley, and dried minced onion. Keep on hand for breading chicken, chops, or fish, or for using in meatloaf. Keep quantities in the freezer.
— from A BOUNTIFUL COLLECTION.

STARTING HERBS FROM SEED

On blustery March days, when you've got spring fever (but spring hasn't gotten the message yet), you can fool Mother Nature by planting perennial herb seeds inside. Find a warm spot, out of direct sunlight, and arrange for consistent moisture from beneath the growing medium. I have had success with commercial indoor miniature greenhouses.

The following *perennial* herbs do well when started from seed about two months before transplanting them outdoors: perennial camomile, catnip, chives, horehound, hyssop, lavender, lemon balm, lovage, pennyroyal, rue, sage, salad burnet, winter savory, wormwood.

These *annual* herbs (or tender perennials treated as annuals in the north) do well when started inside from seed six to eight weeks early: basil, borage, calendula, annual camomile, annual clary sage, coriander, marjoram, rosemary, safflower, summer savory, & sweet wormwood.

Although some *biennials,* such as caraway, chervil, and clary sage, can be started from seed inside in their own peat pots, it is best to plant these seeds outside in late summer in the spot they will stay in, as they need a cold season for best germination. Angelica, sweet cicely, and chervil do not transplant well and should be planted in August or September in moist sand or peat moss in their permanent homes, in a shady spot. (Check my Herb Growth/Use Chart for herbs best purchased as established plants.)

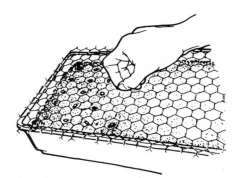

To aid in spacing seeds an inch apart in flats or trays, cut a piece of one-inch-mesh chicken wire the size of the container. Lay it on the soil and plant a seed inside each hole. Or try two-inch or three-inch spacing for larger plants.

If you stand the flat in a tub with water coming about three-quarters of the way up its side, the soil can suck up the exact amount of water it needs and the seeds stay where planted.

For best results, use peat flats (approx. 5" x 7") as the nurseries do, filled with soaked and drained milled (fine) sphagnum moss. *Barely cover* the tiniest seeds with more of the moss. Place the flats in a tray and keep them warm and moist by covering each flat with a clear plastic "tent" and providing heat from the bottom. (Before I had my indoor light reflectors I used the top of my refrigerator, TV, and clothes drier for bottom heat.)

Remove the plastic as soon as greenery appears and place the packs nearer sunlight or indoor growing lights. Feed with a weak 20-20-20 solution of plant food when the seedlings first appear. Do not allow them to dry out. Gradually move the plants closer to the direct sunlight on a window sill or under indoor lights, as now they will seek heat and light from above. (They're like children; we don't expose an infant to all the elements immediately!)

When the second set of leaves appears, transplant the seedlings to small individual peat pots (medium size for fast growers such as basil) filled with sterile potting soil containing plenty of perlite and/or vermiculite, and feed them again. Placing sphagnum moss in the top quarter of the peat pots, or misting with strained camomile tea, will help prevent "dampening off," which can kill seedlings.

If you have a late frost, remove the seedlings from the windowsill during the night so they won't catch a draft. Keep them watered and fed (with weaker solutions than the container directs) until ready to go outside.

If you have a coldframe in a sheltered spot, which you will cover at night or during chilly spells, the plants can be moved to this 2 or 3 weeks before they can be put in the ground. They will start to adjust to outside temperatures and become "hardened off" by this process. When your frost-free date has arrived and your soil is warm, plant each pot directly into the garden, tearing off the wet bottom if the roots are not already through it.

I would recommend early starts with basil, marjoram, rosemary, and summer savory for lusher and longer harvests. If you prefer to start parsley inside from seed, do it early this month or even in February next year. Parsley seeds take several weeks to germinate, but can be hastened by soaking them in warm water for 24 hours before planting. Plant three seeds in each peat pot and thin out to only one seedling, leaving only the strongest in the pot. Plant pot and all into the garden when soil is warm. Like its relative the carrot, parsley has a taproot which must not be damaged while transplanting.

Carefully transplant the seedlings into individual pots filled with sterile potting soil mixed with perlite or vermiculite.

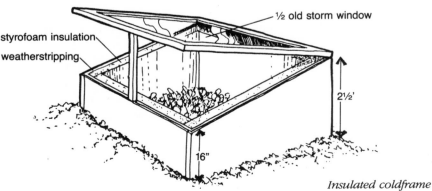

½ old storm window

styrofoam insulation

weatherstripping

2½'

16"

Insulated coldframe

A Word of Caution

Do not make the mistakes I did in my early gardening years and plant too much too soon inside! An overanxious gardener, trying to rush the season, will have too many crowded and spindly plants by mid-April, and tender new plants shouldn't be placed in the garden until all danger of frost is over. If you have a coldframe, however, the seedlings could go out in April to harden before the mid-May planting.

After years of experimenting, the best schedule for me is to start perennial herbs (rosemary, lavender, thyme, catnip, etc.) inside in early March and *tall* marigolds in mid-March, when I start my tomatoes and other vegetables. I start short marigolds and the *annual* herbs (marjoram, summer savory, basil, etc.) toward the end of March. Often I plant only *half* the packet of annual seeds, saving the rest to plant outside in mid-May.

This deliberate delaying eliminates making several different transplantings before outside weather is favorable, and leaves me more time to be outside in the gardens as the weather improves.

Strong seedlings can go into the coldframe by late March if you keep your eye on the weather forecast.

You might want to visit or call local nurseries to ask what herbs they will have in April, so you will know which ones to order by mail now from herb catalogs. Some that are difficult to raise from seed (unless you have an outdoor greenhouse) should be bought by the novice in pots, and later propagated from rootings, layerings, or cuttings the second year. The true varieties of the best mints (see Appendix for botanical names), tarragon, rosemary, oregano, tansy, pineapple sage, the thymes, lavender, comfrey, and the scented geraniums all fall into this category.

Dennis Mawhinney from Pennsylvania suggests recycling an abandoned children's swing set to use as a coldframe by covering it with heavy plastic.

I have had good luck ordering herb plants by mail, but I usually order two or three of each variety, and plant them in different locations. Then, if I lose one or two, I will still have a survivor, and will know where that particular herb grows the best. If I buy herbs locally, or at least from somewhere close with similar climatic conditions, I buy only one plant of each kind.

Improvising a Greenhouse

Several winters ago I found myself with many eager markets for my herbal products — and no more dried herbs! A decision had to be made as to how to meet the demand the next fall. (My products sell like hot-cakes only in October, November, and December, since they are gift-type items that people seldom buy for themselves.) With virtually no money to spend on a greenhouse, we had to "make do" and improvise an indoor greenhouse, where I could raise quantities of herbs from seed the following spring.

Darlene Beauvais (MA 02061) increases her coldframe space with six bales of rotten hay and a second-hand storm window for a cover. She reports great success with this method in spite of the cold weather in Massachusetts, and she uses the hay later for mulching.

For many years I had successfully "wintered over" a few tender herbs in my sunny living room bay window (southern exposure), but there was no room there for the hundreds of seedlings I would soon need. Had we not had an available garage, we would have converted a portion of our cellar into a greenhouse, which might be more feasible for you.

Our garage never gets below 50 degrees because it has an open doorway to the cellar. Heat comes from the furnace as well as from the two windows with a southern exposure. When nights are 10–20 degrees, I place old blankets or rugs at the bottom of the garage door to keep out drafts. We keep an electric heater by the plants, set at 55 degrees, the minimum temperatures at which the growing plants and seedlings can survive.

In addition, my talented husband rigged up an automatic timer on the lights and set this so the lights are on all night, and my herbs get the heat from the lights when the garage is coldest. We draw down the window shades and the dark curtains on the garage door windows. The herbs "sleep" in the darkened garage for 8 hours during the day, and have 16 hours of light and warmth when it is coldest and darkest outside. (This also means the lights are on when I am free to putter around with my plants in the evenings.)

Towards spring, as nights get warmer, we adjust the timing each month to start turning the herbs' "nights" back into "days" in preparation for their April or May entrance to their real world.

We have found very little heating expense with this arrangement. We expected our electric bill to be phenomenally high, but were delighted to discover very little increase...perhaps $3.00 or $4.00 a month from the lights and the electric heater. I doubt that I could heat a greenhouse of any type any cheaper during the coldest months. Also, I don't have to wade through snow drifts in order to visit my plants.

Through friends we found four sets of used 48" fluorescent light fixtures from an office that was being modernized and redecorated. My husband made metal reflectors to cover the lights and keep the heat over the plants. These turned out to be worth their weight in gold when we discovered they were also warm enough on top to dry boxes of herbs.

Our only major expense in setting up the garage greenhouse was the purchase of the "Naturescent" or "Vita-Lite" tubes which simulate the sun's rays and give the herbs the nourishment they'd receive from Old Sol herself. These lights last a year or two and are readily available in different sizes in garden centers, nurseries, and hardware stores.

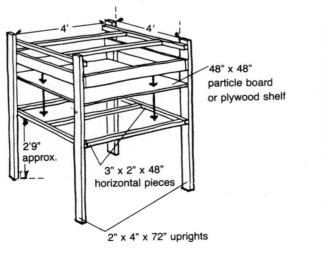

48" x 48" particle board or plywood shelf

2'9" approx.

3" x 2" x 48" horizontal pieces

2" x 4" x 72" uprights

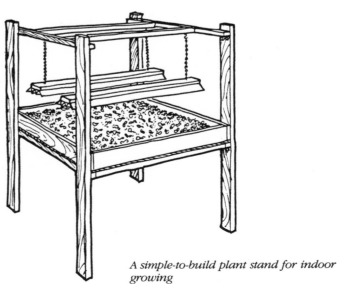

A simple-to-build plant stand for indoor growing

My indoor greenhouse provides me with year-round pleasure. I can't begin to describe the joy of walking into my garage on a freezing January night and finding a cascade of fragrant greenery under the simulated sunlight and warmth.

1. It provides winter protection for all my scented geraniums and the tender herbs such as lemon verbena, rosemary, marjoram, and pineapple sage, and allows me to propagate them for increased yield by cuttings during the slower pace of life in winter.

2. It allows me to start *perennial* herbs from seed in quantity in February or early March so I'll have super harvests by summer.

3. I am able to start *annual* herbs, flowers, and vegetables inside in March for earlier and longer harvests.

4. Lastly, my garage greenhouse becomes my "drying" house in the summer, when we replace the growing lights in June with the cheaper plain fluorescent types and dry the herbs very quickly on top of the metal reflectors.

Rue

I use the rest of the garage to dry herbs in bunches on clotheslines and an old clothes rack. We use a dehumidifier and a fan on the humid days. (This uses more power than the lights do.)

For growing herbs indoors under lights, I suggest using sterile soil, monthly commercial feedings (20-20-20) during the winter when the plants are "resting", and weekly feedings in the early spring when new growth appears. I spray the plants once or twice a week to simulate rainfall, and occasionally I add some blenderized and strained garlic or onion juice, or some strong pipe tobacco solution, to keep garden pests from my sweet-smelling friends. The leaves are rinsed off with clear water and allowed to dry before I do any harvesting. So far we've never had any marjoram tasting like tobacco or rosemary tasting like garlic!

I water the herbs thoroughly once a week and turn the trays around occasionally to expose different sides to the "sun". If I see any sign of insect infestation, I move the herbs, tray by tray, to the laundry for Fels Naptha baths in a weak, tepid, sudsy solution, carefully covering the soil with aluminum foil while I swish the plants around in their "bath water." After letting them drain on their sides for a few minutes I thoroughly rinse them off in another bath of clear tepid water. (You will be amazed at how much greener the herbs will look after this tender loving care!)

The best book I know for indoor herb gardening *without lights* is Adelma Simmons's HERBS TO GROW INDOORS.

Closet "bouquets" of moth-repellent herbs make interesting and timely gifts for the coming season. Dried branches of rue, tansy, wormwood, southernwood, mint, lavender, rosemary, pennyroyal and thyme can be used alone or in any combination. Best if wrapped lightly in cheesecloth (so dried leaves won't mess up the floor) and tied with a colorful looped ribbon for hanging.

More Planting Tips

When starting seeds indoors, some herbs should not have light while germinating; calendula, statice, verbena, and parsley should be shielded with newspaper until sprouts appear.

Plant Sugar Snap peas close to your fences now for June picking. In May your luffa transplants can be placed between the pea plants to climb the fence when the latter are finished.

As soon as the soil is workable (not frosty or muddy), prepare it for your new herbs by tilling in compost, lime, peat, sand, etc. Herbs want a neutral pH (on the sweet side), and a light, friable soil for good drainage.

Savor your first outside excursions if you've been winter-bound. Take vigorous daily walks amongst your gardens, inhaling deeply. (My alternative to jogging.)

Sow parsley and chive seeds outside!

Prune roses and cover tops of cut stems with Elmer's Glue or special paint from the nursery to keep out borers. Gradually remove the winter mulch or "hills" protecting the bushes. If you hilled up the roses in the fall with organic materials, gently smoothe it out at the base of the plants and create circular borders to catch the rainfall.

Start calendula seeds inside now in individual peat pots for June blooms in the garden and if the flowers are kept cut a continuous burst of color all summer. Also called "Pot-Marigold", this is the preferred and official marigold for culinary purposes. *PARK'S SEED CO.,* in Greenwood SC 29647 is an excellent source of calendula seeds, including many dwarf varieties. (This is also a source for baby's breath (*gypsophilia*) plants, so breath-taking in arrangements, tussie-mussies and wreaths.)

Silver king artemisia

Royalty in Your Garden: Silver King Artemisia

You can create stunning permanent arrangements and wreaths from dried Silver King Artemisia *(A. ludoviciana albula),* which is a breathtaking accent or border plant in the perennial bed. The silvery elegance of the dried herb is so versatile that it complements any background wall color, or any shade of candles, ribbons, or other dried flowers and plants.

Silver King is hardy and can be planted in the ground in April in the North. I bought one or two plants 25 years ago, and now have many dozens of plants, as it spreads readily by runners. Like mint, it must be confined somewhat, but I allowed it to go wild in my pink-red-blue-purple perennial flower bed years ago, and it became an exquisite background for my pink to purple phlox, salvias, loosestrife, malvas, and pink yarrows. Now Silver King makes a startling border for my perennial herb garden. As an herb it is used in modern times primarily for decorative purposes. It should be cut at the end of summer when the seedheads and leaves are almost pure white, and before the winds and the rains discolor the feathery crowning glory. The branches can be placed directly in a vase (no water) just as you want them to dry...and you will have a lasting arrangement all winter long. It is beautiful enough to be used alone in an arrangement, but Kim decorated our stereo bouquet with thin Christmas balls and the result was enchanting.

People will pay up to 75¢ a branch for this regal dried plant! Three graceful branches, tied in a bunch with a colorful ribbon, have sold for $2.50 or more at garden club bazaars. This herb can easily be divided within a few years to share with friends, sell in stores or at bazaars. A lovely gift for a gardener in the early fall is a bunch of the dried branches along with a rooting or two for his/her own garden. Do order some plants now. Silver King can be purchased by mail from: *HARTMAN'S HERB FARM MA 01005, THE ROSEMARY HOUSE PA 17055, RASLAND FARM NC 28344, FOX HILL FARM MI 49269,* and *THE HERB PATCH KS 66353.*

Wormwood artemisia

Sweetness in Your Garden: Artemisia 'Annua'

"Sweet Annie", or Sweet Wormwood, is my second favorite artemisia. This intensely fragrant annual can be started from seed inside now in individual peat pots and transplanted outside when the soil is warm. It can grow to a height of 6 feet (but less if transplanted) and the rich fragrance of the foliage will last for years. Once called "Chinese Christmas Fern", it has a Christmas tree shape, adding to its graceful, feathery appearance. The tiny yellow blossoms are barely detectable.

Because of its size, *Artemisia 'annua'* needs plenty of garden space (plants should be 2½–3 feet apart). It will self-sow, once established in the bed, if some plants are allowed to go to seed. (I took some dried branches of this to a lecture, and members of the audience stood in line to get a bunch to take home for seeds for their own gardens.) It is a bonus in the garden because of its lush green foliage in the summer and its reddish-brown hue in the fall, and is super for fresh or dried arrangements and bouquets, lovely in lavender or rosemary sachets, and *great for wreaths.* Requiring full sun, Sweet Wormwood originated in Asia, but is believed to have been naturalized in North America. You can purchase plants of this in late spring from *SANDY MUSH HERBS NC 28748.*

Moth Chaser Potpourri

by Barbara Radcliffe Rogers

It is not enough for a "Moth Chaser" potpourri to repel or discourage moths. It must, of course, accomplish this, but it must do so without repelling and discouraging people as well! Fortunately, this isn't too difficult, since there are only a few herbs and spices whose scents are less than delightful — but those few all belong in the best moth blends. Let's get them out of the way first.

Santolina, although a pretty plant in all its forms, does not please the nose as it does the eye. Harvest it either by pinching tips and drying on a screen, or by cutting long sprigs to hang in paper bags. Since it is fragile when dry, it shouldn't be left hanging loose unless the spot is well out of the way. Southernwood grows taller and more rangey and is also best dried in bags to protect it. Pennyroyal, while not actually unpleasant, is strong and penetrating. Its low growth doesn't make neat bundles, but you can screen dry it or just drop sprigs loosely in a paper bag to dry.

From these, we can move on to the scents *we* love, but *moths* don't....

Cedar shavings (buy this in pet supply departments, where it's much less expensive) provide bulk, creating the air spaces that are essential to good potpourri, and a scent most popularly associated with repelling moths. While it is hard for me to believe, there are actually people who don't like lavender! Its use in moth potpourri is therefore optional because it will always predominate unless it is used very sparingly. *Any* mint, but peppermint in particular, is an essential addition not only for moths, but to discourage mice from nibbling around in stored clothing.

Whole cloves, lemon peel, lemon verbena, tansy, thyme, rosemary, black peppercorns, and bay leaves are secondary ingredients, all effective, and all add to a pleasant, if pungent, blend. Orris root (in chipped, not powdered form) is necessary, since moth bags need to last if they are to be useful. The oils should reflect the ingredients and I blend a special oil just for the moth potpourri. It is two parts each cedar, lemon, and lavender (if used in the blend) and one part each pennyroyal, peppermint, and bayberry. Because the blend needs to project if it is to be useful, use about 50% more oil than you would for normal potpourri.

Pennyroyal

Herbitage Farm's Moth Potpourri

½ cup cedar shavings

¼ cup each pennyroyal, lavender, santolina or southernwood, peppermint, lemon verbena, thyme, rosemary, & orris root

⅛ cup each whole cloves, lemon peel, and black peppercorns

6 drops each cedar, lemon, and lavender oils

It is not necessary to use all the moth-chasing ingredients or even all the oils all at once in the same potpourri. But be sure you have at least two of the primary ingredients (if possible, four) and one of the three major oils listed.

Packaging moth potpourri can be as simple as tying it into squares of old sheet fabric, or as fancy as you wish. But bear in mind that these are no-nonsense household necessities to be hidden away, so frilly little lace or organdy sachets would look a bit silly. I have always packaged mine in wool flannel, which my customers find very amusing if not downright arrogant! So far, none have been found with a moth hole. Use six-inch squares, stitching to form a 3 x 6-inch bag. Turn and fill with potpourri and tie to close.

Be generous with the potpourri. Less than ½ cup each is simply not enough, unless you plan to pack three or four in with each sweater! A bow or loop of some type is handy if the bags are to be put on clothes hangers.

Padded hangers may be filled with the blend, too. Use a wooden coat-hanger without a pants-bar. Measure the wooden part from the center to one end and make a satin tube one inch longer and about 1½" wide. Satin ribbon works well for this, doubled and stitched up each selvedge. Only one end should be left open. Turn and slip over one end of the hanger. Repeat for the other end. Fill each side tightly with potpourri and blind stitch together at the center. Wrap the hook with narrow ribbon, holding it in place over the end with white glue. Wrap the other end once around the hanger to hide the seam and stitch in place. Cover the end with a bow tied around the handle.

There are two bonus uses for moth potpourri, if it is nicely made. It will keep trunks and seldom-used closets and chests from developing a musty smell. And moth bags are wonderful to keep in luggage for both traveling and storage.

A booklet, HERBS: A COMPENDIUM OF HOUSEHOLD USES, is available from Barbara. See Bibliography and Directory. *HERBITAGE FARM RFD 2 RICHMOND NH 03470.*

*Santolina
or lavender cotton*

SACHETS FOR SPRING

" 'Tis the season" in spring to make herbal moth-repellent sachets or closet "Perfume Bags" for yourself, for gifts for Easter, Mother's Day, or June brides, or to sell at fund-raising fairs or bazaars. Soon all conscientious homemakers will be storing woolens for the summer ahead. Each of these recipes is a proven "hit" with the public as the scents are pungent, yet detested by moths!

Phyl's Camphor Spice

4 cups camphor-scented
   southernwood*
4 cups lavender flowers and leaves
4 cups wormwood leaves
1 cup ground cloves
½ cup ground nutmeg

*Or, substitute lemon-scented southernwood and add some lemon peel to make LEMON SPICE. (I use summery floral fabrics in pastels, placing about ½ cup of the potpourri in each 4x6" bag, tied with a looped ribbon for hanging on closet hooks or hangers. If selling "Closet Perfume Bags", it is best to list the ingredients on the label and to state that the herbs are NOT FOR HUMAN CONSUMPTION, especially since so many moth-repellent herbs are toxic to humans. It is also wise not to make any guarantees on the label. We know that our colonial foremothers relied on herbs for moth protection, but we don't know if they were 100% effective! My labels simply state that moths detest the scent. The spices and oils may account for this, even more than the herbs! PVS)

Herbal Acres' Tansy-Bansy

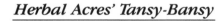

1 qt. tansy
2 cups wormwood
2 cups rue
2 cups southernwood
½ cup EACH of ground cloves,

cinnamon, nutmeg
1 cup vetiver root
2 T. orris root mixed with 10–15
   drops oil of clove or pine

Rosemary-Mint

Tansy

4 cups dried spearmint OR
   peppermint
4 cups dried rosemary
2 cups dried thyme
1 cup ground cloves

Adapted from Ann Tucker's fascinating book, POTPOURRI, INCENSE, AND OTHER FRAGRANT CONCOCTIONS.

Instant Cedar Closet
"In July and again in September, our area has craft shows with log-sawing contests. They always seem to use cedar wood. We gather huge bags of the shavings and use them to fill 8x10" bags of colored netting, tied with a ribbon for hanging, and a label — "INSTANT CEDAR CLOSET". They certainly sell well and the cost is negligible. We also sell this in a plastic bag, so the stuffing won't drip out." *Bertha Reppert, THE ROSEMARY HOUSE, PA 17055.*

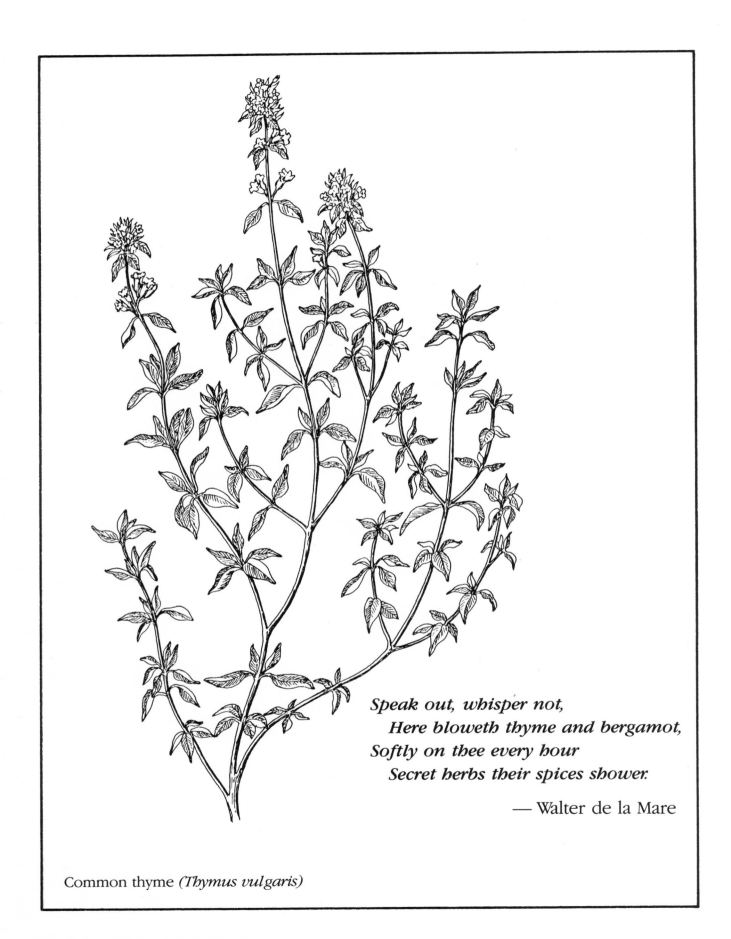

Speak out, whisper not,
Here bloweth thyme and bergamot,
Softly on thee every hour
Secret herbs their spices shower.

— Walter de la Mare

Common thyme *(Thymus vulgaris)*

APRIL

I know a bank where the wild thyme blows,
Where oxlips and the nodding violet grows;
Quite over-canopied with luscious woodbine,
With sweet musk-roses, and with eglantine.

— William Shakespeare,
A Midsummer Night's Dream, II, 1

APRIL IS PRIME THYME for perennial herbs! The already established plants from last year will be popping up vigorously, and lush new growth on woody-stemmed herbs will warm your heart after each April shower. Now is the time to buy potted perennial herbs and place them in a protected area for a few days to adjust to their new environment. Plant them with the dirt from the pot intact, disturbing the root system as little as possible.

All the mints and perennial herbs will need some Tender Loving Care their second and subsequent Aprils. I find this a most joyous task, as these early arrivals in my gardens are as welcome to my soul as the fresh green grass, the faint foliage on the trees, and the first flowering bulbs and shrubs. Winter is over!

All debris that might have blown into the garden should be carefully removed without damaging the new young shoots. The dead stems need to be cut back, and any new rootings that have strayed from their intended neighborhood should be dug up and replanted where you do want them — or potted up to share with others.

Plant hardy herbs in the ground now.

Do not yet, however, cut back sage, thyme, lavender, or tarragon. New growth on woody-stemmed herbs such as these will soon suddenly appear, even though the plants might look like "death warmed over" in early April.

Perhaps you are luckier than I am, but I wage a yearly war with chickweed in my gardens. I spend a great deal of time in April ripping this out by the roots before the flowering seedheads cascade to the ground to become new plants by June.

Solving Space Problems

April showers give us a wonderful opportunity to conserve water by collecting all we can in clean plastic garbage pails, in barrels, or in jars. This can be used to water the gardens during a dry spell. Your roses and vegetables will especially love the saved rain if manure has been added to make manure "tea."

Two cautions: don't feed the mints with the "tea" and be sure to keep the water covered when the weather becomes warm, as it's happy breeding ground for mosquitoes. Place the water-collectors right in the gardens you'll use the water on.

Your second April as an herbalist may find you with scented geraniums and tender perennials that have successfully wintered over inside but are now taking up the sunny window space, which you need for the stretching herb seedlings you started in March.

The other time of the year our indoor winter garden under lights in the garage is not "greenhouse" enough for me is from mid-September till mid-October when I'm still drying harvests in the garage, and am not yet ready to bring the tender plants inside from the garden.

I have devised some solutions for these two times a year when I have a space problem. I do have a small automatic coldframe, which might be very satisfactory for herbing on a small scale, such as you are likely to be doing at least at first. But, since I have an herb *business,* and we are yearly expanding our crops and adding gardens, necessity has mothered my inventions of alternative greenhouses — using my station wagon for trays of sturdy scented geraniums, using Hugh's "junked" Pinto with its big back window, and covering a picnic table with a large sheet of plastic and then a tarpaulin!

The car windows are rolled down each morning and up each cool evening. On windy, cold nights I anchor the tarpaulin down with logs; on mild nights I just place the plastic over the herbs under the table. Thus my wintered-over plants are protected, but are getting fresh air and sunlight in preparation for the May planting.

Once or twice a week on sunny days I set the trays on the ground in the sunlight and give them a drink and a misting. Since they are still in sterile soil, and not yet in garden soil, I feed them occasionally with a 7-7-7 or 20-20-20 ration of chemical gardening fertilizer. This ratio is best for herbs that you want to harvest, since you are not concerned about the flowering of the plants; you want strong foliage growth.

Spring Care of Established Hardy Herbs

Enjoy your first cup of fresh mint tea in April, after you have cleaned up your beds and brushed against the lovely herbs that, like you, have survived the snow and cold.

Clean winter debris such as wind-blown leaves from beds. If last fall you didn't cut back the stems of those herbs that come back up each year from vigorous underground roots (such as Silver King artemisia, bergamot, the mints, rue, tansy, tarragon, and yarrow), do it now. The dead stems can be broken or cut off, if done gently enough to protect the underground growth. Hold the bottom of the stem securely in the soil while breaking or cutting off the top.

Trim lavender, the southernwoods, and upright thyme for good grooming, but don't pull them up, no matter how dead they might appear. New growth will soon pop out of most of the branches. You can cut out the deadwood then.

Divide and conquer! Mints, thyme, sage, hyssop, oregano, chives, lemon balm, and tarragon should be root-divided and moved to new locations if more than four years old. Fresh soil and environs will renew vigor and flavor.

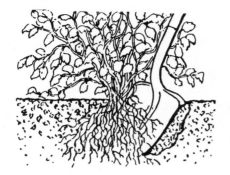

Dividing herbs

1. Dig up a section of the roots of an established plant.

2. Shake off the excess soil and separate the plants into clumps.

3. Replant in new holes to which a 2"–4" layer of compost has been added.

Pass It On

As you clean your beds and pull up the roots of any wandering herbs that may have strayed out of bounds (like the mints, bergamot, artemisias, and other "runner" herbs), pot some up for spring garden club sales or gifts to others. (Always label each plant with botanical and common name.) There's an old gardening adage that one never needs to thank another for a shared plant; the thanking is done by passing it along to someone else.

Divide mint runners to control existing plants and to expand your garden.

See if your local nursing or retirement homes would like some of your rootings. I have found these establishments eager to grow herbs to use as garden therapy, to make potpourri for their fund-raising, and for their own chef's usage. Most program directors are delighted to have volunteer help with herbal programs and projects.

Propagate by Layering

Layer woody-stemmed herbs (upright thyme, lavender, sage, winter savory, tarragon, and the southernwoods) in the spring for new plants by late summer. Take a healthy outside stem and bend it toward enriched soil. "Wound" the part where new roots will develop by gently rubbing some of the under-bark off with a dull knife. Anchor that section of the branch with a wire or a forked tree twig and cover the section with plenty of good soil, and then a brick or heavy stone.

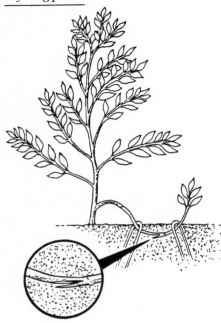

"Wound" the stem by scraping away some of the bark. Cover wound with soil.

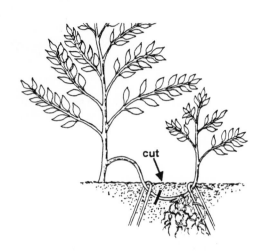

By late summer you can cut the new plants from the parent.

Leave at least 6 inches of the end of the branch exposed to the air. By late summer you should have several "babies" to cut from the mother plant to start lives of their own. (Mulch them well for their first winter.)

Layering can also be done in the late summer for transplanting in the spring, a good schedule because the new plants will have the summer to develop strong roots in their permanent homes.

Stool-layering

Another type of layering, suitable for bushy perennials, is called "stool-layering." Mound the soil up around the center of the plant, burying the center branches. If rains wash soil away from branches, replace it at once. In late spring dig up the plants. Roots should have formed all over the buried branches. Any pieces with a few leaves and some healthy roots can be cut off to be replanted either in pots or directly into beds.

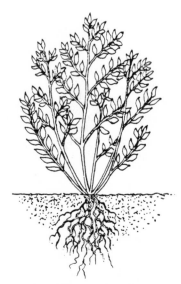

A suitable plant for stool-layering.

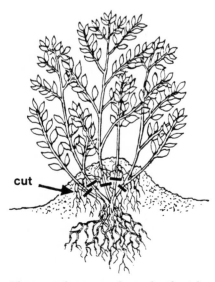

The same plant several months after it has been stool-layered, showing new root growth on buried stems.

Gourmet Gardening — Thyme

THYME is of the essence! Who can do without it? I've had creeping thyme from one original plant for a quarter of a century, and, without any special attention, it's still spreading and just as healthy and hearty as the day I bought it. We thought its flavor and aroma were heavenly, until I discovered lemon thyme and some of the other woody, upright varieties (English Broadleaf and French Narrowleaf). Compared to the lower, creeping, ground-cover varieties, the upright kinds of thyme are a little temperamental. I have grown them from seed under lights with success, but sturdier, larger stock from herb nurseries have definitely wintered over better in our area than the ones I started myself. This could be because greenhouse conditions more closely simulate outside weather than my indoor "nursery" does, and also because the greenhouse plants were started earlier than mine. It is important not to harvest much of the plant after the summer flowering and a protective winter mulch is prudent.

The tiny leaves dry fast and whole sprigs may be stored for winter use. Dried thyme from the garden is unbelievably superior to its grocery store counterpart in a box or tin. I use thyme with most beef, chicken, and fish entrees and most casseroles, soups, and stews. It blends especially well with mushrooms and any mushroom soup/sauce dish. I think so much of this herb that I've added an expert's tribute to thyme to this chapter. Be sure to take a look at the several varieties mentioned in the Encyclopedia in the Appendix. You just may want to have a garden for all thymes!

Thyme

Serve a Spring Tonic from your first fresh mints of the season. Add dried orange or lemon peel for zest.

Roast Beef with Herbs

Since April is *prime* time for herbs, I thought it appropriate here to tell you about my recipe for herbing Prime Rib Roast, or any beef roast. I used to donate this herb blend to local bazaars and fairs, and I've had many requests for it ever since. Some have told me they haven't been able to duplicate the good flavor of beef roasts since they've run out of my mix!

For many years we had roast beef at least twice a month on Sundays. I was then working six days a week, so I devised ways to make cooking easier, especially since Sunday was my only free day for gardening.

I would put the roast in the oven at 325 degrees around 2:00. One of my daughters would peel the carrots and onions while I scrubbed the baking potatoes. Then out to the gardens....

Around 4:00 I'd come in, bringing chives for the sour cream, and put 2 T. of the herb mix on the roast, add the onions to the meat pan, put the pierced and oiled potatoes in the oven and the carrots on the stove *on low,* and go back outside again.

At 5:00 I'd come in and turn the potatoes over (they baked on an old aluminum cookie pan), stir up the onions so they'd brown on all sides, add the carrots to the meat pan, and go back outside.

We were usually all starving and ready to enjoy our gourmet "banquet" by 5:30 or 6:00, even though the "chef" had been gardening all afternoon!

Herbed or Spiced Beef Recipes

Roast Beef Seasoning

3 T. parsley, 2 T. rosemary and chives, 1 T. EACH summer savory, dried minced garlic, and thyme.

Mix well and store in covered jar. Use 2 T. per roast, the last hour or so of cooking.

Here's another family favorite which makes 6 to 9 servings, depending on how hungry we are. I usually stretch it into three meals for the three of us, freezing enough for two quick meals later.

Meat Loaf Parmesan

3 lbs. ground chuck
3 or 4 cups bread crumbs or cubes
3 eggs
1 medium onion, chopped
½ cup grated Parmesan cheese
¼ cup chili sauce or ketchup
2 T. Worcestershire sauce
Dash or two garlic salt
2 T. parsley
1 t. each thyme, oregano, savory

Mix together all ingredients. Place the mixture in a greased pan. Sprinkle more Parmesan on top. Bake at 350 degrees for 1 hour.

The bread in the meat loaf eliminates the need for a starch with the meal, so I just add a vegetable and a salad to the menu.

Heavenly Rolled Round Roast

2 round steaks, a total of 3 lbs.
Salt, pepper, paprika
¼ lb. fresh mushrooms, sliced
1 large onion, sliced
1 jar whole pimentos
Fine bread crumbs
½ cup butter, melted
1 tablespoon boiling water
1 egg
¼ cup minced fresh parsley
1 cup dry red wine

Pound the steaks until thin. Rub in salt, pepper, and plenty of paprika. Overlap the steaks, making 1 large steak. Spread the meat with a layer of mushrooms and blanket them with the onions. Cut pimentos in half and lay over the onions. Cover with fine breadcrumbs.

With a beater, combine the melted butter, boiling water and egg. Immediately dribble this mixture over the crumbs. Add minced parsley over all. Begin to roll the meat lengthwise. Tie the roll firmly in several places and flour the outside.

Brown the roll in butter in a roasting pan. Add the red wine. Roast uncovered at 325 degrees for 2 hours. Serve hot or cold. *Serves 6 or more.*
— From THE CLEMENT FARM HERB COOKBOOK.

Curly parsley

Herbed Burgers

1 lb. ground chuck
½ t. garlic powder
½ t. thyme
1 T. chives
1 T. parsley
2 eggs, slightly beaten

Mix together and form patties. If desired, freeze in individual sandwich bags to be used as needed.

Spiced Meatballs With Gravy

1 lb. ground beef
1 small onion, chopped
1 egg
½ cup bread crumbs
¼ t. each ground cloves, ginger, and allspice
Salt and pepper to taste

Combine all and mix thoroughly with hands. Shape into 12 meatballs. Brown meatballs in 1 T. butter and 1 T. salad oil. Remove from pan and set aside.

Gravy

Sprinkle 1 T. brown sugar and 1 T. flour over pan drippings and stir into the drippings. Stir in 1 cup beef broth and 2 T. red wine vinegar and whisk until smooth. Return meatballs to pan, cover, and simmer over low heat for 15 minutes, stirring occasionally and turning the meatballs to absorb the gravy evenly. You may add more beef broth if needed. Serve over egg noodles. *Serves 3 or 4.*

Surprise Meat Loaf

1 lb. ground chuck
1 cup sliced scallions
1 cup cooked, chopped spinach (well squeezed)
1 egg
1 cup bread crumbs
½ cup grated Parmesan cheese
½ cup minced fresh parsley
¼ cup cream
2 t. salt
½ t. nutmeg
Bacon

Mix together all ingredients except bacon. Line the loaf pan with bacon slices and add meat mixture. Bake at 350 degrees for 1 hour. *Serves 6.*

Herby Roast Beef Marinade
(For a 5-lb. roast)

1 cup red wine (or red wine vinegar)
½ cup olive oil
2 T. parsley
1 t. tarragon (or 2 sprigs fresh)
1 t. thyme (or 2 sprigs fresh)
1 bay leaf, left whole
2 cloves crushed garlic (optional)

Blend all together and pour over the roast. Refrigerate overnight. Drain meat before roasting. Strain marinade and use as base for gravy, with beef broth.

Wild thyme

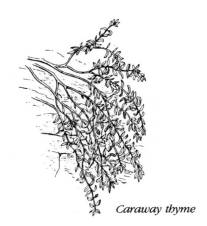

Caraway thyme

Take Thyme to Make it Exciting

by Bertha Reppert

THYME is an ancient herb symbolic of innocence. Centuries ago, maidens wore thyme in their hair to indicate their availability for marriage. Once married, I'm sure they quickly discovered thyme's culinary virtues.

Thyme has certain very definite affinities for foods such as clam chowder, oyster stew, cheese spreads, lamb, mutton, veal, roast pork, lobster, shrimp, scalloped oysters, beets, carrots, mushrooms, onions, peas, chicken salad, omelets, Welsh rarebit, creole sauces, and so on. Such a list allows plenty of leeway for creative cookery with thyme.

Fresh from the garden is best, of course. A healthy thyme plant by the kitchen door will provide snippets of the herb most months of the year, even under the snow. There are a hundred varieties of thyme but the two main categories are upright and creeping. The culinary varieties are mainly upright although all are edible. The creeping thymes are grown as ground covers or between the cracks of flagstone where, 'tis said, "the more it is trodden upon the faster it grows." Thyme makes an outdoor carpet of divine fragrance.

Propagating thyme is easy if you know the secret. Take very small cuttings 3–5" long. Dab each cut end in rooting powder and press the cutting horizontally into good receptive earth. Your little cutting will take off on its own in no time and become a proper thyme plant.

Thyme is believed to be one of the Manger herbs. Time now to think of using your very own thyme harvest in your crèche at Christmas. Leave a thyme plant or two uncut for this important symbolic decoration. You can pick it close to Christmas.

Besides dressing a stew or decorating a crèche, thyme has a long medicinal history. At various times it has been created with relieving melancholy, chasing nightmares, imbuing courage, aiding digestion, and curing hangovers. I think a sprig or two of fresh thyme added to your next pot of tea would be a very good precautionary touch! And it also tastes good.

In France, bunches of thyme are sold in the same manner that we buy parsley. The dried sprigs are also sold by the bunch, neatly covered with cellophane, ready for madam's *bouquet garni*. She will use it generously in soup and stew in the firm conviction that there is never enough thyme.

Take time to practice the culinary arts. Then, for goodness sake, take thyme to make it exciting!

(Bertha sells the varieties of thyme listed in the Appendix, plus five others. Plants are shipped from late April through June.

THE ROSEMARY HOUSE PA 17055

POTPOURRI

"Potpourri" is a French word meaning a blend of spicy flowers, a medley, or an anthology. There are dozens of delightful, fragrant blends you can make from the herbs and flowers you grow yourself, with the addition of oils, spices, and fixatives. Mixing potpourri is to an herb-lover what cooking is to a gourmet. You will soon find yourself making up your own recipes to utilize your favorite scents and plants.

Essential fragrant oils are expensive, but their essence lasts long after the herbs and flowers have lost their original scents. The fixative absorbs and "captures" the essence of the oil and preserves its aroma for many years.

Ground, chopped, or "pinhead" orris root is my favorite fixative (rather than in powdered form) because it magically makes any plant or floral material smell like whatever oil you mix it with. This makes it possible to create a lovely "remembrance" potpourri for someone from a varied collection of the dried flowers from a wedding, hospital trip, funeral, or any special occasion. Just choose the oil most suited to the ingredients and orris root will do the rest! The sachets I made in the 60's are *still* fragrant. Although I sometimes use other fixatives, such as calamus root or gum benzoin, I have not found them as effective as orris root.

Tansy, garlic, chives, and rue planted here and there in the rose bed will distract or discourage Japanese beetles and aphids from inhabiting the rose buds. Control the tansy, however, as it will take over in such fertile soil. (Do NOT plant tansy where livestock graze; it is toxic to cattle.)

Basic Recipe For Potpourri

You can subscribe to a marvelous newsletter, called HERITAGE ROSES, by sending a SASE to Jerry Fellman, 947 Broughton Way, Woodburn, OR 97071, or to Lily Shohan, RD #1, Clinton Corners NY 12514, to find out details. Join the AMERICAN ROSE SOCIETY and receive a monthly magazine abut roses. Write to them for details at P.O. Box 30,000 (yes!), Shreveport, LA 71130. For 50¢ and a SASE, they'll send you their 1986 "Handbook For Selecting Roses."

To 1 quart of crisp-dry flowers and herbs add 3 tablespoons of fixative, to which 1 teaspoon of essential oil has *first* been added, blended, covered, stored for a few days, and shaken occasionally. (I find the herbs and flowers stay drier this way, allowing the orris root to absorb the moisture of the oil and dry out a little, before adding to the petals and leaves.) Add 2 or 3 tablespoons of spices. Mix all together well and store in a covered non-metallic container for 4–6 weeks, stirring or mixing occasionally. The potpourri is then mixed well or "set" to put in jars for gifts, or crushed to a fine consistency, if preferred, for sachets. (I personally like to leave the ingredients whole, so that recipients can identify them if they are curious, as I always am!)

Rose and lavender potpourris seem to appeal to everyone. I include the basics in this chapter, as it's time now to plant roses and lavenders, two primary ingredients of potpourri that you'll want plenty of for this exciting aspect of your herb hobby.

My own basic recipes and variations follow. I hope they whet your appetite to make your own creations and aromatics.

Phyl's Basic Rose Potpourri

Plant new roses in ample holes. Pick the most fragrant of the hybrid teas, floribundas, grandiflowers, and climbers. Try Rugosa roses for their rose hips, used for tea and potpourri. The catalog for old-fashioned roses such as musk and Rugosa (as well as modern roses) is well worth the $2.00 cost, Roses of Yesterday and Today, 802 Brown's Valley Rd., Watsonville, CA 96076.

If you are a beginner, I suggest you divide the basic recipe into parts and try the variations separately. You will soon find which scents are the most appealing.

Blend 1 t. rose oil with 3 tablespoons ground orris root and allow to "set" for a few days, covered (I use empty spice jars for this). Then add mixture to 1 quart crisp-dry rose petals.

Variations

For a *spicy* scent: add 2 T. each ground cloves and cinnamon.

For a very *sweet* scent: add 2 cups lavender blossoms and ¼ cup ground tonka or vanilla beans.

For an exotic *musky* scent: add 1 cup patchouli leaves and ½ cup sandalwood and vetiver root.

For a *fruity* scent: add 1 cup each of dried citrus peel, rose and lemon-scented geranium leaves, and lemon balm or lemon verbena.

Or mix all of the ingredients named in the variations together (plus extra rose petals, oil, and orris root). You will soon find yourself adding "a bit of this" and a "touch of that" as you discover your favorite combinations.

Lavender

In my experience, lavender is the Number One favorite of the public, probably because it is less common in the garden than roses. It is expensive to buy for several reasons. Quite a bit of space is needed for mature lavender plants, which then provide small harvests because the flowers are so tiny. It takes 2 or 3 years before a lavender seedling will bear a decent quantity of flowers.

Hand-picking is time-consuming for the amount of flowers gathered. At our place lavender must be picked at night when the bees are asleep, as they will defend this heavenly nectar with their lives! One can stretch a lavender potpourri with the lavender leaves, which have almost as much fragrance as the blossoms.

I have considered putting our entire back field into lavender, and becoming rich! But then I'd have no time to grow all my other favorites, and I'd have to live in a bee-keeper's outfit in the hot sun.

Basic Lavender Potpourri

Add 1 qt. lavender blossoms to 3 T. orris root pre-mixed with 10 drops lavender oil.

Variations:

Add a cup or two of dried lilac, larkspur, cornflower, or any floral blossoms for an additional color, or rose petals for fragrance, plus double the amount of orris root and oil.

A tablespoon of ground cloves will add a spicy touch.

½ cup of ground vanilla beans will sweeten the blend.

A cup of bergamot leaves and/or mint will add fresh liveliness.

Lavender, rose, cloves, and vanilla (or tonka) beans are all "naturals" together, so for a *super* Lavender-Rose Potpourri, combine the two basic rose and lavender recipes and add 2 T. cloves and 1 cup ground tonka beans.

The enjoyment of lavender and roses extends far beyond their beauty and fragrance in the gardens: as fresh arrangements in potpourri, and for years to come in sweet sachets, bags, or pillows.

Lavender

Blenders for Potpourri

Not enough room to grow roses? Many herbal catalogs sell heavenly French rose buds for potpourri. Or check with local floral shops and greenhouses, funeral homes and cemetery caretakers, to see if you can have their spent flowers.

Once you decide on a basic fragrance for a potpourri (floral, woodsy, citrus, or what you will), this primary scent will be the star of the show and determine everything else to be added to the blend. Blenders, or modifiers, are the "supporting cast" — the harmonious herbs, spices, flowers, seeds, woods, or citrus peel used in smaller quantities. These complement the basic scent, adding zest, variety, balance, color, or texture. The fixatives and essential oils are the "magic," the charisma, the cohesive elements which tie everything together and keep the show on the road for a long run!

If creating your own potpourri, based on what is available to you, a general basic recipe would call for 6 cups of flowers and herbs of the basic scent, a total of 3 cups of blenders, and a ½ cup of fixative(s), in which you have first mixed 1 t. of essential oil(s).

With this recipe (and the fixative chart on the previous pages) in mind, you might want to experiment with some of the following combinations, adjusting the amounts to suit your senses. Some fixatives are also blenders, and vice versa, depending on the holding power, the strength, and the amounts used.

Vanilla Medley

I adore the scent of vanilla, so one of my first amateur attempts many years ago consisted of blending vanilla extract plus orris root with white lilac flowers dried to brown! It didn't work. Now that I know much more about making potpourri, this is my dream blend: tarragon, sweet woodruff, deer's tongue leaf, vanilla bean, tonka beans, calamus, oakmoss, santal, and oils of balsam tolu or peru, or storax.

Fixatives for Potpourri

A fixative is a plant or animal material that activates, absorbs, captures, and preserves the fragrance of potpourri. It retards the evaporation of the volatile oils in the herbs and flowers, releasing

POTPOURRI BLENDING

BASIC SCENT	PRIMARY FLOWERS & HERBS (6 cups)	BLENDERS (3 cups)	FIXATIVES (½ cup of roots or gums; 1 cup woods; 3 cups leaves)	OILS (1 tsp.)
FRUITY	Lemon verbena, lemon balm, yellow/orange flower petals	Citrus-scented geraniums, lemon grass, orange mint, citrus peel	Calamus root, clary sage, oakmoss	Sweet orange, lemon, or bitter almond
FLORAL	Rose petals, lavender, rose-scented geraniums	Tonka beans, patchouli, cinnamon, cloves	Santal chips, calamus root, gum benzoin, frankincense	Ambergris, civet, rose
WOODSY	Any sweetly scented petals	Patchouli, cassia, oakmoss, mace	Sandalwood, vetiver root	Benzoin, frankincense

them more slowly over a much longer period of time and thereby sustaining the blend's quality. Some fixatives have very little scent of their own, but they absorb and "set" the blend. Those having their own fragrances act as both "blenders" and fixatives, adding their own distinctive scents to the potpourri.

I prefer to use fixatives in their cut form, rather than in the powdered state. Powder coats the herbs, clouds glass containers, and leaks through porous fabrics. This causes a "dust" when sachets or pillows are squeezed, certainly an unpleasant experience for someone allergic to orris root, for example. (Powdered orris root and spices *are* best, though, for coating clove-studded orange or apple pomanders.)

I have been experimenting with saturating small pieces of fixatives and spices in essential oils and allowing them to dry out for a few days in a closed container before adding to the dried plant material. Barks, resins, wood chips, orris root chunks, frankincense and myrrh "tears", musk "crystals", whole cloves, and chopped cinnamon sticks all lend themselves to this method. This gives a much stronger, full-bodied aroma to the potpourri and I find it easier than putting the oils directly on powdered fixatives and spices, or directly on the herbs and flowers I have so carefully tended to their crisp-dry state.

Gums and resins (the sap of tropical trees) trap the scent for a much longer period of time than the root fixatives do, and add a delicate scent of their own. If you don't wish to use orris root and essential oils, try these instead.

Now that, happily, we are more enlightened about preserving the wild animal kingdom, most of the fixatives that were formerly obtained from the sexual or scent glands of wild animals are available in synthetic form only. In their original forms, these amplified and enriched the blend and had to be used sparingly as they held their own and other scents for a very long time. I believe the "jury is still out" regarding the long-lasting properties of the new synthetic forms, another good reason to time-test new recipes.

Don't be afraid to include several fixatives in one potpourri for a super long-lasting bouquet. Calamus, orris, and storax combine well, as do benzoin, sandalwood, and vetiver. Just match the fragrances of the fixatives to those of your herbs and flowers. Hope my chart (p. 84) helps!

Save daffodil and hyacinth blossoms for potpourri after you've enjoyed your indoor arrangements.

Instant Potpourri

Make this blender/fixative mix ahead to sprinkle on dried flowers or herbs as they are ready. (Also use on any combination of dried plants saved from special occasions, such as weddings, hospital trips, or funerals.) Store in a covered glass container.

1 cup whole cloves
1 cup cinnamon sticks, chopped
1 cup tonka beans, chopped
1 cup gum benzoin, or storax
2 cups ground orris root, mixed
   first with 2 t. ambergris, civet,
   or musk oils

Since this section is about blenders, use yours to chop up the above!

FIXATIVES FOR POTPOURRI

FIXATIVE AND ORIGIN	PROPERTIES AND AFFINITIES	SOURCES
AMBERGRIS (OIL) from sperm whale, formerly.	Heady, earthy, and subtle. The base of most perfumes. Blends with ANY fragrance!	AT, CM ("bouquet")
BALSAM TOLU (GUM, OIL) *Toluifera balsamum* OR **BALSAM PERU** (GUM, OIL) *Myroxylon pereirae* From evergreen trees in Central & South America & Ceylon	Light and airy. Easier to get oil than resin. Goes nicely with vanilla, honeysuckle, lotus, acacia, heliotrope, and hyacinth scents, especially. **Jeanne Rose rates this excellent for potpourri.	IB, PH (resin) AT, IB, PH (oil)
BENZOIN (GUM RESIN) Formerly, "Benjamin" From tropical spice bush and trees of genus *Styrax* (see below) from Siam and Sumatra.	*Powerful,* balsamic aromatic. Goes with sweet floral scents like lilac. Used for incense. Interchangeable with storax. **Adelma Simmons rates this an excellent fixative.	AP, AT
CALAMUS (ROOT) *Acorus calamus* or *Calamus aromaticus.* Rhizome of American iris, also called sweet flag.	Mellow, violet scent. Mildly spicy. Use with rose, vanilla, fruity, or earthy scents.	AP, AT, PH, TT
CIVET (OIL) Originally from African civet cat *Civettictus civetta* or *Vivera civetta*	Light, floral, delicate. Use for oriental and sweet scents. Valuable fixative in perfumery. **Ann Tucker rates this "unexcelled" as a fixative.	AT, CM ("bouquet")
CLARY SAGE (OIL, LEAVES) *Salvia sclarea* (Easy-to-grow biennial)	Use with any floral or citrus blends, especially with muguet (French Lily-of-Valley), jasmine, lemon verbena, rose geranium, or lavender.	AP, PH, TT (leaves) AP (oil)
FRANKINCENSE (GUM, OIL) *Boswellia carterii* or *B. thurifera* Also called olibanum. From trees in Africa, Arabia, India, Asia.	Sharp, sweet, spicy, balsam odor; yellowish in color. Use in woodsy, spicy, & oriental blends. Used in oriental perfumes and as a natural incense, burned on charcoal.	AT, PH, TT (resin)
MUSK (OIL) Formerly, *Moschus moschiferus* Asian male musk deer	Heavy, sweet, sensual, powerful, and *very* lasting. Used as a perfume by itself or to preserve any sweet or exotic blends.	AP, AT, CM ("bouquet") AP ("crystals")
MYRRH (GUM, OIL) *Commiphoria myrrha* From a tree grown in Arabia and Africa	Brownish-orange in color. Sweeter and less woodsy than frankincense. (When combining the two, use 1 part myrrh to 6 parts frankincense.) For woodsy, spicy, or oriental potpourri. A natural incense when burned on charcoal.	AP, AT, PH, TT (resin)
OAKMOSS (LICHEN) *Evernia prunastri* Found on oak trees in Southern Europe.	Used for the fine cosmetic powder, "Chypre". Adds light-weight bulk, texture, and silvery-gray color to potpourri. Excellent with rose, lavender, orange blossoms, citrus scents, vanilla, patchouli, vetiver, and santal blends, as well as all floral mixes.	AP, AT, PH, TT
ORRIS (ROOT) *Iris florentina, I. germanica,* or *I. pallida* From the dried rhizome.	Mild violet scent, sweeter than the other root fixatives. Esp. nice with lavender, cloves, and vanilla, or woodsy or oriental blends. (I use it, mixed with ambergris oil, in all floral blends.)	AP, AT, PH, TT (cut only)
PATCHOULI (LEAVES, OIL) *Pogostemom cablin* or *P. patchouli* From India and the Philippines.	Heavy, oriental, musky, earthy scent. Very dark leaves. Use with lavender and roses and for *open* jar and long-lasting scent. Esp. nice in rose and oriental blends, or with rose geranium, sandalwood, cloves, cinnamon, vetiver, tonka, or musk blends. Or use by itself! Insect repellent.	AP, AT, PH, TT (leaves)
SANDALWOOD (CHIPS, OIL) *Santalum album* – white or yellow *Pterocarpus santalinus* – red From Asian trees, esp. from India, Malay, & Ceylon.	Doesn't bring out the scent of the blend, but holds what is there, and adds its own sweet, woodsy fragrance. Goes well with rose, lavender, frankincense, heliotrope, vanilla, musk, vetiver, and all floral, oriental, or woodsy scents. Interchangeable with santal.	AP, AT, TT

FIXATIVE AND ORIGIN	PROPERTIES AND AFFINITIES	SOURCES
SANTAL (CHIPS, POWDER) *Sanicula marilandica* (Also called Red Sandalwood) E. Asia	Same properties as sandalwood. Can use interchangeably. Sweet, woodsy scent. Used as a natural dye, and as incense.	AP, TT
STORAX (GUM OR OIL) *Liquidambar orientalis* (Also called styrax or sterax.) From deciduous trees of the Witch Hazel family, including the No. American Sweet Gum, *L. styraciflua.*	True Balsam. Base for many perfumes. Interchangeable with benzoin. Use with floral scents such as lilac, hyacinth, mimosa, carnation, and violet. And with spicy fragrances using cloves and cinnamon. Also blends well with vanilla blends and oriental potpourri.	AP, CM, TT (oil) PH (Sweet Gum Bark)
TONKA (BEANS, OIL) *Coumarouna odorata* or *Dipterix odorata* (Also called Tonquin, Tonqua, or Coumara Nut.) From Cumaru tree of So. America, Africa, and Ceylon.	Black beans. Very heady, powerfully-sweet vanilla (natural coumarin) scent. Intensifies and sharpens the blend, gradually losing some of its own fragrance. Use the beans sliced, chopped, or ground in floral, fruity, or spicy potpourri. Moth-repellent.	AP, AT, TT (beans only)
VETIVER (ROOT) *Andropogon zizanoides* (Also called vetivert or Khus-Khus rhizome) From a tropical grass in India.	Beige, woodsy, earthy scent. Nice with rose and santal, clary sage, violet, mimosa, and patchouli scents. Used as a moth repellent and as an incense.	AP, AT, PH, TT

Note: "Leaves only", etc., means that's all I researched.

AP = APHRODISIA DEPT. PHA 282 BLEEKER ST NEW YORK NY 10014

AT = ATTAR HERBS & SPICES DEPT. PS PLAYGROUND RD NEW IPSWICH NH 03071

PH = PENN HERB CO. DEPT. HA 603 N. 2nd ST PHILADELPHIA PA 19123

TT = TOM THUMB WORKSHOPS PO BOX 322 CHINCOTEAGUE VA 23336

CM = CASWELL-MASSEY 111 8th AVE ROOM 723-HA NEW YORK NY 10011

IB = INDIANA BOTANIC GARDENS PO BOX 5-HA HAMMOND, IN 46325

The first four catalogs listed were used because they each carry at least 14 of the fixatives, and they each offer *smaller* quantities, too, as well as the quoted amounts which allow a savings at the retail level for the hobbyist. The last two catalogs were included because they carry some of the hard-to-find items. They *all* offer their products wholesale, so when you send for their catalogs, include your resale license number on your business letterhead with a request for the wholesale listing.

FURTHER READING
POTPOURRI, INCENSE & OTHER FRAGRANCES, Ann Tucker, Workman Publ., NYC 1972
HERB GARDENING IN FIVE SEASONS, Adelma Simmons, D. VanNostrand, Co., NYC 1964
HERBS & THINGS, Jeanne Rose, Grosset & Dunlap, NYC, 1972
THE RODALE HERB BOOK, Rodale Press, Emmaus, PA 18049, 1974
GROWING & USING HERBS SUCCESSFULLY, Betty M. Jacobs, Garden Way Publ., Pownal, VT 05261

Sweet marjoram (*Origanum majorana*)

MAY

The marigold, that goes to bed wi' the sun,
And with him rises, weeping.

— *The Winter's Tale,* IV, 4

MAY HAS TO BE the most glorious month for gardeners — the month we can finally plant all the seedlings we nurtured inside during the howling March winds. If ever I am impatient, it is during the first two weeks of May, every year. I can hardly wait for the safe frost-free date to plant my annual seeds or to move my tender perennials and my new seedlings to their permanent homes. Early May here can be a balmy 75 or 80 degrees in the daytime, but the temperatures could plunge to 35–45 degrees at night and quickly harm tender young plants.

Whatever your time zone for safe gardening weather, plant the following annuals as soon as your climate allows: basil, dill, summer savory, and marjoram. Also, be sure to plant lemon balm and sage seeds in the garden now. These are perennials and easy to start outside from seed.

Be careful not to let the garden dry out in May. Keep the hose handy and water after the sun goes down. Daytime waterings will cause the soil to bake in the sun and become crusty.

Don't plant all your dill seeds at once. Sow seeds every 2 or 3 weeks from now until early August for a succession of fresh dill all season.

Ornamental Herbs

Dill is breathtaking by August and September, if planted in May in front of tall marigolds. The feathery yellow flower heads next to the golds and the oranges of the sunny marigolds make a spectacular outdoor arrangement.

I have been most successful with dill when it was planted outside in *late* May, and left unthinned and un-transplanted. The fragile plants support each other, making staking-up unnecessary.

Marigold flowers are edible and therefore qualify as herbs — herbs being plants that are useful to humans other than just as decorative or ornamental objects. Calendula or "Pot Marigold" are the pre-

Plant different varieties of Tagetes marigolds (see appendix) for scent, flavor, and nematode control.

Carefully remove the seedling from its pot and place it in the prepared hole.

Trim a few leaves to reduce transplant shock.

ferred variety for culinary use. I dry marigolds for my "Citruscent" potpourris (see FEBRUARY) and also display them in glass jars for winter sunshine in my kitchen. Use the petals sparingly in any sauce, soup, or gravy that calls for saffron or needs a golden coloring. Marigolds can also be used for color in herb teas or to decorate cakes or cookies (see DECEMBER).

I start my tall marigolds inside, so they will bloom sooner and longer, and then plant them to border several of my gardens and hide the wire fences. (Part of our land is a swamp, which harbors all kinds of little rascals who like to nibble on tender young greens. So we fence in most of our gardens.)

I cut and dry the flower heads all summer, and am rewarded with more blooms. The dried petals are cut from the flower head and stored in covered containers. The seeds can be kept in plastic bags in a dark, dry place and planted very successfully next spring.

Rosemary, which is very tender in our area, and the scented geraniums can go outside after all chances of frost are past.

Plant nasturtiums in your herb bed for lovely color and to add to or garnish tossed salads. Both leaves and flowers are edible. I place the stems in a glass of water and refrigerate them until garnishing time.

Red bergamot (bee-balm), or Monarda, is another beautiful herbaceous flower for your herb garden. It is a tall, hardy, spreading perennial, which you should obtain from a nursery and place in the back of your garden. The red flowers bloom for the Fourth of July and are breathtaking in a "fireworks" arrangement with blue bachelor buttons and white roses. The dried flowers and leaves make "Oswego" tea for winter or are wonderful in minty potpourris.

May is the busiest and happiest month for me. Even weeding is a pleasure as I become joyfully reacquainted with the fragrant herbs and the warm fertile soil. Weeding is one job that "shows where I've been," and the results last longer than a scrubbed kitchen floor or a sparkling bathroom sink.

Gourmet Gardening — Marjoram

When I am busiest, I often work outside until dark (thank goodness for DST!) and my patient family is usually willing to settle for a quick eight-o-clock omelet or scrambled egg dish, as we all enjoy the varied flavors we add to eggs with different herbs.

MARJORAM is an herb I simply can't grow too much of. It is sweet and delicate in flavor and fragrance, and the dried leaves have a lasting pungency for my "Sweet Pillows." I start this tender perennial from seed under lights in the spring so I'll have more harvests during the summer, but one can have the same results from buying good-sized plants when the soil is warm enough for outdoor planting. Of course it can be started from seed in the soil then, too, but by the time the plant is sturdy enough to be pruned, the summer will be nearly over. And, if you have a short growing season or an unexpectedly early frost, the plant may never reach the flowering stage — when the flavor is at its best. Full sun, rich soil, and a summer mulch are beneficial to marjoram and I have found that it needs more frequent watering than most herbs, as the leaves will wilt quickly during a prolonged dry spell. I bring plants of it inside each fall, but only a few make it through the season.

Since marjoram is related to oregano (it is sweeter and less strong), it can be used in place of oregano if need be. Marjoram complements any egg dish.

A Note of Caution: If you are not accustomed to eating fresh or home-dried herbs, it would be wise to start out using one herb at a time, to develop an awareness of the individual flavors and to discover your preferences. It would also be best if you use less than the stated amounts at first, adding more each time as your family becomes accustomed to the tastes. Herbs should add a subtle flavor, and not overpower the dish they are embellishing. Better to use too few herbs at first, rather than too many.

Use twice as much as called for when using *fresh* herbs. Most recipes, including mine, intend that you use dried herbs, unless they specify otherwise. Dried herbs contain more concentrated oils than do fresh, because although the volume has diminished as the leaves have shrunk in the drying process, the oils have remained.

Try a wide row of nasturtiums bordering your herb and vegetable gardens to keep small critters away.

Have the children in your life or the scout or other groups they belong to plant a garden of herbs and flowers now to harvest for fall gift-making projects.

Herbed Egg Dishes

Basic Omelet Recipe

4 T. butter or bacon fat heated in pan
4 T. milk mixed with
8 eggs
EITHER:
1 t. marjoram, ½ t. salt, ½ cup shredded Cheddar cheese
OR
2 t. chives, 2 t. parsley, 1 t. marjoram
OR
1 t. each of basil, savory, tarragon
OR
2 t. of any one of the above herbs separately

OR
Use any of the above and add either sautéed mushrooms, diced onions, and/or ½ cup Parmesan cheese.

Now this gives you a choice of 18 different ways to fix omelets or scrambled eggs! (Recipe makes 4–6 servings, depending upon your appetites!)

Greek Omelet

2 T. olive oil
3 tomatoes, chopped (fresh or canned)
1 T. onion, minced (or 3 T. scallions)
1 cup Feta cheese, crumbled
½ t. marjoram (or 1 t. fresh)
8 eggs
½ cup milk
Salt and pepper to taste
3 T. butter

Heat oil in skillet. Sauté tomatoes and onions until soft, stirring occasionally (3 or 4 min.). Remove from heat and stir in cheese and marjoram. Set aside.

Beat eggs until light. Blend in milk and salt and pepper. Cook omelet in buttered skillet until set. Fill with sauce and fold over gently. *Serves 4.*

Summer Savory

Basiled Eggs

8 eggs
½ cup milk
¼ cup crumbled Sweet or Lemon
    Basil (or ½ cup fresh, minced)
Salt and pepper to taste
1 T. butter
1 cup freshly-grated Parmesan
    cheese
Paprika

Beat eggs, milk, and basil together. Melt butter in pan. Scramble until nearly set. Sprinkle with salt, pepper and cheese. Remove from heat. Cover briefly, until cheese melts. Sprinkle with paprika, toss gently, and serve. *Serves 4.*

Strawberry Jar Gardening
"If space is limited, try growing herbs in strawberry jars. Study the soil, water, and light requirements of the herbs you select and group those with similar needs in the same container. Center a piece of perforated plastic pipe down the middle of the jar, fill it up with coarse limestone chips or gravel, and fill around the outside with good, loose potting soil. This will provide a reservoir to take water evenly to all the pockets." (Excerpted from a lecture by Betty Wold, Make a Tiny Fortune From a Tiny Space. *This and other lectures are available from Betty by mail at $2.50 each.*
— *Sequoyah Gardens, Gore OK 74435*

Egg Casserole Brunch for Six

12 hard-boiled eggs, sliced
12 slices bacon, cooked and
    crumbled
2 cans cream of mushroom or
    celery soup
1 cup milk
1 cup mayonnaise
1 T. snipped fresh chives, ½ t. thyme
Paprika
Parsley sprigs for garnish

Layer sliced eggs in buttered

casserole. Blend together soup, milk, mayonnaise, and herbs. Pour over eggs. Bake in 350° oven for 20 minutes. Sprinkle paprika and bacon on top and bake for 10 more minutes. Garnish with fresh parsley sprigs.

Serve with herbed tomato juice, English muffins, and avocado wedges.

Italian Scramble

12 slices bacon, cooked and
    crumbled
1 large onion, minced
20 pimento-stuffed olives, sliced
1 t. each: oregano, basil, thyme
¼ t. allspice
8 eggs
½ t. garlic powder
Paprika (a dash or two)

Cook bacon, drain, and crumble. Set aside. Reserve some of the bacon fat and leave a little in the pan. Sauté onion in the pan. Beat the eggs slightly and add all remaining ingredients. Scramble in a small amount of the bacon fat. Nice flavor surprise! *Serves 4.*

Herbed Pancake Roll-ups

Add fresh sage, chopped chives, and Parmesan cheese to pancake or crepe batter. Roll up thin slices of ham in pancake and serve. Or, add oregano to batter and fold cooked chopped beef inside.

Dill

Egg Seasoning

"Here's my favorite blend for egg salad and deviled eggs — equal parts ground celery seed, onion granules, and dillweed. I make up a quantity and it's ready to use." **DIANE MATHEWS**

COMPANION PLANTING WITH HERBS

Herbs and flowers will not only add color and beauty to your vegetable garden, they will also improve plant growth and health and repel or distract harmful insects. Most are a treat in the kitchen, to boot!

CAUTION: The starred herbs are not edible, but are useful as moth or insect repellents inside the house.

HERB (OR FLOWER)	COMPANION TO:	HERB USES:
BASIL	asparagus, tomato	Serve with all tomato dishes. Patio or pool insect repellent.
BEEBALM	tomato	Tea, bouquets, potpourri
BORAGE	squash, strawberry, tomato	Add to tossed salads
CAMOMILE	cabbage family, onion	Tea, potpourri
CATNIP	border any patch for flea beetle control	Paradise for kitty, tea for you.
CHERVIL	radish	Add to summer salads.
CHIVES	carrot, tomato	Mild onion flavor; freezes well.
DILL	cabbage family	Serve with fish; pickling.
GARLIC	rose, raspberry Japanese Beetle enemy	Dry the bulbs for year-round enjoyment!
HORSERADISH	potato	Harvest the root.
MARIGOLD, *Tagetes erecta or T. patula*	eggplant, pepper, potato, tomato, THROUGHOUT GARDENS	Destroys root-feeding nematodes after 1st yr.; 3-year effect.
NASTURTIUM	cabbage family, cucumber, tomato, squash, melon	Leaves and flowers add Vit. C & pungency to salads.
PARSLEY	asparagus, tomato	Use lavishly. High Vit. C!
PEPPERMINT	cabbage family	Delicious tea. Potpourri.
ROSEMARY	bean, carrot, cabbage, sage	Divine with beef, chicken, etc.
RUE*	rose, raspberry	Japanese Beetles hate it!
SAGE	cabbage, carrot, rosemary	Heavenly with poultry, pork, etc.
SOUTHERN-WOOD*	cabbage family	Moth-preventative. Potpourri.
SUMMER SAVORY	all beans, garlic, onion	Salt-substitute on beans, vegetables.
TANSY*	raspberry, rose, grape, fruit trees	DANGEROUS TO CATTLE! Repels Japanese Beetle; moths and ants INSIDE.
THYME	melon, tomato (attracts bees for pollination)	Superb seasoning for fish, meats, chowders, etc.
WORMWOOD*	use as border	Deters small animals. Moth-repellent.

Some Don'ts: No strong aromatic herbs near cucumbers. Keep dill away from carrots. Keep rue and basil well apart; they are enemies! Give fennel a bed of its own; it's delicious, but anti-social. NO TANSY WHERE COWS GRAZE. Nasturtium *seeds* are toxic to humans.

And Some Do's: Lovage, marjoram, tarragon, thyme, and yarrow can be planted among your vegetables to improve their general health and flavor.

Further Reading: *Carrots Love Tomatoes,* by Louise Riotte (Garden Way Publishing) and *Roses Love Garllic,* same author and publisher.

SEEDING IN THE GROUND

Weed, weed, weed. Get rid of all the spring "bloomers" before their blossoms set seed for summer devastation. Then, if the ground is good and wet, mulch heavily. Even weeding, among fragrant, fresh, and so alive herbs, can be a pleasure.

When your soil is warm to the touch, after the frost-free date in your area, it is time to plant the annual herb seeds in the garden. I've had the best luck with May plantings of marjoram, summer savory, basil, sage, lemon balm, catnip, and dill. It is very important when planting tiny seeds outdoors to use fine, hand-sifted, humusy soil, both under and over the seeds, to add a light mulch, and to give an almost-daily watering with a delicate spray from a bottle or the hose.

When they have two sets of leaves, tranplant the seedlings carefully (to avoid root damage) to their permanent locales, spacing them as recommended on the seed packet. Mulch well, and be sure roots do not dry out. It is wise to label the seedlings with permanent markers through each step of the process. I use plastic markers and a water-resistant felt pen, both available at most gardening centers.

To protect flavorful seedlings from bunnies and other garden visitors, cover the seedbed with chicken wire fencing, held down by rocks or heavy clay pots. I do this now with my young parsley, marigolds, and dill — all of which have been chewed to the ground in earlier years.

Plant annual herb seeds in the garden after all danger of frost is past. This gardener is broadcasting seeds in wide rows to save space and to weed and water less (plants form a "living mulch").

Tamping in the seeds

Raking the soil to cover the seeds

Herbs love raised beds — gardens of enriched, friable soil several inches above ground level, bordered by bricks, concrete barriers, or treated boards. This allows for better drainage and stronger root systems. You can start out with the raised beds, or create them gradually through the use of regular spring and winter mulchings of organic materials, which will eventually rot and become additional layers of soil.

Treat your fall-planted garlic to a spring dose of bonemeal or compost, and your potted herbs to organic fish emulsion or seaweed fertilizer, along with a Fels-Naptha spring bath. (Shave the bar of soap with a potato peeler and swish soap pieces in lukewarm water.) Spray the plants, or dip them in the suds, let sit sideways, then rinse. This is a safe insect-chaser, but any culinary plants should be well-rinsed before consumption.

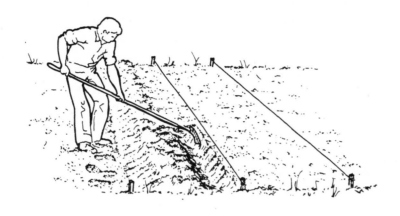

Making a raised bed with hand tools. Mark the bed with stakes and strings. Use a rake to pull soil from the planned walkway to the top of the bed. Stand in one walkway and pull soil toward you from the other walkway. Repeat the process on the other side.

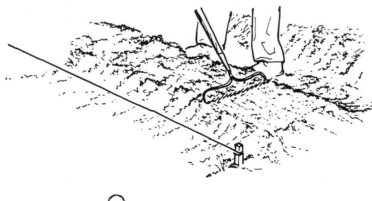

Level the top of the bed with the back of the rake. Sides should slope at a 45-degree angle. A lip around the top edge will help reduce erosion.

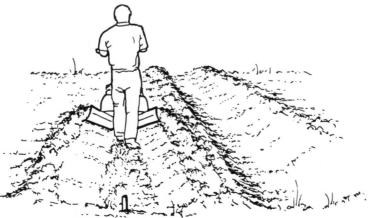

Making a raised bed with a tiller with a hilling attachment, set with hilling wings to the highest position. Line up the center of the tiller in front of your first stake, point it at the stake at the far end of the bed, and guide the tiller directly toward it.

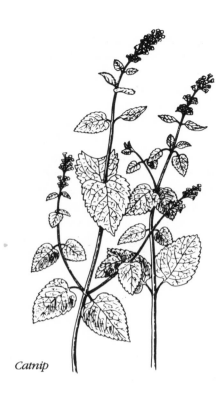

Catnip

Make lovely fresh arrangements from flowering chives and sage, using tansy or mint for the greenery. Cutting the blooms off will stimulate more new growth in the summer.

If you are sure of the identification of your weeds, cut the leaves of chickweed, purslane, and dandelion (no problem of ID here!) into soups and salads for free trace minerals and vitamins.

"Cat-A-Pillers" (Or, *Nip* That *Cat* In the Bed!)

Catnip (*Nepeta cataria*) is an easy perennial to grow from seed. Not only does it survive cold winters, it self-sows, as long as some plants are allowed to flower and go to seed. I urge you to try it whether you have a cat or not. The first year I grew it in a large barrel, imagining our cats wouldn't find it! (The tub has holes for drainage, stones in the bottom, and sterile soil, and the plants are fed 20-20-20 liquid fertilizer during each of the spring and summer months.) We placed other catnip plants in other areas, specifically for our two cats, but they preferred to reach up for the sprigs cascading over the sides of the barrel.

Once catnip is firmly rooted, cats can do it no harm. They simply bite off the leaves and play with them (guarding them jealously), then run up and down trees like crazy or stalk imaginary prey for a while before collapsing into a sleepy "drunk."

Catnip seed can be sown directly in the ground when the soil is warm, but you'll have more harvests if you start it early inside. If the seedlings are firmly rooted in peat pots, you won't have to protect them from your cat for long. We use large plastic or glass soda bottles, after the bottoms have been removed. Not only do these keep cats away, but they also act as miniature greenhouses, allowing air to enter through the mouth of the bottle. (I use these bottles for an early start with tomatoes and tall marigolds, too.)

The large bulk of dried catnip dwindles considerably once the shrunken leaves are removed from the stiff stems. Since my pillows are often bought for new kittens, I don't want any sharp twigs to penetrate the fabric and cause discomfort.

I sew two cups of the soft catnip in a 7x9" muslin bag and then *firmly* stitch this inner pillow into an outer 8x10" case made of percale or flannel "kitty" fabric. The pillows sell for $4.00 or $5.00 in the stores.

Catnip leaves make a marvelous occasional bedtime tea, because the herb acts as a mild sedative for humans — quite the opposite effect that it has, initially, on felines! Europeans use it regularly for a nightcap, often combined with camomile.

"Sweet Pillows"

In colonial times, "Herbal Pillows" or "Sleep Bags" were traditional homemade gifts taken to the ill to induce sleep. My first year in business I experimented with several recipes from herbals and placed "Herbal Sleep Pillows" in my outlets, even though some of the sleep-inducing herbs, such as hops and valerian, were not very fragrant. The shop owners told me that dozens of customers were attracted to the pillows, but they put them back on the shelf saying they knew no one who was ill! Also, my lawyer warned me that making claims to induce a physical or mental reaction could possibly cause problems with the Federal Food and Drug Administration.

So the next year I designed my "Sweet Pillow," which can have a variety of different fragrant combinations from the herbs and flowers I grow myself. The label now states that the pillow contains "A BLEND OF FRAGRANT HERBS, FLOWERS, SPICES, FIXATIVES, AND ESSENTIAL

OILS COMBINED TO CREATE A FRESH SWEET SCENT...to perfume stored linens or clothing in bureau drawers, or to lay one's head upon for pleasant soothing relaxation."

My herbal pillow is a small (11x9") version of a regular bed pillow and its case, but *flat*. It can be slipped between the ticking and the bed pillow case, so that head movement causes a rush of sweet aroma. The 10x8" inner case, made of muslin or organdy, holds two to four caps of potpourri, depending on whether or not I add cotton batting. The outer case, open on one end (so it can be washed if used during an illness), is made of any lightweight cotton or synthetic fabric, and decorated with lace or ribbon.

On my label I list all possible ingredients, and then I simply underline (with colored felt pen matching the fabric) which ingredients are in that particular pillow. The main reason for this is to alert people who may be allergic to orris root, as it can cause eye irritation to a small percentage of the population. (This is also the reason I use pinhead orris root rather than the powdered version.) I also print NOT FOR HUMAN CONSUMPTION on all my products to protect others as well as myself.

Herbal Acres' "Sweet Pillow" Recipes

- 1½ qts. rose petals, 1 pt. lavender flowers, 1 cup patchouli leaves, ½ cup ground tonka or vanilla beans, 20 drops rose oil mixed with 4 T. pinhead orris root.

- Equal parts peppermint, sage, lavender, and lemon balm or lemon verbena. Add generous supply of ground dried lemon or orange peel. OPTIONAL: Lemon or lavender oil with orris root.

- Equal parts lemon or tangerine southernwood leaves, lemon verbena or balm, and rose geranium leaves. For each quart of herbs add a handful of citrus peel and a couple of tablespoons of ground tonka beans. (Variations: Add rose petals and rose oil with orris root. Or, add pineapple mint or pineapple sage, lemon oil and orris root.)

- Equal parts spearmint, lemon balm or verbena, and sweet marjoram. Add generous amounts of blenderized citrus peel.

BE SURE THERE ARE NO SHARP TWIGS IN ANY POTPOURRI YOU USE FOR PILLOWS!

SPRING TREATS

Herbs can aid in the kitchen besides adding flavor to our foods! Dried bay leaves, spread around the food cupboards and even in the canisters themselves, will deter weevils and mealy bugs from flour, pasta, and cereal. And dried tansy branches will keep ants from coming into the house, if placed in the paths of the invading pests, such as at doorways. For more "Pest-Besting," see JULY.

Bertha Reppert's book, HERBS OF THE ZODIAC, contains 70 pages of horoscopes, history, recipes, wreath ideas, potpourri suggestions, and much more for each of the 12 signs plus 12 herbs for each sign! Any herb-lover having a birthday will appreciate it as a gift, and you'll want to see what the stars suggest for *your* herbal birthday party and potpourri. Below is a sampling of some of the delectable recipes in the book. — **THE ROSEMARY HOUSE PA 17055**

Candied Violet Libra

40 violets
2 drops almond extract
1 egg white, beaten frothy
1 T. water
½ cup confectioners sugar

Wash violets and drain. Do not attempt to remove the green calyx. (Impossible!) Add extract to water and softly beaten egg white. Brush on violets, covering each flower well. Lay on wax paper. Sprinkle with powdered sugar, completely covering both sides. They can be dried in the open air in a week or two; in a sunny window in 2 or 3 days; in the oven at 200°F. for 20 to 30 minutes. Store in glass jars. Use as Christmas gifts or on LIBRAN QUICKIES: put a small dab of frozen dessert topping on 3 dozen vanilla wafers or small cookies. Garnish each with a candied violet. Elegant, easy, delicious, and truly beautiful to serve.

Sweet woodruff

Rosemary House "Mai Bowle"

Dry ½ cup sweet woodruff in a 250° oven for 20 minutes. Steep in a small amount of apple juice for several hours or overnight. Strain and add the remainder of a tall can of apple juice and a quart of ginger ale. Sweeten with ½ cup of sugar mashed together with 1 lemon, rind and all. Garnish with sliced strawberries for added color and flavor. (White wine may be used instead of apple juice for a traditional May Bowl.)

Hippocras

½ t. ground ginger
4 cinnamon sticks, broken
4 grains cardamon, ground
½ cup sugar
⅛ t. pepper
1 qt. grape juice (or good red dry wine)
4 blue heliotrope blossoms (for coloring only, optional)
1 lemon, cut in small slivers

Place spices in a large enameled pot and pour in the grape juice or wine. Bring it to a boil and simmer, covered, for 7 minutes. Add heliotrope, if desired, and simmer another 3 min. Remove spices and flowers. Serve warm, garnished with slivers of lemon. *Makes 1 qt.* (Other edible flowers are beautiful floating in this "purple party punch", such as lilacs, violets, borage, pansies, woodruff, etc.) — From the Penn-Cumberland Garden Club Herb Tea booklet, *A Mediaeval Festival.* (See DECEMBER beverages)

Candied Angelica Stems

Cut broad green angelica stems into pieces about ½ inch wide and 2 inches long. Simmer in a simple syrup of 2 cups sugar to 2 cups water for 20 minutes. Drain and put in refrigerator for 4 days, reserving the syrup. Put the angelica back into the syrup and cook again for 20 minutes at 238° until the syrup candies the herb. (Note: you may have to simmer it a third time to candy.) Drain and thoroughly dry. Store tightly covered. Useful as decorations for wedding or holiday fruitcakes.

Angelica

Natural Mouthwash

Steep for 15 minutes in 3 cups boiling water 1 T. each anise seed, dried peppermint, and rosemary. (Double the amounts if using fresh herbs.) Strain, cool, and refrigerate to use as needed. This is not meant to be swallowed, only to freshen the mouth. — **Judy Marcellot, SEVEN ARROWS HERB FARM, MA 02703**

May Bouquets

Make fragrant *edible* May Baskets with bouquets of fresh spearmint or peppermint branches and spring-flowering sage and chives. The mint leaves will make a marvelous tea for a spring "tonic," or, like the sage, can be dried for future culinary use. The chives can be snipped and frozen for use in summer salad treats, especially in cottage cheese. Tie the bunches with pretty pastel ribbons, attaching identifying labels and instructions for use.

Martha Legg of Bella Vista, Arkansas suggests the following, "Many of the alliums are a flower arranger's dream come true. Egyptian onions make fantastic curly-cues and can be used fresh or dried. The seedheads of garlic chives are very beautiful, papery white with black seeds when dried. The tiny herbs, such as Italian oregano and variegated lemon thyme, are lovely in a dish garden, given good drainage, adequate sun, and a large enough container."

JUNE

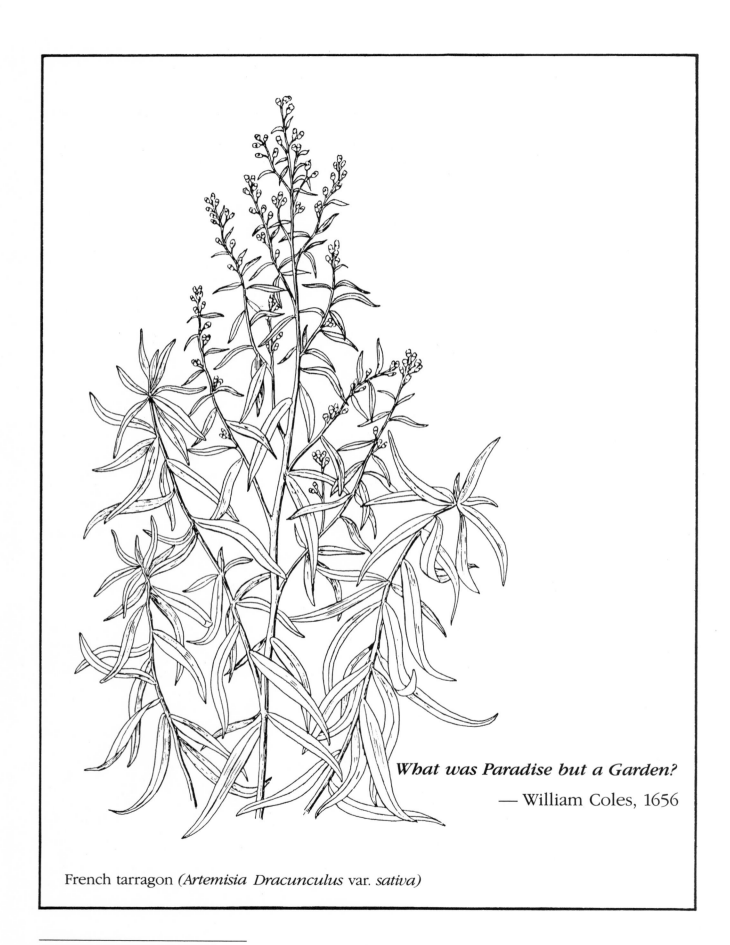

What was Paradise but a Garden?

— William Coles, 1656

French tarragon (*Artemisia Dracunculus* var. *sativa*)

JUNE

When daisies pied, and violets blue,
And lady-smocks all silver-white,
And cuckoo-buds of yellow hue,
Do paint the meadows with delight....

— William Shakespeare,
Love's Labour's Lost, V, 2

B Y EARLY JUNE it is time to start harvesting the mints and other perennial herbs. I do this once a month through September — the final
pruning being the lightest, as I do not want to strip my plants too bare
just before winter.

This regular trimming of the top third of each branch of the herbs
will keep your herb bed trim and neat, as the plants will spread
sideways, adding new branches for *more* harvesting. By mid-June the
annual herbs can be harvested, except for dill, which you will want to
have flower and form a seedhead. The monthly harvesting will delay
or prevent the plants' flowering or going to seed. As a culinary herb
gardener, you will want a cupboard full of herbs to last the winter, so
you won't want to let the plants simply flower and die out in their
natural cycles.

I wash the herbs down with a fine hose spray about an hour
before harvesting, and then, in the late morning or early afternoon, I
prune as soon as the leaves have dried off. I find they retain their full
color this way, rather than if they are washed off after they are cut
from the plant. I usually cut the top 4–6 inches from each branch,
depending on the size of the plant. When I'm about to harvest, I take
a stack of shirt (or gift) boxes lined with paper toweling, and then
write on the paper which herb is in which box.

You might be surprised next winter if you haven't labeled everything. The dried herbs look different and smell stronger than the fresh,
and if you have several varieties, come November you may not be sure
whether you are defoliating orange mint, bergamot, or catnip! Even
though I am now familiar with the dried states of all my herbs, I still
label them, because it is that much quicker to identify them later and
put all the harvests of each individual herb together in one spot.

Drying Herbs

The herbs can be dried right in the boxes in any warm, dark, airy space. An attic is perfect. On dry, breezy days I use empty bedrooms with shades drawn and the windows open.

When I harvest herbs in large quantities, I place the boxes in our garage on top of the indoor light reflectors, which radiate heat. We change our fluorescent "plant growth" lights to standard tubes for summer use, when nothing is under them. We use a fan and a de-humidifier on damp, humid days, and open the garage windows on sunny, dry days.

If the herbs are drying in a box, it helps to stir them occasionally, to expose all sides to the air and hasten the drying process. As soon as they are crisp-dry, cover the box and store until ready to prepare for kitchen uses.

Some tall herbs, such as applemint, oregano, and sage, can be hung in bunches tied together with string, upside down in large grocery bags secured with rubber bands. This dark "tent" keeps the branches dust-free until you're ready to defoliate them.

I've also hung clothesline in my garage and empty bedrooms and hung bunches of herbs from it with twist-ties. And I use an old-fashioned wooden clothes-rack to hang small bunches near the fan.

Different methods of drying herbs

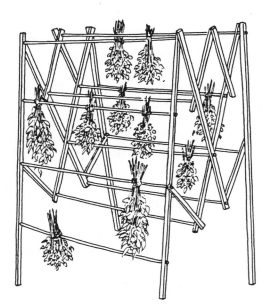

Drying the Harvest — Tips From An Expert

Dody Lyness is a recognized authority on the art of making potpourri and a certified potpourri instructor on the Community College level in her state. Her booklet, POTPOURRI...EASY AS ONE, TWO, THREE!, is an excellent *textbook for potpourri classes. Lecturers will also be interested in Dody's format for conducting potpourri classes. Write for a price list.* **BERRY HILL PRESS CA 90274-4404** *Here are real gems of wisdom from* POTPOURRI, EASY AS 1, 2, 3! *regarding ways to dry your herbs and flowers "as crisp and crackly as cornflakes" to make a dry potpourri:*

Microwave oven. Place one layer of plant materials between two paper towels, setting timer for 2 or 3 minutes. Give additional 30-second shots as necessary. Jot down for future reference how much drying time was needed for each variety.

Conventional Oven. Set temperature no higher than 100° and heat materials on a baking sheet until crisp. (My old oven goes no lower than 150°, so I keep oven door ajar. — PVS)

Food Dehydrator. Set temperature between 95° and 100°.

Gas Oven with constant-burn pilot light. Dispel any moisture in the oven by leaving the door open while heating at the lowest temperature setting that will keep the flame burning. After 2 or 3 minutes, turn off oven, place baking sheet of materials in, close oven door and forget it until you have to heat the oven for cooking. Then you'd better remember that they're in there!

Dehydrating Oast. The oast (drying oven) that my husband built into our former broom closet is my favorite place for drying my harvests. It's 14" high, 14" wide, and 26" deep. Shallow ledges along the sides of its front will suspend three flower presses (also made by him) with room for a fourth to rest on the floor of the oast. In a corner at the back, he anchored a ceramic base for a light bulb. A 60-watt bulb heats the top front of the oast to an ideal 110°, the lower front to 95°. Hardware cloth (an aluminum mesh available from hardware stores) is used for 'shelves' when I dry roses in their whole form. Miniature roses are placed upright on the mesh; larger types are hung head down, their stems pushed through the mesh and secured with small binder clips from the stationer's. Atop the flower presses and/or the hardware cloth shelves, styrofoam trays (from packaged meats) filled with materials can rest.

Storage. Place each type/color of blossoms in a separate glass jar with a screw top, so you can see what you have of what when it comes time to mix a recipe. During the first week after drying the materials, check every few days to be sure they're still crisp. If not, it's back to Square One, the drying tray!

Tip. Spread a white towel on your working surface on which to dump the day's haul of plants to dry or press. That makes it easy to spot the creepy crawlers and UFO's that came along for a free ride. You can use the corner of the towel to help the destroyer types along on their journey to That Great Bug Heaven In The Sky; but be a sport and free the praying mantis, ladybug, or any other carnivore that was tending the garden for you.

Speaking of Bugs. Once in awhile a tiny beetle will escape your attention and will manage to survive the heat of the drying process. You may not even notice the little dude in the mixing and aging process. Then when you've capped the glass container and stand admiring your

Harvest the top half of annual camomile plants when the white petals are falling. Dry upside down in a paper bag. Save the yellow seedheads for tea, the leaves for potpourri.

beautiful creation, up he jumps! Not to worry. Don't empty the container. Leave the jar capped and stick it in the freezer for a couple of days. End of problem. (Altho you should check contents for any moisture from the freezer and re-heat if necessary. PVS)

How I Do It

"What is so rare as a day in June..."? (Unless it's a day in May!) If you should drop in on me (heaven forbid!), you would find me in my bathing suit, sitting on an old blanket by one of my herb beds, with harvesting boxes and clippers on one side and pulled weeds and the digger on the other side. In back will be a bucket or two of mulch materials — probably a mixture of compost, humus, peat, and lime, and maybe cocoa beans or licorice mulch for a neat topping.

I "plant" myself in one area at a time in June and do everything in that spot during that visit: harvesting, weeding, making cuttings, and mulching. If it's a hot June day, I cool off in the pool as often as called for, and I keep a cool drink close by. This is my "heart's content."

As I finish in one spot, I simply pull the blanket farther up the line, take another dip and another sip, and plop myself down again. The weeds can be folded up in the blanket and easily hauled to the swamp when I'm finished.

You will conserve moisture in the soil and protect your flavorful friends from the hottest summer days ahead if you mulch any new plants in June after a good soaking rain. This will also enrich your soil each year and give your new herbs proper summer protection until they have developed healthy root systems.

I keep a tray of peat boxes with some humus and sand or perlite in them under our pine trees all summer, and propagate many of my herbs when harvesting. A shady spot, close to the hose for misting, serves the purpose. The most successful cuttings are taken from new growth in late spring or early summer.

Gourmet Gardening — Tarragon

French tarragon, a scrumptious hardy herb which can be propagated by root divisions from well established clumps in the spring, is most famous for making a flavorful vinegar for salad dressings. It is also a lovely addition, fresh or dried, to tossed salads. When dry, it smells like freshly-mown grass, pungent, yet sweet. It requires good drainage and a cold spell for winter dormancy.

Use the following with an oil and vinegar base, or with any mildly seasoned dressing. Add the herb blend sparingly at first (about 2 t. per head of lettuce or greens). *Salad Herb Blend:* 2 cups parsley, 1 cup each tarragon, basil, and thyme.

For other salad taste treats, add a t. of basil, savory, or marjoram to a tossed salad; or try a ½ tsp. of all three together.

If you are cottage cheese devotees as we are, you can serve it often with different herbs, either as a salad by itself, or whirled in your blender (with 1 or 2 T. milk) to make a dip for raw vegetables or munchies.

French tarragon

Herb Vinegars

by Kathleen Gips

Herb vinegars delight both the palate and the eye and allow you to preserve the harvest in a mellow gourmet blend of flavor and herbs. These vinegars lend themselves to many uses in sauces, marinades, salad dressings, stews, and beverages, and they are as individual as their creator. The herbs enclosed in the bottle can be snipped and used through the winter months when garden herbs are dormant.

The best time to collect fresh herbs is in the morning, after the dew has dried from the foliage but before the hot sun has evaporated the essential oils from the leaves.

Basic Recipe

1 cup (minimum amount needed, more preferred) fresh, firmly packed herbs

3/3½ cups vinegar (5% acidity)
Yield: Approximately 1 quart

Fill a dry, sterilized jar with washed, dried herbs. Store the jars in a cool, dark place for 4–6 weeks.

Wash the herbs by swishing them gently in a basin of cool water, being careful not to bruise the leaves and prematurely release the oils. Remove any discolored or insect-damaged leaves. (Herb stems *can* be used.) Pat the herbs dry or spin in a vegetable spinner to remove excess water. Allow to air-dry *thoroughly* because water will make the vinegar cloudy, although it will not affect the flavor.

Using a wooden spoon, pack the herbs in a dry, sterilized quart jar (due to a chemical reaction, vinegar should not come in contact with metal). Fill the jar with vinegar to within 1″ from the top. With the wooden spoon, push down and bruise the herb leaves in the vinegar. Shake to remove any air bubbles. Cover first with plastic wrap when using a metal lid. Label and date each jar to indicate herbs used.

Some people like to heat the vinegar to just below boiling point before pouring it over the herbs. The advantage of this is that the warmed vinegar releases the essential oils from the herbs more rapidly. The disadvantage is that some acidity will be destroyed if the vinegar becomes too warm, thereby changing its quality. Given the facts, you be the judge, but I have found that unheated vinegar saves time and yields an excellent product.

Store in a cool, dark place for 4–6 weeks, shaking the mixture every few days. If you are impatient for the bouquet to develop, the jars may be put out in the sun. The warmed vinegar may become slightly cloudy. A taste test will determine the right strength for your individual needs. If the flavor is too strong, dilute with unflavored vinegar; if not "herbal" enough, repeat the procedure with fresh herbs.

When you are satisfied with the flavor, strain through a plastic colander to remove and discard the herbs. Then strain through paper coffee filters until the paper is clean. Although it may take 4 or 5 times, this removes all herbal debris and the result is a crystal-clear product.

Pour the vinegar into hot, dry bottles that have been sterilized or put through the hot wash and dry cycle of the dishwasher. Add a sprig or two of fresh, washed and dried herbs to the bottle. When using a variety of herbs in the blend include a sprig of each. (The most eye-appealing herb vinegar bottles contain many herb sprigs!) Cap immediately.

Vinegar/Herb Combinations

Herb vinegars are made perfectly with red or white *wine* vinegar. Preferred is actual wine vinegar, not wine flavored. Both can be obtained in quantity from a wholesale grocer or restaurant supply store. Due to its mellow flavor, wine vinegar allows the full herbal bouquet to be tasted, resulting in a gourmet quality. Any vinegar can be used as long as it has at least 5% acidity, although white and cider vinegars have stronger flavors themselves, masking the herbal flavor.

As a general rule, white vinegar is used when color is important, such as with chive blossoms or opal basil, and red vinegar is used for strong flavors such as basil, oregano, or garlic.

Usually the most popular are vinegars with just one flavor, although I have found the Bouquet Garni (using red or white wine vinegar) to be the favorite and most versatile. The more-experienced herb growers and tasters will be willing to experiment with their own unique blends. The following guide can help determine which combinations would best satisfy your own tastes and needs.

White Wine Vinegars. Marjoram, opal basil (for a light rose result), burnet (a delicate cucumber flavor), chive blossom (a lovely pink), tarragon, thyme, nasturtium (a subtle peppery flavor), rosemary, lavender, rose petal (use pink rose petals from untreated rose bushes), pinks, violet (will turn a pale lavender color), or rose geranium (tint with 4 drops red food coloring). These last six were especially popular in the Victorian era and are useful to flavor beverages and fruit salads, as well as to use externally to soothe headaches, fevers, sunburn, and insect bites!

Red Wine Vinegar. Dill, sweet basil, garlic (mash 6–10 cloves and taste for strength after 24 hours), sage, fennel (if using seeds, allow 2 heaping T. per qt.), lovage, spearmint or peppermint, bay, thyme, chive (foliage only, not blossoms), caraway (2 heaping T. when using seed), or savory.

Pour the vinegar into hot, dry, sterilized bottles, and add a sprig or two of fresh herbs to each.

Herb Blends for Vinegar.
dill/chive//peppercorn
basil/garlic
basil/chive
garlic/chive
sage/caraway (for pork)
mint/rosemary (for lamb)
basil/savory (for beef)
sage/lovage (for poultry)
fennel/bay (for fish)

Here are two favorite blends to try, following the herb vinegar directions and using red or white wine vinegar for either, and fresh herbs (per qt.):

BOUQUET GARNI VINEGAR: 1 cup parsley, ½ cup each thyme, bay, and rosemary

MIXED HERB VINEGAR: ¾ cup each chopped basil and marjoram; ½ cup each chopped rosemary, thyme, and savory

Herb Vinegar Containers — a variety of containers can be recycled for home use by saving bottles from salad dressings, wine, or bottled beverages. Attractive containers for gift samples are small glass juice bottles. Fancy, decorative bottles can be found in dinnerware and gourmet shops. For larger bottle quantities contact a local bottle manufacturer or distributor. An 8-oz. bottle size seems to be preferred for herb vinegars.

Decorative Wax and Ribbon Seal — This adornment gives the delicious herb vinegars the ribbon and seal they deserve! *You will need:* 1 cup of paraffin (available from the grocery canning section), ¼ cup powdered cinnamon (or cloves, nutmeg, allspice, or any combination), and 4–8" of grosgrain ribbon, preferably striped (length depends on size of bottle used). *Procedure:* In a metal can (15½-oz. size is best) placed in 1" of water in a saucepan, melt paraffin and mix in powdered spices. Melt slowly on low heat and watch carefully to avoid fire. Paraffin will ignite on direct heat.

When paraffin is liquid, remove from heat and stir. Dip the capped end of the herb vinegar bottle in the wax a few times, allowing the wax to dry a few seconds between each dip. Put the mid-point of ribbon over cap and push down to secure both ribbon edges to the warm and pliable wax. Holding the ribbon ends out of the wax, dip the top end of the bottle repeatedly in the hot wax until the ribbon does not show through the seal. Dry about 30 seconds between dips or the coating will not build up. If the wax is too clear, add more spices and stir. When the wax in the can starts to congeal, re-heat. More wax and cinnamon may be required to keep the level at 2–3".

Allow wax to dry completely before touching, or fingerprints will be noticeable. Then tie on attractive bow and, if desired, attach a card listing herbs used. Cool remaining wax in can and save for future use.

To open wax-sealed vinegar, score just below cap with a knife and turn lid. Wax and ribbon will remain on the cap, but will allow the bottle to be opened and closed.

Basic Herb Vinegar Salad Dressing

1 cup oil, preferably olive oil
½ to 1 cup herb vinegar of choice
2 T. dried herbs, or the herbs
    preserved in the vinegar
Salt and pepper to taste, if desired*

Combine all ingredients in a glass cruet and shake to mix before using.

*Herb vinegars enhance the flavor of salads without added salt. DO ENJOY!

Basil

Dry small amounts of marjoram, thyme, savory, dill, or rosemary on a paper napkin in your slow cooker on the low setting for a few hours.

Basil, parsley, and chives freeze well for later use. Wash in a cold water bath and remove the stems from basil and parsley. Cut up chives into bits with clean scissors. Place in plastic bags and label.

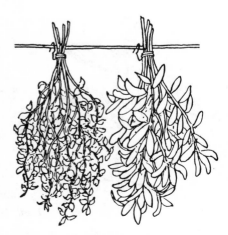

Drying bunches of marjoram and sage

I don't believe it's possible to produce a harvesting chart that's the "last word" for all herb-growers in North America because of our different climates, sub-climates, and growing seasons. Southern and southwestern growers have a long growing season and therefore larger plants and more harvests; northern gardeners have a short season and fewer harvests. And some herbs won't do well in either extreme.

Nevertheless, I have devised this "basic" chart hoping it will be helpful to most of you. Because of our many variations in climate and plant hardiness, I have designated early, mid-, or late spring, summer, and fall as the harvesting times. You can interpret these according to your individual locations. "Early spring" would be a few weeks before your first safe frost-free date; "mid-spring" would be that frost-free date; and "late spring" is when you have warm nights as well as days. Count the months you have consistently warm weather as your summer. "Early fall" would be the period when you have cooler nights before your last safe frost-free date; "mid-fall" would be the first frost, and so on.

Wherever you live, trim your first-year perennials and biennials very sparingly, because the energy should go to the roots rather than to production of new foliage, until the plants are well established. As a general rule you can harvest up to two-thirds of a hardy perennial in the spring and summer, but no more than one-third of the plant in the fall, so that they will have enough protection for the winter. Annuals, on the other hand, can be cut to 4 or 5 inches from the ground whenever there is lush growth.

Most herbals insist that the culinary herbs should be harvested just before flowering (because oil content is highest then), with the exceptions of French tarragon (which never flowers), sweet bay (which produces seed only in warm climates), and dill, coriander, anise, and caraway (if grown for their ripened seedheads). The culinary herbs are flavorful throughout the season, however, and early snitching and snatching of tips and sprigs will encourage new growth, branching out and, eventually, larger harvests.

"S/D" means Screen/Dry in my HOW TO PRESERVE column. For this you could use a screen door or window, a wire rack, or my favorite — the plastic trays with grid bottoms from nurseries. Whichever you use, cover with paper toweling, cheesecloth, muslin, or old nylon curtains (I paste nylon curtains right into my trays). The object is to allow as much air as possible to flow around the herbs. Six of my nursery trays fit on an old-fashioned clothes drying rack, three of which I use constantly all summer in the "herb room," an upstairs ex-bedroom which is kept dark and either dehumidified or air-conditioned.

By "Bag/Drying" I mean tying the stems with a rubber band around the top of a closed grocery bag. "Bunches" means hanging tied branches upside down on an indoor clothesline, pegs, nails, or drying racks. To "Oven-Crisp," briefly and cautiously finish drying in a 100-degree oven, or at 125-150 degrees with the door left open a bit. This should take only minutes, and the herbs should be watched so they don't lose color or flavor. Of course, all culinary and potpourri herbs should be stored in airtight containers when crisp-dry.

Any herbs that are listed for the freezer, or for preserving in oil, vinegar, jelly, or sugar (candying) must be fresh, not dried. They can be frozen whole or snipped in freezer bags, or they can be pureed in the blender with oil or water and frozen in ice cube trays before being labeled and packaged for deep freeze. Later these cubes can be added to soup, sauce, tea, or cooked vegetables as desired. A general rule for blending is 2 cups of washed foliage to 1½ cups of water, or 6 cups of foliage to ½ cup oil (do this in two batches).

Fox Hill Farm (MI 49269) has printed a jewel of a booklet for $3.00, WHAT YOU NEED TO KNOW TO PRESERVE HERBS. Owner Marilyn Hampstead includes a harvest table based on the life cycles of herbs, and directions for preserving them in pastes, oil, vinegar, freezer, and by candying, salting, and jellying. (Add a dollar for Fox Hill's quality catalog, ALL YOU NEED TO KNOW ABOUT HERBS, which includes a classified herb use list. A free plant shopping list will also be sent.)

Tansy leaves

Fern-leaf tansy adds marvelous greenery to summer bouquets of roses and baby's breath.

Harvesting and Preserving Roses

Harvest your roses when they are sun-dry (that is, without moisture from dew or rain). I give mine a quick drying start on absorbent paper in flat boxes in my station wagon, which heats up rapidly on a sunny day. (If you do this, park in the shade to keep the sun from bleaching the petals.) I pull the petals off separately and try to keep them from touching each other. The petals are almost crisp in a day or two of sun.

If I see any signs of "life" (it seems the entire insect kingdom also loves the heavenly aroma of roses), I finish drying the petals in a "prison of spices," an idea I dreamed up in a fit of desperation one year. Insects can't abide spices, which is why effective moth-deterrent sachets always contain a spice or two. Since I use cloves and cinnamon in most of my rose potpourris, I figured it wouldn't hurt the roses to finish drying in a bed of spices in grocery bags, folded tightly shut and placed in a warm room or closet. I don't know whether the vermin suffocate from the "hot" imprisonment or from the spices, but it works! To be absolutely certain, I oven-crisp the petals very briefly on the lowest oven setting.

Mace also helps, if you plan to make an exotic potpourri. One of my readers spreads her rose petals out on newspaper and sprinkles them liberally with pumpkin pie spice! She has never had an insect or moth problem. Another uses her microwave oven to destroy moth larvae on roses.

Still another reader reports that rose petals dry very quickly between paper towels weighted with magazines. The petals come out flat, but with excellent color. And one more swears by her gas stove oven, saying that the heat of the pilot light alone does the job in 2 or 3 days. (She places rose petals and other herbs on absorbent paper in colanders or trays with holes before placing them in the oven.)

Add dried orange peel and lemon verbena to tansy for moth protection.

HARVESTING AND PRESERVING HERBS

HERB	WHAT & WHEN TO HARVEST	HOW TO PRESERVE
AMBROSIA	Flowering stems when green or beige	Dry in bunches or wreath shape
ANGELICA	Side leaf stalks in fall of 1st yr.; more often in 2nd year	S/D leaves; freeze or crystalize stalks
ANISE	Flowers & leaves when seeds turn brown	S/D leaves & seeds
ARTEMISIA (Silver)	Flowering stems when seedheads are whitest in late summer	Dry in bunches, vases, or wreath shape
BASIL	Prune top ½ of plants whenever lush growth before flowering	S/D, then oven-crisp. Or oil, vinegar, freezer or pesto
BAY, SWEET	Individual leaves sparingly until established; then top ¼ when lush or when transplanting to larger pots	S/D
BERGAMOT	Top half of plant when flowering	Dry in vases, bags or bunches
BORAGE	Prune tops for early leaf harvest; then top half when flowering	S/D leaves; candy flowers
CALENDULA	When flowering	S/D
CAMOMILE (Annual)	Top half when flowers turn from gold to brown; leave some to self-sow	S/D, or bags
CAMOMILE (Perennial)	Prune as desired if for ground cover	S/D
CARAWAY	Seedheads when brown	S/D
CATMINT	Top third after flowering for second bloom	Bunches
CATNIP	Top half early and late summer before blossoming	Bunches or bags
CHERVIL	Outer leaves in fall and 2nd spring; preserve central growth and some seed-heads	In butter, oil, or freezer
CHIVES	Snip outer leaves regularly all season; cut flowers in spring	Scissor-snip for freezer; vinegar
CLARY SAGE	When flowering	S/D
COMFREY	Top half, or more, 2 or 3 times during lush summer growth	S/D
CORIANDER	Foliage as needed, but allow some to go to seed; harvest when seeds turn brown.	Seedheads in bags; leaves in oil or freeze
COSTMARY	Leaves in mid-summer and early fall	S/D
DILL	Top half of plants when seedheads are beige; may trim foliage lightly earlier	Bunches or oil; vinegar or freeze
FENNEL	Whole plant when flowering; may trim foliage earlier	S/D or vinegar, oil or freezer
FENUGREEK	Seed pods when ripe in fall	S/D or syrup
FEVERFEW	Flowers when blooming in mid-summer	Bunches
GARLIC	Flowers in spring; bulbs late summer after leaves have died down	Braid, air-dry in nylon; oil, vinegar
GERANIUMS, SCENTED	Prune whenever lush growth	S/D or candy or jelly
HOREHOUND	Top half when flowering, but may prune leaves in spring & early fall	Bunch dry; candy
HYSSOP	Top third in early and late summer	Bunch dry

HERB	WHAT & WHEN TO HARVEST	HOW TO PRESERVE
LADY'S MANTLE	Prune foliage early in season, then when flowering	Screen or bunch
LAVENDER	Cut back top third of branches just before flowers open up	Screen, bunch, vase
LEMON BALM	Top half early, mid, or late summer, before flowering	Bunch or bag; candy, vinegar or jelly
LEMON VERBENA	Top half mid-summer and early fall before bringing inside	S/D, candy or jelly
LOVAGE	Half of top leaves in late spring and early fall	Bunch dry & oven crisp, or preserve in oil or freeze
MARJORAM	Top third mid-summer & early fall before flowering	S/D then oven crisp
MINTS	Top half, or more, in late spring, mid-summer, and early fall	Bunch or Bag-dry. Candy, ice cubes, vinegar, jelly
OREGANO	Cut top half in summer before flowering, then again in early fall	Bunch or bag-dry, then oven-crisp; vinegar, oil
PARSLEY	Outer leaves when lush, leaving central growth	Bunch, oven, or freeze
PENNYROYAL	Prune in early summer; top half when flowering in fall	S/D
PINEAPPLE SAGE	Top third when lush foliage	S/D or bunches
ROSEMARY	Top ¼ when established & lush in northern gardens or pots	S/D, bunches, oil or vinegar or jelly
RUE	Prune top half in spring and when flowering	Bunches or bags
SAFFLOWER	Petals when flowering	Paper bags
SAFFRON	Stigmas in the fall	On white paper towel in dark place
SAGE	Prune top third in early spring and again in mid-summer	S/D or bunches; oil, vinegar or freeze
SALAD BURNET	Prune young leaves often; cut off flowering stalks	S/D or vinegar or freeze
SANTOLINA	Prune in early spring and as necessary for neatness	S/D or bunches
SHALLOT	Bulbs when foliage yellows	Sun-dry; store in mesh or nylon out of light; oil
SORREL	Cut back flowering stems for later crop	Use fresh young leaves for cooking or freeze
SOUTHERN-WOOD	Cut back by a third in early spring; half of plant in late summer	Bunches or in open paper bags
SUMMER SAVORY	Top half in mid-summer and early fall before flowering	S/D
SWEET CICELY	Leaves as needed in late spring and early fall before they darken	S/D, bunches, or freeze
SWEET WOODRUFF	Cut back half of plant when flowering in spring; and repeat in early fall	S/D
SWEET WORMWOOD	Harvest whole plants when flowering in green or brown; leave some to self-sow	Dry in vases or wreath shape

HERB	WHAT & WHEN TO HARVEST	HOW TO PRESERVE
TANSY	Can prune in mid-spring and then cut top half or more when flowering in fall	Bunch or vase-dry
TARRAGON (French)	Prune top half in mid-spring, summer, and fall	Vinegar, oil, or freezer, cubes, or S/D
THYME	Top third in spring when lush and before flowering in summer	S/D or vinegar, oil, or jelly
WINTER SAVORY	Prune tops lightly when lush growth in spring & summer	S/D
WORMWOOD	Cut back top half in late spring, late summer, and mid-fall	Bunches or vases
YARROW	Cut stems when flowering	Bunches or vases

Copies of this chart combined with my HERB GROWTH & USE CHART are available free to subscribers of my newsletter, *POTPOURRI FROM HERBAL ACRES.* Write to me at PINE ROW PUBLICATIONS, BOX 428-POH, WASHINGTON CROSSING PA 18977 for a free brochure telling about obtaining the newsletter and the charts. — PVS

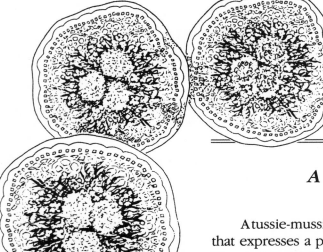

The Tussie-Mussie
A Sentiment From The Past

by Kathleen Gips

A tussie-mussie is a tightly gathered bouquet of herbs and flowers that expresses a personal message through the language of flowers. The custom originated in medieval times, before sanitation, when fresh air was thought to be harmful. Fragrant herbs were held to the nose and became known as nosegays. The strewing herbs, those with medicinal fragrances, were often used to combat germs and to fight the plague.

In the 17th century, herbalist John Parkinson recommended using herbs "to make a delicate tussie-mussie or nosegay for both sight and scent." The origin of the name remains a mystery, but the tussie-mussie soon became necessary in every woman's wardrobe.

The language of flowers came to England in the 1700s, originating from the Middle East where the Turks sent one another fruit and floral greetings representing verses of classical poetry. Each plant had a different meaning, varying according to use, growing characteristics, and religious significance, so that in different areas one plant may have had several interpretations. This very romantic, indirect, and elaborate custom reached its peak in the Victorian era.

Today the giving and receiving of tussie-mussies recalls a time when gifts were handmade and given from the heart. They make personal and welcome gifts for all celebrations, particularly Valentine's Day, Mother's Day, Christmas, bridal or baby showers, and get-well wishes.

Some herbs that can be included in the nosegay and their meanings are: basil (love, good wishes), burnet (a merry heart), rose geranium (preference), marjoram (joy, happiness), rosemary (remembrance), sage (long life and good health), and thyme (happiness, courage).

These meaningful herbs can be combined with flowers such as: roses (love), marigolds (joy, remembrance), pansy (thoughts), pinks (fascination), forget-me-nots (true love), zinnia (thoughts of absent friends), and bachelor buttons (single blessedness).

The herbs and flowers should be gathered after the dew has dried and before the hot sun has evaporated the essential oils in the foliage. If possible, "harden off" the plants to prevent wilting and to preserve freshness by putting them in water in the refrigerator for a few hours or overnight.

The flower symbolizing the most important sentiment should be in the center position with the other flowers surrounding it. Arrange the herbs in groups of three in a circular pattern around the center. Then surround and frame the arrangement with leaves of scented geranium or fern-leaf tansy. Secure the bouquet with a rubber band and trim the stems to 3 or 4 inches.

Cut an X in two paper doilies and slip the stems through. Pin the 4 tips firmly at the base with straight pins. The posy can be put directly into a vase or wrapped as a nosegay. To wrap, dampen a small square of paper towel and wrap around the stems 2 or 3 times. Squeeze out the extra water and surround the stems with a bit of foil. Cover this with florist's tape if desired.

Add two 18" lengths of narrow ribbon tied in a bow at the base with love knots added at the ends, and tie a card to a streamer, explaining the meanings of the herbs and flowers. Mist the foliage and store upright in refrigerator.

A tussie-mussie will last longer than cut flowers and stays fresh without water for 3 or 4 days. Then it can be dried in a dim, dry, warm spot, either hanging or standing upright in a vase.

For a drying method that retains shape and color more perfectly, put the entire nosegay in silica gel (a commercial drying agent found in craft stores) and completely cover the bouquet with the gel in an airtight container for about 2 weeks.

The scent can be preserved and renewed by sprinkling orris root and/or essential oils on the bouquet.

This lasting remembrance can be displayed as a decorative potpourri for years to come. Treat yourself and those around you to an experience of fragrance and beauty that will lift and refresh the spirit.

Fortunately for us, Kathleen Gips enjoys sharing her expertise on herbs with others through writing, lecturing, and her herb business (**Pine Creek Herbs, OH 44022**). *Kathleen's first love is the study of the language of flowers and its expression, especially through her specialty craft, fresh or dried tussie-mussies.*

In June everything I love most in fresh tussie-mussies is ready for plucking in my gardens — roses, lavender, baby's breath, lemon verbena, black peppermint, and rose-scented geraniums.

A Shower of Herbs

by Kathy Goeckel

When we started our herbal business a few years ago, we had no idea it would be year-round! We had planned for fall and Christmas, but our first year in business we ended up having a Valentine Open House, several programs and tours, herbal anniversary and birthday parties, a wedding reception, and three bridal showers — all from my mother's home! Here is a description of one of the bridal showers.

This shower was all done in yellows, the matching parasol and tablecloth made from a delicate print. The Victorian nosegays (tussie-mussies) were made of baby's breath for festivity and gaiety, statice for everlasting remembrance, roses (yellow) for love and youth, camomile for patience, and immortelles for cheerfulness and unfading love. The bouquets were graced by long yellow streamers with "love knots floating down the sides of the table so the love doesn't run out," to quote Lee Whitfield from WHITCHAPPEL'S HERBAL [now out-of-print].

Our shower invitations were designed with pressed herbs, and the guests signed an herbal scroll.

The bride-to-be and both mothers of the couple were presented with rosebud corsages accented by cinnamon sticks, nutmegs, and tonka beans — smelling rather heavenly! We added a honey dipper, nutmeg grater, and measuring spoons to the bride's corsage.

Refreshments consisted of herbal finger sandwiches on a tray lined with lettuce and parsley, a refreshing sunshine salad, and herbal-citrus punch garnished with fresh mint. The crystal punch bowl was set in the middle of a living herb wreath, which left an herbal fragrance in the air. Favors of heart-shaped sachets were given to the guests, as well as herbal tip cards.

We made a potpourri for the bride from the flowers guests were asked to bring from their gardens, and gave a prize to whoever brought the most flowers from the secret list we had made beforehand. We also gave a short talk on herbal wedding customs and then later a prize to whoever first recalled the old-fashioned name for a nosegay ("tussie-mussie"). A "Know-Your-Herb" quiz was based on potted herbs placed in the fireplace. **Herbs Everlasting, Hanover, KS 66945**

Doing It Up Royally

Bertha Reppert and friends threw a "Tea and Tussie-Mussie Party" to celebrate the historic wedding of Prince Charles and Lady Di in 1981. Although this was an August occasion, I have included its description here because of the wedding-related activities.

With the magnificent wedding strains from St. Paul's as background music, the Mechanicsburg, Pennsylvania ladies served 3 gallons of iced herb tea, rose petal sandwiches, lemon balm jelly on saltines, tiny "herbwiches" called "Lady Di's Diamonds," and candied rose petals and royal purple violets.

Guests were given tussie-mussies as party favors, which were the hit of the day. Used earlier as decorations on the festive table, they became lively conversation pieces and then fragrant keepsakes with a touch of England.

Since it was a porch affair, on a "maximum mugginess" August day, the sterling silver and best damask were ruled out in favor of a queen-sized lavender sheet topped with polyester lace. Everything was served on polished mirrors for elegance. A bouffant bouquet of wedding-like Queen Ann's lace from a nearby field was the bridal centerpiece, surrounded by bowls of the beautiful tussie-mussies with their colorful bows, and beribboned baskets of lavender sachets (additional gifts for the guests).

Congratulatory messages were inscribed by all on a scroll ornamented with sprigs of pressed rosemary "for remembrance" to be sent to the royal couple. A dried tussie-mussie was also included in the wedding package to England, consisting of English lavender for luck, mint for joy, yarrow for love that lasts, sage for a long and happy life, rue — the "herb o' grace" of Shakespeare, and pink rosebuds, the symbol of love. (Often in photographs Lady Di and Queen Elizabeth carry tussie-mussies that have been presented to them.)

You can order Scented Pink Wedding Rice with Rosemary and Rosebuds (a Rosemary House original), Bridal Sachets, a Potpourri Kit to Preserve the Bride's Bouquet, and more, from ROSEMARY HOUSE PA 17055

Two of the recipes used at the celebration follow.

Candied Mint Leaves and Violets
Beat 1 egg white and 1 tablespoon of orange juice until frothy. With a small paint brush, paint mint leaves or violets with the mixture. Spoon super-fine sugar over the leaves or flowers so that all sides are covered. Lay on waxed paper and move often enough to keep from sticking to the paper. Dry completely for a few days, then store in sealed glass jar. (This is not a humid-weather project.)

Take some fragrant rose petal potpourri to the wedding to throw on the betrothed instead of rice! Offer to make a potpourri from the wedding flowers for posterity.

Lady Di's Diamonds

1 cucumber, unpeeled
6 red radishes
½ cup chives (or more)
1 generous bouquet of sage, dill, lovage, parsley, mint, basil, oregano, rosemary, savory, and tarragon, fresh from the garden
¼ cup cottage cheese or mayonnaise

Grate or process the vegetables; snip all herbs very finely and mix thoroughly with cheese or mayonnaise to bind it all together. Serve on thin rye bread, cut into diamond shapes with scissors. Makes countless little diamond open-faced herbwiches.

Royal Wedding Herbal Punch

⅓ cup peppermint
⅓ cup sage
⅓ cup rosemary
1 large can frozen lemonade
1 sliced orange

Pour freshly boiled water over the dried herbs in a teapot; steep for 30 minutes and strain. Add lemonade and required water; stir, then pour over ice in a punch bowl. Add the sliced orange, juice and all, along with fresh mint leaves, blue borage flowers, Alpine strawberries, or other garden garnishes. Champagne could be added, of course.

More Herbal Wedding Ideas

Betty Wold suggests that the bridal bouquet should contain the herbs reputed to bring good fortune: laurel (for a long and happy marriage), rosemary (for constancy), and marjoram (for serenity). After her son's wedding, Betty dried the bouquet herbs and made them into a pillow, as a gift to the newlyweds, using crocheted doilies that were family heirlooms. And she sends these tips from **SEQUOYAH GARDENS OK 74435**: to insure peace and harmony in marriage, place pennyroyal and magnolia leaves under the mattress; include lavender and southernwood so the flames of passion will never die!

Jane Dole shares this from her daughter's wedding: "The bridesmaid's nosegays were beautiful with rosebuds, mints, artemisias, lavender, sage, thyme, baby's breath, and even chive blossoms, as Pam had chosen lavender for the color of the bridesmaid dresses. The flower girl was adorable as she went down the aisle dropping rose petals from her white wicker basket. I wanted to re-collect them for potpourri, but restrained myself!" **THE RED CABOOSE SHOP PA 15701**

Rose Rounds had a craft booth in 1981 featuring "Keepsake" sachets made with fragrant herbs used in the British Royal Wedding (rosemary, rose, lemon verbena, pinks, and lavender). As a result, a shop owner asked her to make customized "Keepsake Sachets" for brides to give their attendants, even using the fabric of the gowns when possible.

If you're interested in this topic, you won't want to be without Betsy Williams's booklet, PLANNING AN HERBAL WEDDING. See Bibliography. **BETSY WILLIAMS MA 01810**

The mother of a friend of mine inherited the potpourri made from her own mother's wedding flowers. She added her bridal bouquet and, through the years, freshened the potpourri with roses, lavender, verbena from her gardens, and **CASWELL MASSEY NY**'s heavenly Potpourri Oil. When her daughters were married they wore garterbelt sachets containing the heirloom potpourri for "something old," and now they each have half of the original potpourri, to which their own wedding flowers have been added. Shortly it will be passed on to the 4th generation!

Harvesting Lavender

When harvesting lavender, take the whole stems, rather than just the flower heads. I belatedly discovered this, after seeing some attractive

Lervenia Davidson of Tennessee recommends the following Tube-Rose Sachets for showers, weddings, or anniversaries. Use a 3" square of deep pink net, tulle, or maline; stitch up one side by hand. Twist one of the ends securely and wrap tightly with green florist's tape, inserting a green leaf into the tape. Fill the top of tube with rose potpourri; then tuck sides into one side of the top of the "rose". These are very pretty in a silver or crystal bowl, and appropriate at the guestbook table.

lavender sachets (see below) that included the stems by folding them over into the bag. A month after the harvest my lavender had the most prolific second blooms I'd seen in 24 years!

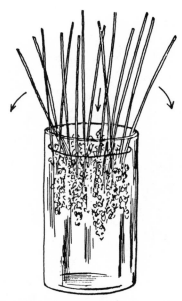

Placing the blossom cluster in a juice glass makes it easy to bend the stems down evenly. (Step 3)

Lavender Wands

by Barbara Remington

To capture summer's magic fragrance in your linens and wool sweaters, make a lavender sachet utilizing the stems as well as the flowers. We like to call these lavender wands (because of the magic lavender scent inside) instead of lavender sticks or, as the British call them, lavender bottles. You will need: *fresh* blossoming lavender stems, 3 to 5 yards of ¼" satin ribbon in soft pastel colors, thread to match, straight pins, toothpicks. (You may use velvet ribbon, which looks nice and doesn't slide easily, but it does cost more.)

To start your wand, pick 13 to 19 stems, always using an uneven number (it is easier to start with 13 and graduate up). Pick the lavender in mid-to-late morning when the dew is off the flowers and the sun has not yet broiled the fragrance into the wind. The stems and flowers must be used immediately; otherwise they will break.

Step #1: Tie the blossoms securely together with thread or a sturdy rubber band.

Step #2: Hold the blossoms with your left hand with the stems upward.

Step #3: Bend the stems down, one by one, very carefully, to form a parasol or umbrella. (See illustrations.)

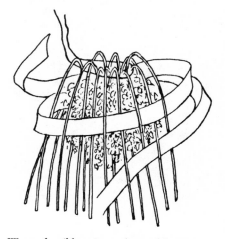

Weave the ribbon in and out of the stems for 2 or 3 rows. (Step 5)

Step #4: Place the ribbon (the length depends on how many stems are used), satin side up, under your left thumb, and hold it securely on top of the blossoms.

Step #5: Weave the ribbon in and out of the stems in a basket weave for 2 or 3 rows.

Step #6: Bend the stems down over the flowers. Now the ribbon will look messy. Simply take a toothpick or crochet hook and tighten the ribbon until a neatly woven effect is achieved. Don't pull so tight that the stems stain the ribbon.

Step #7: Continue weaving ribbon in and out until the blossoms are covered.

Step #8: When you have 4 or 5 inches of woven stems, wrap the ribbon around the stems and secure with a pin. Let dry for two weeks.

Step #9: The stems will shrink while drying. Trim the stems even. Neaten appearance with toothpick as before. Wrap remaining ribbon around stems and secure with matching thread. A bow may be tied at either or both ends of the stems.

Trim the stems evenly. (Step 9)

Barbara's instructions for making what she has termed lavender "wands" were first published in the July 1983 issue of ORGANIC GARDENING Magazine. The owner of the original DUTCH MILL HERB FARM in Oregon, where she has over 250 herbs, one of the largest collections on the West Coast, Barbara is a third-generation Oregon herb grower and has a hybridized lavender named after her! She has recently expanded her business and a SASE to her Puyallup WA 98371 address will bring you information about her current offerings, classes, plants, wedding herbs, and special festivities.

Dwarf lavender

"May the bees buzzing in your lavender bring you contentment."
— *Barbara Remington*

Odds & Ends on the June Agenda

If you **mulch** your gardens heavily after a good, soaking rain as soon as the soil is very warm, you will have very little work to do in the gardens for the rest of the summer. You can just enjoy, gloat, and harvest. A heavy (4–6") mulch will retain heat and moisture in the soil, keep weeds from seeing the sun, combat disease, prevent soil erosion, prolong the growing season by maintaining an even soil temperature, keep your herbs, flowers, fruits, and vegetables clean and dry, provide a support, add valuable enrichment to the topsoil as it decomposes, make your gardens more attractive, and, if all this is not enough, in the winter will prevent root damage from alternate freezing and thawing!

One of my dear friends has an immaculate, weed-free lawn, so she can safely use her grass clippings to mulch her gardens. We aren't so lucky, so we are constantly adding organic materials to our compost pile to use for mulch: ground-up vegetable waste, leaves, pine needles, wood chips, sawdust, used potting soil, our wood ashes, lime, and bonemeal.

If you don't compost, seek out organic mulches available in your area, such as peat moss (plus lime), baled hay or salt hay (for coast dwellers), seaweed, ground-up corn cobs, or peanut, rice, cottonseed, or cocoa bean shells or hulls. Top off your organic mulch or your paths with pine bark nuggets, cocoa bean shells, or licorice bark both for aroma and for very attractive dark backgrounds for the lovely grays, greens, and aquas of your herbs.

Dennis Mawhinney strongly recommends **electric home food dehydrators** with heaters and motorized fans for superior air-dried herbs. The vitamin, mineral, and essential oil contents are better preserved because the drying environment can be controlled. The lack of insects, dust, mold, and other pollutants is highly beneficial. Many herbs can be dried simultaneously since there is no flavor transfer with this method.

Moving? Or traveling through? When Betty Wold started Sequoyah Gardens, her entire growing stock consisted of 18 herb cuttings she safely moved from California to Oklahoma. To transport herb cuttings, fill a quart plastic bag with damp perlite or sponge rock. Seal tightly, poke holes with a pencil, and insert cuttings.

JULY

Summer savory *(Satureja hortensus)*

JULY

Mercury claims dominion over savory. Keep it dry by you all the year, if you love yourself and your ease.

— Nicholas Culpeper

J ULY IS ENJOY MONTH. If the weeding and mulching were done well in the spring, there is little to do in the summer except harvest, and luxuriate in the beauty of the gardens — to enjoy the fruits of one's earlier labor.

Each July morning is a delight. I take my breakfast tea outside with me and sit in a lawn chair to "drink in" my handiwork (and that of the good Lord!). Then I walk about the gardens to plan that day's priorities — what to pick to enhance our dinner, what to cut for indoor arrangements, or which patch to harvest for winter.

Rains seem to bypass us in late June and early July, a time when the developing plants are extra-thirsty. Many a warm summer night finds me watering my gardens by moonlight. After a sultry day, you can feel and smell the plants coming back to life with gratitude as they devour their much-needed drinks.

Gourmet Gardening — The Savories

July seems a most appropriate month to mention the dozens of ways you can liven up the flavor of vegetables with herbs, since garden-fresh varieties are easily available now.

My family never liked green beans of any variety until the first summer I grew SUMMER SAVORY. This peppery little annual adds spice to almost anything, and can be used very effectively as a salt substitute on vegetables, especially green beans, in egg dishes, soups, stews, and with meat, poultry, and fish.

Summer savory does best when started early inside in its own little peat pots or cubes, in order to protect the delicate roots from being disturbed during transplanting. Harvest half of the top of each branch as soon as it has lush foliage and again whenever it begins to

Winter savory

flower. If the plants are started early enough in the spring, three harvests are possible. And, as with any of the annuals, you can uproot the entire plants before the first frost and dry the leaves.

WINTER SAVORY is a hardy perennial and a tiny, attractive bush, but in my opinion its flavor is stronger and less desirable than that of summer savory. You might not agree, so do try both kinds, started inside from seed.

You can spruce up peas or carrots with a few chopped leaves of fresh or dried spearmint added to the butter you'll adorn them with — no salt or pepper needed. Try a pinch of marjoram on cooked spinach or lima beans, rosemary with potatoes, dill in cucumber and sour cream salads, and basil with any and all tomato dishes.

I make herb butter while the vegetables are cooking, giving the herb flavors a chance to permeate the butter before being added to the hot vegetables.

To clarify butter, so it won't burn as readily in recipes calling for high heat, simmer gently in a heavy pot on low heat until a foam forms and the butter bubbles for a time. Carefully skim off the foam and pour the clear yellow liquid into a bowl, leaving any sediment and watery liquid in the pot (the milk solids and water, now eliminated from the butter). Store clarified butter in refrigerator for up to 2 weeks.

Snow Peas a L'Herbe

½ lb. snow peas
2½ T. peanut oil
1 t. fresh tarragon, snipped
1 T. fresh spearmint, snipped
A pinch of cayenne pepper

Wash, drain, and de-vein the peas. Heat oil in pan over high heat. When hot, quickly stir-fry the peas and herbs for 1 minute. Season and serve to 4 immediately.

It's Bean Thyme

½ lb. fresh green beans, snapped
2 T. *clarified butter*
1 T. fresh thyme leaves
Salt and pepper to taste

Blanch the beans in boiling water for a minute or 2, then

plunge them in cold water. Drain. Dry off with paper towel. Heat the butter in skillet until hot. Saute the beans and thyme until warmed through, approximately 2 minutes. Serve immediately. *Serves 4.*

Rice Confetti Salad

Use your own "Fines Herbes" — snip with scissors fresh chervil, chives, parsley, and tarragon. Sprinkle on fish, roasts, salads, casseroles.

3 cups cool cooked rice
1 cup grated carrots
1 cup finely diced celery
½ cup sweet pickle relish
1 large or 2 small fresh basil leaves, minced
1 cup sour cream
Dash of salt and pepper

Blend basil into sour cream and refrigerate to use as sauce. Toss remaining ingredients together and chill. Serve on greens and garnish with sliced hard-boiled eggs, tomatoes and cucumbers. *Serves 6–8.*

Herbed Vegetable Salad

5 cups of fresh vegetables, sliced into bite-size pieces, cooked until crisp-tender, drained, and chilled. (Use carrots, green beans, cauliflower, or broccoli in any combination.)
1 red onion, sliced thinly
½ cup salad oil
½ cup cider vinegar
2 T. lemon juice

1 t. each fresh minced oregano, basil, and rosemary
1 clove garlic, minced
½ cup fresh parsley, minced

Place prepared vegetables in a bowl and toss gently. Arrange onion rings on top. Blend together all remaining ingredients and pour over vegetables. Chill several hours. *Serves 6–8.*

Sprinkle sprigs of rosemary (with beef), thyme (with fish), or sage (with poultry) on barbecue coals near the end of cooking for subtle flavor and aroma.

Broiled Zucchini or Yellow Squash

4 small zucchini (or 2 summer squash)
1 T. salad oil or melted butter
½ t. fresh snipped marjoram
½ t. garlic powder
Dash of pepper
½ cup grated Parmesan cheese

Cut squash lengthwise into halves. Place cut sides up on broiler pan. Mix seasonings with oil and brush on the squash. Broil on top shelf for 5 minutes. Sprinkle cheese evenly over all; broil another 5 minutes. *Serves 4.*

Make a "Bouquet Garni": a fresh or dried bay leaf and sprigs of thyme and parsley to tie in cheesecloth and suspend in soup, stew, gravy, or sauce...and withdraw before serving. (Basil, marjoram, savory may be included.) Make these flavor-sachets as gifts.

Carrot-Parsnip Tarragon

2 cups grated carrots
2 cups grated parsnips
2 T. salad oil (or *clarified butter*)
1 T. fresh tarragon, minced

Fresh parsley for garnish

Quickly stir-fry vegetables and tarragon in butter or oil. *Serves 4.*

Herbal Iced Drinks and Treats

Sip **iced mint tea** in the afternoon when you take a breather, and delight the family and friends by serving it at picnics. Pour boiling water over 4 or 5 tea bags, 8 to 10 fresh applemint or spearmint leaves (6–8 dried), and 1½–2 cups of sugar in a china or Corningware teapot. Steep for 10 minutes, stirring once or twice. Pour into a large (4-qt.) pitcher which is already half-filled with cold water. Pour more boiling water into the teapot to get extra mileage from the tea/mint blend; steep briefly and stir. Squeeze tea bags and herbs into the pot and discard. Add this and ice cubes to the pitcher.

Variation: Add dried or fresh lemon or orange peel (in a tea strainer) and/or lemon balm or lemon verbena leaves to create your own special blend. And, you can use low-calorie sugar substitutes or honey as sweeteners, if preferred.

Sugarless Sun Tea: Place ¼ cup green tea (found in Oriental or specialty shops) and ¼ cup herbs (mint, lemon grass, camomile, hibiscus flowers, lemon verbena or a combination of any of these) in a ½-gallon jar. Fill with cold water and set outside in sunny location. Sun tea brews in 4–6 hours, depending on your taste and the heat of the sun (it takes only 2 hours in Arizona!). This is delicious, mild, and needs

Treat yourself and others to fresh or dried "Mixed Herbs" — equal parts of thyme, savory and parsley with smaller amounts of marjoram and/or lemon thyme. This can be used for everything! Try it instead of salt on meats, fish, vegetables, eggs. Add chives or onions or lemon juice or peel if desired.

no sugar. Great for a garden tea party or picnic, with ice in ice buckets or cooler. (This is marvelous made on the stove, too. Brew 2 tea bags of green tea in 6 cups of boiling water with 1 T. each of *dried* spearmint, camomile, lemon verbena, and hibiscus flowers for 20–30 minutes of simmering on the stove. Wonderful aroma. No sugar or honey needed.)

Lemon Balm Punch: Take two big handfuls of fresh lemon balm leaves and a few sprigs of lemon verbena or lemon grass, if desired, and plunge into 2 qts. of boiling water. Let simmer for 5–10 minutes or steep for 20 minutes. Cool and strain. Use with equal parts ginger ale or with grapefruit-orange juice. Serve with ice. Very refreshing for hot summer days. — Nancy Syme Czak, from a bulletin from MERRYSPRING GARDENS ME 04843 (Catalog, $2.00).

Rosemary-Pineapple Cooler: Simmer 1 cup pineapple juice from a 46-oz. can for 5 minutes with a teaspoon of fresh rosemary and a handful of spearmint leaves. Strain. Add a pinch of salt, 2 cups water, ½ cup sugar, ¾ cup fresh lemon juice, a 6-oz. can frozen limeade, and the rest of the large can of pineapple juice. Chill. Serves 25. Rose Canny

The "Mint Oil Capital of the Midwest", North Judson, IN, sponsors an annual mint festival and cooking contest, the results of which are printed in an 80-recipe cookbook, COOKING WITH MINT. The following recipes calling for fresh mint are from the book.

Pass bowls of chew-sprigs of fresh parsley, peppermint, or spearmint after the barbecue or picnic to demolish garlic or onion breath, or just as after-dinner breath fresheners.

Watermelon Surprise
(Kathy Brown)

1 small watermelon
2 cantaloupes
½ lb. cherries
1 lb. peaches
seedless grapes
1 cup sherry
3 T. fresh mint
1 T. lemon balm

Start in the morning by cutting watermelon in half, length-wise, and removing pulp with a melon scoop. Mix this with the cantaloupe balls, cherries, & any other fresh fruit you like. The peaches must be added last or they will turn dark. Marinate all day in the sherry, to which the mint and balm have been added.

Before serving, return the fruit to chilled watermelon shell. Decorate with sprigs of mint dipped in egg whites and dusted with granulated sugar for a frosted look.

(I've been making a similar watermelon compôte for years, which is a great centerpiece for picnics. I use 1 cantaloupe and 1 honeydew, sliced bananas first dipped in lemon juice to prevent browning, seedless grapes and cherries sliced in two to release juices, blueberries and strawberries, adding lemon verbena and spearmint to the prepared fruit and its juice. A hit! — PVS)

Minty Grape Cooler
(Kathy Brown)

1 cup sugar
1½ cups water
1 cup mint leaves
1 cup lemon juice
2 cups grape juice
12 oz. ginger ale

Cook combined sugar and

water for 5 min. Cool slightly and pour over mint leaves. Add lemon juice. Cover and let steep for 1 hour. Strain. Add grape juice. Just before serving add chilled ginger ale. Garnish with mint sprigs and add ice. *Makes 2 qts.*

BEST THE PESTS ORGANICALLY

Although most herbs are naturally repugnant to insects because of their strong, pungent oils, those that are most fragrant to us are also nectar to the insect kingdom. Homemade organic sprays must be used often and after each rain on such herbs and flowers as roses, scented geraniums, and lemon verbena in my gardens, since I don't want holes in the leaves or insect eggs in my potpourri! Organic sprays are safe to use on the culinary herbs and anything else edible.

Check your local nursery for some excellent new commercial organic sprays now on the market which may prove to be better than my homemade concoctions. Here are some organic remedies easily made at home. (Also see tobacco mix in SEPTEMBER.)

Chive Spray (especially recommended for roses): Whirl lots of chives, with water to cover, in blender; let "sit" overnight; strain through cheesecloth and add 3 times as much water as you have blend. Spray 3 times in one day, then again after heavy rains. Store excess in refrigerator.

For White Fly & Mealy Bug Control on Herbs: "Bring to a boil one quart of water; add 4 cigarettes minus the paper filter, 2 crushed garlic cloves, 2 T. household ammonia, and 2 T. Ivory Soap Flakes. Steep for 3 days, strain, and spray on plants. Culinary herbs are safe to use the next day after a clean water rinse". — printed in the *New York Times,* contributed by Elizabeth Remsen Van Brunt, Honorary Curator of Herbs at the Brooklyn Botanic Garden.

Grasshopper & Garden Bug Repellent: "I have successfully raised dill, basil, sage, and thyme in spite of horned worms and grasshoppers. I boiled tomato plant leaves in a big pot for 10 minutes, strained the liquid through a cheesecloth, and sprayed it on the herbs and other garden plants. (Store this in plastic or glass container.) — Ruby Vanderlinden from Oklahoma.

Spray for Mold, Mildew or Other Fungi Disease (often found on bergamot that doesn't have enough air circulation): "A spray of tea made from camomile and onions or garlic has proved worthwhile in protecting plants or eradicating disease caused by fungi. To make the spray, dry the herb or root and prepare a strong infusion or decoction. Add a pint of this to a gallon of water. Shake well and add 1 T. of liquid soap or mild detergent. Stir gently and use immediately. Observe the results and adjust the strength of your spray accordingly." — from the 1982 catalog of **THE NATURALISTS, P.O. Box 435, Yorktown Hgts., NY 10598.**

Grain Weevil Prevention: "As soon as you bring a package of grain, legumes, pasta, flour, cereal, crackers, or raisins into the house, date it and freeze it. After 2 days empty contents into a clean gallon jar or Tupperware container into which you have first placed a bay leaf or two. (The moth invasion can be recognized in your cupboards by a small cocoon or worm — even under screw lids of jars — or a fluttering gray moth. If not discovered early this nuisance will spread through

Pennyroyal

Pennyroyal is an excellent mosquito repellent. Hanging baskets of pennyroyal on the porch or patio will help keep insects away. Fresh leaves rubbed on picnic guests' arms and legs will keep mosquitoes, bees, flies, wasps, and even chiggers at a distance! Pennyroyal leaves can be applied to the hair of humans or the fur of pets, but should not be used near the eyes or tender facial areas.

Keep an eye on basil. It can "go to seed" practically overnight, depriving you of more harvests. Pinch off any developing seedheads regularly.

Bush basil

Plant sweet basil in pots to place around the patio or swimming pool, on the picnic table, and by the house entrances to dispel flies. Flies will steer clear of the pungent scent.

the house. Although it won't bother cloth, it is upsetting indeed. I also use bay leaf in the bottom of containers for storing dried fruit, roses, and herbs." — Mary Wheeler from California

Ant Deterrent: Rub oil of spearmint around sink pipes to deter ants. — Mary Wheeler

Keeping Pests Off Your Pets

Be careful not to get any of these herbal blends into pet's eyes.

Herbal Pet Aid: Protect your dog with pungent herbs, nature's own flea repellents. For a fragrant and relatively scratch-free pet, bathe the dog weekly with an herbal bath rinse, made by simmering 2 cups of fresh peppermint or pennyroyal in a quart of boiling water for ½ hour. Double the recipe for a large dog. Add the infusion to at least a gallon of warm bath water. The dog may be sponged off with the herb water, or submerged in it, *except* for the face and eyes, which might be irritated by the herbs.

Veterinarian Deva Khalsa of Philadelphia suggests the next three herbal recipes.

Rosemary Flea Rinse/Spray: Steep 1 t. rosemary for each cup boiling water. Cool. Use as an after-bath rinse and as a spray between baths. Allow pet to dry naturally. Use for several days for severe problems.

Herbal Flea & Tick Powder: Pulverize equal amounts of dried rosemary, rue, wormwood, pennyroyal, and eucalyptus, and blend in some citronella oil. Powder your pet outside on a newspaper. Comb the coat carefully with a flea comb. The fleas will be stunned, not killed, so wrap them up in the newspaper and burn them.

Tick Removal: Moisten a cotton pad with oil of eucalyptus, pennyroyal, or rosemary. Rub this on the ticks to stun them and make removal much easier (for you and the pet!).

Natural Dog Flea Collar: Blend together dried pennyroyal leaves, orris root, and oil of pennyroyal. Wrap in fabric and secure with velcro or a stretchable material such as elastic. A cord soaked in pennyroyal oil every two weeks, and wrapped in fabric, is even more effective. WARNING: *oil of pennyroyal is very toxic and must not be consumed by humans or pets.* Ingestion of pennyroyal *oil* can cause spontaneous abortion, illness, and even death to adults if consumed in large doses.

Pet Pillows: To perfume the dog's bed and chase fleas away, make pillows of the following herbs, or a combination of them: camomile flowers, pennyroyal leaves, cedar chips, or rue.

Dog Cologne: To prevent "doggie odor" in the house, mix a few drops of oil of pennyroyal, peppermint, pine, or cedar in warm water in a spray bottle and lightly spray the dog's bedding and hairbrush periodically.

Note: None of these herbal aides should be expected to *destroy* a flea infestation already present. However, starting flea-less from scratch (1), these precautions will prevent or ward off an invasion, without the use of strong chemical commercial preparations.

Supplementing the pet's diet with brewer's yeast (de-bittered variety available at health food stores) and fresh garlic will help to prevent flea infestations, and rubbing the powdered yeast on the pet's fur and bed is also beneficial.

Pest Repellents for Humans

Want to work or play outside without mosquitoes, flies, gnats, or chiggers pestering the daylights out of you? Make your own lotion to rub on your skin before going out. Double strength mint vinegar is effective. Or try oils of pennyroyal, eucalyptus, and/or citronella in an almond oil or rubbing alcohol base, but not near eyes.

Car Perfume. Deodorize your car during the steamy months with a bunch of fresh lemon balm, lavender, scented geraniums or peppermint...or all combined! Take some "car bouquets" as hostess gifts when you travel. (Put in cheesecloth or muslin bags tied with ribbon to hang from car garment bag hooks.) Or, dry roses and herbs in shallow boxes on the back seat of your car on hot days, and you won't need bouquets for auto aroma!

Carpet-Fresh. The colonists perfumed their musty closed-up "parlors" with bowls of fragrant potpourri when guests were expected. They also placed small pillows or bags of sweet flowers and spices between the cushions of chairs and sofas to emit a pleasant scent when a guest sat down. Modern homemakers can use these same "natural" aromatics, as well as homemade carpet fresheners.

In medieval times herbs were "strewn" on cottage and castle floors to combat odors before important festivities. For a current version of this custom, grind up old potpourri in the blender and strew it on the carpet before vacuuming. Or, blend thoroughly ½ cup each of baking soda and cornstarch with 15 drops of a favorite essential oil (such as pine, cloves, lavender, or rose) and allow to dry. Place in an empty powder container and shake on the rug before cleaning. The vacuuming will impart a sweet, fresh scent to the carpet and the entire room! (If fleas are a problem, use oil of rosemary, pennyroyal, or citronella; brush the powder into the carpet and allow to "sit" a while before cleaning.)

Bathroom Deodorizer. Fresh orange mint or peppermint add exotic fragrance to the bathroom and can be grown in a container on the windowsill or in a hanging basket near the light. Or, a fresh mint bouquet from the garden will deodorize the bathroom naturally, and the addition of a few colorful flowers will be enhanced by the rich green foliage of the mint.

Stove-Top Simmers. Although popular in winter, these can freshen up air-conditioned homes that are closed up for weeks at a time in the summer as well. Experiment with blends of fresh mint and camomile and smaller amounts of orange peel, cinnamon, cloves, & bay. Or try fresh lavender and woodruff with patchouli, cloves & vanilla bean. Let simmer in pot on top of stove.

Red bergamot flowers are spectacular by themselves for 4th of July indoor arrangements, as they resemble bursting stars. To add the white and blue of the flag, use white roses or baby's breath, and lavender, larkspur, cornflower, or delphinium for the blue.

Bergamot

Cut your bergamot, lavender, rose, and marigold flower heads often to dry for winter potpourris, and they will reward you by re-flowering for later harvests! (You can pick them for indoor arrangements, if you wish, and dry the flowers after the display is spent.)

Quick Sachets. Edith Bailes' very thorough AN ALBUM OF FRAGRANCE contains complete directions for making perfume, potpourri, & incense at home. Here are samples. "Quick sachets to use in cushions, toys, and so on, can be made with the teabag papers sold in health food stores. Just pour a teaspoon of potpourri into the little paper bag and iron it shut with a warm iron. These are very nice for scenting stationery or to tuck in a greeting card."

Spicy Lemon Potpourri
Edith's #7

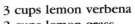

3 cups lemon verbena
2 cups lemon grass
1 cup lemon balm
1 cup lemon thyme
½ cup lemon peel

½ cup oak moss
2 t. crushed cinnamon stick
10 drops lemon oil
5 drops ambergris oil
5 drops lime oil

Jasmine Rose
Edith's #23 Blend

8 cups rose petals, 4 cups jasmine flowers, 2 cups sandalwood, ½ cup each patchouli, orris root, frankincense, & crushed cinnamon stick, ¼ cup each cardamom and coarse grind black pepper, 10 drops each jasmine and musk oils.

Sweet Vanilla
Edith's #8 Blend

4 cups woodruff
1 cup vetiver root
2 vanilla beans, cut

5 drops lime oil
5 drops ambergris oil

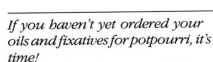

Lemon verbena

If you haven't yet ordered your oils and fixatives for potpourri, it's time!

More July Fragrances

Rose Rounds (Bedford MI) is an herbal consultant, lecturer, and crafter who keeps an "Herb-Lover's Notebook" from which she so generously shares some of her favorite recipes here. A few have been revised by me to make them easier for beginners to follow.

Super-Strength Potpourri

Take morning strolls among your herbs before the heat of the day.

2 qts. of rose petals or lavender or lemon verbena or rose geranium
3 cups orris root chips
½ cup sandalwood chips
1 T. oil of musk
1 T. oil of bergamot
2 t. oil of rose geranium
1 t. oil of rose
1 t. oil of sandalwood

Blend oils with fixatives and mellow in covered jar for a week or two, shaking often. Add the flowers or herbs of your choice from those listed above, or any combination. Then store for six weeks in tightly covered jar, stirring occasionally. Due to the amount of fixatives and oils, this fragrance will last a very long time!

Orange Bergamot Potpourri

16 oz. bergamot leaves and flowers
8 oz. dried orange peel chips
8 oz. dried lemon peel chips
8 oz. orange mint or peppermint
4 oz. orris root
2 oz. benzoin
2 oz. cinnamon bark chips

1 oz. coriander seeds, crushed
1 oz. nutmeg, grated

This one is especially nice for kitchen spice ropes or scented hot pads, etc. Or, omit the orris and benzoin and use as a stovetop simmer!

If drying herbs and flowers in boxes, stir occasionally to expose all sides to air.

Sweet Jar

2 oz. lavender flowers
1 oz. rosemary leaves
2 oz. orris root
½ oz. common salt

½ oz. thyme (optional)
6 drops rose oil

Mix well and store to blend for six weeks.

Rosemary Mix

16 oz. rosemary
8 oz. lemon verbena
4 oz. scented geranium leaves
4 oz. rose petals
1 oz. dried orange peel
2 T. orris root

2 T. gum benzoin
2 oz. common salt
½ each of ground tonka beans, nutmeg, and ginger

Mix well and store to blend for six weeks.

A few drops of rosemary or lavender oil will help retain the fragrance of a sachet.

Suggestion to beginners. Divide mellowed fixatives into 4 equal parts and add 1 pint of *each* of the recommended herbs to each quarter. Store, covered, for several weeks. A "sniff-test" should be very enlightening as to the varying fragrances of the blends. (Lecturers might wish to make the four kinds for demonstrations.)

Sachets
Mix any combination of lavender, rosemary, thyme, and sweet woodruff with ground cloves, gum benzoin or calamus root powder.

AUGUST

Sweet basil *(Ocimum basilicum)*

AUGUST

To have nothing here but Sweet Herbs, and those only choice ones too, and every kind its bed by itself.

— Erasmus

THE EIGHTH MONTH tends to be humid and wet in southeastern Pennsylvania, which probably accounts for the fact that I'm happy to spend a little more time inside in August — providing the air conditioning is working! There are some important kitchen chores this month due to the heavy crops of fresh vegetables now.

But, first, a reminder that in mid- to late August, you should take cuttings when you harvest your herbs, especially tender plants such as scented geraniums, lemon verbena, and rosemary. Placed in a moist soil in a shady spot, they'll make fine plants to bring inside to enjoy this winter.

It is also time to prepare sterile soil for the plants you will bring inside before frost. My recipe is based on many years of experimenting by our local nurseryman, who was kind enough to share with me what he has found best for growing plants inside.

I take equal parts sterile soil, humus (peat), vermiculite, and perlite. I add a cupful or two of lime and some sterile dried cow manure. We mix this up in large plastic garbage cans, tossing the ingredients back and forth to mix them thoroughly. This blend is light, friable, and moisture retaining.

Another job I perform in August is to spend a hot day with the hose and a pail of laundry bleach or other disinfectant solution in hot water, scrubbing my used plastic pots while I'm in my bathing suit! (Doing a scrubbing job in the hot sun merits an occasional hosing-off for reward.)

Gourmet Gardening — Basil

Now it's time to discuss SWEET BASIL, so spicy and such a joy to behold. As I implied in the last chapter, basil goes with tomatoes the way apples go with cinnamon. You haven't stewed a tomato until you've added basil. Try it in tomato salads, or chopped up with mayonnaise in tomato-lettuce sandwiches. Tea made with basil is reputed to be good for the nerves.

Basil is somewhat difficult to dry, as it tends to turn dark (although my Italian hair-stylist tells me his family has used it in the dark dried state for centuries!). If it is dried quickly, however, and the leaves are separated before drying and stirred often, it stays green, for the most part. Basil tends to go to seed early if not pruned each month, but if you keep an eye on it you'll have several harvests.

Pesto Sauce

You don't have to be Italian to fall in love with this delight. But you DO have to have fresh basil.

2 cups washed fresh basil
3 cloves of garlic
4 T. of pine nuts or walnuts (optional)
½ cup olive oil
½ cup grated Parmesan

Pulverize everything in the blender, except the cheese, which is added after the first ingredients are pasty, and then blended again briefly. Serve this on hot egg noodles (or fettucine), or dress up sliced tomatoes, steak, corn-on-the-cob, or cooked zucchini with pesto.

Isabelle Wiand, from ME 04289, suggests freezing pesto in plastic, pre-molded solid ice cube trays, then storing in double plastic baggies. The cubes, containing about 1 T. each, can be used for flavoring vegetables, meats, stews, soups all winter long.

When my children were in their early teens, I found few meals that pleased everyone, and I had a problem of filling up "hollow legs" on a limited budget.

However, one meal that was *always* a hit was spaghetti. So every August I would cook up a storm with my garden-fresh tomatoes and herbs and freeze dozens of quarts of spaghetti sauce for winter use. (I'm Dutch and my husband's Polish, but our children are all Italian!) Lasagna is their *second* favorite meal, or is Pizza second?

The easiest way to make and serve spaghetti is: defrost the spaghetti sauce, cook the ground beef in a large pan, and add the spaghetti sauce and a medium can of tomato paste to the cooked beef to blend the flavors. Simmer gently while the pasta is cooking. Then toss all together and serve with Parmesan cheese.

Phyl's Dutch Spaghetti Sauce

8 quarts tomatoes, quartered
10 onions, chopped
3 green peppers, chopped
10 cloves garlic, chopped
2 cups olive oil
½ cup sugar, or more
2 t. chopped fresh thyme
4 t. chopped fresh basil
4 t. chopped fresh oregano
4 T. chopped fresh parsley
½ cup Worcestershire Sauce, or more
2 T. salt
1 t. pepper
2 12-oz. cans tomato paste (optional*)

Simmer all together, *except* the herbs and the tomato paste, with the cover ajar (not completely tight) in large non-metallic pot for 2 or 3 hours, stirring occasionally. Add the herbs and tomato paste the last hour of cooking, and stir frequently until paste is thinned out. Strain in colander or food mill. Cool and freeze in 6 plastic quart containers.

*If you prefer to eliminate the tomato paste, cook the sauce down until desired thickness (4 or 5 hours total).

More Pesto, Pasta, and Pretenders

The annual Basil Festival at **Fox Hill Farm MI 49269**, catalog $1.00 has received much media attention, and rightly so. Owner Marilyn Hampstead, who has written a book all about basil, shares here one of the winning pesto recipes from the festival.

Colette's Pesto

2 cups fresh basil leaves
1 cup fresh Italian (flat) parsley
½ cup grated imported Romano cheese
½ cup grated Asiago cheese
12 blanched almonds
12 blanched walnut halves
1 T. pine nuts
2 garlic cloves
3 T. softened butter
½ cup olive oil

Place all ingredients (except cheeses) in blender and whirl to a smooth paste; place in a large bowl. Stir in cheese by hand. Cook pasta al dente (Webster says that's "firm to the bite; chewy"). Fork cooked pasta into the pesto. Add 4 T. of hot water from the pot. Stir again. Serve immediately. — **Collette Wismer, FOX HILL FARM**

Ro's Pasta Salad Supreme

Sauté 2 medium zucchini, sliced, 1 cup pea pods, ½ cup peas, 1 small bunch broccoli pieces, ¼ cup chopped scallion, and 2 cloves minced garlic in olive oil. Make a dressing in blender from ¼ cup each of wine vinegar, honey, and lemon juice, 2 T. each of fresh snipped chives and parsley, 3 T. mustard, and salt and pepper to taste. Cook 1 lb. of pasta (fettucini recommended) until al dente. Combine 1 can artichoke hearts with pasta, sautéed vegetables, dressing, and 2 cups of cooked crab or shrimp. Chill. — **Rosemarie Vassalluzzo**

Vegetable Spaghetti (or Spaghetti Squash) is often called "the pasta pretender" because it's subtle-tasting strands so resemble real pasta, but with only one third of the calories! In 1982 I co-authored THE VEGETABLE SPAGHETTI COOKBOOK with gardening expert, Derek Fell. The following two recipes are from the book. (Pierce the squash with a cooking fork on all sides; bake in 375° oven for 45 minutes, turning once. Cool slightly. Cut in two and remove seeds and darker yellow flesh around seeds. Pull strands out of shell with a fork.)

Parsley Pesto Surprise

6 cups cooked vegetable spaghetti (1 large squash)
1 cup fresh parsley, tightly packed (½ cup dried)
1½ cups chopped walnuts
2 cloves garlic, minced
6 T. grated Parmesan cheese
4 t. fresh basil (or 2 t. dried basil)
¾ cup olive oil

Whirl parsley, 1 cup of the nuts, garlic, 3 T. of the cheese, the basil and oil in blender at top speed until well-mixed.. Stir into hot Vegetable Spaghetti and place into greased baking pan. Top with remaining cheese and nuts. Heat through in 350° oven for 15 or 20 minutes. *Serves 4–6.*

Sweet basil

Dieter's Veggie-Ghetti

3 cups hot, cooked Vegetable
  Spaghetti
1 T. safflower oil
½ lb. skimmed milk mozzarella
  cheese, sliced thin
1½ T. snipped fresh chives (or 1 T.
  chopped onion)
2 tomatoes, finely chopped

1 t. fresh oregano, minced

Place the cooked Vegetable Spaghetti in a lightly oiled pie plate or small pan. Mix the tomatoes, herbs, and oil and spoon into the squash. Top with the cheese and broil until cheese is melted. *Serves 2–3.*

Basiled Noodles

Make your favorite herb butters and freeze. Slice off as needed to flavor meats, fish, breads, etc.

Cook 8 oz. of spinach noodles in boiling water per package directions. Melt ⅓ cup butter in low oven. Spoon in 2 T. fresh snipped basil and allow to blend for a few minutes. Stir basil butter and ½ cup grated Parmesan cheese into the drained, hot noodles.

Annie's Vegetable Juice

Cut up 7 qts. fresh tomatoes, 4 onions, 1 stalk of celery, and 3 green peppers. Add 9 T. sugar, 7 t. salt, 3 whole cloves, 8 sprigs of parsley, 3½ bay leaves. Bring all ingredients to the boiling point.

Simmer 5–10 minutes. Correct seasonings to taste and strain. May be canned or frozen. **Bertha Reppert, A BOUNTIFUL COLLECTION, PA 17055**

Jean Givens and Barbara Vanderhoff offer the following two recipes from their newest book, HERBAL HORS D'OEUVRES. (From HERBS BY JEAN GA 30307)

Basil-Tomato Jam

4 lbs. ripe tomatoes, scalded, peeled,
  and cut in quarters
4 cups sugar
2 cups basil vinegar
1 t. whole cloves

½ t. whole allspice
½ T. broken cinnamon stick

Tie spices in cheesecloth. Simmer, stirring frequently until quite clear and thick. *Yield: 5½ pints*

Pickled Herb Carrots

Planning one last barbecue for Labor Day? Grill foil packets on barbecue for 15 minutes of: carrot sticks and dill, sliced potatoes and chives, sliced tomatoes and basil, plus butter and salt and pepper (or garlic powder on the potatoes or tomatoes.)

⅔ cup dry white wine
⅔ cup white wine vinegar
½ cup olive oil
1 t. sugar
1 t. salt
5 fresh sprigs thyme
3 fresh sprigs parsley
1 clove garlic, minced
1 bay leaf
½ t. ground red pepper

⅔ cup water
1 lb. carrots cut ½ inch julienne
1½ T. Dijon mustard

Bring liquids and seasonings to boil in large skillet. Add carrots and cook until crisp-tender. Stir in mustard. (Cover and let marinate 2-3 days.) Serve hot or cold. *Serves 8.*

Garden Kraut Relish

2 T. salad oil
1 clove garlic, minced
1 small eggplant, diced, and
   1 medium onion, chopped
2 cups fresh tomatoes, chopped and
   drained
2 t. fresh basil, snipped
1 cup sauerkraut
½ cup chopped green olives

Sauté garlic, eggplant, and onion in oil in Dutch oven for 5 minutes. Stir in tomatoes and basil and simmer for 15 minutes. Stir in kraut and olives and cook for 5 more minutes. Chill and serve as a sandwich filling or as a topper for meats and cheeses, hot or cold.

Eggplant Caviar

2 good-sized eggplants
3 cloves garlic, crushed
1 medium onion, finely chopped
1½ t. salt
1 t. freshly ground pepper
¼ t. cinnamon
½ cup chopped fresh parsley
1 T. each chopped fresh mint and
   basil
2 T. olive oil
2 T. grated lemon rind
2 T. lemon juice
2 T. vinegar
1 tomato, minced

Bake eggplants whole in a 350° oven for one hour. (Pierce first with a fork so steam will escape.) Peel, and chop very fine. Add the rest of the ingredients and mix well. Chill in refrigerator several hours or overnight. Serve as appetizers spooned on crackers or toast bits. This is a very popular recipe in our area, adapted from the Eggplant Festival in Vineland, NJ.

Late summer or early fall are the recommended times to plant biennial seeds outside in the places they will stay, as most do not transplant well. Try lunaria (the money or silver dollar plant), clary sage and caraway. Angelica, sweet cicely, and chervil prefer the shadier spots and a rich, pliable soil, kept moist. Be sure to label each seedling bed well to avoid confusion in the spring!

Iced Tomato/Herb Soup

4 cups fresh tomatoes, pureed
   in blender
¼ cup salad oil
¼ cup vinegar
½ cup milk
2 T. lemon juice
1 garlic clove, minced
2 T. sugar
1 t. dry mustard
1 T. each fresh chopped rosemary,
   basil and thyme
Salt and pepper to taste
1½ cups chopped cucumber for
   garnish

Combine tomatoes, oil, and vinegar. Beat in milk and lemon juice. Stir in garlic, sugar, and herbs. Chill at least 24 hours. Whirl ½ portions in blender. Strain. Serve with ice and chopped cucumber. *Serves 4 or 5.* — adapted from Rosemarie Vassalluzzo's "BUCKS COUNTY KITCHEN" newspaper column in *The Delaware Valley Advance*

Sweet cicely

Chervil

Nasturtium

Nasturtiums: Summer Jewels in Your Garden and on the Menu

by Bertha Reppert

Nasturtiums are herbs of the first order, being both pretty and tasty. They are a peppery seasoning, particularly good to eat in sandwiches and salads.

Anyone who has grown nasturtiums will tell you they are ridiculously easy to grow. The plump seeds can be pressed into the earth by any available child who will adore the task. In no time they pop through the soil and begin to grow.

From the first few beginning leaves you may harvest enough to season a salad. Chop the green leaves and toss in with the other greens. Nasturtium is very like its close cousin, the true watercress, and therefore may be used in much the same way. If you like watercress sandwiches, you will also enjoy nasturtium sandwiches. The leaves may be used whole in rolled tea sandwiches or the bread may be cut round to fit the leaves.

The flowers are as delicious as they are beautiful. One of the loveliest dishes I have ever seen was pale green freshly made applesauce garnished liberally with bright yellow, orange, and red nasturtiums.

The late General Dwight D. Eisenhower, who enjoyed cooking, added nasturtiums leaves and stems, chopped fine, to his famous vegetable soup. He used about a tablespoon, added near the end of cooking.

The largest nasturtium leaves may be stuffed with a mixture of tuna fish or anchovies, chopped parsley, sweet pickles and mayonnaise. Use about a teaspoonful per leaf, roll up, secure with toothpicks, and cover with French dressing. Marinate before serving as an hors d'oeuvre. A conversation piece!

Mince the flowers and leaves into whipped sweet butter for something new and exciting on dinner rolls.

If the soul of festivity is in the cookery and the soul of cookery in the sauce, or so it has been said, I give you then:

Nasturtium Sauce

1 t. salt
1 qt. vinegar
½ t. cayenne
8 shallots, well bruised
1 qt. pressed nasturtium blossoms

Simmer all ingredients, except flowers, together for 10 minutes. Then pour over flowers and cover closely for 2 months. Strain and bottle. **THE ROSEMARY HOUSE PA 17055**

SUMMER SPECIALTIES

Nasturtium Salad

2 cucumbers
36 small nasturtium leaves
½ t. dry mustard
2 T. wine vinegar
6 T. salad oil
Salt, freshly ground pepper to taste
2 T. chopped fresh tarragon
6 nasturtium flowers with leaves

Peel and slice cucumbers thinly. Wash nasturtium leaves; remove stems and drain. Mix well in blender the remaining ingredients, except for the flowers with leaves. When ready to serve, combine the cucumbers, small nasturtium leaves, and the dressing and toss gently. Garnish with nasturtium flowers with leaves. *Serves 4.* — adapted from HERBS FROM CULTIVATION TO COOKING, the Herb Society of Greater Cincinnati.

August Potpourris

Highland Summer Potpourri

½ cup each heather flowers and silver artemisia
¼ cup each pink fragrant roses, lavender, bay leaves, thyme, and rosemary
4 T. orris root chips
3–4 drops each rose & lavender oil

— from Barbara Roger's **FOLK ARTS QUARTERLY NEWSLETTER, NH 03470**

Woodspirits Pink-pourri

1 cup oakmoss (beautiful gray!)
20 drops clove bud oil
25 drops sandalwood oil
4 oz. pink rosebuds
4 cups red peony petals
1 qt. pink globe amaranth flowers

— from Barbara Bob at WOODSPIRITS HERB SHOP in St. Paris OH 43072, who recommends pre-mixing the oils with the oakmoss.

Tropical Breeze

1 cup patchouli
1 cup rosemary
½ cup thyme
1 cup sandalwood chips
10 white cardamom seeds (crushed)
1 cup marjoram
1 cup coriander seeds (crushed)
½ cup vetiver (cut)
20 drops magnolia oil
20 drops sandalwood oil

Mix well and store for two weeks in a tightly covered ceramic or glass jar. Makes approximately ½ lb.

This potpourri is beige/green in color and has an interesting texture. The fragrance is woodsy, tropical and most delicious. Try it in sachets for men. This blend is especially suited to storage in hand-made pottery.

Rosemary

Moth Repellent I

1 cup rosemary
1 cup vetiver (cut)

1 cup pennyroyal (repels fleas)
10 whole bay leaves (crushed)

Winter Holidays

Grace Wakefield, from **TOM THUMB WORKSHOPS,** *has much to share with us and from her catalog ($1.00). She has written several publications which you will want in your library: DECORATING WITH FRAGRANCE, from which all the luscious recipes on this page are excerpted, PERFUME CRAFTING, SACHET AND POTPOURRI CRAFTING, AN ESSENTIAL OIL CHART, and her latest, FRAGRANT WREATHS AND OTHER AROMATIC BOTANICAL CREATIONS.*

Not only does Grace tell us how to make dozens of wonderful herbal creations, she sells everything necessary for the crafts, from dried flowers and botanicals, herbs, oils and spices...to the accessories and equipment used!

1 oz. cassia chips
1 oz. myrrh gum (small pieces)
1 oz. sandalwood chips
½ oz. cloves (whole)
2 oz. allspice (whole)
2 oz. cedar chips
1 oz. bay leaves
1 oz. star anise (whole)
2 oz. rose hips (whole)
20 drops spruce oil
20 drops frankincense oil
10 drops bay oil

Mix all the above ingredients in a nonmetal bowl. Store in a glass jar with a tightly fitting lid. Allow to blend for two weeks before using. Stir occasionally. Makes approximately 12 ounces of potpourri.

Winter Holidays potpourri is pleasing to the eye and the nose. The sandalwood, cedar wood, myrrh and spices combine to make a reddish-brown background for the green bay leaves and the round, red rose hips. The fragrance is pungent, woodsy and spicy and is reminiscent of forest resins. A jar of this potpourri in a den or near a favorite reading chair is a welcome winter treat.

Strawberry Fair

1 oz. orange leaves (cut)
1 oz. clover flowers
1 oz. orange petals
2 oz. hibiscus flowers (whole)
2 oz. rose hips (cut)
1 oz. calamus root (cut)
1 oz. tonka beans (cut)
1 oz. life everlasting
30 drops strawberry oil
25 drops rose geranium oil
10 drops labdanum oil

Mix all the ingredients together and store in a glass jar with a tightly fitting lid. Allow the potpourri to blend for two weeks before using.

This is a very pretty mixture of flowers and leaves. The bright yellow of the life everlasting and the dark reds of the rose hips and the hibiscus make a striking contrast with the other ingredients. The fragrance is deliciously strawberry.

Sachet Base

4 oz. orris root powder
4 oz. sandalwood powder
1 oz. cedar powder
1 oz. lavender flowers
2 oz. rose petals
2 oz. patchouli leaves
1 oz. vetiver powder
1 oz. benzoin powder
½ oz. tonka bean
1 teaspoon clove powder

Pulverize the rose petals, lavender, and tonka bean with a mortar and pestle. Combine all the above ingredients and store for two weeks. Add any essential oils to this basic mixture to make a long-lasting sachet. Most of the above ingredients are fixatives and make a fine base for sachets.

Kitchen Crafts

Spicy Hot Pads

A spicy hotpad placed under a teapot or a hot casserole will give off a delicious aroma while keeping the heat from the table top. A nice gift for the holidays. The removable spicy inserts can be filled with different spices which can be changed for variety. When the hot pad needs washing, the bag of spices is removed.

Materials

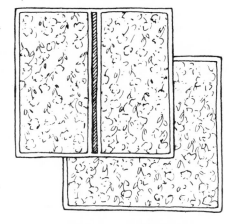

2 6" squares of quilted material
packet of bias tape (or lace for edges,
   if preferred)
2 5" squares of muslin
2 oz. of whole allspice (or whole
   cloves or 1" cinnamon sticks)

Method

1. Sew the two 5" muslin squares together, ½" from the edges, leaving 2" unsewn. Turn the bag inside out and fill with allspice berries so that a layer of berries covers the interior of the bag. Sew up the 2" gap.

2. Cut one of the 6" quilted squares in half lengthwise. Sew an edge of bias tape over 2 of the 6" edges. (This forms the back flap for inserting the spice bag.)

3. Butt the biased edged back flaps together and place them on top of the 6" quilted square with wrong sides together. Tack the top and bottom of the pad together. Attach the bias tape around the 4 sides of the hot pad. (If a lace edge is desired, sew the lace to the right side of the 6" square with the free edge pointing towards the center.) Then sew on the 2 flaps with right sides together and bias flap edges completed. Turn inside out.

4. Slip the muslin bag of allspice into the flap and flatten.

Separate bags containing different spices can accompany this quilted pad. Another idea would be to mix allspice, cloves, cassia bark, and star anise in a spice mixture. — from FRAGRANT WREATHS AND OTHER AROMATIC BOTANICAL CREATIONS, by Grace Wakefield, TOM THUMB WORKSHOPS VA 23407

Spice Rope

Colonial grannies hung spice ropes in their kitchens to absorb odors. These are great for closets, too. Should the little bundles lose their scent after a time, add a drop of clove or cinnamon oil to the back of each bundle.

Materials

9 strands Bulky yarn 52" long

27 strands knitting worsted 52" long

4 circles of 6" wide assorted calico pinked

1 metal ring 1½" wide

3 cinnamon sticks

Mixed spices or potpourri ("Citruscent" is especially nice.)

Method

Fold yarn in half over ring. Divide equally in three and braid tightly, leaving 4" for tassel. Tie with matching yarn. Put about a tablespoon of spices or potpourri on calico circles. Pull ends up and tie securely with a 6" strand of matching yarn. Flatten out making little hats with dangling ribbons. Sew hats on braid leaving room between to tie or insert cinnamon sticks.

(— contributed by Helen Fifield of Rochester, MN.)

Barbara's Kitchen Spice Potpourri

Try this in the spice ropes.

2 oz. orris *chips* (not powdered), pre-mixed a few days ahead with the following oils

20 drops each clove, orange, & cinnamon oils

10 drops each lemon, nutmeg, & coriander oils

¼ lb. star anise

3 oz. whole allspice

¼ lb. whole nutmeg (crush with nutcracker)

½ lb. whole cloves

¼ lb. cinnamon chips

½ lb. hibiscus flowers (Mexican whole)

½ lb. orange or lemon peel

2 oz. whole coriander seed

Barbara Bobo makes several 5-gallon crocks of this every year because it's so poplar! If you are living or traveling anywhere near her, find out about the workshops and activities at her **WOOD-SPIRITS HERB SHOP OH 43072**

HARVESTING

Harvest garlic just as soon as the leaves start to turn yellow. Store in mesh (onion-type) bag, or even in pantyhose, in cool, dry, dark place, not in refrigerator. Preserve some mashed in vinegar, and some minced in oil, for "instant" garlic flavor for salads and cooking.

When harvesting your herbs this month, make cuttings of those you want a larger supply of in the future. Strip all but the top 3 to 5, leaves from cut 4–6" branches and place in wet sand or peat in the shade. Keep moist by light sprays with the hose every few rainless days. Rooted now, lavender and the southernwoods can be planted in your herb beds next month. Scented geraniums, rooted now, will yield lovely indoor winter plants for yourself and others. Lemon verbena and rosemary rooted now will become lovely winter houseplants, which may stay green and fresh until spring, given the proper light and feeding/watering care.

Refer also to the HARVESTING AND PRESERVING CHART in JUNE.

Harvest Silver King Artemisia as soon as the buds are their whitest (before they turn brown). Place in vases, boxes, or baskets, or hang upside down to dry. (It will dry just as it looks!) You may prefer to make wreaths or arrangements while it is fresh and more pliable. If so, see suggestions in fall chapters.

PLAN YOUR INDOOR GARDEN

The best chance for success with some of the culinary herbs indoors for the winter is to start new plants from seed in early August of the following: basil (*Ocimum basilicum* best), chives, coriander, dill (variety "Bouquet" best), parsley, marjoram, rosemary, sage, summer savory, and thyme. Plant in 4" pots which are sunk into the garden up to their necks. Use soil/sand/peat/perlite medium and cover seeds with sand or sphagnum moss. Keep moist and fertilize with fish emulsion or liquid seaweed when sprouts are 3" high. Bring inside before first frost and place in southern-exposure window in a tray filled with pebbles. Feed every 2 weeks as roots cannot spread to find food. — adapted in part from Gilbertie and Sheehan's *excellent* book, HERB GARDENING AT ITS BEST, 1978, Atheneum Press/NYC

Other culinary herbs for indoors, such as the mints, oregano, and French tarragon, are best prepared by potting up root divisions after the last harvest...being sure that sprouts appear on top...and burying the pots in the ground to rest for 3 or 4 good hard frosts. Then bring indoors to a sunny window for winter enjoyment. Spearmint and tarragon will lose some leaves, but will perk up by February. Pennyroyal, peppermint, pineapple mint, orange mint, and oregano should do well from the start. Feed lightly every two weeks, as the crowded roots will deplete the nourishment from the soil since they can't stretch to look elsewhere. The mints need lots of root room; nice in hanging baskets.

Other herbs to consider for inside gardening: aloe (purchase plant), bay tree (purchase), catnip (seed), lavender (L. dentata variety best — purchase plant or seeds), and the scented geraniums, lemon verbena, and the southernwoods from summer cuttings (or purchase plants).

Bay, lemon balm, and the other mints need only partial sun indoors, and can be in east or west-facing windows. The rest need southern exposure or indoor lights for best results.

Lemon balm

SEPTEMBER

Dill *(Anethum graveolens)*

SEPTEMBER

I would heartily advise all men of meanes to be stirred up to bend their mindes, and spend a little more time and travell in these delights of herbes and flowers than they have formerly done, which are not only harmlesse, but pleasurable in their turn, and profitable in their use.

— Parkinson, 1640

EARLY THIS MONTH you should pot up your tender plants to allow them time to adjust to the pots before facing the shock of being taken inside in October. Cut back the foliage by a third before taking the plants from the ground. Place the plants in sterile soil in the clean pots you prepared in August, and put them in a shady spot for a week or so. Then they can be placed back in sunlight until it is time to bring them inside.

Sturdy plants, like two- or three-year-old scented rose geraniums, will tolerate a thorough washing before repotting, to remove any insect eggs nestling among the roots or leaves. Rinse the roots, cut back the root system by one third, and give the foliage and stems a sudsing in a lukewarm solution of mild soapy water. Rinse the foliage off in a bucket of clear water.

I try not to use any chemical sprays on my culinary herbs. Soapy baths are helpful, and I have had good luck with a tobacco spray. Pour boiling water on the strongest pipe tobacco you can find. When cool, dilute the mixture with water and spray the plants once a week throughout September. I find this spray very effective, and it does not harm my plants at all.

A word of warning if you *do* use commercial chemical insecticides on your herbs — don't use them in the kitchen for a few weeks, and be sure to wash the leaves thoroughly first.

Besides the scented geraniums, plan to bring in rosemary, marjoram, bay and any perennials you wish to enjoy fresh. Mints, for example, do well inside in hanging baskets near a sunny window, but they must have room for their spreading roots.

Scatter dill seed saved from the summer harvest in the garden in the fall. If soil and climate conditions are right, it will sprout in the spring.

Gourmet Gardening — Dill

Your DILL should be the picture of perfection in August or September, depending on when and how you planted it, how rich the soil was, and the summer weather conditions. Since dill does not transplant well, it should be started outside in well-fertilized, sun-warmed soil, and watered often until the seedlings are sturdy. Then the patch should be thinned out to give the strongest survivors growing room.

You can lightly snip the leaves as needed during the summer, and then harvest the top half of the plant when the seedheads are beige. Dry in bunches or a bag, or preserve in oil, vinegar, or the freezer.

Not only is dill indispensable for pickling, but it can also be enjoyed in dips, spreads, breads, and most fish dishes. Try dill leaves in a ham and cucumber salad, or make a dilled butter sauce for grilled salmon. Recipes calling for dillweed refer to the leaves and stems, rather than to the seeds or seedhead.

I love to cook, but I seldom have time to enjoy it now that I am so busy with my home businesses. My solution is to double recipes, in order to have a second meal with a different salad and vegetable two days later. The three of us enjoy my herbed fish meals so much that we devour one pound per meal. I cook two pounds at a time, therefore, in a large, rectangular Teflon cake pan. If I am using fresh fish to begin with, then I freeze the second batch for later.

Save herb seeds by cutting the entire dried seedhead (on a dry day) and placing in a paper bag, labeling immediately!

There's Something Fishy Here!

Herbal Acres' Baked Flounder or Haddock

2 lbs. fresh or defrosted flounder or haddock

Heat 6 T. butter or oleo in low oven with 1 T. dill leaves and seeds

Place fish in greased pan and brush both sides with the warm herb butter using a pastry brush.

Bake in a 400° oven for 15 minutes, then sprinkle with grated Parmesan cheese and some paprika for color and broil for 3–5 minutes. (May be covered with aluminum foil and kept warm in low oven until everything else is ready, or everyone is home.)

Variations

Add 1 T. minced onion or some onion salt to the dill.

Use 1 t. each thyme, summer savory, and basil in the herb butter.

Add 2 t. thyme and some grated lemon peel (fresh or dried).

Do try these four different herbed-fish flavor combinations to see which ones you like best. The Parmesan cheese is optional; you may prefer to omit it at times. We love it because it adds "body" to the fish, plus a crispy top without the fish having been *fried*.

You could also add lemon juice or lemon peel to *any* of the herb combinations, not just the thyme variation. I hope you discover how much fun it is to try new flavors and experiment with a "dash of this" and a "dash of that" once you become familiar with which herbs complement which foods.

Dill

Hang bunches of herbs in the kitchen to dry, as our foremothers did. So handy for quick seasoning!

Herbal Acres' Lemon-Balmed Fish Broil

Place 4 cups fresh lemon balm leaves, washed and drained, in a buttered 8x12" Teflon or glass (cake size) baking dish. Spread 2 lbs. fresh or thawed flounder on top of the bed of balm. Brush the fish with herbed butter: 4 T. melted butter or oleo, 1 cup chopped fresh parsley, 1 T. fresh dill, snipped. Sprinkle paprika over all, and a dash of salt and pepper, if desired. Broil 10 minutes, then turn the oven off. Cover and leave in closed oven 15 minutes. Serve on platter with fresh lemon balm garnish. *Serves 4–6.*

Crab-Cucumber Salad

8 oz. frozen or canned crab, drained
1 T. lemon juice
1 T. fresh dillweed (leaves), chopped
1 T. fresh chives, snipped
Salt and pepper to taste
¾ cup sour cream
1 cucumber, cubed
4 tomatoes

Gently mix all ingredients except tomatoes together. Chill. Serve on sliced tomatoes or in tomato cups. *Serves 4 for lunch or 2 for dinner.*

Salmon Quiche

¼ cup chopped leeks or onions
1 T. butter
½ cup smoked or canned salmon, flaked
¼ cup chopped fresh dill
1 cup half & half
3 eggs
¼ cup flour
Dash of salt, pepper, and nutmeg
1 cup shredded Finlandia Swiss cheese
1 unbaked 8" pastry shell

Sauté leeks or onions in butter until tender. Add salmon and dill and toss lightly. Turn into pastry shell. Mix together until smooth the half & half, eggs, flour, and seasonings. Pour over salmon. Sprinkle with cheese and bake at 400° for 35 or 40 minutes or until custard is set. Cut into thin wedges to serve as appetizers or larger slices for lunch servings.

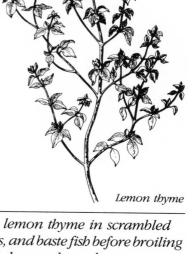

Lemon thyme

Use lemon thyme in scrambled eggs, and baste fish before broiling with lemon thyme butter.

Lemon Butter for Fish

¼ cup each butter, lemon juice, and water, 1 t. chicken bouillon, ¼ t. of dill or thyme, dash of salt, pepper, and paprika. *Enough for 1 lb. of fish (3 servings).*

Crabmeat Stroganoff

1 lb. frozen crabmeat, plus liquid
3 T. butter
8 oz. mushroom pieces
½ cup chopped onion
2 cups sour cream
¼ cup white wine
1 T. chopped fresh dill (1½ t. dried)
½ t. garlic powder
1 t. lemon zest
Paprika and black pepper
8 oz. spinach noodles

Sauté mushrooms and onions in butter in large skillet til lightly browned. Stir in liquid from crabmeat, sour cream, wine, dill, grated lemon rind and garlic powder. Gently cook for a few minutes, stirring often, to blend flavors. Add crabmeat and black pepper (2 shakes) and simmer another 5 minutes or so, stirring occasionally. Serve over buttered green noodles. Sprinkle paprika over the sauce. *Serves 5–6.*

PLANNING FOR THE HOLIDAYS

One of my favorite dried herb arrangements is an all-purple and gray blend featuring flowering purple basil at the center, edged with peppermint and oregano blossoms, dotted with lavender, with purple sage branches bordering the arrangement and baby's breath highlighting it. Spectacular!

This is a month of new beginnings. The weather is cooler, vacations are over, the kids are back in school, and organizational activities are starting up again. It's time to start thinking about fall bazaars and fund-raisers, teas and programs, and, yes, the holidays.

Chances are you've had the holidays in mind before now as you've been harvesting, drying, and preserving your herbs all summer for potpourri, culinary blends, and wreaths or arrangements. Now it's time to get down to business; now it's pay-off time for all your efforts. Creating and sharing your herbal harvests to bring delight to others is the most satisfying and meaningful aspect of herb hobbying.

In fact, this is how most of us who have herb businesses started out — by creating fragrant or tasty treats for gifts or donations to local fundraisers. Before long, individuals, groups, and retailers asked us to sell our unique crafts to them.

My "story" is told in my first publication, *Growing Fragrant Herbs for Profit,* which is reprinted and updated in the Appendix. Some of the ideas mentioned there for preparing, presenting, and displaying fragrant herbs could be helpful to those of you who are planning to donate herbal crafts to holiday bazaars.

You might wish to glance through the remaining chapters of this book now, too, as they all contain holiday craft suggestions. Map out your strategy for the season ahead so you can leisurely enjoy making gifts of love from your harvest, hearth, and heart. Let your children or grandchildren help. They can make simple potpourri and sachets, and they'll *love* getting their fingers into apple pulp pomanders (see OCTOBER).

Wire mesh cones

Lavender Tree

This decoration is my pride and joy. Originally created for a Garden Club lecture on "Decorating with Herbs for the Holidays," it has been well received wherever shown, and even won the Silver Award from the Garden Club Federation of Pennsylvania.

The tree looks particularly stunning on a long dining room table or a grand piano. And it is a pleasure to create in the early fall, to have ready and waiting for the often-hectic holiday season.

Make a large wire mesh cone (14" tall) from ½-inch hardware cloth. (I bought a 2' x 3' piece, which made a large cone and two smaller ones.) Using wire scissors and pliers, intertwist and bend back the cut ends to fasten the cone. Anchor the cone to a circular base — I used masking tape and an old metal pizza pan.

You will need several buckets of Silver King Artemisia for a tree 32 inches tall and 36 inches wide.

Starting at the bottom, place the longest branches through the center of the cone. Working upward, use the next-to-largest branches

Start at bottom, placing longest branches through center of cone.

on the next tier, and so on, leaving the shortest and prettiest blossoms for the top. Reserve three to five medium-length branches to add height to the top.

Then place bunches of ribboned or netted dried flowering herbs in among the branches. They will be kept in place by the curlicues of artemisia. I use bunches of lavender, purple basil, oregano, pennyroyal, peppermint, and orange-mint — all shades of purple or lavender, with matching ribbon and netting.

Sunny O'Neil MD 20812 *is a leading expert on the Victorian uses of dried flowers and everlastings. She has written several books, including DRIED FLOWERS WITH A DIFFERENCE, and now publishes a newsletter on the subject.*

Finished lavender tree with tussie mussies.

As favors to be offered as gifts, I place on the tree and in sterling silver bowls on the table around it, lavender sachets and small tussie mussies made with baby's breath and the herbs mentioned. The tree fits nicely on a card table, which I camouflage with a gray lace tablecloth, topped by three layers of purple netting. I revive it every season with lavender oil on the sachets, and store it in a dark room.

If you have a bulletin board in your herb room, as I do, thumbtack the herbs, placed in manilla folders, to the wall.

Basic Steps in Wreath Making

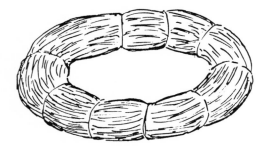

1. Use a straw wreath form (illustrated) or a wire or wood wreath frame.

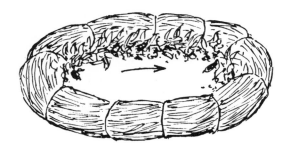

2. Tie together bunches of herbs with floral wire and, starting from the inside of the wreath, insert the bunches with stems all going in the same direction. Use florists' picks if stems aren't stiff enough to hold plants.

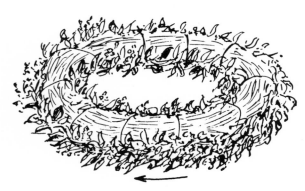

3. Still going in one direction, insert larger plants around outside of wreath.

4. Keep wreath in a dry, dark, airy spot to dry for a week or so.

5. Decorate and hang!

Southernwood Wreaths

One year I had a lecture commitment for which I had very little time to prepare, due to the sudden illness of my father and a consequent unanticipated three-week stay in Vermont. The lavender tree, these southernwood wreaths, and the baskets in the November chapter were the results, since I came home to an abundance of unharvested, blossoming, purple-flowered herbs, and very lush southernwood!

It is best to use *fresh* southernwood, as it is less fragile and more pliable than dried, allowing you gently to bend or break the woody branches to flow in the curved shapes you want.

Tie together several bunches of 10–14" branches with floral wire or twist-ties. Then anchor them to a wire or woody wreath frame, just as if making an evergreen wreath. Overlap the bunches of branches, all going in the same direction.

Southernwood

Or try my simple innovations. Place paper napkins (to absorb the moisture) in any circular containers you can part with for a week or two. Bend and shape the branches in a circle to fit the container. Add several layers of overlapping branches. A large colander is ideal because the holes allow air to hasten the drying. I have also used an angel food cake tin, a round salad mold, and deep cooking pots.

Keep the wreath in a dry, dark, and airy spot for a week or so. Air-conditioning, a fan, or a dehumidifier will facilitate the drying process. When crisp and dry, the wreaths will hold their shape, but they should be transferred to plates or baskets as permanent bases, because they will be fragile.

Decorate as you wish, or try my version. I decorate with bunches of dried silver mound artemisia and red bergamot flowers. The southernwood dries to an olive green, quite a unique hue.

Potpourri Southernwood Wreath: Use two lemon- or tangerine-scented southernwood wreaths, with the smaller on top, on a mat or plate base, and place a bowl of potpourri in the center. Decorate with dried roses, bunches of lavender blossoms, sprigs of lemon verbena, orange mint, and lambs' ears. Enclose a note telling the recipient that the entire wreath can be crumbled up and added to the potpourri when the wreath is "spent." If stored carefully, it could last for several seasons, so you might wish to enclose a small vial of rose oil and some orris root for restoration of fragrances. I have used deep red roses in a deep claret bowl, with matching velvet ribbon and spray-painted mat. It looks nice on a coffee table or as a dining room centerpiece.

Artemisia Wreaths

My second year in business I started making Silver King Artemisia wreaths for a local gift shop. They sold so fast that customers had to be put on a waiting list by October! I decorated them with dried sprigs of culinary herbs, tied with green ribbon, with a pine green candle in the center of the wreath. The silver-gray of the artemisia, however,

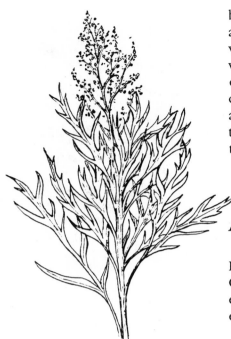

Silver king artemisia

blends with any color scheme. I've since made this wreath with pink and purple glove amaranth flowers and a magenta candle and ribbons, with the browns of whole spices, nuts, and tiny pinecones with a vanilla-scented brown candle. "The Fruit and Spice Wreath" encircles a cranberry red candle and is adorned by dried red cayenne peppers, strings of dried cranberries, pieces of orange peel and vanilla bean, and whole cinnamon sticks, ginger, nutmegs, and tonka beans. The reds, brown, and oranges are very colorful against the white-gray of the artemisia base.

And More Herbal Wreaths

Jane Holliday has co-authored a very informative book with Rachel Hartley, now in its 5th printing — BOTANICAL WREATHS: A Guide To Collecting, Preserving and Designing With Natural Materials. All you ever wanted to know about making herb or floral wreaths is clearly explained and illustrated with step-by-step photos and drawings.

Connie Lewis, owner of **CABINS IN THE PINES Herbs & Everlastings MS 38633** shares with us some of her creations:

Kitchen Herb Wreath. The base is santolina and lamb's ear, adorned with 5 or 6 little Sweet Bags of dried clove basil, cinnamon basil, and lemon basil in a lavender knit fabric, with a deeper purple bow tied to the base.

Grapevine Wreath. Decorate the base with a spray of Concord grapes, brown/rust/beige wild grasses, and the tops of large peacock feathers, with matching ribbon.

Moss Wreath. The base is old woody honeysuckle (bleached by nature to off-white when peeled). Wrap a string of silver sequins on the frame. Add silver-gray moss, letting a silver bead show through every now and then. Add lamb's ears and Silver King artemisia blossoms. Top off with a wide white lace bow. It "twinkles" and catches the eye!

Betsy Williams's catalog ($2.00) is splendent with *full-color* photographs of the loveliest and most exquisite herb wreaths I have ever seen — each one a work of art! Most famous for her original and enchanting FAERIE RING, Betsy's Fall Wreath is equally breathtaking and radiant, and her Halloween and Herb and Grass Wreaths are so imaginative that one can "feel" the intended message just from the catalog! Betsy has also written a booklet, THE HERBS OF CHRISTMAS, and one on planning an herbal wedding. **BETSY WILLIAMS, DEPT. HWH 155 CHESTNUT ST ANDOVER MA 01810**

FALL & WINTER FRAGRANCES

Salted Potpourri

Salt activates and absorbs the perfume in dried flowers and can be used as a fixative if they are crisp-dry. (I wouldn't use this method on a humid day or in a damp house. For added insurance, I heat the roses and herbs in a low oven with the door open for a few minutes before using this method.)

Here's an 18th century recipe used before orris root was popular.

2 cups dried rose petals
½ cup salt (coarse kosher best)
1 T. ground cloves
1 T. mace

Store the roses and salt for a few days in closed jar. Then add the spices and "set" for a month.

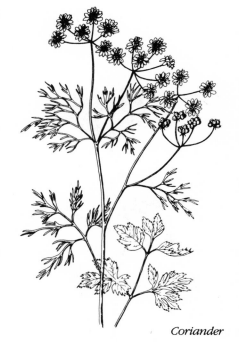

Coriander

Floral Salted Potpourri

The following salted blend can utilize every fragrant flower and leaf and spice on your place!

6 cups of a mixture of roses and at least six of the following: jasmine, lilac, heliotrope, lily-of-the-valley, honeysuckle, mock orange, scented geraniums, lemon verbena or balm, myrtle, or oregano (Sprinkle salt on these as they dry to a crisp.)
2 cups of a ground blend made from at least 4 of these: thyme, angelica, marjoram, peppermint, lavender, and rosemary

1 T. each allspice, mace, cinnamon, coriander, cardamom
2 T. each cloves and orris root
6 bay leaves, cut up finely

Salt bottom of container, then alternate layers of the first two blends, salt, and the spices. Seal jar and let "set" for 4 weeks, shaking it occasionally. (Be sure to include the salt sprinkled earlier on the drying flowers.)

Please don't confuse this with the old-time "wet" or "moist" method of making potpourri with salt and *fresh* flowers! I only tried that method once, many years ago, and I lost my entire summer's harvest to a chronic case of mold!

To add greenery to potpourri, but not change the fragrance noticeably, use dried fern, parsley, or bay.

Oriental Spice

The following is the most exotic potpourri I have made to date. The fragrance is extremely long-lasting (15 years, so far). For this reason, and because of the expense of the fixatives and spices, I only use my most colorful red rose petals and sell it bulk or in jars. It is too lovely visually and sensually to hide in sachets! The browns and reds somehow even remind one of the East Asian countries from which most of the ingredients are obtained, the rich overtones similar to those seen in an oriental rug or a sari. I charge top dollar for this one, $4.00 a cup.

Add your favorite talcum powder to dried flowers of your choice, with some orris root and a spice or two for a really-personalized potpourri!

4 cups roses
4 cups vetiver root (or vetivert)
3 cups patchouli leaves
1 cup sandalwood

2 cups mace
1 cup orris root with
2 t. rose oil

Does Your Potpourri Need "Something"?

For *sweetening,* try cinnamon, jasmine, anise, or vanilla bean.

For *enlivening,* add lemon (verbena or oil), orange rind or oil, mint, lavender, bergamot, or cloves.

For *enriching,* try mace, sandalwood, tonka beans, or vetiver root.

For *toning down* a too strong scent, add sweet grass or a bland flower such as elder.

Calendula

Potpourris for the Holidays

This was one of my first original creations, especially nice because you can use any dried flowers you have on hand for the bulk. Three times I have obtained the same scent, using different flowers each fall to add to the basic base of oils and granules of frankincense and myrrh. The scent, symbolic of gifts to the Christ Child, is very meaningful at Christmas, and the potpourri can be used for sachets to decorate trees or wreaths, to put in glass jars or plastic bags to be used as incense burned on hot coals in the fireplace or woodstove. Any leftover fixatives, oils, or spices can be used in rose or lavender potpourri.

One year I used all yellow and orange flowers, such as calendula, marigold, lilies, daffodils, and orange blossoms. The golden hues were suggestive of gifts of gold to the Babe in the Manger. Another time I used just purple loosestrife (which we have a swamp full of!) and this looked regal, too. But the most beautiful results were from red roses, bergamot, peonies, and geranium flowers. Regardless of the color, this potpourri sells very well at holiday bazaars by the bulk. Recipe is by the cupful so you can easily divide by ½ or ¼ if desired.

Frankincense and Myrrh Potpourri

24 cups of dried flowers
4 cups lavender
1 cup each of vetiver root, sandalwood, and cedar (or 3 cups of any *one* of these)
2 cups oakmoss (optional)
¼ cup each ground cloves and cinnamon
2 chopped vanilla beans
½ cup each ground tonka beans and myrrh
1¼ cups ground frankincense
1 cup orris root mixed with 1 T. frankincense oil

1 cup orris root mixed with 2 t. lavender oil
½ cup orris root mixed with 1 t. myrrh oil

I mix the oils with the orris root with a mortar and pestle first and let this "set" for a few days before adding to the rest of the potpourri. And I grind chunks of vanilla beans, tonka, orris root and frankincense and myrrh in my blender (on "chop").

Children, who could pick and dry the flowers for the above potpourri all summer, might particularly enjoy helping you make this to share with others, because of its symbolism in regard to the Babe in the Manger. Consider also the following recipes for beginning potpourri-makers. The ingredients are readily available from the grocery, pharmacist, kitchen cupboards, and probably *your* gardens. Children can grow many of these herbs and flowers, harvest and dry them, and make sachets for the potpourris. You must stress though that these are non-edible, and carefully supervise the projects if young children are involved.

Mix the spices and herbs together, then carefully blend in the salt. Store in covered jars and shake often for a month.

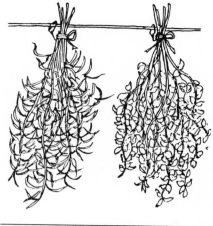

Mari-Mint Gold
(for a teacher's desk)

1½ cups marigold petals*
1½ cups peppermint leaves
1 cup crushed basil leaves
½ cup thyme leaves

1 cup coarse (kosher) salt

*Dry whole flowerheads; cut off petals with scissors from seedheads, saving seeds.

Herb Garden Potpourri
(for Aunt Mary)

2 cups rosemary leaves
1 cup marjoram leaves
½ cup each thyme, sage, summer savory leaves
1 cup each dried orange peel and coarse salt

Note: ¼ to ½ cup orris root may be substituted for the salt in any of these recipes.

Pick bunches of flowering herbs to dry for fragrant winter wreaths or bouquets. Whether flowering or not, fragrant branches of artemisia, lavender, rue, oregano, southernwood, and yarrow will dry without drooping and remain just as placed in vases or baskets. Tansy and most of the mints will dry better hung upside-down in bunches. Use long enough pieces of string or twine to tie the stems together tightly with a knot and to suspend them with a bow from your indoor clothesline, drying rack, hooks or nails. Then it only takes seconds to remove them. With a quick untying of the bow, you'll have room for the next batch! Store in cardboard cartons, separating the varieties with tissue paper.

Spice Surprise

Look what can be made from Mom's cupboards to give Dad for scenting his closet or bureau!

6 nutmegs, chopped up*
5 cinnamon sticks, broken up*
3 vanilla beans, cut in pieces
1 T. each crushed anise seed and allspice

½ cup whole cloves
1 cup coarse salt or ½ cup orris root

*Place in double plastic bags; chop up on breadboard with hammer.

Lemon-Lavender
(for Grandma)

2 cups lavender flowers
2 cups lemon verbena leaves
1 cup marigold petals
¼ cup orris root

Of course, all the potpourris in this book can be used for delightful holiday gifts.

Odds and Ends on the September Agenda

Herb Tea Sandwiches. Need refreshment ideas for an herb program this fall? Check December for herb desserts and punches. If entertaining in early fall, try tea sandwiches made of fresh herbs. Beat softened cream cheese, thinned with milk or cream, to spreading consistency. Cover thin crustless bread with the cheese and place any one of the following herbs on top to cover, and roll up: chives, parsley, watercress, spearmint, nasturtium flowers and leaves, or chemically-free rose petals.

Or cut the bread into various shapes with scissors or cookie cutter and make dainty sandwiches using the herbs diced up and blended into the cream cheese. (Taste-test for proper amounts.) To identify the varieties, spear a whole leaf of the herb used on each sandwich with a colorful toothpick.

Be sure you don't prune more than the top third of your perennial herbs this time of year.

Artemisia Tree. For a breathtaking holiday centerpiece, use a smaller cone for the directions given for my Lavender Tree, and decorate with any or all of these: dried red roses, apple pulp pomanders (next chapter), red bergamot flowers, rose or spice potpourri in red fabrics and net, and baby's breath.

Harvest "Honesty" as soon as the outer layers slip off easily when a seedhead is gently rubbed between the fingers. Do this over a newspaper to catch the seeds, which you can plant in the ground now for next year's new plants. Break off the woody stem at the bottom of the plant to harvest. Set in tall vases or bottles to store to protect the fragile pods. (Remember not to pick the lovely blossoms in the spring!)

Herbal Hot Plate. Connie Lewis (MS 38633) shares this tip, along with her herbal wreath ideas in this chapter. A bestseller of Connie's at craft fairs is her herbal hot plate, quilted fabric stuffed with mint and basil (clove, lemon, and cinnamon varieties). The heat releases the scents when used.

You don't have room to grow all the herbs and everlastings you need for decorations? Never fear. Several of the firms listed in the Appendix sell bunches of dried herbs and flowers, of which a few are named here. Please check the list for the complete addresses and catalog costs:

Jean Cope's POSIE PATCH OH 45371
Joan Choby's BACKYARD HERBS OH 44406

OCTOBER

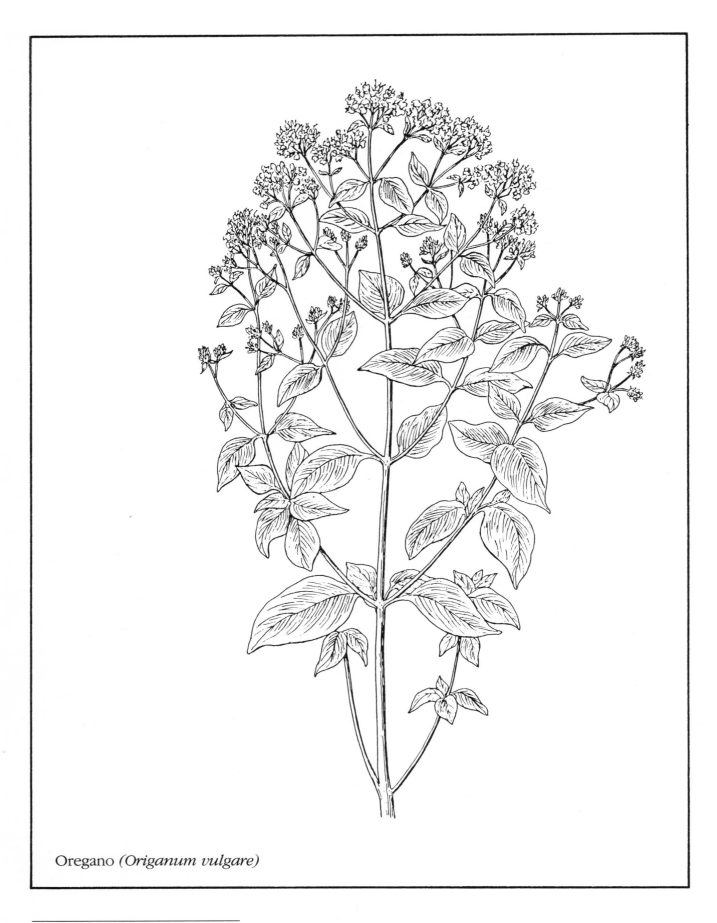

Oregano *(Origanum vulgare)*

OCTOBER

Her parlour window stuck with herbs around,
Of savory smell, and rushes strewed the ground.

— John Dryden

LOVELY OCTOBER! I am ambivalent about this month. The spectacular rainbow of colors against an azure autumn sky thrills the soul, but it is also an omen of what's to follow. The leaves will soon be gone, cool will turn to cold, and the brilliant hues will become brown or gray. But the good earth must rest, and all of nature needs a chance to hibernate for the winter.

Be sure to bring in your potted plants well before the first frost. During the brisker days you can start defoliating your dried herbs harvested last month. Use a large bowl and gently release the crisp-dry leaves from the stems, trying not to crush them. (Whole leaves will retain the flavor better until you are ready to use them.) Remove the woody stems and save them for fireplace fragrance this winter. Place the dried herbs in separate, labeled, air-tight jars.

Gourmet Gardening — Oregano

It's OREGANO'S turn for attention this month. I bought my original plant in 1962 and it has survived drought, neglect, and sub-zero weather, spreading into a nice 3 x 5' area of its own with a southern exposure in front of our house. About eight years ago I moved two clumps of it to new locations, and have been rewarded with much more vigorous growth and tastier foliage.

Buy a well-rooted oregano for late spring planting. It will slowly spread by itself, or you can propagate it by root division in subsequent springs.

I lightly prune oregano all summer as needed, and then in midsummer and again in fall I cut back the plant by half on each side.

The harvested branches dry quickly and are easily defoliated for winter storage. We use at least 2 quarts a year!

I always leave a couple of plants unharvested, as the fragrant, fresh or dried blossoms are beautiful in tussie-mussies or floral arrangements.

I use the "pizza herb" in all lasagna, spaghetti, chili con carne, and meatloaf dishes, and we have used it fresh or dried to make our own "hoagies" for years.

To make hoagies: Chop up and combine half a head of lettuce, one onion, and 1 T. oregano with ½ cup salad oil. Spread mixture on both sides of split hoagie rolls. Add Swiss cheese, boiled ham, and sliced tomatoes, and enjoy.

Before the first frost, bring your potted tender herbs inside and also pull up any annual herbs (such as basil and summer savory) to dry the whole plants by hanging by the roots in a dark, airy place.

HERB JELLIES

Being a cooler month, October is an excellent time to make herb jellies — especially since apple season is upon us. For treats for your family and friends all winter long, spend a day or two making a variety of herb jellies. First pick several sprigs of the herbs you'll want to use, rinse them off well, and dry them on a paper towel.

Make apple jelly according to the manufacturer's directions on the packages of powdered pectin you buy from the grocer. After skimming off the foam from the boiling jelly, divide it into 2 or 3 hot bowls and quickly add a few drops of food coloring until you like the hues. Then pour into the hot, sterile jars which should already contain 2 or 3 leaves of the following herbs, according to your taste...

Mint Jelly. Spearmint; dark green. Nice in pear or peach halves to accompany ham, lamb, or pork.

Thyme Jelly. Light green. Use a sprig — wonderful with beef or fish meals.

Rose Geranium Jelly. Slightly pink. Lovely with cream cheese on hot biscuits; divine on angel food or pound cake with whipped cream frosting!

Orange Mint Jelly. Yellow and red. Orange mint leaves and fresh or dried orange peel; marvelous with Chinese foods or baked chicken.

Lemon Balm Jelly. Yellow. Exquisite with fish and poultry.

Sage Jelly. Slightly yellow. Delicious with turkey, chicken, or pork.

Basil Jelly. Dark orange. Excellent on hot rolls with ANY meals.

Rosemary Jelly. Leave natural amber color. Use a sprig. Perfect with beef.

Lemon balm

Another Method. Here's another method, especially for mint jellies.

Cook all together: 1 cup of mint leaves, 4 cups apple juice, 4 cups sugar, one box of powdered pectin, and 6 drops of food coloring. You can chop the mints up finely and leave them in the jelly, or wrap the whole leaves in a cheesecloth bag, and remove before pouring into the jars.

If you try several different flavors and hues, it will be difficult to hide the results away in a cupboard! The rainbow of your garden creations will be mouth-watering just to look at.

I am very grateful to KATHLEEN GIPS (of **PINE CREEK HERBS OH 44022**) for sharing her expert advice and superior blends in the section to follow. She spent several years experimenting and researching the subject, saving a lot of us much time and energy!

Preserving the Herbal Harvest with Herb Jellies
by Kathleen Gips

Herb jellies capture the essence of fresh herbs in a delicate base of fruit juice or an herbal infusion. The glittering, colorful jars of sweet herb condiments appeal to the sight as well as to the taste, and can be enjoyed long after the herb garden is dormant.

The endless combinations of herbs and spices with fruit juices are a challenge to the herbalist's imagination. Traditional uses for tangy tarragon with poultry or fish, rich rosemary with roast meats, and green mint with lamb are commonly known and used. But those who enjoy the herbal flavors will seek new taste experiences such as rich basil on hamburger, rosy rose geranium with peanut butter sandwiches, delicate orange rosemary on muffins, fennel jelly with grilled fish, sherry rosemary with cream cheese and crackers, or even lemon verbena jelly in a sundae!

General Directions

Fruit juice jelly when made with apple juice will have enough natural pectin from the apples to gel without the addition of commercial pectin. When water or other fruit juices are used as a base for the infusion, however, commercial pectin (either powdered or liquid) must be added to obtain proper consistency. Liquid and powdered pectin are *not* interchangeable in recipes, however.

Although fresh are preferable, dried herbs or seeds may be used. A general rule is 1 cup fresh, ½ cup dried, or ¼ cup seeds. More or less may be used according to taste. The herbs should be gathered in the early morning after the dew has dried from the leaves, but before the hot sun has evaporated the essential oils from the foliage. Wash the herbs by swishing in a basin of cool water, being careful not to bruise the leaves. The herbs for the infusion may be chopped and put in a cheesecloth bag, or the stems tied in a bunch, or, as I prefer, chopped and put into the liquid and then strained before using. Bruise the leaves with a wooden spoon or a potato masher when the herbs are infusing into the juice or water. This, along with the heat, will increase the release of the essential oils into the liquid. If desired, ¼ cup of *fresh* chopped herbs — not those used for the infusion — can be added to the jelly batch before it is poured into the jars. To prevent floating herbs, stir the jelly for 5 minutes before ladling into jars.

A fresh sprig of herbs should be added to each hot jar before the jelly is poured into it, to add flavor and eye appeal. Jelly jars and lids should be sterilized in either boiling water or in the hot cycle of the dishwasher. Screw-top canning jars are preferable to paraffin seals, since new information indicates that the mold which sometimes forms when paraffin is used can be harmful.

The jars and lids should be boiling hot when filled and capped. To do this, run the jars through the hot cycle of the dishwasher and leave closed until the jelly is ready. Or keep the jars hot, after boiling, upright on a cookie sheet in a 250° oven. Boil the lids for at least 5 minutes, and leave them in the hot water while making the jelly.

Fill the jars, leaving ¼ inch headspace to allow room for a vacuum and therefore a proper seal. Turn the lidded jars over, after filling with jelly, to coat the lids. Place them upright on a folded towel for about 8 hours, until set. Jelly will thicken as it cools.

Measurements must be accurate when using jelly recipes. Too little sugar will cause the jelly to be thick and rubbery; too much sugar will cause it to be thin and watery without a proper "set." It is important to remember *not* to exchange the liquid and powdered pectins called for in the recipes; for success you *must* use the form listed.

A large enamel or stainless steel pot should be used when making jelly for correct heating of the sugar mixture and to allow room for the rolling boil. A few drops of vegetable food coloring can be added to the mixture before boiling, if desired, to enhance the color of the jelly. Choose from the colors red, yellow, or green, but use sparingly — just a few drops are needed.

Vinegar can be substituted for all or part of the lemon juice when it is desirable for the jelly to have a tangy, sweet flavor. Use this variation for meat accompaniments with herbs such as tarragon or fennel.

Fennel

One half teaspoon of butter or margarine in the boiling jelly will prevent or decrease foaming, thus eliminating or lessening the skimming process.

Basic Herb Jelly Recipes

First select the recipe you will follow, choosing either apple juice, powdered pectin, or liquid pectin. Assemble ingredients including the herb and fruit juice or herbal infusion combination that you have chosen from the chart that follows, or from your own imagination. Have on hand sterilized tongs and very clean oven mitts or hot-dish-pads for handling the very hot jars and lids. Make your herbal infusion following the directions below, and then proceed with jelly recipe instructions.

To make an herbal infusion: In a covered saucepan combine fruit juice or water with the herbs. Heat to the boiling point, but do not boil. Remove from heat and let steep, covered, for 20 minutes. Strain the liquid through a coffee filter paper or jelly bag, squeezing the herbs left in the paper or bag to include all the flavor. Discard herbs. This is the herb jelly liquid base.

Recipe Using Powdered Pectin

3 cups fruit juice or water (see chart)
1 cup fresh herb
2 T. fresh or frozen lemon juice or vinegar
1 package powdered pectin (1¾ oz.)
4 cups sugar
½ t. butter or margarine
1 fresh herb sprig for each jar used
3 or 4 drops food coloring (optional)

Mix the prepared herb infusion with the lemon juice or vinegar, food coloring, if desired, and pectin & butter. Mix well. Put over highest heat, stirring constantly, until mixture comes to a full rolling boil that cannot be stirred down. Mix in sugar. Continue stirring, return to full rolling boil and boil hard for exactly 1 minute. Remove from heat. Stir and skim off foam with metal spoon. Immediately pour into hot, sterilized jars with herb sprigs in the bottom of each. Seal. *Yield: approximately 40 oz.*

Recipe Using Liquid Pectin

2 cups juice (bottled or canned), wine or water **infused** with
1 cup herb (or proportion of spices suggested on following chart)
3½ cups sugar
2 tablespoons lemon juice
1 pouch liquid pectin
¼ teaspoon butter or margarine (optional)
1 fresh herb sprig per jar (optional)
3 or 4 drops food coloring (optional)

To the prepared herb infusion add the lemon juice or vinegar, food coloring, sugar and butter. Mix well. Over highest heat, stirring constantly, bring mixture to a full rolling boil which cannot be stirred down.

Mix in pectin all at once, and return to full rolling boil. Stir constantly and boil hard exactly 1 minute. Remove from heat. Stir and skim off foam with metal spoon. Add herb sprigs to hot sterile jars. Pour and seal immediately with hot caps. *Yield: approximately 48 oz.*

Recipe Using Apple Juice

4 cups apple juice* (see below)
1 cup herb leaves
3 cups sugar
½ t. butter or margarine
1 herb sprig for each jar used
Few drops red or yellow food
    coloring, if desired

Stirring constantly, bring infusion of apple juice and herbs to a rapid rolling boil; boil hard for 5 minutes. Add sugar, butter, and food coloring. Stirring constantly, boil about 10 minutes until reaching 222 degrees on a candy thermometer, or until jelly stage reached.

Test by placing a spoonful on a dish that has been chilled in the freezer. It should harden to jelly in a few minutes. Remove from heat, skim, and fill jars with herb sprigs in the bottoms. Cap and seal. *Yield: approx. 28 oz.*

Make herbal jellies and apple pulp pomanders from the apple harvest to enhance the months ahead for family and friends.

*To prepare fresh apple juice, cut up tart apples and discard blossom and stem ends. Barely cover with cold water and cook slowly, stirring occasionally, until soft. (Add more water if necessary.) Strain through a jelly bag or several layers of cheesecloth, which can be tied with twine over the edges of a colander to be kept in place, but do not squeeze, as this causes cloudy jelly. Measure 4 cups of juice for infusion. (Save the pulp for pomanders! See following section.)

Herb and Fruit Juice Combinations

BASIL (opal)/basil infusion (this will be a lovely rose color without food coloring)

BASIL (sweet)/basil infusion (add 2 T. cloves to infusion for spicy flavor; strain)

CINNAMON/cherry juice (make infusion with ¼ cup crushed cinnamon; strain)

CLOVE/tangerine juice (make infusion with ¼ cup crushed cloves; strain)

FENNEL/fennel infusion (add vinegar for all or part of the lemon juice, if desired)

LEMON BALM/red grape juice

LEMON THYME/white grape juice

LEMON VERBENA/lemonade

MARJORAM/grapefruit juice

MINT/mint infusion or apple juice

PARSLEY/parsley infusion or dry white wine (add fresh chopped herbs to the finished jelly — see General Directions)

ROSEMARY/orange juice or sherry

SAGE/cider or apple juice

SAVORY/cranberry juice

SCENTED GERANIUM/apple juice or scented geranium infusion

SWEET WOODRUFF/white wine (this is the famous May Wine taste)

TARRAGON/white wine or tarragon infusion (add vinegar instead of all or part of the lemon juice)

THYME/purple grape juice

APPLE PULP POMANDERS

You can make Christmas gifts and decorations from the leftovers while you are producing your winter supply of applesauce, apple butter, and apple jelly. The drained apple pulp left in your colander or food mill can be spiced, shaped, perfumed, and dried to create fragrant remembrances for family and friends. The miniature pomanders can be used as sachets in closets, drawers, or chests to perfume clothing, linens, or blankets, and to keep the moths away, as they detest the strong scent of the spices! But, first, they can be used to adorn your Christmas tree, wreath, or packages and they are useful stocking stuffers, party favors, or hostess gifts.

Most of us think of pomanders as clove-studded oranges or apples which have been rolled in spices and dried. The word *pomander* is derived from the French "pomme d'ambre", meaning *apple of amber,* the amber stemming (pun intended) from ambergris oil...which was the original favorite scent for pomanders historically and is the base of most perfumes. However, since ambergris is from the sperm whale, which is fast becoming an endangered species, synthetic ambergris is now more widely available and used.

The same lasting fragrance can be obtained from using leftover apple pulp, rather than the whole fruit, and many more pomanders can be made with much less time and cost, considering the current high price of whole cloves and fresh fruit, as well as the many hours it takes to completely cover one apple or one orange with whole cloves. Plus, if you make pomanders from the pulp, you will be using the fruit for consumption, and fashioning the aromatic and useful gifts from the waste!

Isabelle Wiand (SEVEN OAKS ME 04361) gave a talk on herbs at a club luncheon for which 150 apple pulp pomander sachets were made to use for the table decorations and then as personal favors for all who attended.

Dry pine branches in a shed or an airy garage for making pine-needle potpourri for the holidays.

My preference is to wrap them in the organdy squares that will be their permanent attire, so that none of the spices will be lost in the drying process. (Also, the oil then permeates the fabric, adding to the strength of the ambrosia.) I tie the organdy squares with looped ribbon to hang from the fireplace mantle, where we already have nail holes for the Christmas stockings. The pungent fragrance from the drying pomanders perfumes the house and the colorful red fabrics give an aura of Christmas long before it is time to decorate! Children are fascinated by this sensual project, especially since they can get their fingers into it while shaping and rolling the pulp. They delight in helping to make their own Christmas gifts for grandmom, auntie, or as "apples for their favorite teachers." (Non-edible, of course.)

Within a week or two the pomanders will shrink slightly and be dry enough to store in plastic bags until you are ready to wrap them for gifts. You can be a jump ahead of your Christmas chores by making these aromatic delights in the fall when apples are most reasonably priced and there is more time to enjoy creating your gifts of love. Recipe follows.

Making Apple Pulp Pomander Balls

De-stem and core the apples before cooking, using all the skin except for blemished areas. Press the pulp against a cheesecloth lined sieve or colander until it is no longer dripping wet. It can be covered overnight in the refrigerator to drain, if you wish to wait until the next day to make the balls, or if you need to add another batch of pulp.

Step 1. To 4 cups of drained pulp, stir in a heaping tablespoon of ground cloves, a tablespoon of ground nutmeg, 2 teaspoons of ground ginger, and 3 tablespoons of ground or powdered orris root. Mix thoroughly.

Step 2. Shape the pulp-spice blend into 1½–2" balls and roll them in the following mixture until they begin to feel dry: 6 tablespoons orris root to which a teaspoon of an essential oil has been added and well blended (oil of rose, cloves, ambergris, apple blossom, or patchouli), and ½ cup each ground cinnamon and ground cloves. *Approximate yield: 50 pomanders.* Recipe may be halved or doubled.

Step 3. Wrap in organdy or other porous fabric that is easily pinked with shears, and hang to dry. Or, if you prefer to adorn them later with fabric, let them rest in a large glass or plastic (non-metallic) container on top of any leftover spice mix. Best if they don't touch each other. Roll them around occasionally to expose all sides to the air and the spices.

I use red organdy and ribbon for Christmas pomanders, as they look so stunning with Christmas greens for decorating. In the spring I wrap any leftover pomander balls in pastel shades and matching net for gifts for Easter, Mother's Day, and June brides.

Recycled apple pulp can give you and others many pleasurable moments of aromatic delight (each time a closet or drawer is opened up!) as well as lasting usefulness over the years. The aroma can be revived in the future, if need by, by adding a few drops of your favorite perfume or an essential oil.

(This article is a revised edition of one written by the author for THE MOTHER EARTH NEWS MAGAZINE, entitled "Apple Pomander Sachets," published in their November-December 1981 issue.)

The pomanders can be packaged in plastic zip-top bags from the grocery, 3–5 per bag, for gift-giving or selling at bazaars. A descriptive label, printed or typed, can be added. Do explain that they can be used for decorations or favors and then stored with clothes or linens for fragrance and moth protection. I always advise that they are *not edible.*

Rake up leaves for compost pile. Will rot faster if shredded first with a mower or shredder (and then could be put directly on gardens as mulch).

GROWING THE SAVORY BULBS

If You Can Grow Crocus, You Can Grow Saffron!

Saffron (*Crocus sativus*) is the world's costliest spice, selling at well over $2,000.00 a pound! But you can pick the precious bright orange stigmas from your own garden each fall, dry them on absorbent paper in a dark place, and store in a tightly-sealed, dark container away from heat and light.

Plant the corms in the fall in a *well-marked spot* (because the grass-like leaves will appear in the spring, and then disappear...with no further signs of life until the flowers suddenly arrive in the fall), in full sun and soil that drains well, 4" deep and 4–6" apart. Once established, the corms can be lifted and divided every few years to increase the harvest.

In cooking with saffron, use only a pinch at a time and follow recipe directions exactly, as a little is good, but a lot can be dreadful.

Bertha Reppert imports saffron corms from Holland each fall and will let you know when they arrive if you are on her "Saffron Bulb List". The ROSEMARY HOUSE sells not only the corms, but the dried saffron threads, at very reasonable prices, as well as a marvelous brochure for a small fee which gives the history, uses, horticulture, and several recipes (samples below) for saffron. Growing instructions are included with each order of saffron corms.

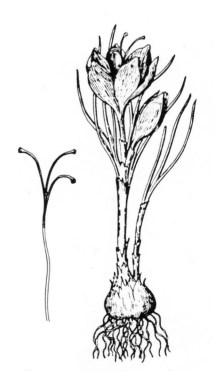

Saffron crocus with close-up of stigma

Risotto

Elephant Garlic, available from NICHOL'S GARDEN NURSERY, 1190 NORTH PACIFIC HWY ALBANY OR 97321, is much larger, has a milder flavor, and is easier to peel than regular garlic. It requires the same treatment except that it is planted at least 8" apart in rows 16" apart in a space of its own, as it will reach 3' in height. Nichol's Nursery has much information to share about this, including how to grow it on a large scale as a business crop. These good folks also offer many herb plants and seeds, as well as a huge selection of unique vegetable seeds. Send for their catalog.

1 t. saffron
2 cups boiling water
2 cups chicken bouillon
⅓ cup butter (or half chicken fat)
1½ cups rice
1 medium onion, chopped
1 t. salt
1 cup cheddar cheese, shredded

Steep the saffron in the boiling water until cool. Bring the chicken broth to a boil. Melt butter in a large pan; add rice and cook and stir until toasted. Add onion to brown. Add hot chicken broth with saffron water and salt. Cover and simmer about 25 minutes, until rice is done. Top with the cheese in the last few minutes, to melt. Stir. *Serves 6.*

Golden Glazed Chicken

6–8 pieces of chicken
1 T. butter
1 can golden mushroom soup
¼ cup cooking sherry
⅛ t. nutmeg
⅛ t. saffron
¼ cup diced pimento

Butter the chicken and place in a shallow pan to bake at 400° for 45 minutes. Combine soup and seasonings, mix well, and spoon over the chicken. Bake 15 minutes more. *Serves 6.*
— THE ROSEMARY HOUSE PA 17055

Garlic

Garlic — Another Remarkable Bulb to Plant Now

Did you know...that 15 lbs. of garlic bought a young, healthy slave in ancient Egypt? That Queen Victoria's chef used to chew on a raw garlic clove, then breathe on the royal salad? Fortunately for us, we can grow this tasty and nutritional plant ourselves, and serve it directly to our families...without benefit of chef's secrets!

Garlic should be planted this month to be harvested next August. Best results if planted a month before your first *hard* frost, allowing time for the roots to develop before the ground freezes. You can use a garlic bulb from the supermarket, but be sure it is firm, plump, and free of brown spots. Plant each clove with skin intact (if possible), pointed end up, about 4 inches apart, in friable rich soil in full sun. A heavy feeder, garlic likes manure and plenty of compost, or a balanced (12-12-12) fertilizer, and must have good drainage. Although it needs a lot of water (until July), garlic mustn't sit in it or it will rot.

Making A Live Wreath

A live wreath started in mid-October will be lush for the holidays. Purchase a 12" planting frame from the florist. Fill with well-soaked spaghnum moss and place in a shallow bowl. Insert cuttings of herbs, using rooting hormones. I have used myrtle on the inside and outside, with culinary/tea herbs in groups of three on the top: scented geraniums, thyme, sage, and rosemary.

I kept the wreath under my Gro-Lights, watered with weak solution of fertilizer, misted it regularly, and trimmed the tops as needed, to keep the plants compact.

Try wintering over rosemary in a cold frame or inside by a cellar or garage window if a cool and damp spot. Do not let dry out but water very sparingly.

How about a fresh bay wreath for a gift to yourself or a special one? Send for Glory Condon's BAY LAUREL FARM catalog, CA 93924. An 18th Century-inspired Victorian wreath? Contact Polly Haynes at **MEADOWSWEET HERB FARM VT 05738.** *Do you want artemisia bases to decorate yourself? Write Sylvia Tippett at* **RASLAND FARM NC 28344.**

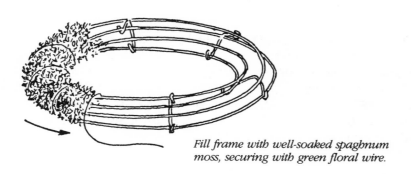

Fill frame with well-soaked spaghnum moss, securing with green floral wire.

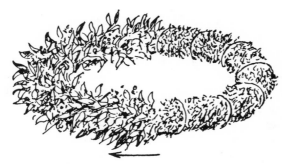

Insert cuttings, with stems all going in one direction as shown.

Finished wreath ready to be placed under indoor lights and watered with weak solution of fertilizer until holiday time.

Defoliate your dried herbs and make culinary blends for easy gourmet cooking all winter long. This is one of the greatest joys of herb-hobbying, savoring their pungent essence as you remove the leaves from the stems. Most of the culinary herbs are small-leafed, requiring more painstaking effort, as you do not want tiny woody twigs to slip into your storage jar to ruin someone's enjoyment of an otherwise-delicious meal. Try to keep the leaves as whole as possible to retain optimum flavor. Bottle and label the herbs separately and store out of sunlight. Save the stems and twigs to toss on dying embers of the fireplace or woodstove coals for a final whiff of the fragrances!

Is your potpourri up to snuff? One of my readers once sent me an SOS because she had made gallons of a potpourri which her shop customers were by-passing. It contained every kind of flower, herb, and spice you can imagine...so I tipped her about my old "stand-by", CASWELL-MASSEY'S "Potpourri Oil". I have used this any time I've had a conglomeration of dried flowers I've wanted to preserve.

This oil is powerfully rich, with long-lasting fragrance, up to 15 years, so far. And it makes any blend smell wonderful when pre-mixed with orris root. Caswell-Massey also has the best synthetic ambergris oil, the base of most elegant perfumes. A drop or two is perfect to add to apple pomander sachets, which are to be re-used each holiday season, as the heavenly scent will permeate the pomanders for years. **CASWELL-MASSEY NY 10011**

There are two other sources of high-quality oils that I recommend heartily. I particularly love Nancy McFayden's Rainforest oil (**GINGHAM 'N SPICE PA 18926**). And Rosella Mathieu's Magic Garden oil is spectacular! (**HERB GARDEN FRAGRANCES OH 45236**). Check the Appendix for catalog fees and full addresses.

Hot Mulled Cider
(from Fallsington Harvest Day)

1 gallon cider without preservatives
½ cup light brown sugar
½ t. salt
¼ t. ground nutmeg
½ t. whole cloves
2 pieces stick cinnamon

Bring all ingredients to boil in a large pot. Boil for 5–8 minutes.

Strain and serve hot or refrigerate to reheat.

Serve in mugs with cinnamon sticks as stirrers. This may be kept warm in crockpot and is nice with spicy molasses cookies using vanilla frosting adorned with crushed, dried orange calendula petals.

Add a dash of ginger to mashed squash or cooked carrots. And rub it sparingly over meat or poultry before broiling or baking.

Poultry Stuffing Herb Mix

Mix well and store in covered quart jars:

2 cups each of celery flakes, dried parsley, and dried crumbled sage leaves
1 cup dried minced onion
1 cup of dried minced chives

Cook giblets in 2 cups salted water; add a chicken bouillon cube or two. Sauté 2 T. of the herb blend in ½ cup butter or oleo. Add the stock, the herb butter, and 2 or 3 eggs to 2½–3 qts. bread cubes. Salt and pepper lightly. *Makes plenty for one large chicken. (Triple the recipe for a large turkey; double it for a small turkey.)*

My chicken recipe is for 6 servings because I freeze 3 for an easy and quick gourmet meal another week!

Phyl's Herbed Parmesan Chicken

Melt one stick of butter or oleo over low heat and add 2 t. each marjoram, thyme, and sage. (Or try the recipe using 4 t. of JUST rosemary, thyme, or tarragon.)

Moisten both sides of 6 chicken breasts with the herb butter using a pastry brush. Place in greased pan and bake in 350° oven for 45 minutes.

Remove from oven and add enough grated Parmesan cheese to cover each chicken breast, and a dash of paprika for crispy color. Broil for 3 to 5 minutes. *Serves 6.*

Variations

We also like the recipe using a teaspoon each of thyme, summer savory, and basil for the herb butter OR using 3 t. oregano and some garlic salt.

So here are 7 different ways to serve baked chicken! You might like to try any of the variations without the Parmesan, or to substitute other cheeses.

I often have frozen chicken breasts in the freezer. In this case, I cook them first in onion and garlic-salted water in a large covered pan on the stove over high heat until boiling, then simmer gently for about 30 to 40 minutes. Then I drain the chicken (saving the liquid for soup stock), and proceed with the herb butter step above and the broiling (eliminating the baking).

Fragrant Holidays Balls
Use sewing remnants to make colorful patchwork or calico Christmas balls for holiday decorations (3–4" wide). Fill with cotton batting stuffed with potpourri and essential oil inside.

Oregano

NOVEMBER

Broad-leaf sage *(Salvia officinalis)*

NOVEMBER

Sage is singularly good for the head and the brain; it quickeneth the senses and memory, strengtheneth the sinews, restoreth health to those that hath the palsy, and takes away shaky trembling of the members.

— John Gerard

M Y LAST labor of love for the year is mulching the herb beds in November after the first hard frost. Tender perennials and any herbs new this year need protection from the icy winds and the alternating freezing, thawing, and heaving of the soil. (If you mulch *before* the first hard frost, field mice and other little pests will burrow under the protection you meant for your plants. By the first real killing frost, however, rodents will have found their winter homes.)

For our winter mulch, we shred leaves, grass clippings, vegetable garden compost, and pine chips, and throw in some peat and some lime. Straw makes a good winter blanket, but requires a big clean-up in the spring. Our blend adds humus to the soil each year, and utilizes the wastes from our own property.

Our herb beds were all started in barren lawn, orchard, or field plots, which were extremely acidic. We have added as much enrichment as possible through our spring and fall mulches. Now our soil is dark, rich, sweet, and friable.

Gourmet Gardening — Sage

I had to save SAGE for November. This is another herb that has survived since the beginning of my hobby. Although our original mother plant of 18 years ago is now long gone, her grandchildren are now filling a large space in one of my beds. A well-established sage can be pulled apart into several new plants in the spring, as long as part of the root or "heel" is included.

Sage can also be easily started inside from seed. The garden soil should be well limed, in advance, for sage, and the soil "sweetened" and fertilized every few years thereafter. Established plants should be

All tender perennials and any newly-planted herbs need a winter mulch after the first hard frost (so the field mice and other critters will have already found their winter homes). Use anything available that will later add enrichment to your soil. We use shredded leaves, grass clippings (without weedseeds from fall mowing), used potting soil, vegetable compost, and lime, all mixed together.

Narrow-leaf sage

pruned in early spring and again in midsummer, taking about a third off the tops each time.

"Garden sage" is prominently used in sausage making, poultry seasonings and stuffings, cheese spreads, and with pork entrées. Other sages are primarily ornamental or fragrant, such as clary, pineapple, and purple sage (see Encyclopedia). Garden sage stays gray-green until mid-December, in mild winters, and starts to revive itself in March.

Any stuffing recipe will be enhanced by using fresh herbs from the garden — and it's a joy to bundle up in November and go out and pick fresh sage (as well as thyme and oregano) for a Thanksgiving stuffing. My favorite recipe, to follow, involves adding sautéed chicken livers, onions, and celery to quarts of bread cubes and lots of chicken broth, plus fresh sage, thyme, parsley, oregano, and a few eggs. My family has devoured this for years without realizing I'm getting *liver* into them. I make huge quantities of it, freezing several loaf pans of the dressing topped with the turkey and gravy leftovers.

Dressing It Up With Sage

Phyl's Chicken Liver Stuffing
(for a large turkey or 2 roasted chickens, plus leftovers)

This takes 2 hours from start to finish, but makes enough to feed a crowd or to freeze for several meals. To cut the time by 20–30 minutes, scrub the celery, cook, crumble, and refrigerate the livers, and cube the bread the night before.

3 cups chopped celery
3 cups chopped onion
1–1½ lbs. chicken livers
½ lb. butter or oleo
Garlic powder
3 or 4 fresh sage leaves, minced
Leaves of 2 fresh sprigs of thyme
Leaves of 1 fresh sprig of oregano
2 long loaves white bread, cubed
6 eggs, blended with fork

1. Start the stock by placing rinsed turkey neck and gizzards in 3 qts. salted water and simmer on stove while preparing dressing. Add 2 chicken boullion cubes and more water as needed.

2. Chop up celery and onions, placing some of the cleaned root-ends plus celery leaves in the stock pot for flavoring.

3. Sauté washed and drained chicken livers in 4–6 T. of the butter (depending on whether you're using 1 or 1½ lbs. livers) in large skillet. Season with a couple of dashes garlic pow-der. Turn for even browning. Remove from skillet and set aside. Leave drippings in pan.

4. Add rest of butter to skillet. Sauté celery first, adding onions in a couple of minutes. As the vegetables become softer, add the herbs and stir well. Turn off heat.

5. Cube the bread, crusts and all, and place in large pot.

6. Chop up the chicken livers finely and add to the bread.

7. Mix in the stirred eggs and the sautéd vegetables and herbs.

8. Strain the stock in colander and pour on as much as needed to make the dressing cohesive. Mix well. Stuff.

9. Bake the extra stuffing for 1 hour at 350°. (I put this in the oven with the turkey, turning the roaster sideways for the first hour of cooking.)

10. Reserve remaining stock for gravy.

More Sage Advice

Sausage Stuffing
(for a small turkey)

1 lb. pork sausage, browned & drained
1 cup butter and sausage fat combined
4 cups onions
4 cups celery
8 cups white bread, cubed
2 eggs, slightly beaten
2 t. dried sage, minced

Salt and pepper to taste

Cook sausage until browned. Remove from pan and drain, reserving drippings. Sauté vegetables in butter/sausage fat. Stir in sage and other seasonings. Mix all ingredients together. Refrigerate until stuffing time.

Use fresh sage, thyme, and oregano in your turkey stuffing, if possible. Sage sprigs placed on top of the roasting turkey or pork roast will emanate aroma and flavor reminiscent of grandma's house! Garnish the platter with fresh sage sprigs.

Oyster Parsley Dressing
(For small turkey or 2 chickens)

2 pts. oysters, rinsed, shucked, and coarsely chopped, reserving oyster liquid
1 cup onion, chopped
1½ cups celery, chopped
1 cup butter
½ cup parsley
2 t. sage
1 t. each thyme, salt, pepper, paprika

¼ t. nutmeg
8 cups bread crumbs
4 eggs
Stock — oyster liquid and milk

Sauté vegetables and oysters in the butter, plus ½ cup of oyster liquid. Stir in the seasonings. Add to the bread and eggs and moisten with stock.

Breadless Dressing
(For roast chicken)

2 lg. cans mushroom pieces, drained
2 med. onions, chopped
4 stalks celery, chopped
1 stick butter or oleo
1 t. sage, minced
½ t. each marjoram and thyme
1 T. parsley, minced

½ t. garlic powder

Sauté vegetables in butter; add seasonings and stir to blend. Stuff chicken before baking. Serve dressing separately to top chicken, or mix dressing in cooked rice.

Tie bunches of dried sage with red ribbons and sell at bazaars in plastic food storage bags. Include a recipe.

Apple/Sausage Stuffing for Pork

Good with roast pork, pork chops or Rock Cornish hens.

½ lb. pork sausage
1 cup chopped onion
1 cup chopped celery
3 cups chopped apples
2 t. sage, minced
1 t. thyme
½ t. rosemary
4 T. parsley, minced
½ t. garlic powder
8 cups bread cubes
Chicken broth

Brown, drain, and reserve sausage. Sauté onion and celery in pan drippings for 3 or 4 minutes. Blend in apples and seasonings. Add mixture to bread and sausage and stir well. Use as filling for stuffed pork chops or bake separately at 325° for 1 hour and serve on a platter under a pork roast or pork chops.

Herbed Chicken & Rice Dishes

Chicken Simon & Garfunkel
"Parsley, sage, rosemary & thyme..."

Serve hot catnip tea with lemon and honey to anyone coming down with a cold. In STALKING THE HEALTHFUL HERBS, *Euell Gibbons* says this is full of vitamins A and C, induces perspiration, lowers fever, and aids rest and sleep!

3 boned, skinned whole chicken breasts
1 stick butter
6 slices mozzarella or Swiss cheese
Flour
Bread crumbs
1 beaten egg
1 T. chopped parsley
½ t. each sage, rosemary, thyme
½ cup white wine

Flatten chicken and spread with half the butter. Season with salt and pepper to taste or garlic powder as salt substitute. Place cheese on chicken; roll and tuck ends. Coat lightly with flour. Dip in eggs and roll in crumbs. Place in baking dish. Melt rest of butter and add the herbs.

Bake chicken at 350° for 30 minutes, basting with the herb butter. Pour wine evenly over the chicken and bake 20 minutes longer, basting occasionally. Rosemarie Vassalluzzo's column, *Bucks Co. Kitchen.*

Kitchen Wreath
Cover a straw or styrofoam wreath base with bunches of santolina or artemisia, using florist wire and picks. Add flowering sprigs of any of the following: peppermint, orange mint, oregano, or purple basil. Tuck in dried sprigs of rosemary, thyme, parsley, and bay. Embellish with garlic or shallot bulbs, whole nutmegs, cinnamon sticks, and dried cayenne peppers, if desired. If for a gift, identify the edible herbs.

Tarragon Chicken Loaf

2 cups soft bread crumbs
1 T. parsley
1 t. dried tarragon
½ t. salt
¼ t. black pepper
2 cups chopped, cooked chicken
½ cup sour cream
3 eggs, beaten
1 T. lemon juice
4 T. butter, melted
1 small onion, minced (about 3 T.)

Mix together bread crumbs, parsley, tarragon, salt, pepper, onion, and chicken. Set aside. Mix together remaining ingredients until thoroughly blended. Stir into bread crumb/chicken mixture and pour into greased loaf pan. Bake at 350° for about 35 minutes, until golden brown and a knife inserted in center comes out clean.
— from **DIANE MATHEWS**

Faith's Indoor Barbecued Chicken

My sister, Faith, serves this with potato salad in the summer. I can't wait 'til summer, so I serve it all winter long with scalloped potatoes that cook along with it during the last hour.

12 chicken thighs
1½ cups ketchup or chili sauce
1½ cups honey
2 or 3 large cloves garlic, minced

Marinate the chicken in a sauce made of the last three ingredients, for about 20 minutes. Place in baking pan, skin sides down, and bake in 400° oven for ½ hour. Turn pieces over, use up marinade on top of chicken, and return to 350° oven for 45 minutes, or until browned on top. *Serves 6.*

Busy Day Chicken-Rice Bake

Arrange 3 or 4 lbs. of frying chicken parts in a deep baking dish. Sprinkle 1 cup raw rice over top, then 1 package of onion soup mix over that. Combine 1 can cream of chicken soup with 1 can water and 1 t. each thyme and Worcestershire sauce. Pour into baking dish and spread well over chicken. Bake 1½ hours at 350° for 6 servings.

Easy Make-Ahead Chicken Bake

A company dish that freezes well.

Cook 3 large chicken breasts in water with celery tops, onion, salt, bay leaf, and rosemary, until tender. Cool and remove bones and skin. Cut in bite-size pieces.

Mix lightly with 1 pint sour cream, 1 can mushroom soup, and 1 can mushrooms (small or large).

For topping, melt 1 stick butter in 1 cup chicken broth and mix with a package of herb stuffing. Bake at 350° for 45 minutes. Serve to 6 with cranberry sauce.

Leftover Turkey Variation

Using above recipe, starting with second paragraph, add celery salt, minced onion, and thyme or sage to sour cream. Proceed with directions using 3 or 4 cups turkey meat.

Rock Cornish Hens With Rice

4 T. vegetable oil
3 T. lemon juice
2 game hens, cut in half
1½ sticks butter, melted
1 garlic clove, minced
4 T. crumbled dried parsley
1 t. dried sage, minced
1 t. dried thyme leaves
Salt and pepper to taste
1 cup rice

Blend together oil and lemon juice. Brush over all sides of the chicken halves. Bake at 350° for 1 hour.

Mix herbs, seasonings, and butter in blender. Baste hen pieces with half the blend during last 20 minutes of baking. Cook rice and season with the rest of the herb butter. Serve chicken halves on a bed of rice. *Serves 4.*

Savory Lemon Rice

2 T. butter
½ clove garlic, minced
1½ cups chicken broth
¼ t. salt
1½ cups long grain instant rice
1½ T. parsley
2 t. lemon juice

In medium saucepan, sauté garlic in butter. Add chicken broth and salt; bring to a boil. Stir in rice. Cover, remove from heat and let stand 5 minutes. Add the parsley and lemon juice. Fluff with fork. *Serves 4.*

Instant Rice Dressing

For whole chicken or turkey breast.

1 cup chopped celery
1 cup chopped onion
¼ cup butter
¼ cup chopped parsley
1 T. sage, minced
2½ cups chicken broth
1 cup instant rice

Sauté vegetables in butter; add dried herbs. Add broth; cover and simmer to a boil, about 6–7 minutes. Stir in rice. Cook and stir for 2 minutes. Remove from heat. Cover and let sit for 7 or 8 minutes. Fluff.

Herb-Rice Mix

1 cup uncooked rice
2 beef bouillon cubes
½ t. each salt, marjoram and thyme
1 t. dried green onion flakes

Place in air-tight plastic bag with these directions: Combine mix with 2 cups cold water and 1 T. butter in heavy saucepan. Bring to boil over high heat, stirring once with fork. Reduce heat, cover and simmer 12–14 minutes, or until all liquid is absorbed. — from PANTRY PRESENTS.

It will soon be the season for the lovely perfume of pine and other evergreens to permeate the house. We are blessed with a row of 40-year-old white pines behind our house, which serve as a windbreak and offer us privacy, shade, beauty, swatches for decorating and wreaths, cones, and needles for potpourri! Fifteen years ago we almost lost row #1 during a field fire, so we planted a second row, for insurance.

Curly parsley

A _NOVEMBER BASKET_

The colonists created homemade remedies from their herb gardens for everything! There's no guarantee that this one will cure a migraine, but you'll have a sweet-smelling handbag each time you open it up! Keep a pouch in your purse of equal parts of dried marjoram, peppermint, lavender, and orange peel, with a few whole cloves. Then, when your Christmas shopping begins to take its toll on you, inhale the pouch for relief from your holiday headaches.

No need to limit gift baskets of flowers and herbs to May Baskets! Try this perfect pre-holiday gift for a Thanksgiving hostess. She can enjoy it throughout the winter and into the summer.

Find an Easter or May basket in the attic and make a "nest" in it of any of the southernwoods, although I prefer dried camphor-scented southernwood branches for this one. Insert short-stemmed dried blossoms (all yellow and orange shades) of calendula, marigolds, yarrow, wormwood, tansy and rue into the southernwood and fit a scented gold candle in the center to blend in with the colors of the herbs. (I intertwined green satin ribbon through my basket to blend with the greens of the southernwood, tansy, and rue leaves.)

Enclose a note advising the recipient not to burn the candle in the basket, as the herbs will be so dry. She can use it elsewhere after the bouquet is "spent", at which time she can crumble up all the other ingredients from the basket and add a few shakes of cloves and nutmeg from her cupboard to become moth protection for her closets and bureaus the next summer!

You can give baskets of re-usable dried herbs at _any_ time of year. How about a "March" basket for your best friend's birthday?

Variations

How about an arrangement of dried lavender branches and foliage, roses, purple basil, Silver King artemisia, and baby's breath for a Christmas or Valentine Basket, from which a sweet potpourri can later be made?

Try an arrangement of dried flowering peppermint, oregano, basil, chives, camomile, etc., for a culinary bouquet to be used as needed. The herbs in this basket should be identified.

This one is my favorite, featuring browns, reds, and golds. Anchor an oasis block in the center of the basket. Make a nest in it of lemon or tangerine-scented southernwood branches, covering the oasis. Insert a bouquet of the lovely *Artemisia Annua* (Sweet Wormwood), dried to the reddish-brown stage. Also insert a few long cinnamon sticks in the oasis. Add short-stemmed dried blossoms of bergamot, calendula, marigold, rue, tansy, and yarrow around the edges of the basket. These will stand up well in the southernwood. Again, the recipient can crumble up the ingredients for moth-chasers.

More Craft Ideas

An artist specializing in ceramics, Bob Clark entered the world of potpourri because fragrances go naturally with his ceramic and porcelain pomanders and figurines. Now potpourris are an integral part of Bob's business, and he sells a large variety of his own unique blends, two of which he shares on the next page. Bob exhibits at craft fairs and has seasonal Open Houses at his shop, which is usually open (but it is best to call first). His retail/wholesale brochure costs 25¢ plus a business-size SASE. **CERAMICS BY BOB CLARK 901 SHERIDAN DR LANCASTER OH 43130 (614/653-6854)**

Here is a visual aid Bob uses for lectures, showing the proportions of the ingredients of one of his potpourri creations. In an attractive decorative jar from a gift shop, he leveled each ingredient in the proper amount, being very careful not to mix it up. Then he ran a wide strap of Scotch Magic Tape™ down one side to label the ingredients, as shown in the sketch (or, one could write on the glass with a china marker.) After Bob gives talks on making potpourri, each person makes about a quart of potpourri, with his help.

Pressed Flowers

If putting potpourri in a glass jar for a gift, Bob suggests you press some flowers, leaves, ferns, or fronds until dry, to decorate the inside of the jar. If you don't have a flower press, place the plant material between paper towels or napkins in an old phone book, or between newspapers, weighted on top.

This method retains the color very well, and is useful for thick leaves like peppermint-scented geranium, or for large leaves like costmary, so they won't turn brown.

Pansies, violas, scented geranium leaves, etc., are very nice to use for jar decor, and dry quickly.

In the clean empty container, arrange the pressed items by holding them against the glass by using a bit of eggwhite. Then, carefully fill the jar with potpourri, and give with pride. Use colors that will complement the blend, but contrast with the color of the potpourri. Or, use the flowers and herb leaves that are *in* the potpourri, as an educational tool.

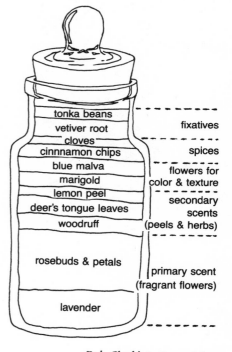

Bob Clark's potpourri jar

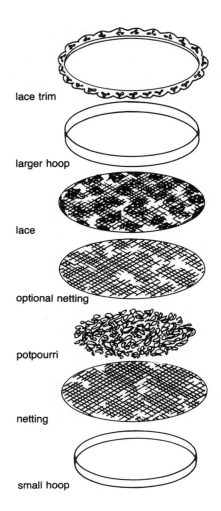

lace trim

larger hoop

lace

optional netting

potpourri

netting

small hoop

Lacy Hooped Potpourri Decoration

(Bob Clark)

Materials. Embroidery hoop (3" for tree ornament, or to hang anywhere; 4 or 5" for wall decor), potpourri, fine lace, tulle or fine netting, gathered lace trim, white or hot glue. Optional: paint or stain and brush, lace motif, gold cord or narrow ribbon for hanging.

1. Paint or stain both hoops, if desired. Dry thoroughly.

2. Cut a piece of netting or tulle slightly larger than hoop and lay it over the smaller ring of hoop.

3. Spread glue on central portion of netting; press potpourri evenly over this.

4. If lace has large openings, place another piece of netting over the potpourri. If lace is fine, omit this step.

5. Lay a piece of lace over all. Press an outer ring of hoop, pulling all layers tight. Tighten screw on outer loop. Trim off excess netting and lace.

6. Optional: glue flat lace design or motif on front with clear-drying white glue.

7. Glue lace trim around outer rim on back of hoop, using white or hot glue.

8. Use gold cord or narrow ribbon to hang the ornament from the hoop screw. Or, sew hanger to back and cover the screw with a bow.

Orange Simmering Potpourri
(Bob Clark)

2 cups orange petals
2 cups orange peel
1 cup lemon peel
20 broken bay leaves
1 cup camomile flowers
2 T. cloves (whole)
6 broken cinnamon sticks (3")
1 cup sandalwood

Add:
10 drops bergamot oil
10 drops lime or lemon oil

Simmer on stove for room refreshment. Use 2 or 3 tablespoons per quart of water.

Peppermint Candy Potpourri
(Bob Clark)

4 cups whole peppermint leaves
3 cups pink rosebuds and petals
1 cup hibiscus flowers
(Optional — red & white peony petals)
1 T. cloves
1 T. cinnamon chips
2 T. orris root
20 drops rose oil

10 drops peppermint oil
5 drops sweet orange oil
1 T. gum benzoin

Add the oils to the ingredients listed above them and stir thoroughly. Then add the gum benzoin and re-stir. This prevents the oils from making a gummed-up mess of the benzoin powder.

November Specialties

Once the sunny crisp of fall becomes the graying cool of winter, our thoughts turn to warming our hearts and hearths with preparations of treats to share during the holiday season. Here are two gems to add to your pantry stock, from Pat Bourdo's **WOODLAND HERB FARM MI 49670**.

Pumpkin Jam

5 lbs. fresh or canned pumpkin
1 lb. dried apricots, chopped
1 lb. seedless raisins
2½ lbs. sugar
2 T. lemon juice
3 T. crystallized ginger, chopped

If using fresh pumpkin, peel, remove seeds and cut into cubes, or cook until tender and mash.

Mix pumpkin with sugar and let stand for 12 hours. Add remaining ingredients and cook slowly, stirring frequently, for 2 to 3 hours. If pumpkin cubes are used, cook longer until cubes are tender and transparent. Ladle into hot sterilized jars and seal. Process in boiling-water bath for 5 minutes. *Makes about 8 pints.*

Fresh Cranberry Chutney

1 lb. (4 cups) fresh or frozen cranberries
1¾ cup water
1¾ cup sugar
1 cup raisins (golden if available)
½ cup red-wine vinegar
1½ T. curry powder
2 T. molasses
2 t. ground ginger
1 T. Worcestershire Sauce
¼ t. Tabasco Sauce
1 t. non-iodized salt

Bring water and sugar to boil; simmer for 5 minutes. Add cranberries and cook until skins just pop, about 5 minutes. Stir in remaining ingredients and simmer uncovered until thickened, about 20 minutes. Stir occasionally. Ladle into hot sterilized jars and seal. Process in boiling-water bath for 5 minutes. *Makes about 2 pints.*

Dilled Snack Crackers

½ cup salad oil
2 t. dillweed, dried (4 t. fresh)
1 pkg. Hidden Valley Ranch Salad Dressing mix (original)
1 pkg. oyster crackers

Mix first 3 ingredients in large bowl. Stir in oyster crackers. Stir occasionally. Refrigerate overnight. Store in airtight container. — from *The Christian Rambler,* contributed by Ruth Mackey of OH who says these are habit-forming, like popcorn...and I agree! So simple and good!

Candied Citrus Peel

Peel fruit, keeping peel in large pieces. Wash and trim off as much of the white as possible. Cut into strips and triangles. For grapefruit, cover with cold water and boil 5 min. Drain and repeat process twice. For limes, oranges, and lemons — cover with cold water and boil for 20 min. Drain the peel and weigh it. Then use the same weight of honey and sugar, using one-half of each. Add ⅓ cup water for each cup of honey and sugar. Add peel and simmer until glazed, about 20 minutes. Drain and roll in sugar. Store in air-tight jars.

Sage Cheese Spread

1 cup dry curd cottage cheese
½ cup extra sharp Cheddar cheese, grated, and at room temperature
4 t. chopped fresh sage (or 2 t. dried)
1 t. prepared mustard

Mix all ingredients in blender or food processor until smooth and creamy. Store in crock in refrigerator at least 24 hours before using. This makes a lovely gift.

I have found that pine potpourri sells extremely well at bazaars and stores all fall, especially in bulk, as customers fancy making their own sachets or pillows. But pine-scented sachets are big sellers, too.

Thyme-Savor   Herb Butter

1 cup softened butter
½ cup chopped celery leaves
½ cup crumbled parsley
1½ t. thyme
½ t. each sage and marjoram
½ t. garlic powder
¼ t. black pepper

Whirl all together in blender or food processor. Refrigerate or freeze in covered container to use for seasoning cooked rice, or to baste chicken or fish before broiling.

Rosemary Needle Sharpener

Rose Rounds from MI advises us that this project sells very well at craft fairs: a small muslin bag packed tight with dried rosemary to hold needles, sharpen them, and keep them from rusting, sold for $1.00. The idea is from the

COOPERATIVE HERBS CATALOG IA 52318, an *excellent source* of bulk herbs at reasonable prices, retail or wholesale. *Superior* catalog is an encyclopedia of herbs — $4.75.

Basic Pine Potpourri

2 qts. ground pine needles
1 cup orris root combined with

1 T. pine oil

Pine-Mint

2 cups pine needles
2 cups spearmint or applemint

½ cup orris root blended with
1½ t. pine oil

If you don't have any pine trees of your own, you may have neighbors who'd be delighted to have you rake up some of their needles from underneath the trees, or to let you have any of the branches they trim from the trees. (We keep our oldest row of pines trimmed on the bottom so we can walk under them.)

Fruity Pine

2 cups each: pine needles
    spearmint
    lemon verbena (or lemon balm)
as much lemon and orange peel as desired

¾ cup orris root blended with
2 t. pine oil and
1 t. lemon oil

Rosepine

2 cups each: pine needles
    rose petals
    rose geranium leaves
    rosemary needles

½ cup orris root blended with
2 t. pine oil
½ cup orris root blended with
2 t. rose oil

November End-of-the-Season Wrap-Up

This is an excellent time of year to test your soil for pH content and to correct it if needed by adding lime, working it into the soil so that it will do its job before spring planting time. Either get a soil-test kit from a gardening center or contact your local county extension service. (They may want you to send a sample to them for testing.) Herbs are happiest in a neutral soil, or slightly above that, so if your soil in the herb garden tests below 6.5 pH level, sweeten it up!

Time to put the roses to bed. If you live in an area with mild winters, prune back the canes of hybrid teas to 24" to prevent the winter winds from snapping them. Then, wherever you live, heap on a good mulch. As with all winter mulches, the purpose is to prevent the soil from freezing and thawing, which heaves plants out of the soil. This is especially important in areas where there is not a steady, heavy snow cover to protect the plants from the extremes of temperature. Mound some garden soil (from another spot; *not* from under the roses) to cover 8–10" of the lower part of the canes. Later, after *several hard freezes,* add a layer of leaves, straw, or any mulch, about 5" deep, to keep the soil layer frozen. (A cup or two of bone meal added to the soil of rose bushes before you "hill" them up will do wonders come spring.)

After a hard frost cut off dead stems of chives, costmary, lovage, mint, sorrel, tarragon, and sweet cicely. Add to the compost pile. Hyssop, sage, and upright thyme benefit from a winter mulch.

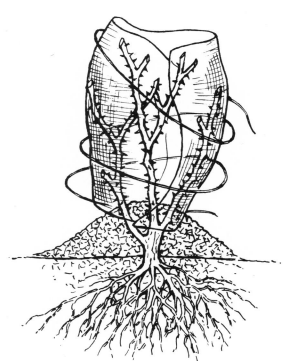

Protecting roses for northern winters

DECEMBER

Rosemary (*Rosmarinus officinalis*)

DECEMBER

There's Rosemary, that's for remembrance.
Pray you, love, remember.

— William Shakespeare, *Hamlet,* IV, 5

EARLY THIS MONTH drop some hints to your Santa that you'd like some indoor lights for growing fresh herbs each winter, and for starting perennials from seed each spring (especially if you don't have a sunny kitchen window). The fluorescent tubes, which are available at most garden centers or hardware stores, simulate the sun's rays. They use very little electricity — the cost is barely discernible on the electric bill.

Wrap up some of your herb blends in plastic bags or pretty jars in December, enclosing directions for use by your culinary-minded friends. Tie with a Christmas ribbon and a sprig of one of the herbs used in the mix. Or give bouquets of dried mint branches with directions for making tea.

Sit back and sip some refreshing and relaxing herb tea of your own when holiday chores loom heavily on your soul. Brew a pot of peppermint tea and add a pinch of cinnamon, a dash of orange peel, and a dab of honey. Between sips recall the quiet sunny day you harvested your peppermint, and envision the first sprouts to burst forth *next* spring.

Gourmet Gardening — Rosemary

Slip some ROSEMARY sprigs in with your Christmas cards. This has to be one of the loveliest culinary herbs of all. Since "rosemary is for remembrance," and December is the time of year we are remembering our loved ones, I have included my favorite herb cake in this chapter.

Rosemary is a tender perennial in the North and should be brought inside or kept in a greenhouse for the winter months. It does not adjust well to change, however, and often dies even if one is very careful.

Place rosemary in a damp, cool place with winter light, such as by a cellar or garage window, for the winter. Do not overwater, but don't let it dry out completely either. Traditionally, one brings the plant back to light and warmth in the late winter to revive it, but sometimes the leaves have all blackened and fallen off by then. I've had better luck getting *new* plants through the winter, plants that were propagated by layering the branches in early summer or by rooting stem cuttings in fall. If this doesn't work either, rosemary is easily started from seed under lights in late winter.

The foliage loves frequent mistings. Harvest the top quarter of the branches when the foliage is lush.

One of the loveliest of the culinary herbs, rosemary is well worth any extra effort it takes to keep a household in good supply and have some extra for "remembrance." It enhances many beef and chicken dishes, makes a lovely jelly, is used in several herb punches, potpourris, and bath blends, and makes a delightful cake.

Here's a fun use for your pine oil (or other oils, such as cloves, lavender, or patchouli): dab the oil lightly with a Q-tip on cool light bulbs. The room will become alive with fragrance when the lights are turned on!

Enclose rosemary sprigs in your Christmas cards for "remembrance".

Rosemary

Holiday Treats

Rosemary Cake

Add 2 t. crushed dried rosemary (or 3 t. chopped *fresh*) to any angel food, sponge, pound or white cake batter.

Add same amount to any kind of white frosting or whipped cream. Tint the frosting to suit the season or match your table decor. This is a unique and luscious way to honor someone special *any* time of year!

Tansy Cookies

Add a teaspoon of crushed dried tansy to any basic white roll-out dough or butter cookie recipe.

Add another tsp. of tansy to any basic white frosting using sherry flavoring for the liquid. Decorate with crushed tansy sprinkled lightly on the frosting.

Molasses Cookies

Add a little crushed anise seed to your favorite molasses cookie recipe and adorn with a confectionery frosting diluted with sherry or rum flavoring. Decorate with dried calendula petals.

Rose Geranium Cake

When baking any white cake, line the cake pan(s) with greased wax paper and place one or two rose geranium leaves on the wax paper before pouring the batter. Remove the baked leaves, but don't hesitate to decorate the frosted cake with some fresh leaves. Serve rose geranium tea with the cake. Lemon-scented geranium leaves may be used in the same way.

Citrus Cheese-Cake

This is one of my favorite herb desserts, and I warn you...it will disappear like magic!

6 egg whites, beaten stiff
¼ lb. plus 2 T. butter
½ cup plus 2 T. sugar
6 egg yolks
12 oz. soft cream cheese
1 cup ground almonds
2 t. chopped dried lemon balm (4 t. fresh)
2 t. each grated lemon and orange rind, or 4 t. either one (either may be fresh or dried)
2 t. finely ground marigold or calendula petals (optional)

Beat egg whites until stiff in small mixer bowl. Cream butter, sugar, yolks, & cheese. Add herbs, rinds, & almonds. Fold in beaten egg whites. Place in greased angel-food tube pan. Bake at 325° for 55 minutes. Cool 10 minutes, then invert on plate.

Lemon balm

More Herb & Spice Desserts

All of the recipes in this section are from the members of the *Penn-Cumberland Garden Club* who have held annual award-winning herbal tea parties for large crowds, and then have published booklets to share the recipes! The themes of some of the booklets are: COLONIAL HERBS, SHAKESPEARE, BIBLE HERBS, PENNSYLVANIA DUTCH, ROSE-MARY, ROSE TEA PARTY, FEAST OF FLOWERS, A COUNTRY HERB TEA, and A MEDIEVAL FESTIVAL. You'll certainly want their DEFINITIVE BOOK ON HERB TEA PARTIES (ideas, instructions, recipes) (See Bibliography).

Cardamom Cookies

3¾ cups all-purpose flour
2 cups softened butter or oleo
1½ cups confectioner's sugar
1½ t. almond extract
1 t. ground cardamom
⅛ t. salt
1 cup chopped walnuts

Measure all ingredients into large bowl and knead until well blended. Shape dough into 1" balls; place 2" apart on cookie sheets. Bake 20 min. in preheated 350° oven until lightly browned. Immediately remove cookies with spatula and cool on wire racks. Roll cookies in additional confectioner's sugar if desired. Store in tightly covered container. *Makes about 6 dozen.*

Nutmeg Cake

1½ cups brown sugar
2 cups flour
½ cup butter, cut into bits
1 large egg, beaten
1 t. freshly grated nutmeg
1 cup buttermilk or sour milk
1 t. baking soda
¾ cup chopped cashews

Preheat oven to 350°. Butter a 9" square baking pan. In a large bowl blend sugar and flour. Add butter and rub into dry ingredients with fingers until small crumbs form. Place half the crumbs into baking pan. To remaining crumbs, add egg, nutmeg, and sour milk which has been mixed with baking soda. Pour mixture onto crumbs in baking pan and sprinkle top with nuts. Bake about 35 minutes, or until a toothpick comes out dry from the center of cake. — **Rosemarie Vassalluzzo**

Granola Pumpkin Bread

1 cup butter or margarine, softened
3 cups sugar
3 eggs
1 t. vanilla
1 can (16 oz.) pumpkin
3 cups sifted flour
1½ t. baking powder
1 t. baking soda
2 t. ground cloves
2 t. ground cinnamon
1 t. ground nutmeg
1½ cups chopped pecans or almonds
1 cup raisins
1½ cups granola

Cream butter and add sugar gradually. Beat in eggs and vanilla. Add pumpkin and mix well. Sift together flour, salt, soda, baking powder and spices. Blend with pumpkin mixture. Stir in nuts, raisins, and cereal.

Preheat oven to 350°. Grease and flour 3 loaf pans (9x5x3). Divide dough evenly between pans, each a little over half full. Bake approx. 60 or 70 minutes, or until bread tests done with toothpick. Let stand 10 min.

Remove from pans & cool on racks. Wrap and store for several hours before slicing. This freezes well. Chopped candied fruit and cherries should be added for color and decoration.

Ask Santa for indoor lights, for herbal books on your "wish list", or for essential oils and fixatives for your year-round hobby.

Clove Cookies

½ cup melted butter
1 cup sugar
1 t. vanilla
1 egg
1 cup flour
1 t. ground cloves

Stir the sugar into the melted butter until blended. Stir in vanilla; beat in the egg until smooth.

Stir flour and cloves together; then stir into the butter mix until blended. Drop batter by level teaspoon on cookie sheet 2" apart. Bake 12 min. at 350° or until edges are golden and puffy. Tops start to crinkle and collapse. Cool on pan 30 seconds, then cool on wire rack. *Makes 4 dozen.*

Taurus Mint Cookies

1 cup butter (or ½ cup butter & ½ cup shortening)
½ cup sugar
½ t. peppermint extract
2 T. crushed dried mint leaves
2 cups flour
¼ t. salt

Cream butter and sugar; add extract, mint leaves, flour, and salt. Mix thoroughly. Chill dough. Form 1" balls and roll in sugar. Press with your thumb. Bake at 350° for 12–15 minutes. Makes 3 dozen cookies or 6 dozen small ones.

Variations

Add chocolate chips or nuts; roll in mint sugar; ice with milk chocolate candy while warm; glaze with pale green icing. (For an interesting plate of cookies, why not use several variations and let people taste-test? — PVS) — from Bertha Reppert's **HERBS OF THE ZODIAC** (see MAY)

Rosemary Squares

Beat 2 eggs vigorously. Gradually add 1 cup brown sugar, then 2 t. vanilla and 1 cup flour that has been sifted with ½ tsp. salt and 1 tsp. baking powder, and into which ½ tsp. rosemary has been stirred. Fold in ⅔ cup of pecans and 1 cup candied fruit and raisins. Bake in 8x8" pan first buttered and dusted with flour for 30 minutes at 350°.

Remove from pan while warm; cool and cut into bars. *Makes 30 squares.* — from Rose Canny

Chewy Cranberry Gingers

2⅓ cups all-purpose flour
2 t. baking soda
½ t. salt
1 t. cinnamon
½ t. ginger
1 cup sugar
¾ cup shortening
1 egg
¼ cup molasses
½ cup whole cranberry sauce
  (cooked or canned)

In large mixing bowl combine all ingredients except cranberries. Blend well. Stir in cranberries; mix thoroughly. Chill dough at least 1 hour. Shape into balls using a rounded teaspoon. Coat with additional sugar. Place on un-greased cookie sheets. Bake at 375° for 12–15 minutes. Remove from cookie sheets immediately. Makes 60–66 cookies.

(High altitude adjustment — 5200 ft. — decrease soda to 1 tsp., sugar to ¾ cup, shortening to ½ cup.)
— **Penn-Cumberland Garden Club**

Minted Grapefruit

Empty 2 cans of grapefruit into a bowl, reserving juice separately. Mix ½ cup juice, 1 cup sugar, and 2 T. mint in saucepan and boil for about 5 min. Add green food coloring, if desired. When cool, add to fruit and let stand for 2 or 3 hours. If you prefer sweeter sauce, add more sugar. Try the different kinds of mint each time you make this — spearmint, peppermint, apple, orange, or pineapple mint.
— from **ADA RICKENBACKER.**

More Holiday Treats

The following recipes are from Pat Bourdo's new 78-page book, HERBS & SPICES, *created with the working woman and the "not so domestic" lady in mind, since time and simplicity in preparation of a meal are of equal importance to both. Most of the recipes can be made a day or two ahead to eliminate last minute rush. 95% of the recipes are salt-free.* JON & PAT BOURDO, WOODLAND HERB FARM, MI 49670

Basic Seed Cookies

1 cup softened butter
1½ cups sugar
2 eggs
3 cups unbleached flour
2 t. baking powder
1 t. salt
2 t. vanilla extract
1 t. grated lemon peel
1–2 T. crushed herb seeds

Choose from one of the following herb seeds: 2 T. coriander; 2 T. dill; 1 T. caraway; 1 T. anise, 1 T. fennel; or 1 T. cumin. Sift together flour, baking powder, and salt. Cream butter and sugar; add eggs and mix well. Work in flour mixture well blended. Add lemon peel, vanilla, and seeds and blend well. Chill for at least 4 hours or overnight. Roll thin and cut into shapes with cookie cutter. Bake on greased cookie sheet about 10 min. at 350°.

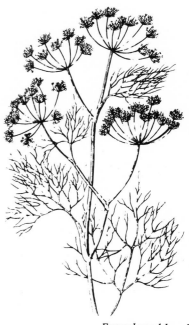

Fennel seed heads

Lemon thyme

Lemon Thyme Cookies

1 cup soft butter
1½ cups sugar
2 eggs
2½ cups unbleached flour
1 t. cream of tartar
½ t. salt
3 T. dried lemon thyme

Sift together flour, cream of tartar, and salt. Cream butter with sugar; add eggs and mix well. Work in flour mixture until well blended; stir in lemon thyme. Chill overnight. Roll into walnut-size balls. Bake on greased cookie sheet about 10 minutes at 350°.

Herb Candy

4 cups boiling water
2 cups leaves with stems and blossoms or 3 seeds*
3 cups each granulated and brown sugar
½ T. butter

Pour boiling water over herbs or seeds and steep for 10 min. or longer for a very strong tea. Strain. Add sugar and butter and bring to boil over medium heat. Cook until syrup hardens when a small amount is dropped in cold water. Pour into a buttered shallow pan. Score into squares before it sets or break up into pieces as soon as it is hard. Wrap each hardened piece in waxed paper and store in an airtight container.

*Herbs to try include: peppermint, horehound, spearmint, orangemint, applemint, wintergreen, lemon verbena and lemon catnip. Seeds to try include: fennel, anise, caraway, coriander, and star anise. For variation: add 1 T. mint leaves or 1 t. crushed anise seeds to horehound for a horehound candy.

Herb & Spice Beverages

Mulling Spices

Mix 6 inches coarsely broken stick cinnamon, 4 t. *each* whole cloves and whole allspice, 2 T. shredded dried orange peel, and 2 shelled cardamom seeds, crushed slightly. Pack in 2 bags made from several layers of cheesecloth and tie snuggly shut with string. Or use a stainless steel mesh teaball or Stuff & Seal Teabaglets (both available from our shop). Store in airtight container. Add to hot cider, wines, coffee, tea, or apple juice.

Spicy Punch

Add 2 qts. boiling water to 8 teabags, 4 sticks of cinnamon, 6 whole cloves. Steep 10 minutes. Remove tea bags. Add ½ cup sugar, 1 cup lemon juice, 1 cup orange juice, 1 qt. pineapple juice, 2 cups cranberry juice, and 2 qts. cider. Heat just to boiling, stirring to blend. Remove cloves. To serve, pour into 2-gal. punch bowl and add 2 qts. ginger ale. (For smaller punch bowl, use 1 qt. ginger ale to half the tea.) Can be served hot.
— from **Rose Canny**

Hot Spiced Cranberry Punch

2 lemons, sliced thickly
24 whole cloves
3 pints cranberry juice
1 pint lemonade
½ t. each ground cloves, cinnamon,
   & allspice
1 cup sugar or honey
12 cinnamon stick swirlers
   (optional)

Stud the lemon slices with whole cloves to float on top of punch. Simmer all other ingredients for 15 minutes. Serve in 2-qt. punch bowl, or deep chafing dish or crockpot to keep warm. Offer cinnamon sticks as swirlers and/or favors. *Serves 12.*

Red Herb Punch or Tea

3 gal. water
1 lb. Rosa de Jamaica flowers
   (Hibiscus)
3 lbs. honey

Boil water; add dried red hibiscus flowers and simmer for 10 minutes. Add honey.

This "concentrate" can be added to 4 gallons of hot or cold water to be served as a hot tea, or poured over ice rings and served as a cold punch. It is a sparkling red punch and takes kindly to the addition of red wine. *Makes approx. 175 tea or punch cup servings.*

Rose Hip Tea

Blend rose hips (the seed pods of Rugosa rose bushes) and hibiscus flowers for a delicious, citrusy tea, pretty and pink.

(Hibiscus flowers and rose hips are available from THE ROSEMARY HOUSE and both the last two recipes are shared by the Penn-Cumberland Garden Club.)

Annie's Rosemary Fruit Punch

1 can pineapple juice (46 oz.)
5 sprigs fresh rosemary (1 T. dried)
½ cup sugar
1½ cups lemon juice
2 cups water
Pinch of salt
1 qt. ginger ale
Lemon slices and mint leaves for
   garnish

Heat 1 cup pineapple juice in small pan until boiling. Add rosemary and steep 8–10 minutes. Dissolve sugar and pinch of salt in hot juice. Then strain into pitcher containing remaining pineapple juice, lemon juice, and water. Chill before serving and adding ginger ale and garnishes. (This may also be served hot.)

Hot Spiked Punch for 40

Simmer 1 gal. cider with 3 sticks of cinnamon, ½ t. each of whole mace and allspice for 1 hour. Add 1 cup each dark rum and cognac and stir until heated through. Remove spices.

Herbal Acres' Orange Mint Spiced Tea

Place 2 t. orange mint or peppermint, ¼ cup orange juice, 2 T. finely-grated orange peel, ¼ t. ground cloves, ½ t. cinnamon, and 2 T. of honey in 1 qt. hot tea. Keep warm over low flame for 20 minutes before serving.

Pomander Pebbles
Mix ½ t. essential oil with 2 T. all-clay litter and leave in glass jar, covered, until oil is absorbed, shaking occasionally. Use to refill china pomanders and closet baskets.

— GINGHAM 'N SPICE PA 18926

Herbed Appetizers and Dips

Herbed Cheese

1 8-oz. package cream cheese, softened
3 cloves garlic, crushed
1 t. each dried basil, chives, caraway seed, and dillweed
2 t. dried parsley, crushed

Freshly ground black pepper, to taste

Thoroughly mix all together in blender and mold into any shape desired. Cover and refrigerate at least overnight.

Creamy Cottage Cheese Dips

These dips are all especially good with celery and carrot sticks and cauliflower and broccoli flowerets. (Also great with crackers.)

1 lb. creamed cottage cheese
1–3 T. milk, whatever needed for desired consistency
½ t. salt
Dash of freshly ground black pepper

Whirl all in blender after adding any 1 of the following, and refrigerate a few hours before serving:

Chives — 3 T. snipped fresh (2 T. dried)

Oregano — 1 t. dried oregano and ¼ cup grated Parmesan flakes
Dill/tuna — whirl 1 small can tuna, drained, and 1 t. each of dill and lemon juice into the cheese blend.
Garlic/clam — 1 6–8 oz. can minced clams, drained; 1 small onion, chopped; plus ¼ t. (or more) garlic powder.

Barbara Bobo from WOOD-SPIRITS HERB SHOP *in Ohio (43072) shares this tip: "Find real licorice sticks to tuck into the Christmas stockings. The remarkable licorice root is fantastically sweet — 52 times sweeter than white sugar — yet it is the only sweet that quenches thirst. It erases a sore throat and is good for the entire system, including your teeth!"*

Dilly Shrimp Dip

8 oz. cleaned and chopped shrimp
8 oz. cream cheese, softened
2 T. sour cream
1 T. each ketchup, mayonnaise, mustard
2 dashes garlic powder & Worcestershire
1 cup celery, chopped fine

1 T. onion, chopped fine
½ t. dill
1 t. parsley
½ t. horseradish

Whirl all in blender until smooth and creamy. Chill before serving. (Adapted from The Penn-Cumberland Garden Club.)

Penn-Cumberland's Sausage Balls (100)

Work 1 lb. uncooked bulk sausage into 4 cups biscuit mix, ½ lb. grated sharp cheese, and 2 t. crumbled sage. Roll into balls.

Bake on ungreased cookie sheet at 350° for 15–20 min. These are wonderful and freeze well.

Rose Canny's Sage Sticks

Sift together 1 cup sifted flour, 1½ t. baking powder, and ½ t. salt into a medium bowl. Stir in ½ t. sage and ½ cup grated cheddar cheese. Cut in 2 T. butter until crumbly. Sprinkle ⅓ cup water over top; mix lightly with fork just until pastry holds together.

Roll out to a rectangle, 12x10, on lightly floured board. Divide in half lengthwise, then cut each half crosswise into ½" wide strips. Place an inch apart on ungreased cookie sheet. Bake at 425° about 10 minutes. Cool on rack.

Sage

Super Holiday Cheese Wafers

1 lb. cheddar cheese, grated
½ lb. butter
2 cups flour
1 t. each red pepper and sage
1 cup finely-ground pecans

When cheese and butter are at room temperature, mix all ingredients together thoroughly. Form in 4 small long rolls. Chill overnight. Slice thin and bake on ungreased Teflon pan at 350° about 10–12 minutes, until light brown. Makes over 250 wafers! You can't buy a better cracker! Store in air-tight can.
Adapted from Penn-Cumberland Garden Club.

Spread the wealth from your kitchen to your neighbor's. Here's my "December Basket". Tie up small bunches of the culinary herbs with red ribbons and place in a basket tied on top with Christmas red, too. This looks nice on kitchen table as centerpiece.

A Christmas Yule Log

Blend together 8 oz. cottage or cream cheese with 8 oz. grated cheddar. Add and mix well: 2 t. chili powder, ¼ t. each thyme and rosemary, 1 t. each garlic powder and grated onion, ½ cup chopped nuts, salt and pepper to taste.

Form into 2 rolls and sprinkle with paprika for wooden log effect. Chill. Slice thin and serve on crackers.
Adapted from a Rose Canny recipe.

December Projects

Scented Dough

This makes interesting and fragrant decorations for the tree or to adorn packages or a wreath. And, children would enjoy helping! (Caution: these are not edible, however.)

2 cups white flour
1 T. powdered orris root
2 T. powdered sandalwood
¼ cup salt
¾ cup strong Sacred Basil tea
Red food coloring, if desired
Assorted ground and whole spices
    (cinnamon, nutmeg, allspice, cloves)

Mix first 5 ingredients well. (The final results will be various shades of off-white, beige, and brown. I wanted some pink, so added red food coloring to a third of the batch.) Roll the dough into 2" balls.

Place ground spices on little mounds on plates. Roll some balls in one spice, some in others. Insert loop for hanging. (I used Christmas ball hangers.) Decorate with whole spices. Dough may also be rolled and cut with cookie cutters.

Bake in a very slow oven until completely dry (about 1½ hours at 150°.) *Makes about 30.*
— adapted from PANTRY PRESENTS, from **HERBS BY JEAN, GA 30307**

Fireplace fragrance can be created with the dried branches of basil, lemon balm, lavender, lemon southernwood, peppermint, rosemary, or scented geraniums. Tie several branches together of any one of these to be placed on the dying embers of a fire for a pungent household aroma.

Instant Christmascent Simmer

3 T. ground cinnamon
2 T. ground cloves
1 T. ground nutmeg
1 T. anise seed (optional)
1 t. ground ginger
1 qt. water

Simply raid your kitchen cupboard to make this household perfume. Stir all together and bring to a boil, stirring occasionally. Then simmer on lowest heat. This can be stored in refrigerator and re-used several times. Add water as needed. The pre-mixed spices, together with directions for use, make a lovely gift.

Frankincense & Myrrh:
Symbols of Gift-Giving and Reverence

by Ruth Chambers

Frankincense, also called olibanum, has for centuries been used to perfume the air in religious rites and services in the Catholic Church and in Jewish Synagogues, and is frequently mentioned in the first five books of the Old Testament. It was used in Asia to treat internal and external ailments. Since it was a precious commodity of ancient trade, it was a fitting gift for the Christ child. It is a gummy resin found in several varieties of small thorny trees growing in East Africa, Yemen, and the Red Sea countries. The aromatic white "sap" oozes from cuts made in the bark, forming pea-sized "tears", which gradually harden in the air and turn yellow. After four months these are stripped from the trees and shipped worldwide.

Myrrh was used extensively by the ancient Egyptians and Hebrews for incense, cosmetics, perfume, medicine — and especially for embalming. It, too, was considered a rare treasure and therefore an apt gift for the Baby Jesus. Myrrh has many modern-day uses, both medical and commercial. It also is a gummy resin and exudes from the bark of a shrub called *Commiphora,* found in Arabia and Abyssinia.

Bedstraw

Horehound

Rue

Advent and Manger Herbs

Kathy Goeckel, of **HERBS EVERLASTING KS 66945** shares the Biblical lore that is the basis of the Advent Wreath of Living Herbs made by her family. "Featured on the wreath are Juniper, which represents life and hope, and protected the Holy family when they were pursued by Herod's soldiers; Our Lady's Bedstraw, used to provide a bed for the Christ Child; Costmary, used by Mary Magdalen to make the precious ointment; Horehound, a Palestinian herb which offers a wish for good health; Rue, a symbol of virtue which banishes evil; Sage, a symbol of health, immortality, and domestic happiness; Thyme, a manger herb symbolizing bravery; Rosemary, which kept silent as the Holy family fled from Egypt while the branches of other bushes crackled; Lavender, beloved by Mary, representing purity, cleanliness and virtue; and true Myrtle, symbol of the highest good, love, domestic happiness and virtue."

Cinnamon Stick Wreath

by Dody Lyness

Dody Lyness teaches potpourri-making, retails potpourri and flowercraft supplies (catalog, $1.50 refundable), fashions floral home decor items which are sold nationwide, and writes a delicious newsletter full of craft instructions, a quarterly, POTPOURRI PARTY-LINE, an outgrowth of her keeping in touch with her customers and students. Here's a sample of Dody's expertise. **BERRY HILL PRESS CA 90274-4404**

You'll need to work with hot glue for this project, and you'll need to work with a "pattern" of a circle drawn on a newspaper. Using 3" cinnamon sticks, line them up 4 abreast and glue the four together. Make up a dozen or so quartets of sticks in that fashion; then lay them on your circle pattern with each quartet overlapping the last. Don't glue the 4-on-4's to each other until you've made as perfect a circle as possible by using the same measurement of overlap. You may need to glue more quartets of sticks together; that depends on the size of wreath you want. If you're going to make a *big* wreath, form quintets or sextets of the sticks; you don't want a skinny-looking wreath. But keep the weight of the finished product in mind, too.

When you have a uniform look, then anchor the overlaps with hot glue. If this is your first romance with hot glue, know that it dries with an extremely shiny finish. The mark of the pro is never having to say you're sorry that your masterpiece shines in a few places. TIP: Keep a dish of ground cinnamon within grabbing reach. If any hot glue oozes to the surface, sprinkle it immediately with ground cinnamon. A big plaid bow and a dash of cinnamon oil brushed on the sticks is sufficient for the finishing touch. For a Christmas Cinnamon Stix Wreath, a green velvet bow looks elegant; a few touches of dried pods and cones or holly are nice, too.

Add fresh or dried herb sprigs to your manger display.

A Potpourri Tree or Wreath

Florists, gardening centers, and craft shops usually have the equipment needed for these projects. Start with a styrofoam cone or wreath and cover the surfaces that will show with sphagnum moss, securing with floral picks or pins. (Or, using a can of spray glue, cover the form with glue and stick the moss in place.) Now spray-glue the moss and cover with potpourri. (The cone may be rolled in the potpourri; the wreath may be laid in the potpourri.) You may need to repeat this procedure several times before the tree or wreath is completely covered. Using straight pins, pin dried rosebuds and other flowers around the tree or to the wreath. (Or tiny cones, etc.) Small sprigs of baby's breath will be easily inserted in the moss for highlighting. Add a circle of greens to the bottom of the tree, and a lacy bow to the wreath. Dot the rosebuds or other flowers with essential oil.

Don't give all your potpourri away! Keep samples of each batch you have made, labeled with the date, ingredients, and amounts. I do this for "quality control"...to test fragrance endurance and to decide what might improve the next batch.

Bay leaves

A Bay Leaf Wreath

For this one you need a glue gun and hot glue sticks (mine is from Sears), a 10" wire wreath base, about 8 oz. of whole bay leaves, florist tape, and dried hot red peppers for adornment. After wrapping the frame with the tape, glue the leaves to the tape, always overlapping each one in the one before, and always going in the same direction. There will be about 3 or 4 leaves from side to side. As with making most wreaths, it's best to start on the inside. Place a cluster of 5 to 7 red peppers in one of the top corners and glue to the wreath. This will last for several years, fragrance and all!

> *Make a kitchen table wreath and adorn with cheesecloth bags of culinary mixes tied with red bows, for seasoning soups, omelets, bread, meats, etc.*

> *Decorate your door wreath or swatch with colorful, fragrant sachets or apple-pulp pomanders.*

'Tis the Season....

Many years ago we bought a "Faith Tree", called a false Cypress by the nurseryman. Its soft blue-gray boughs are my favorite greens for our annual Advent wreath (which bears little resemblance to the ones described in religious literature). Since our family heritage is a blend of many religions, our wreath is an ecumenical one, fashioned with the colors and adornments of our choosing. And this does not seem to effect the spiritual intent in any way. I have a permanent base which makes it very easy to assemble the wreath quickly each year. (A 9½" Advent candle ring is anchored with wire to the top of a 10" straw wreath base, which sits neatly on a 12" plate, to which it can be anchored with masking tape if desired.) First soak and drain the straw wreath as well as the cut branches of evergreens. Then stick the branches all in one direction through the wreath wires of the candle ring, pressing the cut ends of the branches close to the wet straw. (The wreath stays quite fresh throughout December because of the moisture.) Then I add the candles and the adornments, and, in less than an hour from start to finish our wreath is ready. The prettiest I've ever made was done last December, and unfortunately I was too busy writing this book to bother with photography. It was wide with red candles and apple pomander sachets, a single strand of alternating cranberries and popcorn, scalloped around the wreath, and breath-taking sprays of baby's breath throughout. Simple. Quick. Fun. Lovely.

> *"And sitting down to eat bread, they saw some Israelites on their way coming from Gilead and with their camels, carrying spices, and balm and myrrh to Egypt."*
> — *Genesis 37:25*

In recent years we have had all-natural Christmas trees because the girls and I have so enjoyed the fellowship and relaxation of stringing the fresh cranberries and popcorn, often done while listening to Christmas music together or watching holiday specials on TV. (Keeping the strings you are working on right in the bowls with the cranberries or popcorn, use heavy duty red thread and large-headed needles. Leave extra thread on both knotted ends of 3–4' "ropes," to tie several of them together. Refrigerate the cranberry ropes until ready to decorate the tree. These can be made up to a week in advance.)

Aside from using twinkling white lights on our tree, we try to keep it "natural." It's fun finding pretty Christmas fabrics for the sachets and pomanders to blend with the red and white candy canes and cranberry and popcorn ropes. Lately I've been highlighting the tree with sprigs of baby's breath, which I highly recommend. It is lovely having a tree that looks as beautiful in the daylight as it does at night with the lights.

Burn frankincense and myrrh on slow-burning embers in your fireplace.

Christmas Morning Fruit Punch

I've been making this since the children were little and didn't want to stop for Christmas breakfast. This is a "Mom-Saver". Family and guests can serve themselves during gift-opening or on New Year's during Rose Bowl parade and games.

Up to a week early, make a spearmint or orange mint ice ring in gelatin ring mold. Steep the mints in boiling water for ½ hour. Cool. Add orange and lemon or lime slices, and lots of maraschino cherries, drained. Freeze. At zero hour, pour 3 qts. ginger ale over 1 qt. of lime, lemon, or orange ice (sherbet). Float ice ring on top — as it melts the fruits will be released into the punch. This makes 20 punch bowl servings. Add orange or pineapple juice, if desired.

I serve this with broiled ham and cheese on English muffins for a quick hearty brunch, and because it's easy to make a lot at one time in the oven. Our Christmas serve-yourself brunch became one of our traditions most-loved by the children.

Simplicity is the rule at our house; holidays are for everyone to enjoy, even Mom.

Herbal Christmas Tree Ornaments

by Barbara Radcliffe Rogers

Tiny Tussies for the Tree. Miniature tussie-mussies make elegant Christmas tree ornaments and are easily made from tiny dried rosebuds, little sprigs of baby's breath, pieces of statice, and other dried flowers. Cut a piece of styrofoam sheet (well-washed meat trays work perfectly) about the size of a nickel. Push a 4-inch length of doubled florist wire through it to make a handle in the center. Push the stems of herbs into the styrofoam, using a single little rosebud in the center and other rosebuds or tiny sprigs around it. This is a perfect way to use the pieces that have broken off in the process of making herbal wreaths! Use single florets of statice, tansy, etc. When you have a tiny bouquet, fill in the spaces with little whole cloves, tiny sprigs of baby's breath, leaves of boxwood, or other tiny blossoms. Glue these in place with a tacky white glue. When the bouquet is dry, you can glue a small piece of gathered narrow lace around the edge, or you can glue little ruffles cut from paper doilies to the edge. Cover the back with a circle of white paper, snipping off any stem ends that come through the bottom. Wrap the stem with florist tape and finish off with a tiny bow of ¼" wide satin picot ribbon in a complementary or matching color. Add a loop of nylon thread for a hanger.

If you don't have rosebuds, you can use a very small strawflower for your center or you can simply group your other flowers. If the flowers have stems ½ inch or longer, you can bundle your blossoms into a bouquet, tie with heavy thread, and wrap with florists' tape. Then add the ruffle using a slightly wider lace or eyelet, gathered into a circle and glued at the base of the stem. Although full-sized tussie-mussies can be used on the tree, these miniature ones are so delicate and dainty that they are certain to steal the show.

Miniature Lace Wreaths. Using a white florist weight wire, form a circle around a bottle, or other round object about 1½–2" in diameter. Leave about an inch of wire on either end. Using one end of the wire as though it were a needle (you may have to smooth it slightly with steel wool), thread ½ to ¾ inch wide ecru or white lace onto the wire, using about ½ yard of lace, or enough to form a full gathered circle. Loop the ends of the wire together and trim off excess. If the lace is not fairly stiff, give the wreath a quick spray of starch and allow to dry thoroughly. Decorate by gluing tiny dried herb blossoms, such as individual chive blossom florets, little clusters of marjoram flowers, tansy or costmary buttons, feverfew, leaves of thyme, germander, boxwood, and seeds or berries such as bay and coriander. Finish by attaching a loop for hanging and a bow ⅛" satin ribbon in a complementary color.

Pressed Herb Ornaments. As herbs bloom, save the tiny blossoms and a few leaves in your flower press. Good subjects for this are thyme, sage, lavender, marjoram (especially Pot Marjoram with its bright magenta flowers), the individual florets of chive and beebalm, rue, hyssop, and the smaller leaves of bay and costmary. Arrange these carefully on a glass microscopic slide and secure with tiny droplets of glue applied with the point of a pin. When glue is dry, cover with another slide and secure at corners with additional glue droplets. Press until dry. Using a ⅛" satin or grosgrain ribbon in a color to match or blend well with the flowers and foliage, make a 1" loop and glue it to the very edge at the top center. When the loop is dry, make a border with the ribbon, covering the raw edges of the glass. Work from the top center, all the way around and end at the center, leaving 4–5" of ribbon at each end. Glue ribbon in place. When glue is thoroughly dry, tie ends in a bow around the hanging loop and trim ends to an attractive length.

Miniature Herb Wreaths. Tiny herbal wreaths can be made from Silver King or Silver Queen Artemisia when it is fresh and pliable. Use about 6 or 8 inches, as far down as the stem will bend in a round shape without being too stiff. Wrap several of these around one or two fingers, entwining them or tying them with gray sewing thread or invisible plastic thread. Make plenty of these little bases while the Artemisia is fresh and pliable. Later, when they have dried, decorate them with very small flowers, florets, and leaves, gluing them in place. If you have a microwave oven, try tying several sprigs of thyme into a ring, as above, creating a very full, but tiny wreath. Place it inside a folded paper towel and microwave for 15 seconds. Check results and continue to microwave in 5–10 second intervals until leaves are crisp and dry. They will retain a fresh green color and may be decorated with tiny sprigs of red or other colored dried flowers. A tiny satin bow may be added to any of these wreaths, along with a loop of nylon thread for hanging. Try experimenting with other tender herb tips, for a series of fragrant and lovely Christmas tree decorations.

These herbal Christmas tree ornaments, plus many other herb decorations for the holidays are included in a booklet, "DECK THE HALLS WITH ARTEMISIA: Christmas Decorating with Herbs", which may be ordered from Barbara for *$3.00* at HERBITAGE FARM RFD2 RICHMOND NH 03470.

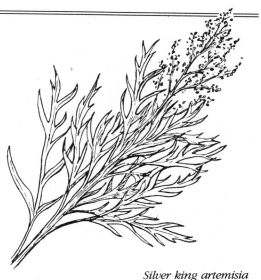

Silver king artemisia

Simmering Potpourris

by Dody Lyness

Many people think of these only at holiday time, but I use them all year long to keep the house smelling fresh. These are meant for simmering on the stove or in the oven with the door slightly ajar. (Some people just dump the mixture onto a piece of foil and stick it in a warm oven with the door open a bit.) They can be re-heated several times, until the scent is gone. A ⅔ or ¾ cup of any mixture is about right for 1 simmering portion in 2 or 3 cups of water. Like any potpourri mixture, let your personal taste dictate the choice of ingredients; each should have an aroma, however. Here are a few recipes to get you started. (*C/S = Cut & Sifted*)

Christmas Spice

This is the most popular mix that I sell. I change its name, depending on the season of the year that I package it for sale: YULETIDE, SPICE TREE, etc.

1 cup of each: whole allspice, star anise, ginger, root, C/S, & Sassafras Bar, C/S.

2 cups of each: orange peel, lemon verbena leaves, rose buds and petals.

30 drops Allspice Oil, stirred into the mixture 5 drops at a time.

When I package this, I tuck two 3" cinnamon sticks in the front of the package and make sure that some rose buds and verbena leaves are front and center, too.

Mulling Spice Simmer

Equal parts whole allspice, broken cinnamon sticks, whole cloves, orange peel. Optional: orange, clove and/or cinnamon essential oil(s) — a few drops.

Orange Blossom Special

2 cups each Orange flower petals and orange peel

½ cup rose hips, pre-steeped in Bitter Orange oil for 5 days

2 T. powdered Orris Root pre-mixed with Orange Spice Oil

Cinnamint

1 cup each broken cinnamon pieces & peppermint leaves. Divide into three ⅔ cup portions. C/S

Excerpted, with permission, from Dody's newsletter, POTPOURRI PARTY-LINE. All of the necessary ingredients for the above recipes are available from Dody; send a *SASE* for her price list of potpourri supplies. **DODY LYNESS DEPT. PFHA 7336 BERRY HILL DR PALOS VERDES PENINSULA CA 90274**

APPENDIXES

A BRIEF
ENCYCLOPEDIA OF HERBS

Herbs Commonly-Grown in the USA —
Their Ancient Lore, Cultural Needs, & Present Uses

---

by Ruth H. Chambers

KEY TO SYMBOLS: (   ) — Botanical Name   **A** — Annual   **P** — Perennial
B— Biennial   **TP** — Tender Perennial   MD — Medicinal   CUL — Culinary
ORN — Ornamental   [   ] — Height   Exposure Needs

AJUGA *(Ajuga reptans)* or Bugleweed   **P**   Groundcover [under 1 ft.]   Sun or shade.

An excellent groundcover, making a thick, attractive mat which prevents weeds from growing. Spreads rapidly. Root produces a black dye for woolens.

ALOE *(barbadensis,* formerly Aloe Vera) First Aid or Medicine Plant **TP** MD [6 to 24 in.] Sun or bright shade.

A versatile succulent famous for its gelatinous sap which has enjoyed for centuries the reputation of being a miraculous skin healer (bites, stings, poison ivy, burns, & sunburn), skin softener and moisturizer. Legend tells us this was Cleopatra's beauty secret! Alexander the Great is said to have gone to war over aloe. He was persuaded by Aristotle to conquer the island of Socotra for the sole purpose of obtaining sufficient amounts of aloe to heal the wounds his soldiers suffered in their frequent battles. Although Aloe Vera is not the "bitter aloes" mentioned in the Bible, used with myrrh to embalm the body of Jesus (John 19:39), it is interesting to note that herbs are mentioned in the Bible more than 3,000 times! The US Navy once stockpiled Aloe Vera for use against the terrible radiation burn danger of atomic attack. A recent product made from aloe is known as Tennis Elbow Cream, reportedly successful in healing muscle ailments, scrapes, wounds, etc. To use your own Aloe plant, simply cut a piece from one of the leaves and apply the sap directly to the affected area. Winter indoors, water infrequently except in hot weather.

AMBROSIA *(Chenopodium botrys)* or Jerusalem Oak or Feather Geranium **A** ORN [2 to 3 ft.] Sun.

An intensely fragrant plant of unusual color. Leaves are olive-green above and purple-red below, and deeply cut, like those of an oak. The tall arching plumes are sweet-smelling and a favorite for flower arrangements and wreaths.

ANGELICA *(Angelica archangelica)* **B** CUL ORN [4–6'] Part sun.

Angelica is a giant relative of parsley and, as its name implies, has religious associations. Legend tells us that an angel presented the plant to man as a cure for the plague. In the Middle Ages, the roots were chewed to cure numerous diseases and it was also thought to protect against witchcraft. The hollow stems may be candied to decorate cakes and other desserts, cooked to flavor such fruits as rhubarb, or jellied. The boiled roots and stems may be eaten like celery. The oil from the plant is used as a flavoring for vermouth, chartreuse, and benedictine. In addition to using the handsome stalks for dried arrangements, one can use the leaves as a fixative in potpourri. Moist, rich soil and part shade are preferred.

ANISE *(Pimpinella anisum)* **A** CUL [to 2½'] Full sun.

Anise has been grown for centuries for its pungent, licorice-flavored and scented leaves and seeds. It is used in cakes and confections, toiletries and medicines. Mentioned in ancient Egyptian records, it was brought to Europe and England by the Romans who used it for a rich cake served at feasts and weddings. In Biblical times, anise was an acceptable payment for taxes. "Woe unto you scribes and Pharisees, hypocrites! For ye pay tithes of mint and anise and cummin, and have omitted the weightier matters of the law, judgement, mercy and faith; these ought ye to have done, and not to leave the other undone." (Matthew 23:25) Edward I of England reportedly needed money to repair London Bridge, so put a tax on this highly-priced herb which, in addition to its many virtues, was said to be excellent for bait in mousetraps! Currently, pungent anise flavors liquors such as anisette, pernod, chartreuse, etc., as well as medicines, notably paregoric. Chewing anise seeds is said to sweeten the breath and aid digestion. Leaves may be used in salads, especially with apples. In Holland the seeds are steeped in milk to induce sleep.

ANISE HYSSOP *(Agastache Foeniculum)* "Licorice Mint", "Anise Mint" **P** CUL [3']

Although often tabbed a mint, this plant does not spread like mint. Lovely, delicious anise scent and flavor of the leaves. Lavender flowers. Used for tea and potpourri.

ARTEMISIA (Silver, decorative forms. See also: tarragon, southernwood, and wormwood.) **Silver King** *(Artemisia Albula)* **P** ORN [to 3'] Full sun.

When dried, this is the basis for many Christmas wreaths and arrangements. Cut the stalks in late summer or early fall whenever seed heads are pure white. You may hang stalks upside down to dry, or lay them in baskets to dry in natural curved form. Wreaths can be more easily shaped with freshly-cut pliable stems. A striking garden accent plant, Silver King needs plenty of space to grow and spread. Plants should be divided every 3 years.

Silver Mound *(Artemisia Schmidtiana)* **P** LANDSCAPING [to 12"] Sun.

Grown mostly for its lovely color and feathery foliage, Silver Mound is particularly beautiful when viewed in the moonlight.

Silver Queen *(A. Ludoviciana var. Albula)* **P** ORN [to 18"] Sun.

Used in landscaping for accent, the deeply cut white leaves create a striking appearance. Winters over remarkably well. Wreath-making.

BASIL *(Ocimum basilicum)* Sweet Basil **A** CUL FRAGRANCE [1' to 2½'] Full sun.

Basil is one of the most popular culinary herbs today, numbering over 50 species. Rich in historical lore and legend, it is a passport to paradise in India, one of its forms considered sacred by Hindus and signifying reverence for the dead. Its name is said to derive from the Greek word for king — *basileias* — as well as from a fantastic monster, the basilisk. Basil was once used to make royal unguents, perfumes, and medicines. Today basil is the favorite herb for flavoring tomato dishes, with which it seems to have a special affinity. It is an essential ingredient in spaghetti sauce and pesto *(pistou* in France), an inspired green sauce for pasta. Basil is also reputed to repel mosquitoes and flies which is why the French often put pots of it in their sidewalk restaurants. Anise or clover-like flavor. Rich soil preferred. Some of the most popular varieties: (Note: "cv" = cultivar, cultivated variety)

Bush *(O.B. cv "Minimum")* **A** [1'] Good for pot culture and as a houseplant. Small, bushy, pretty shade of green with white flowers and tiny very aromatic leaves. (Miniature form known as "Greek")

Camphor *(O.B. cv kilimandscharicum)* **A** [3½'] Not culinary. Woody stems. Excellent mosquito and moth deterrent.

Cinnamon *(O.B. cv "Spice")* **A** [18"] Spicy scent and flavor.

Holy or "Sacred" *(O.B. 'sanctum')* **A** CUL/Asian This is a hairy Indian basil (hoary basil similar) with a very pungent and long-lasting spicy fragrance. Used as a fixative and for dried arrangements.

Lemon *(O.B. cv "Citriodorum")* **A** [18"] CUL From Thailand, this basil is lighter green with narrow leaves. Nice in pea soup and in potpourri and tussie mussies.

Lettuce Leaf *(O.B. cv "Crispum")* **A** [2'] Best variety for pesto and freezing. Similar to Sweet Basil.

Licorice *(O.B. cv "Anise")* **A** [2'] Darker green leaves, lavender flowers. Scent of fennel.

Opal *(O.B. cv Purpurascens)* **A** [2'] CUL Showy purple leaves and flowers. Lovely in dried arrangements. Place in white wine vinegar for a colorful and piquant herb vinegar! Opal Basil is the first and only herb to have won the All-American Award for Excellence. It was hybridized in 1962, combining a colorful Turkish species with the aromatic Sweet Basil, and can be used for all recipes calling for basil.

BAY, SWEET *(Laurus nobilis)* True Laurel. **TP** CUL MED AROMATIC Sun.

For pot culture [2–6'] in cold climates, where it is not likely to flower. (Winter inside; greenhouse best.) Leaves repel fleas, lice, moths, and the bugs found in flour or cereal. Wonderful flavoring for fish or meat stock, soups, and sauces. Caution: Always remove the leaf before serving soup or sauce, etc. The sharp edges can injure the intestinal tract! Also a frequent ingredient of potpourri and in wreaths. Bay Leaf crowns were used for centuries to honor scholars, victors, and heroes, and as a part of weddings and funerals. (*Baccalaureate-Bacca* + *laureus* = berry from laurel...and, one "earns her laurels," meaning honor and praise.) Greeks dedicated the Bay Tree to Apollo as an emblem of the Sun God's powers; believed to protect man from evil and guard his social well-being. Delphic priestesses held bay leaves between lips when making prophesies. "Neither witch nor devil, nor thunder nor lightning will hurt a man in a place where a Bay Tree is." — Culpepper.

BERGAMOT (*Monarda didyma*) or Bee Balm or Oswego Tea **P** CUL ORN [3'] Sun.

This handsome plant produces colorful flowers in many shades of red, from pink to purple, and may attract bees and hummingbirds. It is known as one of the "Freedom Teas" dating back to the Boston Tea Party, when patriots threw the highly taxed English tea into Boston Harbor, in protest. Indians of the Oswego tribe in New York State, in sympathy, showed the colonists how to use this plant to make a delicious, minty substitute tea from its fragrant leaves. This tea from a native American plant became one of the most popular teas of the American Revolution times. The leaves are also used in potpourri, jellies, and fruit salads. The red flowers are attractive in fresh or dried arrangements or in wreaths and potpourri. Fresh leaves rubbed on the skin are said to deter gnats and mosquitoes. May be grown in part shade.

BETONY (*Stachys officinalis*) Woundwort **HP** Grown for flowers & foliage. See Lamb's Ears, "Woolly Betony"

BORAGE (*Borago officinalis*) or Bee Bread **A** ORN [1–2½'] Full sun; rich soil.

Noted for its brilliant blue flowers which are floated in summer beverages or candied for dessert trimmings, the tender, young, hairless leaves and stems of borage are used for the cool, cucumber flavor they impart when chopped and added to salads, spreads, and drinks. *Warning:* Although high in potassium and calcium, borage also contains toxic substances which may cause liver damage if consumed in large quantities over a long period of time. Caution should be exercised in the internal use of this herb, at least until further studies prove it safe for human consumption. For fun with borage, throw its leaves on the dying barbecue coals for a small firecracker display. Sparks and pops will result, due to the nitrate of potash in borage!

BURNET (*Poterium Sanguisorba*) or Salad Burnet **P** CUL MD [1–2'] Full sun.

Historically, burnet was valued for its herbal healing qualities. It was thought to slow the blood in the veins. A tea made from its leaves is said to have been taken by Revolutionary soldiers the night before a battle so that if wounded, they would not bleed to death. Today it is a favorite salad herb and ingredient in herb cheeses, butters, and dips. It has a pleasant cucumber flavor with no unpleasant after-effects. Burnet will stay green in the garden all winter and is also a lovely houseplant.

CALENDULA (*Calendula officinalis*) or Pot Marigold **A** CUL ORN [12 to 18"] Sun.

A showy herb, this is easy to grow and presents a colorful display all summer if blossoms are cut off when spent. (Northern gardeners should start seed inside in individual peat pots for a longer harvest.) Flowers range from pale yellow to deep orange and are sun-worshippers, opening at dawn and closing at dusk. The petals are used for coloring foods and as an inexpensive substitute for saffron. Try the dried petals in rice for a lovely tint and in mixed herb teas for color and flavor.

CAMOMILE (*Matricaria recutita*) or German Camomile **A** CUL [18"] Sun.

There are two plants called camomile, but they are not botanically related. German Camomile is an erect herb that was once believed to be the "garden's physician" — that it would cure sick or dying plants when grown next to them! The blossoms are used to make tea, no doubt the camomile tea made for Peter Rabbit after one of his close calls in Mr. McGregor's garden. It is used to flavor a Spanish sherry wine called *manzanilla*, the Spanish term for camomile. (Camomile may be spelled with or without the "h"; I have dropped it for the sake of pronunciation — PVS) This form is also used medicinally, as a dye plant, insect-repellent, and in potpourri.

(*Chamaemelum nobile*) or Roman Camomile **P** [6 to 14"] Groundcover Sun.

This is a favorite groundcover, especially on large estates in Europe. If mowed regularly it grows in a thick mat. The grounds of Buckingham Palace are said to be planted with camomile to withstand the foot traffic. When walked upon, it emits the fragrance of ripe apples, hence its common name, ground apple. Old-fashioned garden seats made of hardened earth were covered with camomile, creating their own ambiance when sat upon! This form is used as a rinse for blonde hair, as an insect repellent, and in cosmetics.

CARAWAY (*Carum Carvi*) **B** CUL [1–2'] Full Sun.

A very ancient herb, seeds of which were found in the prehistoric lake dwellings of Switzerland. This herb, according to folklore, is credited with the power to keep lovers true and to cure hysterics. German and Austrian recipes particularly feature the seeds in their cakes, cookies, bread, and cheese. In some countries the leaves and tap roots are cooked as a vegetable. The white mature root looks like a carrot and has the same food value. It may be eaten raw, boiled or baked and is highly nutritious. Caraway seeds are used to flavor the liquor, kummel, and are a delicious seasoning for apple pie, apple sauce, cabbage, and boiled potatoes.

CATMINT (*Nepeta Mussinii*) **P** [18"] ORN SUN.

This is noted for its delicate and showy spring blossoms of purple and grayish foliage. Although cats are attracted to it and will nestle in it, catmint is not as appealing nor as devastating to the feline population as its cousin, catnip. Its unusual scent deters insects and attracts bees in the garden. Can be used as an ant and insect repellent.

CATNIP *(Nepeta Cataria)* **P CUL MD** [1½–2'] Sun or Semi-sun.

A member of the mint family, catnip causes the most sedate of cats to gambol with ecstasy and hilarious abandon. Even larger felines such as mountain lions are similarly affected. According to ancient legend, chewing catnip root gave humans prodigious courage and the tale is told of hangmen relying on this herb to face up to their gruesome task. Today catnip tea is greatly enjoyed for its flavor and also as a sedative and antidote for feverish colds. Dried catnip leaves are used to stuff "toys" for kitty.

CHERVIL *(Anthriscus Cerefolium)* **A** [to 24"] Part shade.

Often called "the gourmet cook's parsley" for its fragrant, anise-like flavor and delicate appearance, chervil is one of the *fines herbes* of French cooking. It makes a pretty and edible winter houseplant. A self-sowing herb.

CHICORY *(Cichorium intybus)* or Belgian Endive **P CUL** [over 5'] sun.

A common roadside plant, chicory is best known and used for its taproot which, when ground and roasted, is added to several well-known brands of coffee to reduce the bitter taste of caffeine. The bright blue blossoms open and close with clock-like regularity each morning and evening. Linnaeus, the great Swedish botanist, found their timing so reliable he included "chickory" in a floral clock that marked the hours with blooms. The blossoms open and close even when cut for a flower arrangement!

CHIVES *(Allium Schoenoprasum)* **P CUL** [to 12"] Full sun and rich soil preferred. *(Allium tuberosum)* — Garlic or Chinese Chives — same properties and culture as above.

Chives have been grown and used in the Orient for over 3,000 years. Smallest of the onion family, chives grow in clumps and may be raised in the house with equal success. Chives complement cheese, soups, salads, egg dishes, dips, spreads, and any food you would use onions with. The lovely lavender blossoms make this plant a favorite in the garden and for cutting. Garlic chives add a delicate garlic flavor to food. Their long flat leaves are unlike those of the ordinary chives (which have tubular leaves), and their blossoms are white. Romanian gypsies are said to have used chives in their fortune telling rites, hanging clumps in their wagons to drive away evil spirits. Combined with two or more herbs, chives are an essential ingredient in *bouquet garni* and *fines herbes.*

COMFREY *(Symphytum officinalis)* or Knitbone **P CUL MD** [to 3½'] Full sun; rich, moist soil.

Comfrey is related to borage and according to one writer has the following virtues: it is a vegetable, a tea, a healing herb, compost activator, a supplemental feed for livestock, and a soil conditioner! It has been grown for centuries as a medicinal plant and all-around tonic. While unable to actually knit broken bones, it was thought that an infusion made from its leaves helped the body to repair such injuries more speedily. Also, poultices were used for the same benefits. Comfrey is said to be a good source of calcium, potassium, vitamins A and C, and trace minerals. (*CAUTION:* There is currently some question about the safety of *consistent, long-term* use of comfrey internally. Until research proves otherwise, internal use of *mature* comfrey *leaves* only is recommended. Comfrey has been a well-documented healing herb for many centuries. Hopefully, it will be vindicated soon. — PVS)

CORIANDER *(Coriandrum sativum)* or Chinese Parsley or Cilantro **A** CUL [1 to 3'] Sun.

Coriander has been known and used for over 3,000 yeas. In Exodus 17:31 of the Bible, manna is described as "small, round and white like coriander seed and the taste of it...like wafers made with honey". It is widely used in East Indian curries and Chinese stir-fry dishes. In the Scandinavian countries the crushed seeds are used to make a special bread.

COSTMARY *(Chrysanthemum Balsamita)* or Bible Leaf or Alecost **P** CUL [1 to 3'] Sun.

The fragrance of mint, lemon, and balsam seem pleasantly combined in costmary leaves which, when young and tender, can be used in salads. Dried, they may be added to potpourri. They were once used to flavor beer, hence the name, alecost. It was called "Bible Leaf" in the olden days because the early settlers used the leaves as Biblical bookmarks. These served a double purpose, as they would nibble on the peppery-tasting leaves to keep awake when sermons were dull. Costmary will grow, but not blossom, in shade.

CURRY PLANT *(Helichrysum)* **P** ORN [1½'] Sun. Not for culinary use!

The fragrance strongly resembles real curry (which is a mixture of many spices). An attractive garden plant with gray foliage and yellow blossoms, the curry plant is nice to use for floral arrangements and wreaths.

DILL *(Anethum graveolens)* **A** CUL [1 to 3'] Sun. Rich soil preferred.

The magician's herb to thwart witches and cast spells, there were many ancient superstitions concerning dill. The earliest record of it appears on an Egyptian papyrus from 5,000 years ago. Dill was much treasured by the Greeks and Romans who used it to decorate their banquet halls and crown their heroes. Recipes calling for dillweed refer to the leaves and stems rather than the seeds. The seeds are practically synonymous with pickles but are also a delicious seasoning for breads and apple desserts. Dill leaves go well with most fish dishes and in dips and spreads. There is a variety of dill called "Bouquet" which produces shorter and bushier plants than the better-known tall type.

FENNEL *(Foeniculum vulgare)* **A** CUL [to 4'] Sun; well-limed soil. Grow away from other plants.

One of the oldest-known culinary herbs, we are told that the famous Battle of Marathon was fought in a field of fennel...the Greek word for which was Marathon. Thus fennel gave its Greek name to both the place and the long-distance run. The plant has a bulbous root which can be cooked as a vegetable. The anise-flavored stalks may be cooked also and are delicious raw in salads.

FENUGREEK *(Trigonella Foenumgraecum)* or Bird's Foot or Greek Hayseed **A** CUL MD [1 to 2'] Full sun; rich soil.

A member of the pea family, fenugreek was used by the ancient Egyptians as a spice. While recommended often for losing weight, fenugreek is eaten by Lybian and Eritrean women for gaining weight! The celery-flavored seeds have a spicy odor when crushed and are a common ingredient in curry powders, chutneys, and a famous Middle East candy called halvah. Commercially it is used for flavoring candy, ice cream, meat products, baked goods, and an artificial maple syrup. Oil from the seeds is used to create maple, vanilla, and butterscotch flavors in puddings. The seed pods resemble string beans (but grow upright) and reach 6" in length, containing about 16 yellow-brown seeds. The entire plant has a strong, sweet-clover scent and is often mixed with stored grain as an insect repellent.

FEVERFEW *(Chrysanthemum Parthenium)* **P** ORN MD [18 to 20"] Sun.

The flowers are made into a biological spray to kill insects. No culinary use but the flowerheads should be cut off and may effectively be added to dried winter arrangements. May not survive winters in wet soil or if allowed to go to seed.

GARLIC *(Allium Sativum)* **P** CUL MD [to 2'] Sun; moist rich soil.

One of the oldest-known foods and seasonings, garlic was traditionally thought to be a strength-giving herb and was fed in great quantities to the slaves working on the Egyptian pyramids. Greek and Roman athletes ate garlic before their contests and it was included in the K-rations of the Roman legions. Garlic in the diet is highly recommended for everyone today. Just chew lots of parsley after each indulgence!

GERMANDER *(Teucrium Chamaedrys)* **P** Groundcover or Hedge [to 18"] Full sun.

Formerly a highly esteemed treatment for gout in a blend of herbs, germander is grown today as a groundcover and an attractive hedge or border plant. A favorite among herb growers because it can be kept pruned neatly for knot gardens.

HELIOTROPE *(Heliotropium arborescens)* **TP** Sun.

Called 'Cherry Pie' in Victorian Days, this plant has sweet purple flowers. Not to be confused with *perennial* Valerian which has a floral fragrance similar to the scent of Heliotrope.

HOREHOUND *(Marrubium vulgare)* **P** MD CUL [2 to 3'] Full sun.

The leaves of this plant have provided the home remedy for coughs, colds, and sore throats for many generations. Horehound is the principal ingredient in many candies and cough drops today. The Greeks used it as an antidote for mad-dog bites, thus the common name, "hoarhound". The herb was used in England for beer-making and for snuff, when dried and ground. It was one of the bitter herbs used by the Jews during Passover. Do grow horehound to try your luck with syrup or candy. It's fun!

HYSSOP *(Hyssopus officinalis)* **P** ORN [to 18"] Sun or partial shade. Well-limed soil.

In the days before air-fresheners and room deodorizers, hyssop was one of the aromatic herbs strewn on floors of homes and churches to emit a pleasing fragrance when walked upon. Known as a "strewing" herb, it provided a more agreeable atmosphere, often masking an unpleasant one. It was also used as a flavoring for gamy meats, as a cough syrup, and an antiseptic. Today it flavors the liquor, chartreuse. An attractive shrub-like herb with appealing blue blossoms, hyssop is often used in hedges and knot gardens. Other modern uses include hyssop as a fixative in potpourri, a white fly or cabbage butterfly deterrent, and in cosmetics.

LADY'S MANTLE *(Alchemilla vulgaris)* **P** MD Sun.

According to legend this herb will promote quiet sleep for ladies who place it under their pillows. An easy-care plant, Lady's Mantle is used in colonial beds and for dried arrangements.

LAMB'S EARS *(Stachys byzantina)* or Woolly Betony **P** ORN [2'] Sun.

During the Middle Ages, the large leaves of this herb were used to bandage wounds, hence its name "woundwort". Today it is grown as an ornamental which never fails to become a conversation piece. Garden visitors will enjoy the incredible softness of its leaves and the strong likeness to real lamb's ears! The near-white foliage makes it an appealing plant in the garden, as well as in nosegays and wreaths.

LAVENDER *(Lavendula angustifolia)* or English Lavender **P** FRAGRANCE MD [2 to 3'] Full sun.

Probably the all-time favorite fragrant herb, the Greeks and Romans bathed in lavender-scented water and it was from the Latin word, lavo (to wash) that the herb took its name. Washerwomen in England were once known as "lavenders". Highly-esteemed by royalty, it is said that Queen Victoria kept the castle filled with its scent. Charles VI, Emperor of France, used satin cushions stuffed with lavender, and Napoleon is said to have used 60 bottles of lavender water a month, pouring it over his neck and shoulders whenever he washed. It is now the basis for numerous commercial and homemade products such as perfumes, soaps, sachets, and potpourri. (Pronounced po-poo-ree) Even tobacco mixtures include lavender. Other popular varieties of hardy lavender include 'Hidcote' (a deep purple blossom) and 'Munstead' (shorter and more hardy for coldest climates). The *Tender-Perennial* lavenders are more suitable for the warmer climates; Spanish (Lavendula stoechas); Lavendula 'Lanata' (almost white foliage with rose-purple blossoms; and French (Lavendula dentata), which grows up to 3' in frost-free regions and has indented green foliage. This variety is nice for hanging patio plants in cold climates, but needs richer soil and more moisture than other lavenders.

LEEK *(Allium porrum)* **B** CUL [to 3'] Sun.

Leeks rank with shallots as the aristocrats of the onion family. Considered a 'gourmet' vegetable, they are expensive to buy. Rich in several minerals, leeks may be used as cooked vegetables, in soups, or served raw in salads.

LEMON BALM *(Melissa officinalis)* or Balm **P** CUL [to 3'] Sun.

Lemon Balm is a must for every garden. Its fragrant lemon-minty leaves make a delicious caffeine-free herb tea (or tisane), sweetened with honey, if desired, and served either hot or cold. The leaves are also used to flavor jellies, fruit cups, salads, and desserts. Easy to grow from seed, lemon balm comes back dependably, year after year. Add the dried leaves to potpourri for their lemon fragrance.

LEMON GRASS *(Cymbopogon citratus)* **A** CUL [4'] CUL

Containing Vitamin A, lemon grass makes a fine tea with cloves, and is used in Indonesian cookery. It can be grown in pots in northern areas and is a fine addition to potpourri.

LEMON VERBENA *(Aloysia triphylla)* **TP** CUL [3 to 10'] Sun.

Unexcelled as far as lemon fragrance and flavor are concerned, lemon verbena is more difficult to grow than lemon balm in the North because it doesn't winter over very well when brought inside in the Fall. But it is worth the effort to buy new plants each summer, as it is wonderful in potpourri and in any recipes calling for a lemon flavor. In 1864 Emperor Maximilian and Empress Carlotta planted lemon verbena in the superb gardens around Montezuma's palace in Mexico. He was so fond of it that he named it "Yerba Louisa" after Carlotta's mother. In Spain today, Herba Louisa Tea, sweetened with honey, is still a popular drink, as it is in France, there called "Vervein". The Victorians used the leaves in finger bowls.

LOVAGE *(Levisticum officinale)* **P** CUL [3 to 7'] Sun or part-shade.

The giant among herbs, lovage resembles celery in appearance and taste; the tender, young leaves being used in salads or other dishes requiring a celery taste. The seeds may be used, and the hollow mature stalks make good drinking straws for vegetable and tomato juice cocktails. The Greeks and Romans chewed on lovage seeds to aid digestion, and legend tells of seeds put into potions to conjure up love spells, thus giving the plant its name of lovage or love parsley. Caution: consumption of large amounts of lovage can harm kidneys.

LUNARIA *(Lunaria biennis)* or Money Plant or Silver Dollar **B** ORN [to 2'] Full sun.

Strictly an ornamental, lunaria produces bright purplish blossoms in the Spring and transparent seed pods the size of quarters in the Fall. The latter are much prized for dried flower arrangements.

MARIGOLD *(Tagetes lucida)* Sweet-Scented or Anise-Flavored Marigold **TP** [6"–36"] Sun.

Native to Mexico, where it is called "Cloud Plant", this variety of marigold is perennial in warm climates, but tender in northern regions, where it makes a delightful potted plant to bring inside for the winter. The leaves of this variety are used for tea and flavoring. A taller variety from this family (3'-from Africa) and a smaller 'Tagetes patula' have been found to be the most effective marigolds to dispel nematodes in the soil where they are planted. 'Irish Lace' (Tagetes filifolia) is a tiny 6" white-flowered marigold with ferny foliage.

MARJORAM, SWEET *(Origanum Majorana)* or Garden Or Knotted Marjoram **TP CUL** [1 to 2'] Full sun.

Cultivated in ancient Egypt and adored by the Greeks and the rest of the Eastern world, marjoram was an almost-universal symbol of honor and joy, used as a food, medicine, and perfume. It is one of the sacred herbs of India and Shakespeare compared it to a "virtuous gentlewoman". Marjoram was also used as a strewing herb, a washwater scent, and to clean furniture. Once used in beer-making before hops were discovered, marjoram's fresh or dried leaves are now added to meats, salads, eggs, soups, sauces, vinegars, vegetables, teas, and jellies. However, the flavor is pervasive, especially when the herb is dried, so it should be used with discretion. Pot Marjoram (Origanum Onites) is a tender perennial suited for pot culture, with a sharper fragrance and flavor than Sweet Marjoram or Oregano.

MINT *(Mentha,* Family, *many* varieties) **P CUL MD** [1 to 2'] Part shade, moist soil.

All mints are spreading plants and must be kept separated from each other to prevent cross-pollination and interrooting, which will weaken their fragrances and flavors. They are used in scenting potpourri and in flavoring drinks, candies, vegetables, and a host of commercial products including toothpaste, chewing gum, and medicines. Strong-smelling mint leaves are rubbed on the skin to repel insects. The most commonly used mints of the dozens of varieties are listed below.

Apple Mint *(M.suaveolens)* Soft-leaved, white-flowered, fruity fragrance, apple flavor.

Orange Bergamot *(M.piperita citrata)* Citrus-flavored, nice for tea or potpourri.

Pennyroyal, English *(M.Pulegium)* Not recommended for culinary use today but is a very fragrant addition to mint potpourri and tussie mussies and an effective insect repellent for cats and dogs. Once used by royalty to combat body lice; hence its name! The most powerful mint as an insect-chaser.

Peppermint *(M. x piperita)* or White Peppermint in contrast to the next kind. This is the regular peppermint most likely found in nurseries. Wonderful flavor.

Peppermint, Black-Stemmed *(M.piperita var.)* From England or Yugoslavia, this is the loveliest mint of all in terms of fragrance and flavor, and the one used for commercial trade. Not black-stemmed at all, but a darker purple stem and veins in the leaves than found in regular peppermint or orange peppermint, all of which are purple-flowered.

Pineapple Mint *(M.S.var.)* Pineapple fragrance when young. Flavor does not equal fragrance. Stunning garden and fresh arrangement conversation piece because of creamy patches on leaves.

Spearmint *(M.spicata)* This is the mint meant when recipes call for "mint". The classic flavoring for mint juleps, it is also the most-used mint for culinary purposes.

NASTURTIUM *(Tropaeolum majus)* or Indian Cress **A CUL ORN** [1 to 2'] Sun.

Cultivated for their showy garden display of bright color, nasturtiums also provide peppery-flavored leaves and flowers to be eaten as a salad or part of a green salad. These are high in vitamin C content. However, the seeds *(only)* contain oxalic acid and should not be consumed.

OREGANO *(Origanum vulgare)* or Wild Marjoram **P** CUL [2'] Sun.

Oregano has a fragrance and taste similar to marjoram, but stronger and less sweet. It may be used fresh or dried in the same foods you would use marjoram or thyme for, especially in Italian, Spanish, or Mexican dishes. Oregano is the pizza herb and was popularized in America by the GI's returning from Italy and Greece after World War II. It is particularly good in beef dishes, and a special ingredient of hoagies. There are several varieties from England, Greece, Spain, Mexico, and Sicily (the grocery variety may be a blend of several), so the flowers range from white to purple. Greek Oregano (O. prismaticum) has a stronger, more pungent flavor than the others. 'Dittany of Crete' (O. dictamnus) is an annual variety with pink flowers and a marjoram flavor. (An ingredient of vermouth, this variety only grows to 9" and wants shade!) Fresh or dried oregano blossoms are a joy to behold in fragrant tussie mussies or arrangements.

PARSLEY *(Petroselinum crispum)* French or Curly Parsley **B** CUL [to 1'] Rich soil. *Petroselinum neapolitanum)* Italian or Plain-Leaf **B** CUL [to 2'] Rich soil.

Both varieties of parsley can be grown in sun or part-shade. Unfortunately, this highly nutritious (rich source of iron and vitamins A and C) herb is often regarded as a garnish only and is left on the plate untouched! While the curly variety is more decorative, the plain-leafed parsley has a higher vitamin content and is considered by many to have more flavor. One of the few pests that attack parsley is a handsome green caterpillar with black stripes. If you find one on your parsley, please don't be tempted to do him in! This visitor, known as the parsley worm, will become a stunning black swallowtail butterfly, an endangered species! So please plant extra parsley plants, just in case!

PYRETHRUM *(Chrysanthemum coccineum)* or Painted Daisy **P** Insecticide [1'] Sun.

Pyrethrum flowers are used to make a biological spray or dusting powder to kill insects. Attractive pastel blossoms.

ROQUETTE *(Eruca vesicania sativa)* or Rocket **A** CUL [to 12"] Sun; rich, moist soil.

Roquette is a French salad herb with a distinct but puzzling flavor. It has been described as mushroomy, turnipy, and mustardy and should be used more as a seasoning, although many Italians eat it by the bowlful. It may be cooked as a vegetable or chopped fine to use in melted butter as a sauce for seafood, pasta, etc.

ROSEMARY *(Rosmarinus officinalis)* **TP** CUL [3 to 6'] Sun or part-sun; loves misting.

The joy and dispair of many herb growers, rosemary was a favorite of the ancients, its use going back 3,000 years. Legends concerning it are legion and it has been the symbol of fidelity, friendship, and remembrance for centuries. Its name seems to have come from its affinity for growing by the sea, *ros* meaning dew and *marinus* meaning of the sea. Perhaps the name alludes to rosemary's silvery-blue flowers as well as its love of moisture. A native of the Mediterranean where it grows wild on rocky hillsides, its intense fragrance can be smelled 20 miles at sea during the harvest season when the wind is right! The Queen of Hungary bathed in an essence of rosemary daily and was so beautiful at 72 that the enchanted King of Poland begged for her hand. This "Hungary Water" is the oldest-known perfume and is still made today. Rosemary is sometimes difficult to raise but is worth every effort. It generally does not easily winter over indoors in the North, but it makes an attractive houseplant which can be shaped in the bonsai manner if you have a green thumb. Layer the branches in early summer for fall houseplants.

RUE *(Ruta graveolens)* or "Herb of Grace" **P** ORN [1 to 3'] Sun or part-sun.

Rue is more important today for its distinctive blue-green foliage, yellow-button flowers, and erect stance in the garden than for its usefulness (although it can be used as an insect and moth deterrent). This charming and graceful plant can be used for a hedge in the garden. Once a medicinal herb, bunches of it were used to ward off the plague, and King Mithridates is said to have taken small doses of rue and other poisonous herbs to make himself immune to assassination attempts. The word rue means sorrow, pity, or forgiveness. At one time its leaves were added to holy water used to bless sinners. Unfortunately some individuals are allergic to rue and contact with the plant in the hot sun may cause a rash.

SAFFLOWER *(Carthamus tinctorius)* or False Saffron **A** [2½'] Sun.

The orange petals of this herb are used for coloring and flavoring food. The plant is also used in cosmetics and as a dye plant.

SAFFRON *(Crocus sativus)* Autumn or Spanish Crocus **P** CUL [1½'] Sun or part-sun in sheltered location. Rich soil.

A Fall-flowering plant, saffron is the world's costliest herb. For centuries it has been grown for the flavoring known as saffron. It takes about 8,000 flowers to produce only 3½ oz. of the uniquely fragrant and flavorful dried stigmas. Nero is said to have ordered saffron sprinkled on the streets of Rome for one of his extravaganzas. Saffron is grown mainly in Europe and Asia today as a food coloring and flavoring agent, but in the USA it is a favorite plant since it blooms in the Fall when most flowers are gone. Each bulb or corm will produce several 3 to 4" stems and each stem will produce a single star-shaped flower. Left undisturbed, the corms will multiply and the flowers increase in beauty each year. Saffron is most often used to add spice and a golden hue to rice.

SAGE *(Salvia officinalis)* Garden Sage **P** CUL [2½'] Sun or part-sun.

Garden sage is a favorite seasoning for pork, sausage, poultry seasoning, and cheese. In bygone days sage enjoyed a reputation as being a cure-all for ailments ranging from wounds and broken bones to stomach disorders and loss of memory. It was so highly regarded by the Chinese that they would trade 4 units of China tea for 1 of sage. Sage tea is said to have digestive virtues and to slow down the aging process. Some of the other sages (which are primarily ornamental) are fun and useful to grow.

Clary Sage *(Salvia viridis)* The *Biennial* ("true Clary Sage") type grows to 5' with blue or white flowers, and is lovely for hummingbirds and beauty in the garden. Its oil is used as a toning-down fixative in perfumes. The *Annual* Clary Sage grows to 2', has white, pink, or purple flowers, and no scent. But it is stunning in the garden and in arrangements. Both types like dry sandy soil.

Pineapple Sage *(Salvia 'elegans')* **TP** ORN CUL [3'] A real conversation-piece, the leaves of this ornamental, when rubbed, emit a sweet truly-pineapple fragrance. Its red blossoms in late summer are striking. Roots easily from cuttings for houseplants which make delightful winter gifts. The leaves are used in tea, fruit cup, or minced in cream cheese.

Purple Sage *(Salvia O. 'purpurascens')* **TP** ORN [2'] Sun. Lovely for color in the garden, fresh or dried arrangements, and houseplants, rooted from cuttings. Ditto for *Tri-Colored* (S. horminum).

SANTOLINA *(Santolina chamaecyparissus)* or Lavender Cotton **P** [18 to 24"] Sun. Gray foliage. *(Santolina virens)* The same properties except for the color, which is bright green.

Both varieties of santolina are grown for their fine appearance in the garden. They can be trimmed as hedges and are especially effective in knot gardens.

SAVORY *(Satureja hortensus)* Summer Savory **A** CUL [18"] Sun. Sow seeds inside early, in peat pots. *(Satureja montana)* Winter Savory **P** CUL [2'] Sun. Sow seeds inside early, in peat pots.

Best to start the seeds in individual peat pots early for a longer harvest season and so the roots won't be disturbed by transplanting. Propagate winter variety by spring layering. Both kinds are grown as a food seasoning, the "peppery" taste qualifying Savory as a salt-substitute herb. Known as "the bean herb", Savory adds zest to all bean dishes, the winter variety having a stronger flavor.

SCENTED GERANIUMS *(Pelargoniums)* **TP** CUL ORN [to 4'] Full sun.

These sensual plants are a marvelous way to introduce the delights of fragrant plants to the novice gardener. The aromatic leaves are used for flavoring beverages, jellies, and desserts; for fragrant fresh or dried tussie mussies; and for sachets and potpourri. They must be brought in before frost, but mid-summer cuttings make wonderful winter houseplants. A few of the most popular varieties are rose, lemon, apple, orange, strawberry, cinnamon, nutmeg, and peppermint scented-leaf geraniums. The main difference between scented geraniums and zonal geraniums, besides the fragrance, is that the flowers are tiny on the scented ones.

SESAME *(Sesamum indicum)* or Benne **A** CUL [to 24"] Sun.

Sesame is cultivated in Asia and Africa for its oil and nut-flavored seeds which are used whole in cakes, cookies, and breads. Seed pods are borne in pretty, trumpet-shaped white flowers which wither in late summer. When fully ripened the pods suddenly burst open, scattering the seed. The magic password, "Open Sesame", used by Ali Baba in "The Arabian Nights" tale probably originated from this characteristic of sesame.

SOAPWORT *(Saponaria officinalis)* or Saponaria **P** COSMETIC [to 12"] Sun or part-sun.

This herb contains saponin which creates a foam in water. It can be used as a mild shampoo.

SORREL *(Rumex acestosa)* **P** CUL [to 2'] Sun.

Sorrel has sour taste but has high amounts of vitamins A and C. The small, tender leaves may be used in cole slaw and mixed salads. Mature leaves are excellent for the classic sorrel soup and for sauces and dips.

SOUTHERNWOOD *(Artemisia abrotanum)* **P** LANDSCAPE, INSECT REPELLENT [3 to 6'] Sun.

Southernwood dates back to Roman times when it was used medicinally for an array of diseases and ailments. At one time it was thought to prevent baldness. Once known as "Old Man" and "Lad's Love" and "Maiden's Ruin", it was considered to be an aphrodisiac and was used to make love potions. Use sprigs of it in your storage bags and blanket chests to repel moths. Extremely aromatic, a few fresh sprigs placed in a hot oven will allegedly kill kitchen odors. Every garden should have at least one of each of the exciting varieties: lemon, camphor, and tangerine-scented southernwoods. *All* are conversation pieces, especially the camphor — which elicits memories of childhood home cold remedies. The tangerine-scented is the "Tree Southernwood", growing to 6'. These are shrubby, woody-stemmed plants with delicate foliage.

TANSY *(Tanacetum vulgare)* **P** ORN INSECT REPELLENT [to 3'] Sun.

Medieval herbalists recommended this plant as a cure for, among other things, gout, the plague, colic, and cramps. The leaves applied as a poultice were said to remove freckles and sunburn. Tansy is presently an ornamental whose foliage is used in fresh and dried arrangements and it is also used as an aromatic moth deterrent. Fresh leaves strewn at the doorstep will repel ants. *Caution: tansy is toxic to cattle. Do not plant where livestock graze!* Not recommended for regular or consistent human consumption. (Occasional use in minute amounts is not considered harmful.) "Fernleaf" tansy *(T. vulgare "crispum")* is a lovely variety to use for fresh or dried arrangements or tussie-mussies.

TARRAGON, FRENCH *(Artemisia dracunculus "sativa")* **P** CUL [3'] Sun; part-sun.

If you like the flavor of licorice, this herb is for you! The leaves are used both fresh and dried in a variety of dishes. To make tarragon vinegar for salad dressing, place 2 or 3 sprigs in a bottle of red wine vinegar, seal tightly and set aside in a warm place for a month. Tarragon is the third herb used in *fines herbes* blends, along with chervil and chives. Be sure to purchase *French* tarragon *plants, not* the Russian variety as it is tasteless (even though this kind can be grown from seed)! Propagate *established* French Tarragon plants by root divisions in the spring. Survives best with good drainage. It is difficult to grow in warm climates because it needs a cold spell for dormancy between seasons.

THYME *(Thymus vulgaris)* Common Thyme **P** CUL MD Sun or part-sun; good drainage.

The upright, woody-stemmed varieties of thyme, such as English Broadleaf or French Narrowleaf are the preferred thymes for culinary use, although *all* are edible. The upright types grow from 10–18" tall and have numerous valuable flavoring and scenting uses outside of the kitchen, too. They are used in soaps, medicines, perfumes, sachets, and incense. The low-growing groundcover or "creeping" thymes are sometimes grouped together as "Mother-of-Thyme" to distinguish them from the upright varieties. All are excellent for use in rock gardens, raised beds, or on banks or hills. Here are just a few of the more than 400 varieties of thyme to consider for your garden enrichment, of both the upright and creeping types, depending upon the height.

Albus *(T.praecox)* [5"] Early-blooming, white flowers. Good for flagstone paving.

Caraway *(T.Herba Barona)* [5"] Rose-purple blooms; culinary substitute for caraway seeds.

Coconut *(T.Pulegiodes 'Coccineus')* [4"] Crimson blooms. Excellent for groundcover.

Creeping *(T.Serpyllum)* [6"] Mother-of-Thyme or Wild Thyme. Pink spring blooms. Stepping stones.

Creeping, Golden *(T.S.'Aureus')* [8"] ORN Yellow-green leaves; groundcover.

Lemon *(T.x citriodorus)* [18"] CUL Heavenly lemon-thyme scent and flavor.

Rosy *(T.S.roseum)* [3"] Dark rose blooms in early summer.

Silver *(T.V.'Argenteus')* ORN [18"] Silvery leaves. Especially nice for rock garden.

Woolly *(T.pseudolanuginosis)* [3"] Showy grayish wooly-looking groundcover.

VALERIAN *(Valeriana officinalis)* Phew Plant **P** MD [2 to 5'] Sun.

Above ground, this is an attractive plant with feathery foliage and sweet-smelling flowers with the fragrance of heliotrope. However, its carrot-type root has an unpleasant odor so pronounced that the herb has come to be known as the Phew Plant! Nevertheless, cats find the smell of the root irresistible. According to legend, it was the secret weapon carried by the Pied Piper of Hamlin! Valerian has several medicinal uses and its oil is a favorite in perfumes.

WINTERGREEN *(Gaultheria procumbens)* or Teaberry **P** MD [to 6"] Shade.

This is a lovely wild plant bearing shiny green leaves and scarlet berries. Its oil has been used to flavor beverages, chewing gum, and candy in the past but its current use is primarily pharmaceutical. A terrarium favorite.

WOAD *(Isatis tinctoria)* or Dyer's Weed **B** ORN [to 4'] Sun or part-sun.

Woad is a yellow-flowered member of the mustard family, the leaves of which produce a rich indigo blue dye used by some weavers and spinners to tint wool. The ancient Britons (Celts) stained designs on their arms and legs with it.

WOODRUFF, SWEET *(Galium odoratum)* **P** CUL GROUNDCOVER [to 1"] Shade.

Woodruff is a most attractive groundcover which spreads rapidly and bears dainty white star-shaped blossoms in the spring. The dried leaves are sweet-smelling, the fragrance often compared to that of newly-mown hay or of vanilla, and are being used increasingly as a fixative in potpourri. The flowers are used in making the famous German May Wine. Historically, Teutonic warriors wore woodruff in their helmets to promote success in battle. In the Middle Ages, garlands of woodruff were hung in houses as air-fresheners and Elizabeth I is said to have honored favored individuals with a sprig of this delightful herb. *Caution:* toxic to humans if consumed in large amounts.

WORMWOOD *(Artemisia absinthium)* **P** ORN MD [to 4'] Sun.

Wormwood's name is derived from its medicinal property of expelling worms, for which it has been known since ancient times. It is still used for worming animals. An Egyptian papyrus dated 1,600 years B.C. describes this herb and later it was one of the bitter herbs mentioned in the Bible. It is the principal ingredient in the dangerous drink, absinthe, which is now illegal world-wide because it destroys the nervous system. However, it is now an ingredient in vermouth and other liquors as well as liniments. And it is a reputable moth-chaser. **Sweet Wormwood** *(Artemisia annua),* or "Sweet Annie", is a hardy *annual* because it self-sows vigorously when established. Growing to 3 or 4' in the shape of a feathery Christmas Tree, this fragrant delight is used for fresh or dried arrangements, wreaths, potpourri, and as an aromatic moth deterrent.

YARROW *(Achillea millefolium)* or Milfoil **P** ORN [to 3'] Sun.

A pleasing addition to the flower or herb bed, yarrow is cultivated today mainly for use in fresh or dried arrangements. Common yarrow was an old-time medicinal herb, receiving its generic name from Achilles who is said to have used it as a styptic to stop the bleeding of his wounded men in the Trojan Wars. Sometimes used to cure cuts, it has been called woundwort, nosebleed, and sanguinary. A tea brewed from its leaves was said to relieve colds. There are several varieties of yarrow bearing white, yellow, pink, or red flowers.

GROWING FRAGRANT HERBS FOR PROFIT

By Phyllis V. Shaudys

*This booklet is
gratefully dedicated
to my husband and children
who have lovingly and patiently
endured my preference for spending more
time in the garden than the kitchen so often!*

First Published by PINE ROW PUBLICATIONS, Box 428, Washington Crossing, PA 18977

Introduction

In July 1976 I started selling sachets in two gift shops, and by November I had eleven outlets. By July of 1977 I was turning down requests from new merchants because the local demand for my herbal products exceeded my supply. The second year my profits have doubled. It will be some time before we can live off of my herb business, but my dream is to double my profits each year until we reach the point where my husband can retire early from the industrial rat-race and enjoy sharing the outdoor work with me in the herb gardens!

Friends and acquaintances have deluged me with questions about how I managed "so quickly and easily" to break into the marketplace with my product. There is so much revived interest in herbs these days that I decided to write this booklet to share my experience with other herb lovers.

It has never seemed like "work" to me, since every contact with herbs is a sheer sensual and spiritual delight. If you already know the joy of drinking your own hot peppermint tea, the fragrance of a pineapple sage leaf crushed between your fingers, the pungent aroma of picking thyme or camphor southernwood, or the gourmet taste of fresh summer savory or basil on your garden vegetables, then you are ready to embark on a career which will reward you many thousands of times in terms of health, delight, economy, *and profit!*

How It Began...

My love for herbs began in 1960 when I visited Adelma Simmons's herb farm in Connecticut during a vacation. Mrs. Simmons cheerfully stopped her weeding and guided me through her herb gardens, lovingly introducing me to the delightful scents of dozens of herbs. For several subsequent summers our vacation itinerary and our vacation budget included enough time and money for me to treat myself to a few new herbs and Mrs. Simmons's newest pamphlet or book during my annual "pilgrimage" to *Caprilands*.

Soon I was making sachets of fragrant herbs for gift-giving and creating my own seasoning blends for culinary use. It wasn't long before friends were requesting that I sell my sachets for *them* to use as unique gifts for others. So for many years my hobby paid for itself. I was not seeking markets, but was pleased to be able to pay for my fabrics, oils, and fixatives with the "pin money" from orders from friends and Women's Exchanges.

Even while I was working at a full-time job for five years, I tended my gardens and dried my herbs and flowers. In fact, this *was* my relaxation on weekends — to drink in the beauty and fragrance of nature's perfume while I picked the herbs in the summer, or cleaned the dried leaves off the stems on a cold winter's night.

In June of 1976 three members of our family found ourselves jobless. Our two oldest children were college students and were unable to find summer jobs, and I had just resigned my position. Half-jokingly, one of the children suggested we make "Bicentennial" sachets out of the dried flowers and herbs I had stored over the years. Our historic community expected thousands of tourists over the summer, so maybe we could merchandise sachet souvenirs. It didn't take me long to find the right red, white, and blue flowery prints and velvet ribbons for our "local" souvenirs. Even our youngest, our then 13-year-old daughter, entered into the spirit of the venture, and one week later we had our sachets made, labeled, packaged, and selling in two local gift shops!

A month later, (because it took this long for a new batch of fresh potpourri to "set" and blend), heady from repeat orders from our first two outlets, I was confident enough in our product to become a traveling saleswoman. I felt compelled to succeed for the sake of the children, as they had all spent many hours helping me pick and dry herbs, propagate new plants, establish an herb bed, weed, cut and sew material, and fill, label, and package the sachets. Their concerted and enthusiastic effort prodded me into becoming aggressive with the sachets.

So it was with a large gulp that I headed for the marketplace with my wares, not *daring* to fail, as I had three children expecting some kind of wage for their efforts. I went to several surrounding towns, carefully selecting gift shops that carried unique, hand-crafted, or "back-to-nature"-type items. Out of thirteen attempts in a two-month period, my product was rejected by only two store-owners. And one of the rejections was on the grounds that the store already carried enough bicentennial items, and the merchant warmly accepted other items later. In fact, on the basis of samples I *mailed* to her, since I did not want to face a second rejection, her first order was for over $70 worth!

In the fall I changed my sachet fabrics to reds and greens for the holidays, and found eager reception from all of my summer merchants. I also added a few different products, to test their sales appeal, such as potpourri in jars and herbal wreaths. Some of the merchants were so enthusiastic about my products that they gave me many suggestions for items I could experiment with in their stores. It wasn't long before I began to enjoy making deliveries, as the store-owners were now "friends" and almost co-partners in my business venture!

To one proprietor I happened to mention that I couldn't bear to throw out any part of my herb plants, and that I even saved the fragrant dried stems after defoliation. She replied, "Well, figure out a way to sell the stems and bring them in the next time!" So I labeled and tied bundles of twigs with red or green yarn, placed them in a plastic bag labeled FIREPLACE FUN WITH FRAGRANCES, and explained that after identifying the individual scents, one should burn the twigs in the fireplace for additional aroma. This item sold out in one week. Some grandparents bought sets for all their grandchildren, and most of the rest were sold to Sunday School and elementary school teachers by the dozens!

By mid-December, when many of the stores were still calling me for repeat orders, I had used up all of my herbs. So I became committed to expanding my gardens and continuing my business the coming year. I had found marketable products, and the demand exceeded the supply. My Christmas present from my husband was a set of indoor lights so I could grow perennial herbs from seed and increase my produce many-fold for the future.

I must admit that my "business" took a loss the first year, since I never fully re-paid myself for the initial investments in materials, or for my own labors. All "profits" were used to pay the children, amounting to $1.67 per hour for each of them. (Most new home businesses will not start out employing so many helpers!) But this second year was a different story, since I did all the work alone...devoting most of my time year-round to the business. The children found more lucrative employment the second summer. I was free to invest profits into improving the quality of my products, developing new ones, and finding better packaging methods.

There are many advantages to having a home business. You are your own boss, your hours are your own, and your future is your own. I'd like to share some tips from my own experience which might be helpful to any of you who are considering such a venture, or to those of you who might want to make herbal products to be sold at bazaars or fairs to bring "profits" to the organizations you belong to.

How To Proceed

Plants

Unless you have been drying herbs and flowers for years, as I had been, and have gallons of potpourri already made up, as I did, it will take you longer than one year to introduce a finished product to the market from your garden. (Unless you buy dried herbs wholesale — but my own experience has been that commercially dried herbs do not *begin* to compare in fragrance and color with those dried slowly and naturally at home.)

That first fall I feverishly propagated my 16 established herbs, by cuttings and division, in order to start production on a larger scale the next year. My three original lavender plants became 25 new plants by the next season. But it was a couple of years before the new plants produced blossoms lavishingly. I also only had 6 rose bushes, but friends and neighbors soon began drying their rose petals for me after I explained how easy it is to dry them after the vase arrangements are "spent." (Simply place petals on a paper towel or napkin out of the sunlight!) A local nursery also saved its rose petals for me after each weekly trimming. I spread them out on trays of toweling in any room I had air-conditioning in, as this quickly removed the moisture from the petals.

Your first investment should be to establish some of the hardy perennial herbs in your garden. Lavender is, by far, the most popular fragrance. If you have lots of time and little money, just buy 2 or 3 English Lavender plants the first spring, as "mother" plants for future propagation. If you have a coldframe or indoor lights, you can start lavender and nearly all perennial herbs from seed in February or March, but it will take a few years before there'll be a profusion of blossoms from young plants.

You will not need a field of herbs to launch a business. Mine was started from 16 well-established herbs which were located in various small gardens surrounding our house walls, and in one perennial border. During the summer of 1976 and the spring of 1977 my family helped me establish 3 herb beds, one 15' x 30', and two of them 5' x 45'. I could have managed with less space, but I wanted to experiment with many other herbs.

In addition to lavender, you should certainly start out with members of the reliable mint family. My favorites are peppermint, applemint, spearmint, pineapple mint, orange mint, and pennyroyal. (These pungent leaves make a heavenly base for my "Sweet Pillows".) All mints will spread rapidly, even the first year, if not allowed to dry out. Be sure to keep the various kinds separated so they will not grow together and become less distinguishable in scents and flavors. I have my mints either in separate gardens, or well-separated by deep dividers in the ground. You will probably need only one mint plant of each kind if you purchase the plants locally when you are starting out. The mints will grow well *anywhere,* but some sun is beneficial. Mints like wet feet and are the main exception to the general rule that herbs prefer dry, well-drained soil. (Of course, any new plants of any kind should not be allowed to dry out before the roots become well-established.)

Other fragrant perennials to start out with are: bergamot, catnip, camomile, lemon balm, lemon verbena, rosemary, rue, sage, the southernwoods (camphor and lemon primarily), tansy, thyme (French and lemon thymes the best for potpourri), and wormwood. Of these I have found catnip, camomile, lemon balm, sage and wormwood EASY to raise from seed.

Annual fragrant herbs which are well worth the easy yearly planting are basil, marjoram, and summer savory. These lists are not intended to be all-inclusive; they simply reflect my own preferences and experience.

All herbs (except mints) require as much sun as possible, well-drained sweet soil (egg shells or carefully added lime), with sweet woodruff being the only exception that I'm aware of. This grows in the shade and in acid soil. Most herbs will flourish (and in fact produce more of a harvest) with 2 or 3 cuttings per year. I cut and dry the top 4 to 6 inches from most branches in July, August, and September.

If you can bring plants inside for the winter to a sunny window, do try scented geraniums, especially rose geranium. Their lovely, fragrant leaves are marvelous in potpourri, and they are easily propagated from cuttings.

If 2 or 3 of your friends are also interested in starting herb gardens, you might wish to share the initial investments by each buying a few herb plants and seeds, and then trading cuttings and transplants later.

Drying

Most herbs and flowers dry well on absorbent paper towels or napkins spread out in any dry, airy room, out of the sunlight. An attic is perfect. (It will smell divine!) Larger branches, like the mints, will dry well in bunches hanging upside down or in paper bags, the stem ends held together with the same rubber band used to close the large grocery bags. Or you can dry herbs on old screens in the garage or shed. We tied clothesline in our garage, and added a clothes-rack, a fan, and a de-humidifier in order to handle my volume of herbs the second summer. The herbs dried fast in boxes on top of the aluminum reflectors of my indoor lights. I was able to pack away large amounts of dried delights every 4 or 5 days and quickly move in a new batch. Oven drying has not produced satisfactory results for me due to loss of color and scent from the artificial heat. Once the herbs are crisp-dry, they should be stored in air-tight plastic bags or glass bottles away from the sunlight (which will fade the hues).

Fabrics

You should always be on the lookout for lightweight fabrics for your sachets or herbal pillows. I check the fabric department of every store I'm in, and go to fabric sales and factory outlets whenever possible. Many of the materials I have used recently were purchased months or years ago, whenever I happened to see *thin,* but not sheer, fabric in tiny, flowery prints in pretty colors. (Heavy materials will not allow the scents to permeate through.) I use pastels for my spring-summer "line", and tiny dark colonial prints for fall and winter, with color-coordinated velvet satin, or lace ribbons to match. It is helpful to build up a supply of fabrics and ribbons to coordinate later color-wise, mood-wise, and season-wise! The eye-appeal is as important as the fragrance for successful marketing.

Sachets may be made very simply by just pinking the edges of 6 X 6" squares, placing 2 or 3 tablespoons of potpourri in the center, and pulling the corners up and tying them securely with heavy colored thread. A pretty velvet or satin ribbon is the finishing touch. Or, you can machine-stitch valentine hearts or oblong or circular shapes to create your own special bags.

Labeling and Packaging

Many of my retailers have complimented me on my labeling and packaging methods. This has not been easy! I spent much time searching for plastic bag companies for the right sized bags to fit my sachets. After much frustration I finally fit my sachet size to fit the bags I could buy! I now consider the packaging possibilities before I design a new product. (It is no accident that my Sweet Pillows fit perfectly inside of kitchen storage plastic bags, which are always available and cost me 5¢ per pillow!) Plastic bags allow the customer to see the product, but they protect the fragrance and keep the item clean for the eventual buyer.

I would guess that my labels have sold my products more effectively than any other single factor. The public seems so interested in how herbs were used in colonial times, that I include information about the past history of the items, as well as suggested present-day usage. (Fragrant herbs were used as "natural" deodorizers, room fresheners, moth preventives, etc.) Some of my best sellers this year were packaged bunches of herbs to be hung in homes for decoration with instructions on how the colonists had used the herb for seasoning, tea, or fragrance. I have also coined a phrase which is on most of my labels and expresses my wish for the recipient: "A REMEMBRANCE FROM LAST SUMMER'S GARDEN TO REMIND YOU OF NEXT SPRING'S PROMISE".

Most of my merchants prefer hand-printed labels because of the wide appeal of home-crafted products. My husband and my son are both excellent printers, so they have done most of my labels which are later cheaply reproduced by the "offset" process at local copying shops. I found a paper cutter indispensable for the purpose of cutting up 5 pagesful of various labels at a time.

I do type up labels when either the product is small or when I want to convey a lot of information with a particular item. I also list ingredients whenever possible, to add to the appeal of the item and to comply with the Federal Trade requirements. Often the appearance has been improved by the hand-printing of the scent in a color matching the fabric (ROSE with red or pink felt pen, LAVENDER with purple ink, CITRUS in orange.)

Display

When I first approached store-owners with my sachets, they often asked if they could display my product right in the box or container I had brought it in. (I was careful to initially show my sachets in an attractive display, whether it was a large apothecary jar, a wicker basket, or just a flat box with pastel tissue paper surrounding the matching-colored fabrics.) At first I sold or loaned my containers to the merchants, but now I use boxes with tissue I can easily part with.

Pricing

I must admit that I *underpriced* my products at first, as I wanted to create a demand for them. I think I could have made more profit in the beginning, but it was psychologically beneficial to both myself and the retailers to have picked quick "winners." As soon as items were moving fast and customers were returning for more of the same,

I knew that I could safely raise the prices in order to pay myself more adequately for my labor.

The types of outlets you have will help to determine your prices, because some gift shops mark up the price nearly 100% from what you want for the product! You have no control of the price once your product is purchased outright. So, if you charge a high price, and your merchant wants 100% profit, your product may not "move" at all, no matter how lovely it is!

I have two storeowners who are pleased enough with my wares that they have changed their regular mark-up policy for me in order to insure the success of my items in their shops! And I have eliminated some of my original outlets...replacing them with the more accommodating merchants.

Pricing is also determined largely by the initial production costs, as well as by "what the traffic will bear" in any given geographic location. It is wise to check on the price competitors are charging. I receive $3.50 or $4.00 for my Herbal Sweet Pillows, which sell well in the various stores for $5.00 to $6.00. My sachets sell for a dollar, bringing me from 60 to 80 cents, depending on the outlet. (Note: 1978 prices; doubled by 1981)

Outlets

I have found women's exchange shops to be the best outlets because they are usually church or charity-related and they allow the handcrafter from 70 to 80% of the profit. The articles are sold "on consignment", which means you get paid *after* the items are sold.

Historical associations are also often interested in herbal products because of the tie-in with colonial times. I have used fairs, bazaars, and craft shows as one-shot outlets annually. It generates a lot of good will (and interest in your products) if you donate a good percentage of your profits at "benefits." I have done this at garden clubs, the YWCA, and church and school bazaars, and the experiences have been mutually beneficial. The contacts have usually resulted in requests for me to speak to the organizations, or to give demonstration workshops. I now have had enough experience to charge a fee for this service.

Gift shops that specialize in unique or natural items probably offer the most opportunities in most areas. Be innovative! You don't have to restrict yourself to your own locale. I originally had 3 outlets in Vermont because my family lives there, and they suggested tourist gift shops to me. I hadn't thought tourists would buy Pennsylvania herbs as souvenirs from Vermont, but store-owners told me that the skiers who come back year after year are often looking for gifts other than maple syrup to take home to their wives, mothers, or daughters! Keep in mind that sachets and herbal pillows are lightweight and easy to ship by mail.

I have been asked by several merchants to limit the sale of my products to *their stores only* in their particular locale, to eliminate price competition and to bring all my business to them. So I would advise against trying to deal with more than one shop in the same mall or small town. I am constantly directing my friends and acquaintances (and lecture audiences) to my outlets, as I cannot sell directly to them myself when they inquire. So a unique product-line WILL bring business to the merchant!

Promotion

My son or husband have often made promotional posters to accompany my displays at stores or bazaars, and the results verify the power of suggestion and positive thinking. Sachets at Christmastime make wonderful "stocking-stuffers," "gift-wrap decorations," or "reasonably-priced gifts for children to buy for teacher, mother, and grandmother," etc. Similar posters are helpful for Valentine or Mother's Day sales.

I plan to introduce my herbal pillows to hospital and nursing-home gift shops, and I will certainly use posters to draw attention to them.

Scope

You will need to check into your local zoning ordinances before you decide the scope or extent of your home herb business. In our area, I am allowed only to sell wholesale, and only what I grow on our property. I cannot sell my herbs retail from my house or do anything that will affect the neighbors, cause increased traffic, etc., without a zoning variance (which is most difficult to obtain in our suburban area).

Other necessary steps include checking into permits and licenses needed locally, and on the county, state, and federal levels. These requirements vary from region to region, depending on what type of business you wish to have. Accurate records must be kept for tax purposes by home businesses. I have found SMALL-TIME OPERATOR, by Bernard Kamoroff, to be extremely helpful with good legal and tax advice for a small beginning business. (Bell Springs Publishing Co., Box 640/POH Laytonville, CA 95454, $10.95 pp)

My business is limited to the *fragrant* herbal products for now because of the additional time, expense, and equipment needed to sell *culinary* herbal products. (The Federal Food and Drug Administration and the county and state agricultural agencies have a great deal of control over edible products — fortunately for the consumer, but unfortunately for new, small businesses!) One of my goals for the future is to expand into this area, when I have the time and money to convert a portion of our home or land into a *spotless* and pet-free workshop to meet the required standards for culinary products.

If you have limited funds, I would suggest you check your local library and government agencies for books and pamphlets related to starting your own business before you make any major investment.

In Conclusion...

I have written this booklet with two types of readers in mind — peers who might already have a gardenful of herbs and may wish to earn a second income (or make products to donate to their favorite charities), and younger people just starting out who may wish to produce income from the land. I hope that others can benefit from my experience with the fragrant herbs as a launching pad for all kinds of business opportunities.

My husband edited the first draft of this booklet, and his first comment was, "You didn't caution the readers to guard their enthusiasm!" So here, for Hugh, is a word of caution....

I tended to be so zealous and optimistic when I started out, that I was too diversified; I tried to market every conceivable item I could dream up! Consequently I was dabbling in a different project every day and spending a great deal of time preparing for a project and cleaning up after it, only to start in on another one. I was fulfilling several different orders for several different merchants all at the same time.

Admittedly, I was coming and going in all directions, and not coordinating my work. *NOW* I concentrate on my four best-sellers (sachets, herbal pillows, potpourri in bags, and packaged branches of herbs), and I spend several days making a lot of each item, one at a time. Therefore I am always prepared to fill re-orders promptly, and to take along other items in case they are wanted. But this is hard to do until you have experimented with a number of different products and tested them in the marketplace. Perhaps you won't be in as much of a hurry as I was to bring in an income — I just couldn't let my children down!

Fragrant herbs will open up a whole new world for you, whether or not you wish to profit *financially* from them. You will benefit aesthetically every time you visit your garden or come in contact with your dried herbs!

If you gain nothing else from my booklet, I hope you will learn to more than "double you fun;" to TRIPLE your garden pleasure, as I do. I savor the beauty and essence of my flowers and herbs *at least* three times....in the garden, in the house (in arrangements or drying in bunches), and indefinitely in potpourri or sachets!

May *you* experience the year-round joy of becoming close friends with fragrant herbs and have constant winter reminders of next spring's promise. I assure you riches one way or the other...if not both!

Recommended Catalogs (for herb plants, seeds, oils, books, products)
Caprilands Herb Farm, No. Coventry, CT 06238
Aphrodisia, 28 Carmine St., NYC 10014
Nichols Garden Nursery, 1190 Pacific Hwy., Albany, OR 97321
Caswell-Massey Co., 21 Fulton St., South St. Seaport, New York, NY 10038
Herb Products Co., P.O. Box 898, No. Hollywood, CA 91601
Penn Herb Co., 603 No. 2nd St., Philadelphia, PA 19123

1986 Update to "Growing Fragrant Herbs for Profit"

Little did I know, eight years ago, the direction this modest little booklet would take me. I hadn't heard of "spin-offs" then, nor did I know how to promote my booklet, except through classified ads, which I placed in three gardening magazines, with money borrowed through VISA! I didn't expect to get rich from my little booklet, and that's a good thing, because the response *barely* covered the costs of the ads.

But one advertising executive liked the booklet I had enclosed enough to send it over to the head of the magazine! Imagine my shock to receive a phone call from an executive at THE MOTHER EARTH NEWS MAGAZINE, wanting to know if they could fly up an editor and a photographer to interview me for an article on HERBAL ACRES for the magazine! Still naive as the hills, I asked how much they'd pay me. "Nothing," I was told, "but the 'boss' wants to promote your booklet through the article and we guarantee you many more sales of it than your ad generated." He explained that it would be a feature article, announced on the front page, and that most subscribers read the feature articles, whereas a lot of readers ignore the classified ads.

It wasn't as easy as it sounds. The phone call came in March of 1978, and the interview didn't take place until September, and the article didn't appear until March 1979! For five months we tried to keep our lawn and gardens spotless for the photographer, and I kept the house as clean as a whistle — as I knew they'd be taking pictures inside and out, and I would be serving them refreshments and lunch. The long wait was nerve-wracking, to say the least! Then came another 6-month wait for the results. But it was all worth it. Over 3,000 people ordered the booklet over a period of one year, and the orders are still coming in from MOTHER EARTH readers, six years later!

I've had no training in the business field, but I was not too naive to know that I had a gold mine of a mailing list sitting in my lap! 3,000 people interested in learning about herbs! And many of them asking to be notified when the *next* booklet was ready, one I was planning to publish on culinary herbs that the magazine was kind enough to mention. With such an opportunity I took a few giant leaps. I quit my job, wrote GOURMET GARDENING — A Monthly Herbal Primer For Gardeners Who Love To Cook, and sent an announcement of the new book, along with a free copy of the introductory issue of an herbal newsletter I was starting, POTPOURRI FROM HERBAL ACRES, to everyone on my mailing list. (The proceeds from my first booklet financed these next steps, this in itself a giant leap.)

The response to that mailing was fantastic and now my career had taken a totally new direction — I was now doing more writing and mail-order fulfillment (newsletter and books) than gardening and potpourri-making. I started writing articles for magazines, as this publicity was free promotional work which increased sales of my newsletter and books. (Yes, MOTHER EARTH printed my "APPLE PULP POMANDER SACHET" article in 1981, reprinted it in a Christmas Craft issue, and offered reprints of it in radio advertisements on 1200 stations!)

Now a few additional tips for those of you contemplating an herb business.

1. Just as in show business, there is no such thing as an "overnight success" in a small family business. Even with my quick early start, I had been growing and drying herbs, making potpourri and sachets, studying and experimenting for 15 years before that fateful bicentennial "year of the sachets." It usually takes 3–5 years for a small business of any kind to show a profit, or longer if there is no initial financial backing. And it takes between 5 and 10 years to build up a small business successful enough to support a family. Many of my newsletter readers who have herb farms that are highly successful, occupying both the husband and wife *now,* started out in a small way with the wife making herbcrafts as a hobby or a side-line. In several cases, the husband has been able to quit his

job or his farming to join the wife full-time, only after several years of the wife's gradual building of the herb business, creating a reputation, a following, and a need for her products. So, one must "pay one's dues" in one way or the other, before expecting miracles. Even then, herb farming demands long, hard hours of effort and energy. But the rewards are well worth it for those who love living in the country and off the land and enjoy working together in a family venture.

2. You must check with your local, state, and federal officials before you can plan your scope of operations, and how and where and to whom you will sell products. For example, after consulting our State Agricultural Department, I decided that selling the culinary herbs (such as teas and blends) was not for me. I learned that I would have to pass State inspections in my place of work. We have three beloved pets who own our house, and I had found dog or cat hairs in my potpourri enough times to know that a culinary business was out-of-the-question as long as we had the pets. And, at least in Pennsylvania, very specific requirements must be met if one is going to sell bottled edible products, such as herb vinegar or herb jelly. Not only are the kitchens, equipment, and place of selling subject to periodic inspection by the Ag Dept., but the labels on the jars must meet strict standards. (Company name and complete address, ingredients in a special order, and weight must all appear on label.) So, don't take chances. Check with your State agency first!

3. You should be very knowledgeable about all aspects of herbs before you try to sell them in any state, whether fresh, dry, or the plants themselves. There are many herbals you should study and have on hand for reference (listed elsewhere in the Appendix) and you should keep up-to-date on the latest developments in the world of herbs. The Federal Food and Drug Administration announces new warnings about unsafe herbs with increasing frequency. In many cases, it is just that these herbs need further scientific testing, according to the FDA. But if you are in the business of herbs, it is vital that you are aware of the latest herb news. The best way to do this is to subscribe to the periodicals listed on the next page, and to purchase every new reliable herbal as it is published. These newsletters and books are professional necessities for your business and can be tax write-offs.

4. Do not be easily discouraged. Bertha Reppert once wrote me, "In the early years we were having so much fun we didn't know we weren't making any money! Then all of a sudden our business boomed, miraculously." I think most businesses have "breakthrough" years. After experimenting and diversifying, one almost stumbles into his/her niche, whether from a best-seller, a spin-off (an unexpected result from another endeavor), or just from an ever-widening circle of satisfied customers. Eventually you will find that you'll earn just as much money, but spend much less time and energy, if you limit your line to those products that sell well, and only sell them where you can make a good profit.

Take small leaps at first. Be flexible and open to spin-offs and new trends. If things aren't going well, improve your product, or try a new one. Grow with your business. Iron out the wrinkles. Clear your mind of cobwebs and negative thinking, so that every moment can be productive. Patience, determination, know-how, instinct, hard work, and good judgment — all play a part in a successful business. Do what you love, and love what you do — and you can't lose!

As for me and my dream of Hugh's early retirement, I'm still optimistic! I now am earning much more than I did when I worked away from home. Meanwhile, we are both very confident about our security in our retirement years, because I will not *have* to retire! GOOD LUCK TO YOU!

1986 Recommended Reading List for Herb Businesses

HOMEMADE MONEY, The Definitive Guide To Success In A Home Business, by Barbara Brabec, Betterway Publications, 1984. This will tell you everything you need to know regarding starting, maintaining, and expanding your own business. *Barbara Brabec Productions, PO Box 2137-POH, Naperville, IL 60566.*

CREATIVE CASH, How To Sell Your Crafts, Needlework, Designs, & Know-How, by Barbara Brabec. (Address above.)

NATIONAL HOME BUSINESS REPORT, Barbara Brabec. A very informative bimonthly newsletter. (Address above)

GROWING AND USING HERBS SUCCESSFULLY, Betty M. Jacobs, Garden Way Publishing, Pownal, VT 05261. (Formerly titled PROFITABLE HERB GROWING AT HOME, the revised edition still includes this information.)

BU$INESS OF HERBS, edited by Portia Meares. An extremely informative bimonthly newsletter devoted solely to herb businesses! *Rte. 2, Box 246-P, Shevlin, MN 56676*

POTPOURRI FROM HERBAL ACRES, Phyllis Shaudys. Quarterly newsletter networking tips, crafts, recipes, experiences from business-owners and hobbyists. Free "Herb Blurb" and listings in Herbfest column for subscribers. Starts 8th year in 1986. *Pine Row Publications, Box 428-POH, Washington Crossing, PA 18977*

POTPOURRI PARTY-LINE, edited by Dody Lyness. Constant supply of floral and craft instructions and potpourri recipes from this quarterly newsletter, embellished with a sure chuckle or two in each issue from this talented and witty writer. *Berry Hill Press, 7336 Berry Hill Dr., Palo Verdes, CA 90274.*

AMERICAN HERB ASSOCIATION QUARTERLY NEWSLETTER, edited by Kathi Keville, published by The American Herb Association. Emphasis is on the medicinal uses of herbs. Up-to-date information on safe and unsafe herbs, etc. Subscription includes four issues and membership in the AHA. *(PO Box 353-POH, Rescue, CA 95672)*

HERBALGRAM, edited by Mark Blumenthal and Rob McCaleb and published by The Herb Research Foundation and The American Herbal Products Trade Association. Quarterly newsletter emphasizing herbal research and merchandising on a large scale. *Herb News, PO Box 12602-POH, Austin, TX 78711.*

CATALOG SOURCES FOR CREATIVE PEOPLE, Margaret Boyd. A directory of over 2,000 sources of patterns, plans, kits, and materials for arts, crafts, hobbies, and needlework. *Boyd's, PO Box 6232-POH, Augusta, GA 30906.*

THE HERB MARKET REPORT, monthly newsletter and THE POTENTIAL OF HERBS AS A CASH CROP newsletter and book by Richard Alan Miller. *O.A.K./POH, 1305 Vista Drive, Grants Pass, OR 97527*

Wholesale Sources & Additional Resources for Business Owners

If owning or opening a shop, I strongly recommend you order all the catalogs on my source list that offer wholesale products. (Write on company letterhead and include re-sale license number.) Note that the following companies specialize in wholesale only: The **HERB PATCH VT 05757** (culinary blends), **SILVA FARMS FLORIST 02764** (decorative dried herbs & flowers), **GINGHAM & SPICE 18926** (oils & fragrances), and **FRONTIER COOPERATIVE HERBS 52318** (bulk herbs). **THE ROSEMARY HOUSE 17055** offers the largest variety of wholesale items. Also, please refer to wholesale sources of fixatives, spices, & oils on page 85.

Accessories: Gifts & Decorative Accessories, 51 Madison Ave., New York, NY 10010 (Catalog published by Geyer-McAllister Publications)

Craft Outlets: National Directory of Shops, Galleries, Shows & Fairs, published by WRITER'S DIGEST BOOKS, 9933 Alliance Rd., Cincinnati, OH 45242. This is published every two years, lists thousands of craft markets, telling what each is looking for, and should be available at your local book store.

Craft Supplies: LHL Enterprises, Box 241/POH, Solebury, PA 18963

Culinary Mixes: Mari-Mann Herb Co., RR4, PO Box 7/POH, Decatur, IL 62521 (Listing — SASE)
Herb Patch VT 05757

Custom-made die-cut labels of all kinds: United Label Corp., 2120 S. Green Rd., S. Euclid, OH 44121

Dried Flowers & Herbs (decorative): POSIE PATCH OH 45371, CRAMER'S POSIE PATCH PA 17512, and SILVA FARMS MA 02764

Fabrics: Gohn Bros., Box 111/POH, Middlebury, IN 46540-0111

Gift and craft accessories: New York Gift Market, 225 Fifth Ave., New York, NY 10011

Herbcraft Kits: HERBITAGE FARM NH 03470

Imprinted gift boxes, bags, ribbons, wrapping needs: Tobin Howe Specialty Co., 600 Main St., Paterson, NJ 07503

Pin-head orris root: Tatra Herb Co., PO Box 60-HA, Morrisville, PA 19067 (Ask for price list for pinhead orris root specifically.)

Plants: These well-established firms specialize in selling herb plants wholesale by mail for re-sale: **FOX HILL FARM MI 49269, TAYLOR'S HERB GARDENS CA 92083, CARROLL GARDENS PO BOX 310 WESTMINSTER MD 21157, and SUNNYBROOK FARMS 9448 MAYFIELD RD CHESTERLAND OH 44026**

Plastic Bags: Polybags Plus, Dept. POH, Grassmere Rd., Elk Grove Village, IL 60007
The Milvan Co., Dept. POH, 7799 Enterprise Dr., Newark, CA 94560
Cello-Print, Dept. POH, McKeesport, PA 15131 (custom-made)
Polybags, Crystal Springs Packaging Co., PO Box 658/POH, Belmont, CA 94002

Resource Guides: The Herb Gardener's Resource Guide, Paula Oliver, Northwind Farm, Rt. 2, Box 246-P, Shevlin, MN 56676

Traveler's Guide to Herb Gardens, The Herb Society of America, 9019 Kirtland Chardon Rd., Mentor OH 44060

Ribbons, laces, notions: Home-Sew Inc., Dept. POH, Bethlehem, PA 18018 (Bargain rates)
Newark Dressmaking Supply, PO Box 2448/POH, Lehigh Valley, PA 18001
Valsco Enterprizes, PO Box 269/POH, Midway City, CA 92655

Seeds: Sandy Mush Herbs, Rt. 2, Dept. POH, Leicester, NC 28748
Nichol's Garden Nursery, Dept. POH, 1190 No. Pacific Hwy., Albany, OR 97321
Park's Seed Co., Dept. POH, Greenwood, SC 29647
Otto Richter Seeds, Dept. POH, Goodwood, Ontario, Canada LOC IA0

Straw hats (and many other items): Strikes My Fancy, Dept. POH, 2206 Hickory Ridge Dr., Bossier City, LA 71111
Bolek's Craft Supplies, Box 465/POH, Dover, OH 44622-0465
Coast Wholesale Florist, PO Box 10/POH, San Francisco, CA 94101

Supply Distributor for Small Businesses: Dick Margulis, Dept. POH, RD1, Box 24B, Poland, NY 13431

Vinegar bottles: Supplies Service, Dick Margulis, RD 1, Box 24B, Poland NY 13431 ($2.50 for 4 listings per year).

Also, if you live near a large city, check your yellow pages for "Containers-glass". Many such firms can supply small orders for cash and pick-up, such as the one listed below.

Israel Andler & Sons, Murray Andler, 376 Third St., PO Box 148/POH, Everett MA 02149 (617/387-5700) (Pick-up trade only for small orders)

PLEASE NOTE: Publishing such a comprehensive and informative listing as this is helpful to both the buying and traveling public as well as the businesses involved. **However**, the list has been abused in the past and has caused some problems for both readers and businesses. Some people have paid no attention to the careful coding under each business and have requested catalogs from those who do not even offer mail-order items. Many others fail to send the required amount or the stamped, self-addressed envelope (SASE) required to receive a listing or catalog. **In both cases you are wasting postage because most of the businesses will not respond if you ignore the coding.** So please pay strict attention to what the business offers. If there is no MO under the listing, they send nothing by mail—so do not expect an answer. If their catalog costs $1.00, and you do not send it, do not expect a reply. One more explanation. Many herbal businesses put out seasonal catalogs, so you may not receive an immediate response. If you should order a catalog in the summer, chances are good that the spring catalog is now out-of-date, and you will hear from the firm when the fall or winter catalog comes out. The best time to order seed and plant catalogs is in late winter or early spring. And gift catalogs usually come out in the fall. In many cases you will receive future mailings free, especially if you have ordered from the first catalog sent you. Please realize that in our very mobile society addresses, prices, and the nature of businesses change often. To the best of our knowledge, the data provided in this book is current as of November 1994.

DIRECTORY OF HERB GARDENS AND BUSINESSES

This list has been assembled to assist you in finding herbal products, people, and places to enhance your knowledge of the herb world. It is arranged by zip codes within the states so that you can quickly identify those places located close to each other — in case you are planning a trip. Many places are open to the public only "during the season", which in many cases means the gardening season, from May to October. For this reason, it is essential that you write ahead for brochures or catalogs before you travel any distance for a visit!

The large majority of businesses listed here are owned by subscribers to the author's newsletter, POTPOURRI FROM HERBAL ACRES, and will be happy to know that you learned of them through this book. Members of "The Potpourri Family," as the readers call us, are listed with the owner's names included. (If you add "Dept. POH", short for Pleasure of Herbs, to the envelope address — the recipients will know of the source.)

SH — retail shop, store or studio

AO — by appointment only

GD — garden(s), herb, of course, for viewing or touring.

MO — mail order, with the cost of the catalog included if known.

SASE — self-addressed stamped envelope

WH — wholesale listings available if inquiry is written on business letterhead and state tax exempt license number is included.

VA — variety of products offered.

PL — plants are sold.

ALO — plants sold at the location only, not by mail even if mail-order is offered.

LE — lectures, classes, or workshops are given.

If a company specializes in one aspect of herbs, this specialty is included near the name of the business. (If there is an **asterisk** by the specialty, other products are also offered.)

If you know of a business or garden that should be added to the list, the information would be welcomed by the author for future directories.

ALABAMA

Calmac Nursery
160 Ryan Rd
Cullman AL 35057-2754

SH WH LE VA

ARIZONA

Nordic Haus
Maryon Nordenstrom
238 S Wall St
Chandler AZ 85224

SH VA

ARKANSAS

Clement Herb Farm
Diane/Ed Clement
19690 Clement's Lane
Rogers AR 72756

SH GD MO .50 WH VA PL-ALO LE

CALIFORNIA

The J Paul Getty Museum Bookstore
17985 Pacific Coast Highway
Malibu CA 90265

SH GD VA

Los Angeles State & County Arboretum
301 North Baldwin Ave
Arcadia CA 91007

SH GD VA

Herb Products Company
11012 Magnolia Blvd
PO Box 898
No Hollywood CA 91601

SH MO VA

Mountain Herb Co
Maureen Austin
PO Box 532
Alpine CA 91903

SH AO GD VA PL-ALO LE SASE

Taylor's Herb Gardens
Kent/Dorothy Taylor
1535 Lone Oak Rd
Vista CA 92084

SH GD MO 1.00 WH VA PL

Good Scents
Donna Metcalfe
101 South 6th Street
Redlands CA 92373

AO MO .50 VA LE

Barb's Country Herbs
Barbara Sausser
15665 Russell
Riverside CA 92508

SH AO GD VA PL-ALO LE

Heart's Ease
Sharon Lovejoy
4101 Burton Drive
Cambria CA 93428
800-266-4372

SH GD VA LE

Bay Laurel Farm (Wreaths*)
Glory Condon
W Garzas Rd
Carmel Valley CA 93924

SH AO MO 1.00 WH VA

Filoli Center (National Trust Property)
Canada Rd
Woodside CA 94062

SH GD VA

New Age Creations/Aromatherapy
219 Carl St
San Francisco CA 94117

SH AO GD MO 1.00 WH VA LE

Nature's Herb Company
1010 46th St
Emeryville CA 94608

SH MO VA

Saso Herb Gardens
14625 Fruitvale Ave
Saratoga CA 95070

SH GD AO VA LE

Oak Valley Herb Farm
Kathi Keville
14648 Pear Tree Lane
Nevada City CA 95959

MO 1.00 VA LE

COLORADO

Turtle Island Herbs Inc
(Herbal Extracts*)
4949 N. Broadway #101A
Boulder CO 80304

SH MO WH LE

Rocky Mountain Center for Botanical
 Studies (Herb School)
PO Box 19254
Boulder CO 80308-2254

LE

Herb Companion Magazine
Interweave Press
201 East Fourth St
Loveland CO 80537

MO

CONNECTICUT

Lucky Acres Herb Farm
Mona (Sandi) Distin
Rt 202
New Hartford CT 06057

GD VA PL

Village Herbs
Susan Krane
5 Chapel St
Enfield CT 06082

SH WH VA PL LE

Caprilands Herb Farm
Silver St
Coventry CT 06238

SH GD MO .50 VA PL LE

Logee's Greenhouses
Joy Logee Martin
141 North St
Danielson CT 06239

SH GD MO 3.00 WH PL LE

Catnip Acres Herb Nursery
Gene Banks
67 Christian St
Oxford CT 06478

GD SH VA PL LE

Gilbertie's Herb Gardens
Sylvan Lane
Westport CT 06880

SH VA PL GD

DISTRICT OF COLUMBIA

The National Herb Garden
National Arboretum
3501 New York Ave NE
Washington DC 20002

GD

The Herb Cottage
Washington Cathedral
Mt St Alban
Washington DC 20016

SH GD MO .25 VA PL-ALO

FLORIDA

Kanapaha Botanical Gardens
4625 SW 63rd Blvd
Gainesville FL 32608

GDS PL-ALO VA LE

GEORGIA

The Herb Connection (Topiary)
Barbara L Vanderhoff
2627 John Petree Rd
Powder Springs GA 30073
404-943-4871

SH AO ALO LE

Herbs by Jean (Cookbooks*)
Jean Givens
1161 Oakdale Rd NE
Atlanta GA 30307

MO SASE VA LE

Atlanta Botanical Garden
Piedmont Park at South Prado
Atlanta GA 30309
404-876-5858

GD

HAWAII

Heartscents
Barbara Irwin
PO Box 1674
Hilo HI 96721

SH MO 1.00 WH VA

ILLINOIS

Chicago Botanic Garden
PO Box 400
Glencoe IL 60022

SH GD

Scentiments (Wreaths/Baskets*)
Gail Klingberg
2041 Chestnut
Wilmette IL 60091

SH AO WH VA

Meadow Everlastings (Dried Flowers*)
Sharon/John Challand
16464-PH Shabbona Rd
Malta IL 60150

SH GD AO MO 2.00 WH VA

Stone Well Herbs
Jan Powers
2320 W Moss Ave
Peoria IL 61604

SH GD VA PL-ALO LE

Elegant Designs
Sheri Ohmes-Heusel
RR 1 Box 23A
Hudson IL 61748

SH GD VA PL LE

The Potpourri Patch
Rosma Eugea
500 Union Ave
Belleville IL 62220

SH AO VA

Mari-Mann Herb Co Inc
Michael L King
RR 4 Box 7
Decatur IL 62521-9404

SH GD MO SASE WH VA PL-ALO LE

Aura Herb Farm (Everlastings*)
Lynda Boyd
RR 1 Box 127
Iuka IL 62849

WH ONLY

INDIANA

Herbs & Clay Pottery
Patti Beck
RR 2 Box 356
Sharpsville IN 46068

MO 1.00 WH SASE

Indiana Botanic Gardens
PO Box 5
Hammond IN 46325

SH MO 1.00 VA

Greenfield Herb Garden
Arlene Shannon
Depot & Harrison Box 9
Shipshewana IN 46565

SH GD MO .50 WH VA LE

Victorian Rose Everlastings
John & Rose Hanna
RR 3 Box 20
North Vernon IN 47265

SH GD AO MO SASE WH ALO LE

Cactus Patch Herbs
1158 US 31N
Seymour IN 47274

SH AO GD MO SASE WH PL LE

Cabin Creek Herbs
Barbara Medler
R2 Box 196
Farmland IN 47340

SH GD VA PL LE

Carolee's Herbs & Flowers
Carolee Bean Snyder
3305 S 100 W
Hartford City IN 47348

GD AO MO SASE PL

IOWA

Sandi's Herb Patch
Sandi Moran
420 NW 65th Lane
Des Moines IA 50313

MO 1.00 WH LE

Little Prairie House
Lorne & Christine Gano
1007 Highway C-43
Alta IA 51002

SH GD WH VA

Prairie Pedlar
Jane Hogue
1677-270th St
Odebolt IA 51458

SH MO 2.00 GD WH VA PL-ALO LE

Frontier Cooperative Herbs
Box 299-PHA
Norway IA 52318

SH MO 4.75 WH VA

KANSAS

Herbal-Scent Sations
Ernestine Schrepfer
1329 S 51st Terr
Kansas City KS 66106

AO VA LE

Ebert's Herbs & Wheat
Carol Ebert
14415 Louisville Rd
St George KS 66535

SH MO 1.00 WH

A Season's Harvest
Kathy Goeckel
PO Box 323
Hanover KS 66945

AO MO VA LE

KENTUCKY

Dabney Herbs
Box 22061
Louisville KY 40252

MO 2.00 WH VA PL LE

Bluegrass Pottery (Beehives)
Carol & Mary McKenzie
PO Box 172
Paris KY 40361

MO 2.00 WH SASE VA LE

Country Herb Farm
Joyce Butsch
788E Stevens Branch Rd
Alexandria KY 41001

GD AO PL LE

The Separator Room
Sue Kate Berkshire
8100 US 42
Florence KY 41042

SO VA PL LE

LOUISIANA

Good Scents
Arlene Kestner
11655 Highland Rd
Baton Rouge LA 70810

SH AO 1.00 WH VA LE

MAINE

Hedgehog Hill Farm
RFD 2 Box 2010
Buckfield ME 04220

SH GD MO 1.00 VA PL-ALO LE

Maine Balsam Fir Products*
Wendy Newmeyer
Box 123
West Paris ME 04289

AO MO SASE WH VA

Photocraft's Herb Lady
Isabelle Wiand
RR 1 Box 3090
Weeks Mills ME 04361

LE

Fox Fern Herb Farm
Margaret M Smith
588 Bremen Rd
Waldoboro ME 04572

GD PL-ALO

Merry Gardens
Mary Ellen & Irvin Ross
PO Box 595
Camden ME 04843

SH GD MO 2.00 WH VA PL LE

MARYLAND

St. John's Herb Garden (Oils*)
The Perfume Garden
7711 Hillmeade Rd
Bowie MD 20715

GD SH MO WH VA PL LE

Willow Oak Flower & Herb Farm
Maria Price
8109 Telegraph Rd
Severn MD 21144

SH GD MO .50 WH VA PL LE

Carroll Gardens
PO Box 310
Westminster MD 21158

SH GD MO 2.00 WH VA PL

Sinking Springs Herb Farm
Bill/Ann Stubbs
234 Blair Shore Rd
Elkton MD 21921

SH GD MO 1.00 WH VA PL-ALO LE

MASSACHUSETTS

Hartman's Herb Farm
Lynn/Pete Hartman
Old Dana Rd
Barre MA 01005

SH GD MO 1.00 VA PL

The Herb Farm
Carol Pflumm
Barnard Rd
Granville MA 01034

SH AO MO 1.00 VA LE

Hancock Shaker Village Inc
PO Box 898
Pittsfield MA 01202

GD LE

Serenity Herbs
Susan LePrevost
Box 42 Monterey Stage
Gt Barrington MA 01230

MO 1.00 VAR

Stockbridge Herbs & Stitches
MaryEllen Warchol/Denise Lemay
18 Stockbridge Rd
South Deerfield MA 01373

AO MO SASE WH

Old Sturbridge Village
One Old Sturbridge Village Rd
Sturbridge MA 01566

SH GD MO VA

Whipple House Gifts
Fountain Plaza
Rt 9 at Bergson's Restaurant
Westboro MA 01581

SH VA

The Herb Patch
Paula/Bob Johnson
429 Hill Rd
Boxborough MA 01719

AO GD PL-ALO LE

The Proper Season
Betsy Williams
68 Park St
Andover MA 01810

SH VA

Old Hill Herbs
Barbara Hawkes
29 Norman St
Marblehead MA 01945

SH AO MO 1.00 VA PL-ALO LE

Cricket Hill Herb Farm Ltd
Glen St
Rowley MA 01969

SH GD VA PL-ALO LE

Church Hill Herbary
Darlene Beauvais
26 Church St
Norwell MA 02061

SH GD VA LE

Herb Country Collectables
Paula/Bob Johnson
63 Leonard St
Belmont City MA 02178

SH VA

Plymoth Plantation
PO Box 1620
Plymouth MA 02360

SH GD LE

Ye Crafty Owl Shoppe
Lee/Henri Jobert
755 Plymouth St Rt 58
Whitman MA 02382
617-447-4584

SH GD MO SASE VA PL-ALO LE

Thornton W Burgess Museum
4 Water St PO Box 972
Sandwich MA 02563

SH GD VA LE MO

Heritage Plantation
Box 566 Grove St
Sandwich MA 02563

GD

7 Arrows Herb Farm
Judy/Michel Marcellot
346 Oak Hill Ave
Attleboro MA 02703

SH GD WH PL LE

Hidden Brook Herbs
Elizabeth Timmins
1067 Middle St
North Dighton MA 02764

MO SASE WH VA LE

Silva Farms Whls Florist Supply Co
The Silva Family
1098 Tremont
North Dighton MA 02764

MO WH ONLY

MICHIGAN

Edison Institute/Greenfield Village
Dearborn MI 48120

GD SH LE

Rafal Spice Co
2521 Russell St
Detroit MI 48207

SH MO VA

Grand Oak Herb Farm
Beulah Hargrove
2877 Miller Rd
Bancroft MI 48414

SH GD AO VA PL LE

Heavenly Scent Herb Farm
Kathy Matthews
13730 Whitelake Road
Fenton MI 48430

SH GD MO VA PL ALO LE

The Gathered Herb
Shelley Carlson
12114 N State Rd (M-15)
Otisville MI 48463

SH GD VA PL LE

Nature's Cottage
Joan Erbe
381 Applegate Rd
Sandusky MI 48471

SH GD VA

Dow Gardens
1018 West Main St
Midland MI 48640

SH GD VA LE

Herbally Yours
Gloria Rodammer
8600 State St
Millington MI 48746

SH VA LE

The Sassafrass Hutch
Joyce Kebless
11880 Sandy Bottom NE
Greenville MI 48838

SH GD MO 1.00 VA PL-ALO LE

Thyme In The Country
Kreft/Howell/Pastoriza
3668 West Grand River Rd
Owosso MI 48867

SH GD VA LE

Heaven's Herbal Creations
8202 West ML & Kalamazoo
Kalamazoo MI 49009

SH GD MO WH PL-ALO LE

May Apple
Eugene Kirsch
211 North Center St
Hartford MI 49057

SH AO MO 1.00 VA

The Herb Cottage Inc
700 Anderson Rd
Niles MI 49120

SH GD VA PL

Fernwood Botanic Garden
13988 Range Line Rd
Niles MI 49120

SH GD VA PL-ALO LE

The Little Farm
Susan Betz
146 W Chicago Rd (US 12)
Allen MI 49227

GD AO VA PL LE

Fox Hill Farm
Marilyn Hampstead
PO Box 9-PHA
Parma MI 49269

SH GD MO 1.00 VA PL

Spencer Farms
Jack/Gerry Spencer
4675 Bender Rd
Middleville MI 49333
616-795-7815

MO SASE WH

Willow Tree Farm
Margaret Young
3886 Butterworth SW
Grand Rapids MI 49504

GD PL LE

The Swallow's Nest
Burdette Chapman
3378 W Harbor Hwy
Maple City MI 49664

SH GD VA LE

Woodland Herb Farm
Pat/Jon Bourdo
7741 N Manitou Trail West
Northport MI 49670

SH GD VA PL-ALO

MINNESOTA

Geranium Treasures
Alice Cowley
2718 Frontier Blvd
Becker MN 55308

SH GD AO VA PL LE

Northwind Farm's Herb Resource Dir.
Paula Oliver/Northwind Farm
Rte 2 Box 246-P
Shevlin MN 56676

MO WH

The Business Of Herbs
The Olivers/Northwind Farm Publications
Rte 2 Box 246-P
Shevlin MN 56676

MO

MISSISSIPPI

Stover Herb Gardens
Jewel Stover
PO Box 100
Red Banks MS 38661

SH GD VA PL LE

MISSOURI

Gatherings (Dried Creations*)
Carol Wilson
800 S First
Odessa MO 64076

The Herb Shoppe
Karen Miller
111 Azalea Box 395
Duenweg MO 64841

SH MO 2.00 WH VA PL-ALO LE

Hummingbird Hills Herb Nursery
Ann & Rodger Lenhardt
Rt 2 Box 351A
Ashland MO 65010

GD AO MO .50 WH SASE PL LE

ABC Herb Nursery
R 1 Box 313
Lecoma MO 65540

SH GD MO .25 WH PL

NEBRASKA

Statice Acres (Baskets/Statice*)
Sharon Kraeger
7908 Mill Rd
Plattsmouth NE 68048

SH AO VA

NEW HAMPSHIRE

Pickity Place
Nutting Hill Rd
Mason NH 03048

SH GD VA PL-ALO

Attar Herbs & Spices
Playground Rd
New Ispwich NH 03071

**MO 1.00 VA (WH only $50
minimum order)**

Sleepy Hollow Creations
Joyce Loszewski
34 Sharon Rd
Windham NH 03087

AO MO SASE WH VA

Tanglewood Gardens/Herbal Boutique
Louise Komisarek
424 Rte 101 RFD 13
Bedford NH 03102

SH GD SASE VA PL

Canterbury Shaker Village
Shaker Rd
Canterbury NH 03224

SH GD VA LE

Salisbury Corner Shop
Shirley Goss
PO Box 10 South Rd
Salisbury NH 03268

AO WH VA

Flower Press Publishers (Botanical
    Wreath Book*)
Box 222
Warner NH 03278

MO SASE WH

Andalina Ltd (Potpourri*)
Janet Scigliane
Troy Hill
Warner NH 03278-0057

SH GD AO MO SASE 1.00 VA PL-ALO

Heritage Herbs
Peg Mastey
1 Hannah Dustin Rd
Concord NH 03301

SH GD VA PL LE

Herbitage Farm
Barbara Radcliffe Rogers
686 Old Homestead Highway
Richmond NH 03470

MO 1.00 WH 1.00 VA LE

NEW JERSEY

Herbally Yours Inc
PO Box 26 Changewater Rd
Changewater NJ 07831

SH MO .50 WH VA LE

Well-Sweep Herb Farm
The Hyde Family
317 Mt Bethel Rd
Port Murray NJ 07865

SH GD MO 1.00 VA PL LE

Elisabeth Woodburn/Garden Books
Booknoll Farm Box 398
Hopewell NJ 08525

AO MO 2.00

Whiskey Run Herb Farm
Mary Schenck
RD 2 Box 281
Flemington NJ 08822

SH GD VA PL-ALO LE

NEW MEXICO

Plants of the Southwest (Seeds*)
Agua Fria Rt 6 Box 11-A
Santa Fe NM 87505

SH GD MO 1.00 WH

NEW YORK

Aphrodisia
282 Bleecker St
New York NY 10014

SH MO 2.50 WH VA

Caswell-Massey Co Ltd
518 Lexington Ave
New York NY 10017

SH VA

Caswell-Massey Co Ltd
21 Fulton St
South St Seaport
New York NY 10038

SH MO 1.00 WH VA

New York Botanical Gardens
Southern Blvd at 200th St
Bronx NY 10458

SH GD MO SASE PL-ALO

Boscobel Restoration
Rte 9-D
Garrison-on-Hudson NY 10524

GD SH

Brooklyn Botanic Garden
1000 Washington Ave
Brooklyn NY 11225

SH GD VA PL

Queens Botanical Garden
43-50 Main St
Flushing NY 11355

SH GD VA PL

Mr Spiceman
210–11 48 Ave
Bayside NY 11364

SH MO 1.00 VA

Old Westbury Gardens
71 Old Westbury Rd
Old Westbury NY 11568

SH GD PL LE

Peconic River Herb Farm
310-C River Rd
Calverton NY 11933

GD PL-ALO LE

Gooseberry Honey & Herb Farm
48 Westel Rd
Troy NY 12182
518-235-1068

SH GD MO SASE VA PL LE

The Fresh Herb Farm
Pitcher Lane
RD 3 Box 466
Red Hook NY 12571

SH GD MO SASE WH VA PL-ALO

Gatehouse Herbs (Bed & Breakfast)
Carol Gates
98 Van Buren St
Dolgeville NY 13329

GD VA LE PL-ALO

Aster Place Herbs
Beth/Dick Margulis
RD 1 Box 24 B
Poland NY 13431

SH GD AO MO SASE WH VA PL-ALO

Wholesale Supply Distributor
Dick Margulis Dept P
RD 1 Box 24 B
Poland NY 13431

MO WH ONLY 2.50 VA

Frog Park Herbs
455 Frog Park Rd
Waterville NY 13480

SH MO VA PL-ALO

Back of the Beyond (Bed & Breakfast*)
Shash Georgi
7233 Lower E Hill Rd
Colden NY 14033

SH GD AO MO .50 VA PL-ALO LE

Rue Jas Herb Collection
Ruth Stryker
1849 Woodard Rd
Webster NY 14580

GD AO VA PL

Jane's Herb Farm
Jane Kuitems
1042 State Rd
Webster NY 14580

GD AO VA PL

Rochester Museum & Science Center
657 East Ave
Rochester NY 14610

GD

The Helmer Nature Center
154 Pine Grove Ave
Rochester NY 14617

GD

Garden Center of Rochester
  Herb Garden
5 Castle Park
Rochester NY 14620

GD

Robison York State Herb Garden
  at Cornell Plantations
1 Plantation Rd
Ithaca NY 14850

GD

NORTH CAROLINA

Griffin's
5109 Vickrey Chapel Rd
Greensboro NC 27407

SH SG MO 2.00 WH VA PL LE

Country Cottage Creations
Tamara Davida Leonard
12068 Falls of Neuse Rd
Wake Forest NC 27587

SH AO GD WH VA PL-ALO LE

Rasland Farm
Sylvia Tippett
NC 82 at US 13
Godwin NC 28344

SH GD MO 1.00 WH VA PL LE

Sandy Mush Herbs
Kate Jayne
316 Surrett Cove Rd
Leicester NC 28748

SH GD AO MO 4.00 VA PL

OHIO

Woodspirits Ltd Inc
1920 Apple Rd
St Paris OH 43072

SH AO MO SASE WH (soaps) VA LE

Herb N' Ewe
Barb Wade/Sue Mills
11755 Nat'l Rd SE
Thornville OH 43076

SH WH MO GD VA PL LE ALO

Swisher Hill Herbs
4089 Swisher Rd
Urbana OH 43078

SH GD VA PL LE ALO

Pine Creek Herbs (Tussie Mussies*)
Kathleen Gips
152 South Main St
Chagrin Falls OH 44022

GD AO SH MO 2.50 VA LE

Village Herb Shop in The Market
   at Coach House Square
49 W Orange St
Chagrin Falls OH 44022
216-247-0733

SH VA

Sunnybrook Farms Nursery
9448 Mayfield Rd
Chesterland OH 44026

SH GD MO 2.00 VA LE

The Herb Society of America
9019 Kirtland Chardon Rd
Kirtland OH 44094

Cleveland Botanical Garden
(formerly Garden Center-Greater
   Cleveland)
11030 East Blvd
Cleveland OH 44106

GD

Forgotten Thyme Gardens
Joann Myers
6253 Norwalk Rd
Medina OH 44256

SH GD VA PL

Backyard Herbs
Joan Choby
4101 Canfield Rd
Canfield OH 44406

**SH GD AO MO 1.00 WH VA PL-ALO
LE**

Holborn Herb Growers Guild
   Herb Gardens
Western Reserve Village
Canfield Fairgrounds on Rte 46
Canfield OH 44406

GD

Carlyle Farms (Herbal Weaving*)
Nancy J Quinn-Simon
2110 Carlyle NE
Massillon OH 44646

SH AO GD MO 1.00 VA LE

Bittersweet Farm
1720 St Rt 60
Millersburg OH 44654
216-276-1977

SH GD MO 2.00 VA

Tole House Craft Shop
Elaine Arnold
1052 Perkins Drive
Wooster OH 44691

SH VA

Kentucky Babe
Mary Beth Henthorne
1727 Burbank Rd
Wooster OH 44691

SH GD AO VA

Quailcrest Farm
2810 Armstrong Rd
Wooster OH 44691

SH GD VA LE

Lewis Mtn Herbs & Everlastings
Judy Lewis
2345 ST RT 247
Manchester OH 45144

SH GD WH PL LE

Herb Garden Fragrances (Oils)
Rosella Mathieu
3744 Section Rd
Cincinnati OH 45236

AO MO SASE LE

Cox Arboretum
6733 Springboro Pike
Dayton OH 45449

SH GD VA PL LE

Centerville Historical Society
89 W Franklin St
Centerville OH 45459

GD

Bunch's Everlastings
Kathie Bunch
65 N Paint St
Chillicothe OH 45601

SH WH MO 2.00

Companion Plants
7247 N Coolville Ridge Rd
Athens OH 45701

SH WH MO 2.00 GD PL

The Herb House Catalog
Rebecca Fowler
340 Grove St
Bluffton OH 45817

MO 1.00 VA PL-ALO

OKLAHOMA

Sequoyah Gardens
Betty Wold
Rt 1 Box 80
Gore OK 74435

SH GD AO MO SASE VA PL-ALO LE

OREGON

Dutchmill Herbfarm (Organic*)
Barbara Remington
6640 NW Marsh Rd
Forest Grove OR 97116

SH GD AO MO 1.00 VA PL-ALO LE

Nichols Garden Nursery
Rosemarie Nichols MsGee
1190 N Pacific Hwy
Albany OR 97321

SH GD MO WH VA PL

Winchuck Herbals
Jeff & Connie Gallemore
14612 Munson Lane
Brookings OR 97415

SH GD MO VA PL LE

Organization for Advancement
    of Knowledge
218S SE Portola
Grants Pass OR 97526

MO WH

Windy River Farm/Cottage Garden
    Herbs (Organic*)
Judith Weiner
PO Box 312
Merlin OR 97532

GD MO WH VA

Goodwin Creek Gardens
PO Box 83
Williams OR 97544

AO GD MO 1.00 WH VA PL

PENNSYLVANIA

Four-Leaf Clover Herb Farm
Doris B Bachman
RD 1 Ridge Rd
Natrona Heights PA 15065

SH GD MO 1.50 PL-ALO VA LE

Carmen's Acres
Janet Carmen
1135 Braun Rd
Bethel Park PA 15102

SH AO PL LE

Woodworks & Sagecoach
Mary Thomas
RD 7 Box 378
Greensburg PA 15601

SH GD AO VA PL

The Nicolette House of
    Herbs & Everlastings
Dorothy Nicolette
725 Walnut St
Mt Pleasant PA 15666

SH GD AO VA PL LE

The Herb Merchant
Tim Newcomer/Paul Mertel
70 W Pomfret St
Carlisle PA 17013
717-249-0970

SH WH MO 3.00 PL LE GD VA

Cramer's Posie Patch
Whls Dried Botanicals
116 Trail Rd N
Elizabethtown PA 17022

SH MO WH SASE

Twin Ponds Herbal Heaven
Terry Kunst
RD 1
Lykens PA 17048

SH AO MO WH VA PL-ALO

The Rosemary House
Bertha Reppert
120 South Market St
Mechanisburg PA 17055

SH WH GD MO 2.00 VA PL LE

The Spice Cupboard
Evelyn Jennings
104 North Franklin St
Palmyra PA 17078

SH VA

Fort Hunter Mansion
5300 N Front St
Harrisburg PA 17110

GD

The Strawberry Patch
Ellen Blocher
658 Idaville York Spring Rd
Gardners PA 17324

SH GD AO VA PL LE

Alloway Gardens & Herb Farm
456 Mud College Rd
Littlestown PA 17340

SH GD VA PL LE

Village Herb Shop
Dorothy Weaver
Box 173
Blue Ball PA 17506

SH MO VA PL GD LE

The Herb Shop
20 E Main St
Lititz PA 17543

SH MO VA

Martin's Greenhouse
Marian H Martin
1516 Division Highway
Narvon PA 17555

SH GD PL

Pequea Trading Co
10 East Main St
Strasburg PA 17579

SH MO VA

The Herb Barn
Sandy Nelson
HC 64 Box 435D
Trout Run PA 17771
717-995-9327

MO PL

Little Farm (Herb Etchings)
Jane Conneen
820 Andrews Rd
Bath PA 18014

AO MO 3.00

Gingham 'n Spice Ltd (Oils*)
Nancy M McFayden
PO Box 88
Gardenville PA 18926

Retail/WH MO 2.00 VA

Potpourri From Herbal Acres
(Newsletter)
Box 428
Washington Crossing PA 18977

MO

Pennsbury Manor
400 Pennsbury Memorial Rd
Morrisville PA 19067

GD

Penn Herb Company
603 North 2nd St
Philadelphia PA 19123

SH MO 1.00 WH VA

Dilly Duo Herbs
2015 Potshop Rd RD 2
Norristown PA 19403

SH GD SASE WH PL-ALO LE

Spice Smuggler
Linda Mack
835 W Main St
Lansdale PA 19446

SH MO VA

Blue Mountain Herbals
Shirley L Dierolf
7 North 4th St
Hamburg PA 19526

SH MO SH VA PL-ALO

RHODE ISLAND

Cherry Valley Farm Crafts
Sue Carpenter
RD 2 Box 531
N Scituate RI 02857

AO VA

Daze-End Herb Farm
Loretta McMahon
Abbott Run Valley Rd
Cumberland RI 02864

SH GD WH PL LE

Hi-on-a-Hill Herb Farm
836 Old Smithfield Rd
No Smithfield RI 02896

SH AO VA PL

Meadowbrook Herb Garden
Rte 138
Wyoming RI 02898

SH GD MO 1.00 WH VA PL-ALO LE

SOUTH CAROLINA

Park Seed Company
Cokesbury Rd
Greenwood SC 29648-0046

MO VA

TENNESSEE

Butterflies 'n Blossoms
Janice Logan
125 Lynchburg Highway
Fayetteville TN 37334

SH AO MO 2.00 WH VA

McFaddens' Vines & Wreaths
Joe/Betty/Tammy McFadden
Rt 3 Box 2360
Butler TN 37640

SH MO 1.00 WH VA

Owen Farms
Rt 3 Box 158A
2951 Curve-Nankipoo Rd
Ripley TN 38063

SH MO 2.00 VA PL

Log Cabin Herbs
Jean Dixon
676 Grinders Creek Rd
Hohenwald TN 38462

SH GD AO VA PL LE

TEXAS

Ladybug Press (Heavenly Herbs Book)
Lane Furneaux
7348 Lane Park Court
Dallas TX 75225

GD AO MO SASE WH LE

Hilltop Herb Farm
PO Box 1734
Cleveland TX 77327

SH MO 2.00 VA PL

VERMONT

Rathdowney Herbs & Crafts
Louise Downey Butler
3 River St
Bethel VT 05032

SH MO VA WH 1.00

Shelburne Museum
Apothecary & Fragrance Shops
Route 7
Shelburne VT 05482-0010

SH GD

Meadowsweet Herb Farm
729 Eastham Rd
Shrewsbury VT 05738

SH GD MO WH VA PL-ALO LE

The Herb Patch
Richard & Diane Copley
PO Box 1111
Middletown Springs VT 05757

MO WH VA

Le Jardin du Gourmet (Seeds)
PO Box 275
St. Johnsbury Center VT 05863

MO

VIRGINIA

Nature's Finest
Mike/Jen Mescher
PO Box 10311
Burke VA 22015

MO 2.00 ref WH VA

Mount Vernon
Historic Home of George Washington
Mount Vernon VA 22121

GD

T DeBaggio Herbs
923 North Ivy St
Arlington VA 22201

GD PL

Country Manor
Rt 211 PO Box 520
Sperryville VA 22740

SH GD MO 2.00 WH VA

Faith Mountain Company
Main St PO Box 199-PH
Sperryville VA 22740

SH GD MO VA PL-ALO LE

Colonial Williamsburg
Williamsburg VA 23185

SH GD VA LE

Agecroft Hall
4305 Sulgrave Rd
Richmond VA 23221

GD LE

Tom Thumb Workshops
Grace Wakefield
14100 Lankford Highway (Rt 13)
PO Box 357
Mappsville VA 23407

SH GD MO 1.00 WH VA LE

Antique Orchid Herbary
Linda Baltimore Morgan
Rt 6 Box 734
Abingdon VA 24210

SH GD MO 1.00 WH VA PL-ALO LE

WASHINGTON

The Herbfarm
Ron Zimmerman
32804 ISS Fall City Rd
Fall City WA 98024

SH GD VA PL LE

Alpine Herb Farm Products
Linda Quintana
PO Box 262
Deming WA 98244

SH MO 1.00 WH PL-ALO LE

Giannangelo Farms
5500 Limestone Pt Rd
Friday Harbor WA 98250

SH AO GD VA

Island Farmcrafters
(Everlastings/Wreaths/Garlic*)
Waldron Island WA 98297

MO .50 VA

Silver Bay Herb Farm
9151 Tracyton Blvd
Bremerton WA 98310

SH GD VA PL-ALO LE MO 1.00

Cedarbrook Herb Farm
Toni/Terry Anderson
1345 Sequim Ave South
Sequim WA 98382

SH GD MO 2.00 VA LE PL-ALO

Bears, Herbs, Hearts & Flowers
Arlen & Verona Latta
81 E Raymond-Willapa Rd
Raymond WA 98577

SH GD AO MO 2.00 PL-ALO VA LE

Trout Lake Farm (Organic*)
149 Little Mountain Rd
Trout Lake WA 98650

WH VA

WISCONSIN

Hidden Hollow Heriary
Elaine Vandien
N88 W 18407 Duke St
Menomonee Falls WI 53051

GD AO MO 1.00 VA PL-ALO LE

Boerner Botanical Gardens
5879 S 92nd St
Hales Corners WI 53130

GD

The Magick Garden
Linda Gannon
5703 Country Walk
McFarland WI 53558

SH AO VA LE

Wood Violet Books (Herbs &
Gardening*)
Debbie Cravens
3814 Sunhill Dr
Madison WI 53704

MO 2.00 AO

Dried Floral Creations
Denise Solsrud
N5583 Rangeline Rd
Tony WI 54563

SH MO SASE WH VA

Victorian Heirloom Gifts from
God's Green Acres Herbary
Terry Kemp
N6086 SN
Onalaska WI 54650
608-783-7526

WH MO 2.00 VA LE

US VIRGIN ISLANDS

Sunny Caribee Spice Company
The Gunters
Box 3237
St Thomas US Virgin Islands 00803

SH WH MO 2.00 VA

CANADA

Richters Herbs
357 Highway 47
Goodwood Ontario
Canada, L0C 1A0

SH GD MO 2.00 WH VA PL LE

Tansy Farm
RR 1
Agassiz B.C.
Canada V0M 1A0

MO 1.50 PL

Royal Botanical Gardens
PO Box 399
Hamilton Ontario
Canada L8N 3H8

GD

Country Green
Jeannette Verheist
Box 178
Radville Saskatchewan
Canada S0C 2G0

SH GD VA PL ALO LE

Kiln Farm
RR 3
Puslinch Ontario
Canada N0B 2J0

SH GD VA PL ALO LE

Alberta Nurseries & Seeds Ltd
PO Box 20
Bowden Alberta
Canada T0M 0K0

SH MO 2.00 VA

The Blossoms Bed & Breakfast
Berna Critchlow
RR 1
Westfiled (Morrisdale) NB
Canada E0G 3J0

SH GD LE

BIBLIOGRAPHY OF
BOOKS AND PERIODICALS

Herbs — General

American Herb Association Quarterly Newsletter, Kathi Keville, ed. The American Herb Association, P.O. Box 353-POH, Rescue, CA 95672. Subscription includes membership in the AHA.

THE BEGINNER'S HERB GARDEN. The Herb Society of America, 9019 Kirtland Chardon Rd., Mentor, OH 44060

FUN WITH GROWING HERBS INDOORS, Virginie and George Elbert. Crown Publishers, New York (1974)

GROWING HERBS IN POTS, John Brimer. Simon & Schuster, New York (1978)

GROWING AND USING HERBS SUCCESSFULLY, Betty E.M. Jacobs. Garden Way Publishing, Pownal, VT 05261 (1981)

Herbalgram, Mark Blumenthal and Rob McCaleb, ed. The Herb Research Foundation and The American Herbal Products Trade Association, pub. Quarterly newsletter emphasizing herbal research and large-scale merchandising. Herb News, P.O. Box 12602-POH, Austin, TX 78711

THE HERB BOOK, John B. Lust, ed. Bantam Books, New York (1974)

HERB GARDEN DESIGN, Faith Swanson and Virginia Rady. University Press of New England, Hanover, NH (1984)

HERB GARDENING AT ITS BEST, Sal Gilbertie. Atheneum, New York (1978)

HERB GARDENING IN FIVE SEASONS, Adelma Simmons. Dutton, New York (1977)

HERB GARDENS OF DELIGHT, Adelma Simmons. Dutton, New York (1979)

The Herb-of-the-Month Club. A monthly package containing the featured herb with recipes and lore. P.O. Box 1,000, Atkinson, NH 03811

HERBS AND THINGS: JEANNE ROSE'S HERBAL, Jeanne Rose. Grosset & Dunlap, New York (1972)

HERBS: HOW TO SELECT, GROW, AND ENJOY, Norma Lathrop. HP Books, Tucson (1981)

HERBS OF THE ZODIAC, Bertha Reppert. Rosemary House, 120 So. Market St., Mechanicsburg, PA 17055

HERBS TO GROW INDOORS, Adelma Simmons. Dutton, New York (1969)

PARK'S SUCCESS WITH HERBS, Foster and Louden. George W. Park Seed Co., Greenwood, SC 29647

Potpourri From Herbal Acres, Phyllis V. Shaudys, ed. Quarterly newsletter networking tips, crafts, and recipes from business owners and hobbyists. Free "Herb Blurb" and listings in Herbfest column for subscribers. Pine Row Publications, Box 428-POH, Washington Crossing, PA 18977

THE RODALE HERB BOOK. Rodale Press, Emmaus, PA (1976)

WHAT YOU NEED TO KNOW TO PRESERVE HERBS, Marilyn Hempstead. Fox Hill Farm, Box 7-HA, Parma, MI 49269

THE WORLD OF HERBS AND SPICES. Ortho Books, San Francisco (ND)

Herbs — Regional

HERB GARDENING IN THE SOUTH, Sol Meltzer. Pacesetter Press (1977)

HILLTOP HERB FARM Catalog. Hilltop Herb Farm, P.O. Box 1734, Cleveland, TX 77327 (includes comprehensive plant guide).

HOW TO GROW HERBS IN THE MIDWEST. Missouri Botanical Gardens, St. Louis, MO 63166

Roses

Heritage Roses. Jerry Fellman, 947 Broughton Way, Woodburn, OR 97071 or Lily Shohan, RD 1, Clinton Corners, NY 12514. Send SASE with inquiry.

ROSES OF YESTERDAY AND TODAY catalog. 802 Brown's Valley Rd., Watsonville, CA 95076

Herbal Crafts

AN ALBUM OF FRAGRANCE, Edith Baile. Cardamom Press, Box D, Richmond, ME 04357.

BOTANICAL WREATHS: A GUIDE TO COLLECTING, PRESERVING AND DESIGNING WITH NATURAL MATERIALS, Jane Holliday and Rachel Hartley. Flower Press, RFD 1, Box 222-P, Warner, NH 03278.

CATALOG SOURCES FOR CREATIVE PEOPLE, Margaret Boyd. P.O. Box 6232-POH, Augusta, GA 30906.

DECK THE HALLS WITH ARTEMISIA: CHRISTMAS DECORATING WITH HERBS, Barbara Radcliffe Rogers. Herbitage Farm, RD 2, Richmond, NH 03470

DECORATING WITH FRAGRANCE, Grace Wakefield. Tom Thumb Workshops, P.O. Box 332-HA, Chincoteague, VA 23336

DRIED FLOWER DESIGNS (#76). Brooklyn Botanic Garden, 1000 Washington Ave., Brooklyn, NY 11225.

DRIED FLOWERS WITH A DIFFERENCE, Sunny O'Neil. P.O. Box 137, Dept. POH, Glen Echo, MD 20812.

DYE PLANTS & DYEING (#46). Brooklyn Botanic Garden, 1000 Washington Ave., Brooklyn, NY 11225

FRAGRANT WREATHS AND OTHER AROMATIC BOTANICAL CREATIONS, Grace Wakefield. Tom Thumb Workshops, P.O. Box 332-HA, Chincoteague, VA 23336

GIFTS FROM YOUR GARDEN, Scobey and Myers. Bobbs-Merrill Co., Indianapolis and New York (1975)

HERBS AND THEIR ORNAMENTAL USES (#68). Brooklyn Botanic Garden, 1000 Washington Ave., Brooklyn, NY 11225

THE HERBS OF CHRISTMAS, Betsy Williams, Dept. POH, 155 Chestnut St., Andover, MA 01810

NATURAL PLANT DYEING (#72). Brooklyn Botanic Garden, 1000 Washington Ave., Brooklyn, NY 11225

PLANNING AN HERBAL WEDDING, Betsy Williams. Dept. POH, 155 Chestnut St., Andover, MA 01810

POTPOURRI, INCENSE, AND OTHER FRAGRANT CONCOCTIONS, Ann Tucker. Workman, New York (1972)

SOAP: MAKING IT AND ENJOYING IT, Ann Bramson. Workman, New York (1975)

Cooking With Herbs

BACKDOOR HERB GARDEN RECIPES, Paulette and Peterson. Fernwood, Inc., 1720 Range Line Rd., Niles, MI 49120

A BOUNTIFUL COLLECTION. Rosemary House, 120 So. Market St., Mechanicsburg, PA 17055

CLEMENT HERB FARM COOKBOOK, Diane Clement. Rogers, AR 72756

COOKING WITH MINT, Box 33-PFHA, No. Judson, IN 46366

COOKING WITHOUT A GRAIN OF SALT, Elma Bagg. Doubleday, New York (1964)

CRAIG CLAIBORNE'S GOURMET DIET, Craig Claiborne and Pierre Franey. Ballantine Books, New York (1981)

THE DEFINITIVE BOOK ON HERB TEA PARTIES, Rosemary House, 120 So. Market St., Mechanicsburg, PA 17055

HERBAL HORS D'OEUVRES and PANTRY PRESENTS, Givens and Vanderhoff. Herbs by Jean, 1161 Oakdale Rd. NE, Atlanta, GA 30307

HERBS AND SPICES, Pat Bourdo. Woodland Herb Farm, 7741 No. Manitou Trail West, Northport, MI 49670

HERBS FROM CULTURE TO COOKING. Herb Society of Greater Cincinnati, P.O. Box 14763, Cincinnati, OH 45214

SALT-FREE HERB COOKERY, Edith Stovel. Garden Way Publishing, Pownal, VT 05261

THE VEGETABLE SPAGHETTI COOKBOOK, Derek Fell and Phyllis V. Shaudys. Pine Row Publications, P.O. Box 428-POH, Washington Crossing, PA 18977

Herbs for Good Health

BACK TO EDEN, Jethro Kloss. Back to Eden (1985)

THE COMPLETE HERBAL GUIDE TO NATURAL HEALTH AND BEAUTY, Dian Buchman. Doubleday, New York (1973)

DON'T EAT YOUR HEART OUT, Joseph Piscatella and Bernie Piscatella. Workman, New York (1983)

The Herb Report. Newsletter devoted to the progress of herbal medicine. P.O. Box 1568, Hobe Sound, FL 33455

THE HONEST HERBAL: A SENSIBLE GUIDE TO HERBS AND RELATED REMEDIES, Varro Tyler. George T. Stickley Co., 210 W. Washington Sq., Philadelphia, PA 19106

SALT-FREE HERB COOKERY, Edith Stovel. Garden Way Publishing, Pownal, VT 05261

SHAKER HERBS AND THEIR MEDICINAL USES, Dee Herbrandson. Shaker Heritage Society, Albany-Shaker Rd., Watervliet, NY 12189 (1985). Archival materials, including records and journals of Shaker herbalists, are also available by appointment at Shaker museums and libraries.

STALKING THE HEALTHFUL HERBS, Euell Gibbons. David McKay Co., New York (1970)

WEINER'S HERBAL: THE GUIDE TO HERBAL MEDICINE, Dr. Michael Weiner. Stein & Day, New York (1980)

Herbal Businesses

See Reading List following Appendix B, "Growing Fragrant Herbs for Profit."

Herb Resources

THE HERB GARDENER'S RESOURCE GUIDE, Paula Oliver. Northwind
Farm, Rte. 2, Box 75A-P, Shevlin, MN 56675

THE HERB SOCIETY OF AMERICA, 9019 Kirtland Chardon Rd.,
Mentor, OH 44060. Send 50¢ for list of publications, including
information about the "Traveler's Guide to Herb Gardens."

The newsletter, POTPOURRI FROM HERBAL ACRES, published by
Phyllis Shaudys, may be purchased from *PINE ROW PUBLICATIONS
BOX 428-POH WASHINGTON CROSSING PA 18977* for $18.00 for the
current Fall through Summer series, including the past issues.

INDEX

Numbers in italics indicate that illustrations appear on that page.

A

Advent herbs, 202
Advent wreath, 204
Ajuga, 213
Albus thyme, 228
Alecost. *See* Costmary
Allspice, 13
Aloe, 213
Ambrosia, 214
American Heart Association, 15
American Rose Society, 80
Angelica, *99*, 214
  stems, candied, 99
Anise, 214
Anise hyssop, 214
Anise mint. *See* Anise hyssop
Anne's vegetable juice, 138
Annie's dilly bread in a casserole, 57
Annie's rosemary fruit punch, 199
Appetizers. *See also* Dip
  Christmas yule log, 201
  eggplant caviar, 139
  herbed cheese, 200
  Penn-Cumberland's sausage balls,
    200
  pickled herb carrots, 138
  Rose Canny's sage sticks, 200
  sage cheese spread, 188
  super holiday cheese wafers, 201
Apple
  pulp pomander balls, 169 – 171
  /sausage stuffing for pork, 181
Applemint, 8, *11*, 223. *See also* Mint
  tea, 11
April, 69 – 85
Artemisia, 214 – 215
  silver king, *64*, 64 – 65, 214 – 215
    harvesting, 145
  silver mound, 215

Artemisia (*continued*)
  silver queen, 215
  sweet Annie, 65
  sweet wormwood, *65*, 65
  tree, 160
  wreaths, 155 – 156
August, 133 – 145
Autumn crocus. *See* Saffron

B

Bacon
  egg casserole brunch for six, 92
  Italian scramble, 92
Bag drying, 110 – 111
  chart, 112 – 114
Balm. *See* Lemon balm
Barbara's kitchen spice potpourri, 144
Basic herb vinegar salad dressing, 109
Basic lavender potpourri, 81
Basic omelet recipe, 91
Basic pine potpourri, 188
Basic recipe for potpourri, 80
Basic seed cookies, 197
Basic sweet bag potpourri, 51
Basil (sweet), *134*, 135 – 139, 215
  basiled eggs, 92
  basiled noodles, 138
  bush, 215
  camphor, 215
  cinnamon, 215
  Colette's pesto, 137
  holy, 215
  jelly, 164
  lemon, 215
  lettuce leaf, 215
  licorice, 215
  opal, 215
  pesto sauce, 136
  -tomato jam, 138

Basiled eggs, 92
Basiled noodles, 138
Baste. *See also* Marinade
  double-duty salt-free dressing, 19
  herbed fish, 19
  rosemary chicken, 19
Bath
  bags, 22
  bubbles, scented, 23
  decoction, 22
  herbal love, 49
  infusion, 22
  lavender, 23
    beauty, 23
  oil
    dispersible, 22
    floating, 22
  sachet, 23
Bathing with herbs, 21–24
Bathroom deodorizer, 129
Bay (sweet), *35*, 215 – 216
  leaf wreath, 204
Beans. *See also* Green beans
  dried, seasoning, with herbs/
    spices, chart, 17
  soup, overnight hearty, 50
Beauty scrub, oatmeal, 24
Bee balm, 90, 216. *See also* Bergamot
Bee bread. *See* Borage
Beef
  chowder, 35
  heavenly rolled round roast, 76
  herbed burgers, 76
  meat loaf Parmesan, 76
  roast
    with herbs, 75 – 76
    marinade, herby, 77
    seasoning, 76
  seasoning, with herbs/spices,
    chart, 17
  spiced meatballs with gravy, 77

Beef (*continued*)
    surprise meat loaf, 77
Beginner's Herb Garden, 46, 261
Belgian endive. *See* Chicory
Benne. *See* Sesame
Bergamot, *46*, 216. *See also* Bee balm
    orange. *See* Orange bergamot
Berry-nice, 50
Betony, 216. *See also* Lamb's ears
Bible leaf. *See* Costmary
Bird's foot. *See* Fenugreek
Biscuits, herb, 58
Black peppermint tea, 10
Borage, 216
Botanical Wreaths, 156
Bouquet garni vinegar, 109
Bouquets, May, 99
Bourdo, Pat, 197
Bread(s), 56 – 57
    Annie's dilly, in a casserole, 57
    crumbs, seasoned, 59
    granola pumpkin, 196
    oregano cheddar, 58
    quick caraway cheese, 57
Breadless dressing, 181
Bridal showers, 116 – 118
Broiled zucchini or yellow squash,
    125
Brunch. *See also* Main dishes
    basic omelet recipe, 91
    basiled eggs, 92
    egg casserole, for six, 92
    Greek omelet, 91
    herbed pancake roll-ups, 92
    Italian scramble, 92
Buchman, Dian Dincin, 21
Bug repellent, 127. *See also* Insect(s),
    repellents
Bugleweed. *See* Ajuga
Burnet, 216
Bush basil, 215
Butter, 56 – 57
    chive, for chicken or fish, 19
    clarified, 124
    herb, 16, 59
    lemon, for fish, 151
    slim gourmet's lemon-garlic, 59
    thyme-savory herb, 188
    whipped garlic, 57
Butterfly sachets, 97

C

Cake
    citrus cheese-cake, 195

Cake (*continued*)
    nutmeg, 195
    rose geranium, 194
    rosemary, 194
Calendula, *13*, 217
Camomile, *21*, 217
    jell soap, 21
    skin toner, 24
Camphor basil, 215
Candied angelica stems, 99
Candied citrus peel, 187
Candied violet Libra, 98
Candy, herb, 198
Canny, Rose, 18
Car perfume, 129
Caraway, 217
    cheese bread, quick, 57
    thyme, 228
Card sachets, 24 – 25
Cardamom, 14
    cookies, 195
Cardomon. *See* Cardamom
Carnation spice potpourri, 49
Carpet-fresh, 129
Carrot(s)
    -parsnip tarragon, 125
    pickled herb, 138
Casserole, eggs, brunch for six, 92
Cassia. *See* Cinnamon
Catalogs, 239
Catmint, 217
Catnip, *96*, 96, 218
    tea, 12
Caviar, eggplant, 139
Cedar closet, instant, 68
Chamomile. *See* Camomile
Charts
    companion planting with herbs, 93
    fixatives for potpourri, 84 – 85
    harvesting and preserving herbs,
        112 – 114
    herb growth & use, 42 – 45
    potpourri blending, 82
    seasoning poultry, fish, meat &
        other proteins with herbs/
        spices, 17
    seasoning vegetables with herbs/
        spices, 16
    varieties of mint, 9
Cheddar bread, oregano, 58
Cheese
    bread
        oregano cheddar, 58
        quick caraway, 57
    herbed, 200
    spread, sage, 188

Cheese (*continued*)
    wafers, super holiday, 201
    wedges, herb, 58
Cheese-cake, citrus, 195
Chervil, *33*, 218
Chewy cranberry gingers, 196
Chicken. *See also* Poultry
    bake, easy make-ahead, 183
    baste, rosemary, 19
    chive butter for, 19
    Faith's indoor barbecued, 182
    golden glazed, 172
    liver stuffing, Phyl's, 180
    loaf, tarragon, 182
    Parmesan, 175
    -rice bake, 182
    Simon & Garfunkel, 182
    soup...plus, 35
Chicory, 218
Chinese Christmas fern, 65
Chinese parsley. *See* Coriander
Chive(s), *56*, 56, 218
    butter for chicken or fish, 19
    spray, 127
Chowder. *See also* Soup
    beef, 35
    fish, 35
    herbed corn, 34
Christmas morning fruit punch, 205
Christmas spice potpourri, 208
Christmas tree ornaments, 205,
    206 – 207
Christmas yule log, 201
Chutney, fresh cranberry, 187
Cider, hot mulled, 174
Cilantro. *See* Coriander
Cinnamint potpourri, 208
Cinnamon, 14
    basil, 215
    stick wreath, 203
Citrus cheese-cake, 195
Citrus peel(s), 30
    candied, 187
Citruscent potpourri, 49
Clarified butter, 124
Clark, Bob, 185
Clary sage, 226
Climatic differences in herb growth
    patterns, 47
Clove cookies, 196
Coconut thyme, 228
Cold frame, 60, 61
Colette's pesto, 137
Cologne, dog, 128
Comfrey, *12*, 45, 218 – 219

Common thyme. *See* Thyme
Companion planting with herbs,
　chart, 93
*Complete Herbal Guide to Natural
　Health & Beauty*, 21
Cook Without Salt, 18
Cookies
　basic seed cookies, 197
　cardamom, 195
　chewy cranberry gingers, 196
　clove, 196
　lemon thyme cookies, 198
　Libran quickies, 98
　molasses, 194
　rosemary squares, 196
　tansy, 194
　Taurus mint cookies, 197
Coriander, *157*, 219
Corn chowder, herbed, 34
Cosmetics, kitchen, 24
Costmary, 219
Cottage cheese dips, creamy, 200
Crab-cucumber salad, 151
Crabmeat Stroganoff, 151
Crackers
　dilled snack, 187
　super holiday cheese wafers, 201
Cranberry
　chutney, fresh, 187
　gingers, chewy, 196
　punch, hot spiced, 199
Creamy cottage cheese dips, 200
Creeping thyme, 75, 228
Creeping, golden thyme, 228
Cucumber salad, crab-, 151
Curry plant, 219
Cuttings, 30 – 31

D

December, 191 – 208
Decoction, 22
Dehydrating oast, for drying herbs,
　105
Deodorizer, bathroom, 129
Desserts
　basic seed cookies, 197
　cardamom cookies, 195
　chewy cranberry gingers, 196
　citrus cheese-cake, 195
　clove cookies, 196
　granola pumpkin bread, 196
　herb candy, 198
　lemon thyme cookies, 198
　Libran quickies, 98

Desserts (*continued*)
　minted grapefruit, 197
　molasses cookies, 194
　nutmeg cake, 195
　rose geranium cake, 194
　rosemary cake, 194
　rosemary squares, 196
　tansy cookies, 194
　Taurus mint cookies, 197
　watermelon surprise, 126
Diet soup, 34
Dieter's veggie-ghetti, 138
Dill, 89, *148*, 150, 219
Dilled snack crackers, 187
Dilly bread in a casserole, Annie's, 57
Dilly shrimp dip, 200
Dip
　creamy cottage cheese, 200
　dilly shrimp, 200
　herbed cheese, 200
Dispersible bath oil, 22
Dog cologne, 128
Double-duty salt-free dressing, 19
Dough, scented, 201
Dressing. *See also* Salad, dressing;
　Stuffing
　breadless, 181
　double-duty salt-free, 19
　instant rice, 183
　oyster parsley, 181
Dried herbs, storing, 105
Drinks
　Anne's vegetable juice, 138
　Annie's rosemary fruit punch, 199
　Christmas morning fruit punch,
　　205
　Herbal Acres' orange mint spiced
　　tea, 199
　herbal iced, 125 – 126
　herbs of Shakespeare tea, 20
　hippocras, 98
　hot mulled cider, 174
　hot spiced cranberry punch, 199
　hot spiked punch for 40, 199
　iced mint tea, 125
　lemon balm punch, 126
　minty grape cooler, 126
　red herb punch or tea, 199
　rose hip tea, 199
　Rosemary House "Mai Bowle", 98
　rosemary-pineapple cooler, 126
　royal wedding herbal punch, 118
　spice tea, 14
　spicy punch, 198
　sugarless sun tea, 125 – 126

Drying herbs, 103 – 106
Dyer's weed. *See* Woad

E

Easy make-ahead chicken bake, 183
Eggplant caviar, 139
Eggs
　basic omelet recipe, 91
　basiled, 92
　casserole brunch for six, 92
　Greek omelet, 91
　Italian scramble, 92
　seasoning, 92
　with herbs/spices, chart, 17
Eggshells, 30
Elephant garlic, 172
English lavender. *See* Lavender
Essential fragrant oils, 79

F

Faith's indoor barbecued chicken, 182
False saffron. *See* Safflower
Feather geranium. *See* Ambrosia
February, 27 – 51
Fennel, *166*, 219
Fenugreek, 220
Feverfew, 220
Fireplace fragrance, 201
Fish. *See also* Seafood
　baste, herbed, 19
　chive butter for, 19
　chowder, 35
　Herbal Acres' baked flounder or
　　haddock, 150
　Herbal Acres' lemon-balmed fish
　　broil, 151
　lemon butter for, 151
　Phyl's, 19
　salmon quiche, 151
　seasoning, with herbs/spices,
　　chart, 17
Fixatives, 79, 80 – 81
　chart, 84 – 85
Flea & tick powder, herbal, 128
Flea rinse/spray, rosemary, 128
Floating bath oil, 22
Flounder, Herbal Acres' baked, 150
Flower baskets, 184 – 185
Food dehydrators, 105, 120
Footbath, herbal, 23
Frankincense, 202
　and myrrh potpourri, 158 – 159

French tarragon, *102*, 106, 227
Fresh cranberry chutney, 187
Fruit. *See also* specific fruit
  juice, herb and, combinations, 168
  punch
    Christmas morning, 205
    rosemary, Annie's, 199
Fruity pine potpourri, 188
Fungi disease spray, 127

G

Garden. *See also* Gourmet gardening;
    Herb(s), bed; Herb(s), garden
  bug repellent, 127
  indoor, planning, 145
  kraut relish, 139
  sage. *See* Sage
Garlic, *172*, 220
  elephant, 172
  growing, 172
  butter
    slim gourmet's lemon-, 59
    whipped, 57
Garnish
  candied angelica stems, 99
  candied violet Libra, 98
Geranium(s), scented, 31 – 33
  rose, *28*
    cake, 194
    jelly, 164
    potpourri, 49
  TLC formula for, 32
German camomile. *See* Camomile
Germander, 220
Gift baskets, 184 – 185
Gingers, chewy cranberry, 196
Golden glazed chicken, 172
Gourmet gardening
  chives, 56
  dill, 150
  marjoram, 90 – 91
  mints, 8 – 10
  oregano, 163 – 164
  parsley, 56
  rosemary, 193 – 194
  sage, 179 – 181
  scented geraniums, 31 – 33
  summer savory, 123 – 124
  sweet basil, 135 – 139
  tarragon, 106
  thyme, 75
  winter savory, 124
Grain weevil prevention, 127 – 128

Granola pumpkin bread, 196
Grape cooler, minty, 126
Grapefruit
  minted, 197
Grapevine wreath, 156
Grasshopper repellent, 127
Greek hayseed. *See* Fenugreek
Greek omelet, 91
Green beans
  it's bean thyme, 124
Green salad, 18
Greenhouse
  improvising, 61 – 63
  space problems, 72
Growing Fragrant Herbs for Profit,
  231 – 245

H

Haddock, Herbal Acres' baked, 150
Hamburgers, herbed, 76
Harvesting
  herbs, 110 – 114, 144 – 145
  lavender, 118 – 119
  roses, 111
Health, using spices and herbs for,
  14 – 15
Heavenly rolled round roast, 76
Heliotrope, 220
Herb Garden Design, 46
Herb Gardening at Its Best, 145
Herb Society of America, 46, 244
Herb(s)
  beds. *See also* Herb(s), garden
    planning and plotting, 36 – 39
    preparation, 55
    "specialty", 46
  biscuits, 58
  blend, no-salt, 18
  businesses
    1986 recommended reading list
     for, 242 – 243
    wholesale sources & additional
     resources for, 243 – 245
  butters, 16, 59
  candy, 198
  catalogs, 239
  cheese wedges, 58
  companion planting, chart, 93
  cuttings, transporting, 120
  defined, 13
  dried, storing, 105
  drying, 103 – 106, 110 – 111
  and fruit juice combinations, 168

Herb(s) *(continued)*
  garden. *See also* Herb(s), beds
    designing your first, 40 – 41
    potpourri, 159
  growing for profit, 231 – 245
  growth & use chart, 42 – 45
  growth patterns, regional and
    climatic differences in, 47
  hardy
    propagation of, 72 – 74
    spring care of, 72
  harvesting, 110 – 114, 144 – 145
    chart, 112 – 114
  jellies. *See* Jelly(ies)
  lore for lovers, 48
  meanings of, 115
  mix for soups and stews, 33
  of Shakespeare tea, 20
  ornamental, 89 – 90
  preserving, 110 – 114
    chart, 112 – 114
  reputed to bring good fortune, 118
  rice mix, 183
  seasoning poultry, fish, meat, &
    other proteins with, chart, 17
  seasoning vegetables with, chart, 16
  soap balls, 22
  starting from seeds
    indoors, 59 – 64
    in the ground, 94 – 96
  tea sandwiches, 160
  using for better health, 14 – 15
  vinegars. *See* Vinegar(s), herb
Herbal Acres' baked flounder or
  haddock, 150
Herbal Acres' household spice, 25
Herbal Acres' lemon-balmed fish
  broil, 151
Herbal Acres' orange mint spiced
  tea, 199
Herbal Acres' tansy-bansy, 68
Herbal flea & tick powder, 128
Herbal footbath, 23
Herbal hot plate, 160
Herbal infusion, 167
Herbal love bath, 49
Herbal notebook, 20 – 21
"Herbal pillows", 96
Herbal skin oil, 23
Herbed burgers, 76
Herbed cheese, 200
Herbed corn chowder, 34
Herbed fish baste, 19
Herbed pancake roll-ups, 92
Herbed popcorn, 17
Herbed vegetable salad, 125

Herbitage Farm's moth potpourri, 66
Herbs & Spices, 197
Herbs of the Zodiac, 98
Herbs to Grow Indoors, 63
Herby roast beef marinade, 77
Heritage Roses, 80
Highland summer potpourri, 141
Hippocras, 98
Holidays
    planning for, 152 – 156
    potpourri for, 158 – 159
Holy basil, 215
Horehound, *202*, 220
Hot mulled cider, 174
Hot pads, spicy, 143
Hot plate, herbal, 160
Hot spiced cranberry punch, 199
Hot spiked punch for 40, 199
Hyssop, 221

I

Iced mint tea, 125
Iced tea, 11. *See also* Tea(s)
    mint, 125
    red herb, 199
    sun tea, sugarless, 125 – 126
Iced tomato/herb soup, 139
Incense, winter spice, 25
Indian cress. *See* Nasturtium
Indian-flavored popcorn, 18
Infusion, 22
Insect(s), 105 – 106, *105*
    repellents for humans, 129
    repellents for pets, 128 – 129
    repellents for plants, 127 – 128
Instant cedar closet, 68
Instant Christmascent simmer
    potpourri, 201
Instant potpourri, 83
Instant rice dressing, 183
It's bean thyme, 124
Italian scramble, 92

J

Jam. *See also* Jelly
    basil-tomato, 138
    pumpkin, 187
January, 5 – 25
Jasmine rose sachet, 130
Jelly, 164 – 168. *See also* Jam
    basic recipes, 167
    basil, 164

Jelly (*continued*)
    lemon balm, 164
    mint, 164
    orange mint, 164
    recipe using apple juice, 168
    recipe using liquid pectin, 167
    recipe using powdered pectin, 167
    rose geranium, 164
    rosemary, 164
    sage, 164
    thyme, 164
Jerusalem oak. *See* Ambrosia
Juice
    Anne's vegetable, 138
    fruit, herb and, combinations, 168
July, 121 – 131
June, 101 – 120

K

Kitchen cosmetics, 24
Kitchen crafts, 143 – 144
Kitchen herb wreath, 156
Knitbone. *See* Comfrey

L

Lace wreaths, miniature, 206
Lacy hooped potpourri decoration,
    186
Lady Di's diamonds, 117
Lady's mantle, 221
Lamb, seasoning, with herbs/spices,
    chart, 17
Lamb's ears, 221
Laurel, true. *See* Bay (sweet)
Lavender, *32*, 80 – 81, 221
    bath, 23
        beauty, 23
    cotton. *See* Santolina
    harvesting, 118 – 119
    potpourri
        basic, 81
        lemon-, 159
    tree, 152 – 153
    wands, 119 – 120
Layering, 74
Leek, 221
Lemon balm, 11, *164*, 222
    Herbal Acres' lemon-balmed fish
        broil, 151
    jelly, 164
    punch, 126
Lemon basil, 215
Lemon butter for fish, 151

Lemon grass, 222
Lemon herb tea, 11
Lemon potpourri, spicy, 130
Lemon thyme, 75, *151*, 228
    cookies, 198
Lemon verbena, 11, *130*, 222
Lemon-garlic butter, slim gourmet's,
    59
Lemon-lavender potpourri, 159
Lettuce leaf basil, 215
Libran quickies, 98
Licorice basil, 215
Licorice mint. *See* Anise hyssop
Liver, seasoning, with herbs/spices,
    chart, 17
Lovage, 222
Love potions, 48
Lunaria, 222
Lyness, Dody, 104–105, 203, 208

M

Mace, 14
Main dishes. *See also* Salad
    basic omelet recipe, 91
    basiled eggs, 92
    casserole brunch for six, 92
    chicken Simon & Garfunkel, 182
    chicken-rice bake, 182
    Colette's pesto, 137
    crabmeat Stroganoff, 151
    dieter's veggie-ghetti, 138
    easy make-ahead chicken bake, 183
    Faith's indoor barbecued chicken,
        182
    golden glazed chicken, 172
    Greek omelet, 91
    heavenly rolled round roast, 76
    Herbal Acres' baked flounder or
        haddock, 150
    Herbal Acres' lemon-balmed fish
        broil, 151
    herbed burgers, 76
    Italian scramble, 92
    meat loaf Parmesan, 76
    Parmesan chicken, 175
    parsley pesto surprise, 137
    Phyl's fish, 19
    Risotto, 172
    roast beef with herbs, 75 – 76
    Rock Cornish hens with rice, 183
    salmon quiche, 151
    spiced meatballs with gravy, 77
    surprise meat loaf, 77
    tarragon chicken loaf, 182

Manger herbs, 202
March, 53 – 68
Mari-mint gold potpourri, 159
Marigold(s), 89 – 90, 222
Marinade. *See also* Baste
    herby roast beef, 77
Marjoram (sweet), *88*, 89, 90 – 91, 223
    wild. *See* Oregano
Massage oil, 49
May, 87 – 99
    baskets, 99
McFayden, Nancy, 23
Mealy bug spray, 127
Meat. *See also* specific meats
    seasoning, with herbs/spices, chart,
        17
Meat loaf
    Parmesan, 76
    surprise, 77
Meatballs, spiced, with gravy, 77
Medicinal uses of herbs, 12 – 13
Mexican-flavored popcorn, 18
Microwave oven, for drying herbs, 105
Mildew spray, 127
Milfoil. *See* Yarrow
Miniature lace wreaths, 206
Mint, 8 – 10, 71, 223. *See also* specific
        varieties
    containing, 8
    cookies, Taurus, 197
    jelly, 164
        orange, 164
    spiced tea, orange, Herbal Acres',
        199
    tea, 10 – 12
    varieties of, chart, 9
Mintcense potpourri, 25
Minted grapefruit, 197
Minty grape cooler, 126
Mixed herb vinegar, 109
Molasses cookies, 194
Mold spray, 127
Monarda, 90
Money plant. *See* Lunaria
Moss wreath, 156
Moth chaser potpourris, 66 – 68
Moth repellent I, 142
Mouthwash, natural, 99
Mulch, 106, 120
Mulled cider, hot, 174
Mulling spice simmer, 208
Mulling spices, 198
Myrrh, 202
    frankincense and, potpourri,
        158 – 159

N

Nasturtium(s), 90, *140*, 140, 223 – 224
    salad, 141
    sauce, 140
National Herb Garden, 46
Natural mouthwash, 99
Needle sharpen, rosemary, 188
New Year's potpourri, 24
Noodles, basiled, 138
No-salt herb blend, 18
Nosegays. *See* Tussie-mussie
Notebook, herbal, 20 – 21
November, 177 – 189
    baskets, 184 – 185
Nutmeg, 14
    cake, 195

O

Oast, for drying herbs, 105
Oatmeal beauty scrub, 24
October, 161 – 175
Oil-free popcorn, 18
Oils. *See also* Bath oil
    essential fragrant, 79
    massage, 49
    skin, herbal, 23
Omelets
    basic, recipe, 91
    Greek, 91
Opal basil, 215
Orange bergamot, 223
    potpourri, 131
Orange blossom special potpourri,
        208
Orange mint, *11*, 11. *See also* Mint
    jelly, 164
    spiced tea, Herbal Acres', 199
Orange simmering potpourri, 186
Oregano, *162*, 163 – 164, 224
    cheddar bread, 58
Organic insect repellents
    for humans, 129
    moth, 142
    for pets, 128 – 129
    for plants, 127 – 128
Oriental spice potpourri, 157
Ornamental herbs, 89 – 90
Orris root, 79
Oswego tea. *See* Bergamot
Ovens, for drying herbs, 105
Overnight hearty bean soup, 50
Oyster parsley dressing, 181

P

Painted daisy. *See* Pyrethrum
Pancake roll-ups, herbed, 92
Parmesan
    chicken, 175
    meat loaf, 76
Parsley, *54*, 56, 224
    dressing, oyster, 181
    pesto surprise, 137
Parsnip tarragon, carrot-, 125
Pasta salad supreme, Ro's, 137
Peas
    dried, seasoning, with herbs/
        spices, chart, 17
    snow, a l'herbe, 124
Penn-Cumberland's sausage balls,
        200
Pennyroyal, 45, 66, *127*. *See also* Mint
Peppermint, *6*, 223. *See also* Mint
    candy potpourri, 186
Perfume, car, 129
Pest repellents
    for humans, 129
    for pets, 128 – 129
    for plants, 127 – 128
Pesto
    Colette's, 137
    sauce, 136
    surprise, parsley, 137
Pet(s)
    insect repellents for, 128 – 129
    pillows, 128
Phew plant. *See* Valerian
Phyl's basic rose potpourri, 80
Phyl's camphor spice, 68
Phyl's chicken liver stuffing, 180
Phyl's Dutch spaghetti sauce, 136
Phyl's fish, 19
Pickled herb carrots, 138
Pine potpourri
    -mint, 188
    basic, 188
    fruity, 188
    rose, 188
Pineapple cooler, rosemary-, 126
Pineapple mint, 11, 223. *See also* Mint
Pineapple sage, 226
Planning an Herbal Wedding, 118
Plants, insect repellents for, 127 – 128
Pomander balls, apple pulp, 169 – 171
Pomander pebbles, 199
Popcorn
    herbed, 17

Popcorn (*continued*)
  Indian-flavored, 18
  Mexican-flavored, 18
  oil-free, 18
  spiced, 18
Pork, apple/sausage stuffing for, 181
Pot marigold. *See* Calendula
Potpourri: Easy As 1, 2, 3...!, 104
Potpourris. *See also* Sachets
  Barbara's kitchen spice, 144
  basic lavender, 81
  basic pine, 188
  basic recipe, 80
  basic sweet bag, 51
  berry-nice, 50
  blenders for, 82
  blending, chart, 82
  carnation spice, 49
  Christmas spice, 208
  cinnamint potpourri, 208
  citruscent, 49
  decoration, lacy hooped, 186
  defined, 79
  enlivening, 158
  enriching, 158
  essential fragrant oils, 79
  fixatives, 79, 82 – 83
    chart, 84 – 85
  for holidays, 158 – 159
  frankincense and myrrh, 158 – 159
  fruity pine, 188
  herb garden, 159
  Herbal Acres' household spice, 25
  Herbal Acres' "sweet pillow"
    recipes, 97
  Herbal Acres' tansy-bansy, 68
  Herbitage Farm's moth, 66
  highland summer, 141
  instant, 83
  instant Christmascent simmer, 201
  in jars, 185
  jasmine rose, 130
  Lemon-lavender, 159
  mari-mint gold, 159
  mintcense, 25
  moth chaser, 66 – 68
  moth repellent I, 142
  mulling spice simmer, 208
  New Year's, 24
  orange bergamot, 131
  orange blossom special, 208
  orange simmering, 186
  oriental spice, 157
  peppermint candy, 186
  Phyl's basic rose, 80

Potpourris (*continued*)
  Phyl's camphor spice, 68
  pine-mint, 188
  reminiscent, 24
  rose geranium, 49
  rosemary mix, 131
  rosemary-mint, 68
  rosepine, 188
  sachet base, 142
  salted, 157
  simmering, 208
  southernwood wreath, 155
  spice surprise, 159
  spicy lemon, 130
  strawberry fair, 142
  super-strength, 130
  sweet jar, 131
  "sweet pillows", 96 – 97
  sweet vanilla, 130
  sweetening, 158
  toning down, 158
  tree, 203
  tropical breeze, 141
  vanilla medley, 82
  winter holidays, 142
  winter spice incense, 25
  woodspirits pink-pourri, 141
  wreath, 203
Potting soil, sterilizing, 29 – 30
Poultry. *See also* Chicken
  Rock Cornish hens with rice, 183
  seasoning, with herbs/spices, chart,
    17
  stuffing herb mix, 174
Preserving
  herbs, 110 – 114
    chart, 112 – 114
  roses, 111
Pumpkin bread, granola, 196
Pumpkin jam, 187
Punch(es)
  Annie's rosemary fruit, 199
  Christmas morning fruit, 205
  hippocras, 98
  hot spiced cranberry, 199
  hot spiked, for 40, 199
  lemon balm, 126
  red herb, 199
  Rosemary House "Mai Bowle", 98
  royal wedding herbal, 118
  spicy, 198
Purple sage, 226
Pyrethrum, 224

Q

Quiche, salmon, 151
Quick caraway cheese bread, 57

R

Red bergamot, 90
Red herb punch or tea, 199
Red wine vinegar, 108
Regional differences in herb growth
    patterns, 47
Relish, garden kraut, 139
Reminiscent potpourri, 24
Reppert, Bertha, 98
Rice
  bake, chicken-, 182
  confetti salad, 124
  instant, dressing, 183
  mixed, herb, 183
  risotto, 172
  Rock Cornish hens with, 183
  savory lemon, 183
Risotto, 172
Ro's pasta salad supreme, 137
Roast beef
  with herbs, 75 – 76
  marinade, herby, 77
  seasoning, 76
Rock Cornish hens with rice, 183
Root division, 72 – 73
Rose Canny's sage sticks, 200
Rose geranium. *See* Geranium(s),
    rose
Rose hips, 80
  tea, 199
Rose(s)
  harvesting, 111
  potpourri, Phyl's basic, 80
  preserving, 111
  putting to bed, 189
Rosemary, *192*, 192, 193 – 194,
    224 – 225
  cake, 194
  chicken baste, 19
  flea rinse/spray, 128
  fruit punch, Annie's, 199
  jelly, 164
  -mint, 68
  mix potpourri, 131
  needle sharpen, 188
  -pineapple cooler, 126
  squares, 196
Rosemary House "Mai Bowle", 98
Rosepine potpourri, 188
Rosy thyme, 228
Round roast, heavenly rolled, 76

Royal wedding herbal punch, 118
Rue, 225
Russian tarragon, 227

S

Sachet(s), 131. *See also* Potpourris
    base, 142
    butterfly, 97
    card, 24 – 25
    for spring, 68
    jasmine rose, 130
    making, 50 – 51
    quick, 130
    spicy lemon potpourri, 130
    sweet vanilla, 130
Safflower, 225
Saffron, 14, *171*, 225
    growing, 171
Sage, *178*, 179 – 181, 225 – 226
    cheese spread, 188
    clary, 226
    jelly, 164
    pineapple, 226
    purple, 226
    sticks, Rose Canny's, 200
Salad
    crab-cucumber, 151
    dressing
        basic herb vinegar, 109
        double-duty salt-free, 19
    green, 18
    herb blend, 106
    herbed vegetable, 125
    nasturtium, 141
    rice confetti, 124
    Ro's pasta, supreme, 137
    seasoning blend, 18
Salmon quiche, 151
Salt-less salt, 20
Salted potpourri, 157
Sandwiches
    herb tea, 160
    Lady Di's diamonds, 117
Santolina, 66 – 67, *67*, 226
Saponaria. *See* Soapwort
Sauce(s)
    Colette's pesto, 137
    nasturtium, 140
    pesto, 136
    Phyl's Dutch spaghetti, 136
Sausage
    balls, Penn-Cumberland's, 200
    stuffing, 181
        for pork, apple/, 181

Savory, 123, 226
    bulbs, growing, 171
    herb butter, thyme-, 188
    lemon rice, 183
    summer, *122*, 123 – 124, 226
    winter, *124*, 124, 226
Scented bath bubbles, 23
Scented dough, 201
Scented geraniums, 31 – 33, 226
Seafood. *See also* Fish
    crab-cucumber salad, 151
    crabmeat Stroganoff, 151
    dilly shrimp dip, 200
    oyster parsley dressing, 181
Seasoned bread crumbs, 59
Seasoning
    egg, 92
    roast beef, 76
Seed cookies, basic, 197
Seeds, starting herbs from
    in the ground, 94 – 96
    indoors, 59 – 64
September, 147 – 160
Sesame, 226
Shrimp, dip, dilly, 200
Silver dollar. *See* Lunaria
Silver king artemisia, *64*, 64 – 65, 214 – 215
    harvesting, 145
Silver mound artemisia, 215
Silver queen artemisia, 215
Silver thyme, 228
Skin oil, herbal, 23
Skin toner, camomile, 24
"Sleep bags", 96
Slim gourmet's lemon-garlic butter, 59
Snack crackers, dilled, 187
Snow peas a l'herbe, 124
Soap, Making It and Enjoying It, 22
Soaps, 21 – 22, 24
    balls, herbs, 22
    camomile jell, 21
    oatmeal beauty scrub, 24
Soapwort, 227
Soil pH, 189
Soil preparation, 55
Sorrel, 227
Soup
    beef chowder, 35
    chicken, ...plus, 35
    diet, 34
    fish chowder, 35
    herb mix for, 33
    herbed corn chowder, 34

Soup (*continued*)
    iced tomato/herb, 139
    overnight hearty bean, 50
    tomato, for six, 19 – 20
Southernwood, 66, *155*, 227
    wreaths, 155
        potpourri, 155
Spaghetti squash. *See* Vegetable spaghetti
Spanish crocus. *See* Saffron
Spearmint, *11*, 11. *See also* Mint
Spice(s), 13 – 14
    defined, 13
    rope, 144
    seasoning poultry, fish, meat, & other proteins with, chart, 17
    seasoning vegetables with, chart, 16
    surprise, 159
    tea, 14
    using for better health, 14 – 15
Spiced meatballs with gravy, 77
Spiced popcorn, 18
Spicy hot pads, 143
Spicy lemon potpourri, 130
Spicy punch, 198
Squash
    vegetable spaghetti, 137 – 138
        dieter's veggie-ghetti, 138
        parsley pesto surprise, 137
    zucchini or yellow, broiled, 125
Stews, herb mix for, 33
Stove-top simmers, 129
Strawberry fair potpourri, 142
Stuffing
    apple/sausage, for pork, 181
    breadless dressing, 181
    chicken liver, Phyl's, 180
    herb mix, poultry, 174
    instant rice dressing, 183
    oyster parsley dressing, 181
    sausage, 181
Sugarless sun tea, 125 – 126
Summer savory, *122*, 123 – 124, 226
Sun tea, sugarless, 125 – 126
Super holiday cheese wafers, 201
Super-strength potpourri, 130
Surprise meat loaf, 77
Sweet Annie, 65
Sweet bags. *See also* Potpourris
    potpourri, basic, 51
Sweet basil. *See* Basil (sweet)
Sweet bay. *See* Bay (sweet)
Sweet jar, 131
Sweet marjoram. *See* Marjoram (sweet)

"Sweet pillows", 96 – 97
    Herbal Acres' recipes, 97
Sweet vanilla sachet, 130
Sweet wormwood. *See* Wormwood

T

Tansy, *68*, 227
    cookies, 194
Tarragon, 106
    carrot-parsnip, 125
    chicken loaf, 182
    French, *102*, 106, 227
    Russian, 227
Taurus mint cookies, 197
Tea(s), 10 – 13
    Herbal Acres' orange mint spiced, 199
    herbs of Shakespeare, 20
    iced mint, 125
    red herb, 199
    rose hip, 199
    spice, 14
    sun, sugarless, 125 – 126
Teaberry. *See* Wintergreen
Thyme, *70*, 71, 75, 78, 228
    albus, 228
    caraway, 228
    coconut, 228
    creeping, 228
      golden, 228
    it's bean, 124
    jelly, 164
    lemon 75, *151*, 228
      cookies, 198
    propagating, 78
    rosy, 228
    -savory herb butter, 188
    silver, 228
    woolly, 228
Tick powder, herbal flea &, 128
Tick removal, 128
TLC formula for geraniums, 32
Tomato
    /herb soup, iced, 139
    jam, basil-, 138
    Phyl's Dutch spaghetti sauce, 136
    soup for six, 19 – 20
Transporting herb cuttings, 120
Tropical breeze potpourri, 141
True laurel. *See* Bay, sweet
Tussie-mussie, 114 – 115

V

Valerian, 228
Vanilla
    medley, 82
    sweet potpourri, 130
Veal, seasoning, with herbs/spices, chart, 17
Vegetable juice, Anne's, 138
Vegetable salad, herbed, 125
Vegetable spaghetti, 137 – 138
    dieter's veggie-ghetti, 138
    parsley pesto surprise, 137
Vegetable Spaghetti Cookbook, 137
Vegetables, seasoning, with herbs & spices, chart, 16
Vinegar(s), herb, 107 – 109
    basic recipe, 107 – 108
    blends for, 108 – 109
    bouquet garni, 109
    containers, 109
    mixed, 109
    red wine, 108
    salad dressing, basic, 109
    white wine, 108
Violet(s), candied, Libra, 98

W

Wafers, cheese, super holiday, 201
Watermelon surprise, 126
Wedding ideas, 116 – 118
What You Need to Know to Preserve Herbs, 111
Whipped garlic butter, 57
White fly spray, 127
White wine vinegars, 108
Wild marjoram. *See* Oregano
Winter holidays potpourri, 142
Winter savory, *124*, 124, 226
Winter spice incense, 25
Wintergreen, 228
Woad, 228
Woodruff, sweet, *98*, 229
Woodspirits pink-pourri potpourri, 141
Woolly betony. *See* Lamb's ears
Woolly thyme, 228
Wormwood, *65*, 65, 229
Wreath(s)
    advent, 204
    artemisia, 155 – 156
    bay leaf, 204
    cinnamon stick, 203
    grapevine, 156

Wreath(s) (*continued*)
    kitchen herb, 156
    live, 173
    miniature herb, 207
    miniature lace, 206
    moss, 156
    potpourri, 203
    southernwood, 155
    southernwood, potpourri, 155
    steps in making, 154

Y

Yarrow, 229
Yellow squash, broiled, 125
Yule log, Christmas, 201

Z

Zucchini, broiled, 125